Theatre, Time and Temporality

Theatre, Time and Temporality
Melting Clocks and Snapped Elastics

David Ian Rabey

intellect Bristol, UK / Chicago, USA

First published in the UK in 2016 by
Intellect, The Mill, Parnall Road, Fishponds, Bristol, BS16 3JG, UK

First published in the USA in 2016 by
Intellect, The University of Chicago Press, 1427 E. 60th Street,
Chicago, IL 60637, USA

A catalogue record for this book is available from the
British Library.

Series: Theatre & Consciousness
Series editor: Daniel Meyer-Dinkgräfe
Series ISSN: 1753-3058

Cover designer: Holly Rose
Copy-editor: MPS Technologies
Production manager: Katie Evans
Typesetting: Contentra Technologies

Print ISBN: 978-1-78320-721-3
ePDF ISBN: 978-1-78320-722-0
ePUB ISBN: 978-1-78320-723-7

Printed and bound by Bell & Bain Ltd, UK

This is a peer-reviewed publication.

To
Charmian Savill
with
whom
never
enough

'What is this place?' Bevan was silent
a second. 'This isn't solid ground
but a place of potential, actions that resound

forward through time and, sometimes, echo
back to affect events. This island floats
through space and time. Here we foreknow
the future's genome. It's like a boat
riding the waves of an implicate
ocean behind the things we see.
things can happen and unhappen at once,
then happen again. Probability
waves break on our beaches, the first surge destroys,
the second restores. Nobody knows

how such flux happens. Uncertainty is this island's principle.

Gwyneth Lewis, *A Hospital Odyssey* (2010: 125–126)

Contents

Acknowledgements   xiii

Introduction   1

Part I:	**Theatre in Time**	**7**
Chapter 1:	*Whose* **Time Is It?**	9
	What fundamental things apply?	11
	Time is ticking (clock of the heart)	14
	Temporality: What *is* 'the time'?	16
	Intensifying combinations: Theatrical time	19
	Melting clocks and snapped elastics	21
	Wild mercury	24
	Points of departure	25
	Creative tension	27
	Stretch and flow	28
	Cause and effect	29
	Slaves to the rhythm	29
	Morality and money	31
	(Un)Doing the maths	32
	Beating the bounds	33
Chapter 2:	**Theatre in Time**	39
	Starting the day	41
	Interlude: Ways of speed	41

Starting the night 42

Chronos and *kairos* 48

Bachelard and *The Dialectic of Duration* 53

Prigogine and theatre as dissipative structure 56

Theatre as diffusive resonance: green's *random* 58

Theatre as dissipative structure: Wesker's *The Kitchen* 60

Theatre as chaotic map: Beckett's *Krapp's Last Tape* 62

Barbara Adam and quantum theatrics 66

Chronos v. *kairos*: Thomas's *Flowers of the Dead Red Sea*: 70
'THE WHOLE FUCKING SHIT PALACE FALLS ON OUR HEADS'

Theatrical timescapes 72

Interval: **A Hole in the Night** 77

Part II: **Time in Theatre** 83

Chapter 3: **Shapes of Time** 85

Everything must change 87

Distinctions in time 89

Models of theatrical time: A survey 89

Temporal 'thickness' in morality plays 92

Dr Faustus: 'The double motion of the planets' 94

Shakespeare: Too long for a play 98

Dislocations in dreamtime 105

Wilder: Stygian perspectives on the passing world 107

Priestley: Hinges in time 115

Wesker: Disillusion and dynamism 121

Comical-historical-tragical 128

Interlude 1: **'Why don't you all just f-f-fade away'?: Further Thoughts** 139
on Staging Ageing

Chapter 4: **Principles of Uncertainty** 145

Beckett: Marking time/shoring up the debris 148

Contents

Pinter: In search of lost time   156

Barker: 'The sheer suspension of not knowing'   165

Complicating shadows   176

Ed Thomas: Memory, desire and the parts you throw away   180

Butterworth: Time past and time present   183

Breaking the loop: McDowall's radical uncertainty   185

Interlude 2:   **The Clock in the Forest: *Jerusalem* Unenclosed: A Case History**   191

Chapter 5:   **Time Out of Joint**   197

Timebends and countermyths   200

Bond: Time as blood money   204

Neilson's *The Wonderful World of Dissocia*: 'Inside-between the carvings of the clock'   209

Once upon a time: Churchill's traumatic dystopias   212

The time that does not heal   214

Rudkin: The once and future   220

Rifkin: Searching for the new 'time rebels'   228

Reverse engineering: *The Radicalization of Bradley Manning*   230

Inconclusion: **Repent, Harlequin …**   239

Stolen moments   241

Envoi: Give me just a little more time   245

References   247

Index   257

Acknowledgements

My thanks to: Gwyneth Lewis and Anthony Harwood Limited for permission for my choice of epigraph; Daniel Meyer-Dinkgräfe; Michael Mangan; Lara Kipp; Katie Evans. *Bon temps roulez...*

Introduction

The function of an Introduction might include an identification of what the book does, and what it does not.

David Wiles describes his self-styled 'short book', *Theatre & Time*, as not concerned with 'plays *about* time', but with 'performance'; and with 'the way in which plays are neither *in* time nor *about* time, but are *of* time' (Wiles 2014: 3).

This book, *Theatre, Time and Temporality*, is, in distinction, concerned with ways in which drama, theatre and performance are in time, and also often about time.

Rebecca Schneider points out how the title of her short book *Theatre & History* contains a central conjunction that is not only coordinative but also copulative, suggesting different and varying arrangements of 'interest, emphasis, importance, pleasure and so on': where things and people demand care, but may well also become complicating, confusing and sticky (Schneider 2014: 1). Schneider's approach seems salutary for our own projects (of writer and reader). She also considers the possible consequences of emphasis and direction, had her central conjunction been 'in', rather than '&' (5–6).

This book, *Theatre, Time and Temporality*, will indeed incorporate some considerations of Theatre in Time (how and where Theatre may be located in an ongoing stream of events in Time, and what it self-consciously does with and about that), and also, to a larger extent, some considerations of Time in Theatre (how Time may be presented, communicated, contemplated and transformed – condensed, stretched, subverted, displaced and transposed – in Theatre by dramatists, directors, performers, scenographers and audiences). However, this book cannot claim to consider all of these things exhaustively, across time and space. Rather, it focuses on a surprisingly neglected relationship, on how theatrical performances offer a time-based hinge in the imagination, through a time-based hinge in perception.

As J. B. Priestley remarks, the subject of Time has been principally the work of 'mathematicians, physicists or philosophers', attempting an objective approach to a subject that is 'at once large and yet peculiarly elusive, like a Moby Dick that may be a spectre', and that is also likely to indicate that 'any attempt at an objective manner' is impossible (Priestley 1964: 12), or else, tellingly limited by Time itself, in another of its mythological facets, 'a crouching Sphinx' (78). I suggest that these images for Time are also applicable to Theatre, which is also large, elusive, mysteriously paradoxical, identifiably limited and yet calling into question all claims to objective authority.

This book will explore various aspects of signs and contradictions, connections and disconnections, in a (necessarily selective) variety of dramatic, theatrical and performative forms, scripts and events; and how, and to what effects, these forms of drama, theatre and performance may re-present our usual senses of Time. It will also ask how an unusually attentive focus to issues of Time may prove particularly informative in drama, theatre and performance studies, and for the relationship of these things to wider ways of imagining possibilities.

My selection of texts and performances for consideration is admittedly and manifestly subjective, informed (inevitably) by my particular location in time (1958–) and space (Europe, Britain, Wales). It draws primarily upon the western dramatic canon, contemporary British theatre and contemporary performance practices, exploring the relationships of selected plays, performances and practices to their social, cultural and ideological contexts.

Michael Mangan begins his book *Staging Ageing* by indicating how any kind of theatrical performance 'brings into play both the body and the mind, together with the signifier and signified, with the physical/biological organism that is the performer and with the questions of self and identity which the performance generates' (Mangan 2013: 5); and how time (specifically age, in the remit of Mangan's study) brings a particular sharpness to these questions (as, indeed, may considerations of gender and sexual orientation) of self and identity in various social circumstances.

A heightened awareness of Time in theatrical performance also activates considerations and questions of *consequence*: frictions between what might be identified as natural rhythms and human, scientific, historical and political narratives (including religious, national and ideological foundation myths); personal (dis)orientation through (un)familiarity and (in)comprehension; and time as a political resource and currency, to be dispensed and distributed, given and taken, according to principles of social justice. These three facets provide the starting points for each of my chapters in Section II on Time in Theatre.

It strikes me as apt to borrow some terms of profession from Barbara Adam: like hers, my study 'does not culminate in a polished new theory but merely a first step in that direction; it identifies points of departure and indicates the potential for future development' (Adam 1990: 149). It aims to progress by what Gould describes as the interplay of 'internal and external sources': 'theory informed by metaphor and observation constrained by theory' (Gould 1987: 8). I agree with Thornton Wilder that literature 'has always resembled more a torch race than a furious dispute between heirs' (Wilder 2007: 687), and believe that scholarship also proceeds best in these terms.

I wish to record my particular thanks to Jay Griffiths, whose writing inspired me and set me on this trajectory of endeavour, and to Barbara Adam, whose writing inspired me to sustain it. Here, as elsewhere, the words (and music) of Gil Scott-Heron prove salutary to me:

Life inevitably translates into time. That is why the sum total of it is called 'a lifetime'. Freedom is the potential to spend one's time in any fashion one determines. [...] It is very important to me that my ideas be understood. It is not as important that *I* be understood. I believe that this is a matter of respect; your most significant asset is your time and your commitment to invest a portion of it considering my ideas means it is worth a sincere attempt on my part to transmit the essence of the idea. If you are looking, I want to make sure there is something here for you to find.

(Scott-Heron 2000: xiii, original emphasis)

This is the last survey of a wide range of theatrical and dramatic forms that I will undertake. It involves me in new points of focus, and also reconsiderations of some material and events with which I have engaged earlier, but I do so now from crucially different perspectives, afforded by a different and keener awareness of time.[1] If, during my discourse, things seem to warp, stretch associatively and even burst out of initial structures and categories, then that too is probably appropriate to the topics. Priestley notes how there is something not just challenging but paradoxical in devoting time to the apprehension of time: 'pursuing Time, we are like a knight on a quest, condemned to wander through innumerable forests, bewildered and baffled, because the magic beast he is looking for is the horse he is riding' (Priestley 1964: 81). Consequently, Priestley advises the reader of his own book, *Man and Time*, to regard the contents as the observations of a 'Time-haunted man', encouraging others who may be similarly 'Time-haunted' (12) to be alert to her/his own specific glimpses, which may develop her/his observations. My own frequent response to a performance, play, event, idea associated with this study has been to think or say 'yes, *and* ...', whilst trying to prevent the hinge of associated dialectical possibilities mutating into an unassailable hydra, becoming instead a powerful and trustworthy – if many-headed and not always predictable – steed.

Similarly, I hope your responses to this book will flow and fly further.

Note

1 As Paul Weller observes, 'If you try to hang on to who you think you were, you end up being a parody of yourself': a situation I am similarly concerned to avoid. http://www.theguardian.com/music/2015/may/10/paul-weller-miss-the-chaos-and-madness accessed 17/08/2015.

Part I

Theatre in Time

Chapter 1

Whose Time Is It?

What fundamental things apply?

When we consider both time and theatre, we are brought into contact with issues of perception, speculation and action, which are fundamental – and fundamentally contentious. The significantly mercurial qualities of time and theatre make them difficult to discuss, either separately or in combination. Any attempt to establish a single authoritative perspective on, or arising from, either time or theatre will rightly be suspect. Both time and theatre provide forms of definition, which are also indefinite; time and theatre both intrinsically indicate alternatives and adjacencies, even as we perceive their moments of highest precision.

One useful starting point is provided by Stefan Klein (succinctly paraphrasing Aristotle): 'Time comprises the state of everything around us, and of how everything changes'; furthermore, we experience and identify every moment as specific to its time (Klein 2008: 255). However, if (as Kant suggested) our perception of time is an inherent part of human life, our experience of time is dialectical: our 'encounter with time is quite unlike colour or shape, since our experience is not just of time, but also manifestly in time' (Arstila and Lloyd 2014: 143). Similarly, theatre invites us to focus our perceptions, communally but from different subjective angles, on what is before and, to some degree, around us: how these things change, and can be made to change; what may be specific to the present, in its relation to the past and the future; and what might be the limitations inherent in confinement to a single perspective. It is one of the ways in which we try to define and structure the world around us, and to imagine how (and why) it might change; and it works through creating particularly dialectical experiences, of time, in time.

Ilya Prigogine proposes that time is 'our basic existential dimension' (Prigogine 1997: 13). Similarly, Eva Hoffman observes, 'we live in time', with the resonant addendum that it comprises 'the one dimension of experience we cannot leap out of, at least until the final act' (Hoffman 2009: 10). Barbara Adam characterizes Time as not '*a* fact of life' but as something that is 'implicated in *every* aspect of our lives and imbued with a multitude of meanings' (Adam 1990: 2). Adam notes how concepts of time are 'inextricably bound up with human reflexivity and the capacity for self-knowledge', but also observes how 'contemporary industrialised societies' insist on their own fundamental systematized sense of time, as means 'not merely to synthesise aspects of mind, body, nature and social life', but also something 'employed' 'on a world-wide basis as a standardised principle for measurement, co-ordination, regulation, and control' (9).

Theatre, by contrast, is something we are only sometimes 'in' (even if we work in it professionally). Theatre is an event (or series of events) with particular co-ordinates: it is designated spatially to occur in a specific space (or series of spaces) identified to host the event, involving specific participants, and designated temporally to commence at a specific time (or series of times).[1]

Gaston Bachelard proposes that if we decide to 'think time', to confront or foreground or reassess what we generally construe as the forms and claims of time, 'it means that we place life in a framework' (Bachelard 2000: 92), which also provides a basis for thinking (about) theatre, or any art. Marvin Carlson suggests that 'the major feature generally separating a work of art from other activities of the consciousness lies in the particular way it is framed', as 'an activity or object created to stimulate interpretation' and invite interaction: an interaction that will 'in turn be primarily based upon their previous experience with similar activities or objects', 'upon memory' (Carlson 2003: 5).

However, when a theatre event occurs within (and/or around) its specified space (usually a building), we, as attending audience members, are unlikely to be the regular central focus of the event. We might be, if we were the professional theatre artists or active amateurs, presenting the production, or might be, more regularly than usually, if we were spect-actors in a participatory programme constituting one dimension of an Applied Theatre or Theatre of the Oppressed performance: such as one that might overtly acknowledge and respond to our immediate reactions, by way of reconstituting 'observers' as embodied participants and creators of their observations, knowledge and historical situation, and reflecting the unavoidable centrality of the constitutive self in analysis.

Each theatre performance is contextually situated: it has its own spatial and temporal co-ordinates, of its start and duration (and sometimes an interval), by which that performance is locatable, even as it sets one idea of time against another, fictionally and/or experientially. In the process, it 'faces the uncertainty, indeterminacy and contingency of its own making' in ways that fulfil Ermarth's criteria for modes of invention that exercise responsibility and freedom (Ermarth 1992: 23). Susan Bennett remarks how, at 'its core, theatre is both live and transient' (Bennett 2013: 42). Harry Burton reflects on theatre's 'maddening ephemerality' that may also be the source of its 'powerful ritual magic': perhaps several times a week, in a specified location, 'the lights dim as the actors (supported, lest we forget, by a director, a designer and a team of technicians) create the illusion of an often familiar story being told for the very first time' (Burton 2014: 210). Alan Ayckbourn succinctly observes how, during a theatre performance, (at least) two time schemes run simultaneously, which he calls 'stage time and real (theatre foyer) time' (Ayckbourn 2002: 21).[2] The latter is the duration of the convening of practitioners and spectators, whether for a continuous 75 minutes or three hours (including a 15-minute interval). The former refers to the temporal span of the fictional action (which may encompass several years of a family or country's history), though it might also apply (experientially) to how long that action *feels* under sustained and detailed focus (the last scene of *King Lear* unfolds an astonishing *extent* of strenuous experience, for characters, performers and audience alike, beyond the fictional time of its enactment).

Theatre aims to focus our eyes, ears and imaginations selectively, and draws our attention to things, people, actions and consequences. It invites us to focus, to an unusual degree, on process in relation to outcome, and to entertain and consider hypothetical situations (which may inform future decisions). The objective of theatre is not the same as the goal of science, which Stephen Hawking describes as a quest for 'nothing less than a complete description of the universe we live in' (Hawking 1988: 15); rather, theatre deals and delights in partial truths, incomplete descriptions, highlighting and playing with the *provisionality* of everything.[3] However, another observation by Hawking may indicate some occasionally shared terrain: 'since the dawn of civilization, people have not been content to see events as unconnected and inexplicable' (15). Theatre often examines and explores prevalent connections and explanations – and often finds and shows them wanting, and sometimes attempts new ones. Theatre, like science, addresses questions of human purpose and meaning.[4] However, it is distinctively *intersubjective* in its form, thematic concerns and effects, which are manifested through different frames of foregrounded subjective time – and through considered and resonant estrangements of linear time – in a specifically dynamic space, to create an event. An intriguing comment attributed to Tom Waits is the observation: 'If you don't change time in some way, it's not theatre – it's real' (Waits 2014: 91).[5]

Rebecca Schneider claims that theatre (like history) is an art of time; indeed, perhaps theatre is '*the* art of time', because time is 'the stuffing of the stage – it's what actors, directors, and designers manipulate together' (Schneider 2014: 7), working in a space to create and embody practice where 'then and now' (and, sometimes, living and dead) can become unusually simultaneous (3), extending the frame of a single perspective and lifetime: theatre 'cites, and replays, other places and other times' (24), in startlingly embodied ways, from a multitude of angles. As Patricia Schroeder observes, theatre often offers an investigation of how the prior events of the past are related to the present (and, I would add, how these might relate to the future), but in the process may indicate how the past is 'not entirely', or only, 'a sequence of objective facts but a matter of recollection and interpretation' (Schroeder 1989: 12), a process into which the audience is incorporated. At its best, theatre may be a form of *praxis*: a form of joint exploration, which 'presents as an integrated whole what institutional knowledge and professionalization have set apart: academic knowledge, practical activity, embodied sense experience and aesthetic sensibilities', an embodied knowledge conceived not 'as inscription but incorporation' (Adam 1998: 5). This book is also a manifestation of *praxis*, which 'reflectively acknowledges the theorist as part of her[/his] story and analysis', as someone who is inescapably physically implicated in time (7). Indeed, theatre reminds all involved of our physical implication in time: as Kalb points out, because 'theatre confronts us with the physical, real-time pressure of toiling performers as well as fellow audience members, it provokes a greater awareness of the body – and of the ticking clock of mortality – than recorded performances can'; Kalb identifies the 'palpable exertions of living performers', 'replenishing our energy with theirs as we watch them', as 'theatre's signature feature' (Kalb 2011: 17). Here, the 'intense physical exertion' behind 'the prolific flow of demanding techniques' may become 'a poignant, tactile trope for the perseverance of mortal bodies – fragile flesh caught but still wriggling in the implacable fact of time' (Kalb 2011: 63). This might also be identified as energy transferred (not lost) from one system of perception/action to another.

Theatre demands an unusual intentness of focus on the parts of audiences and performers,[6] although – or because – it elicits this through an unusual variety of forms (human and object), presented in unusual three-dimensional spatial combinations.

Theatre is also three-dimensional, in temporal terms: it involves intense layerings of synchronized *and* responsive behaviour, often attempting enlargement of a sense of present possibilities, by activating social awareness of the past and/or future.

Thus, theatre raises questions of value: of what should be communicated, endured and changed over time. From a neoliberal economic perspective that conceives of power in exclusively monetary terms, theatre might be condemned or dismissed as a 'waste of time', without immediately visible or predictable consequences in terms of exchange or investment (according to the presumption that 'any time that is not translatable into money tends to be associated with a lack of power', Adam 1998: 68). However, theatre's different power is how precisely its speculations and transpositions may throw signs and values (inevitably including the terms of power) into play, thus showing itself to be an ostensible 'waste' of time that may nevertheless prove paradoxically plentiful.[7]

Time is ticking (clock of the heart)

G. J. Whitrow remarks on the difficulty of discussing time objectively, even though it is something that we all unavoidably and inevitably go on experiencing whilst alive: 'only time has this peculiar quality which makes us feel intuitively that we understand it so long as we are not asked to explain what we mean by it' (Whitrow [1972] 2003: 1). Hoffman notes how, nevertheless, 'time is to the mind what air is to the lungs: invisible, ubiquitous and absolutely necessary' to perform mental acts such as meaningful recall and informed self-orientation; the waking question, what time it is, seeks to establish 'where we are in the day and how we should pitch ourselves towards it' (Hoffman 2009: 63). Strikingly, Adam points out that while 'space is associated with visible matter and sense data, time is the invisible "other", that which works outside and beyond the reach of our senses' (Adam 1998: 10). But perhaps this notable observation might be further developed: time works outside and beyond the *complete* or *comprehensive* reach of our senses, as it is possible to sense and perceive aspects of time, fortunately, even though we have no single sense organ dedicated to it; rather we are required to use several senses in complementary combination with imagination, to approach the senses of time, with which we experience and organize our lives.

Nature itself is intrinsically temporal: at their most basic level, all living organisms, plants and animals contain cells that measure time – most discernibly in the instances of a pulse or heartbeat – as a requirement for life: the principle of *rhythmicity*. We sense and feel time's passages through the periodic rhythms of our biological metabolisms: breathing, heartbeats, pulses, digestion, reproductive and menstrual cycles, nervous reflexes, sonic location, all of which can be affected by our feelings in relation to our environment (and its changes, seasonal or otherwise). A physiologically sensed variation in tempo, in relation to some environmental and/or internal change, often prompts, and registers as, our unusual awareness of a sense of time. We not only sense and act, but interact, with others and with our environment, rhythmically: focusing on bodily rhythms will throw into relief how we 'eat, sleep, breathe, use energy, digest, perceive, think, concentrate, communicate and interact in a rhythmic way' (Adam 1990: 73), within larger contextual cycles of day and night, tides and seasons. This is given vividly erotic dramatic expression by the protagonist in Kaite O'Reilly's play *Woman of Flowers*, when she proclaims her lover

> [...] touches me and flowers bloom against my skin. Meadowsweet, broom, the flowers of the oak. All the petals, stamens, the cells, feathers, the claw and hollow bone, all the ticking in a clock, the pulse of life beating, beating, beating of wings, of time passing, of life, all this is him.
>
> (O'Reilly 2014: 61)

In highly contrasting terms, Michon characterizes human time in terms of information exchange, 'the manifestation of the need to exchange experience with the environment' (Michon 1985: 47). Barbara Adam notes that Michon's paradigm allows for 'prediction, anticipation, self-observation and modificatory behaviour', but this information exchange is not a prerogative of the human, but a general characteristic of the biological order (Adam 1990: 92). From the human perspective, it may seem that animals live more in the present (though pets can demonstrate that they have learnt lessons and expectations from past experiences, and bees are particularly notable in performing their waggle dance, during which a scout communicates the proximity of food to a colony through indicating direction and distance over time needed to attain it). Though Fraser contentiously suggested a concern with posterity, or even an afterlife, was the decisive manifestation of the 'fully human' (Fraser, introduction to Whitrow [1972] 2003: x), it may be more appropriate to begin by noting how all 'rhythmically organised beings' extend their sensibilities 'beyond the present' (Adam 1990: 126). As far as we can see and tell, humans seem to be particularly equipped (imaginatively) and inclined (temperamentally and socially) to construct and rehearse images of a possible future (sometimes by way of a possible past, very occasionally by an alternative present, or alternative immediate future), as their imaginations project beyond the more immediately observable cyclical rhythms of day and year to those of other generations, centuries, millennia. This is one aspect of their biological capacity for self-renewal (the internal abilities to heal, regenerate and self-replicate, morphogenetic processes that machines lack), in dynamic offset of discernible decay.

However, all forms of life are united by the fact of death. The foreknowledge of death is something that human beings seem, according to current knowledge, 'to share with only a few of the "higher" animals such as elephants'; and human beings seem, again according to current knowledge, to be 'the only beings that express that knowledge symbolically' (Adam 1990: 128); and that, moreover, posit an existence beyond death, in terms and relationships that vary between individuals and cultural contexts in different ages.

Temporality: What *is* 'the time'?

Sean Carroll helpfully provides three identifications of different aspects of time:

1. *Time labels moments in the universe.*
   Time is a co-ordinate; it helps us locate things.
2. *Time measures the duration elapsed between events.*
   Time is what clocks measure.
3. *Time is a medium through which we move.*
   Time is the agent of change. We move through it, or – equivalently – time flows past us, from the past, through the present, towards the future.

(Carroll 2010: 10)

'Space/time' – or perhaps more elegantly, 'spacetime' – is here used in Carroll's first sense of an objective co-ordinate, helping us to locate things in the universe by identifying the presence of something through reference to the three dimensions of *space* (located in both horizontal and vertical axes[8]), and the fourth dimension of *time*.

However, because it is difficult to apprehend precise nuances of Time directly by the senses, we tend to rely on the mediations of various indicators, such as the clock or calendar, which superimpose a sense of social time on our biological rhythms. This means that (though a world without time is unimaginable) 'the meaning of time is relative to its system of measurement' (MacNaghten and Urry 1998: 143) and the priorities of the social context. Rifkin identifies six distinct temporal dimensions in social interaction: every 'thought, event, occurrence or situation is definable in terms of sequential structure, duration, planning, rate of recurrence, synchronization, and temporal perspective', factors present within every culture, although the ways that a society chooses to define and use 'each of these building blocks of time determines the overall temporal orientation of the culture' (Rifkin 1987: 48).

Furthermore, in its (fortunately unpredictable) permutations of limitations and flexibilities, time is also relative to the individual, for whom an event (rather than a specified quantification of seconds or minutes) may generate emotional and physiological repercussions, which slow or prolong a sense of inner time. Subjective time, or *temporality*, is time defined in primarily personal terms, the experience of a surprising and mysterious elasticity in contrast and counterpoint to clock-time that more reductively measures out minutes and hours. Klein suggests that the 'twin gauges' of this inner time are 'movement and memory', which combine to some degree in any conscious sense of an event, which is constructed subjectively, although he also claims 'we experience time exclusively against a background of events' (Klein 2008: 53, 55). Arstila and Lloyd are more precise when they identify subjective time as 'the *experience* of temporality, the phenomenology of duration and passage' where every detail of experience is idiosyncratically 'surrounded by some sort of awareness or remembrance of what has just happened, and some sort of anticipation of what is to come'; therefore subjective time 'comprises both embedded temporality and explicit (conscious) timing', a socially defined and implicit 'fabric of perception' and experiments in 'explicit temporality' in which 'time moves to centre stage', with attendant target of intervals and durations and 'responses are signals of an awareness of passing time as such' (Arstila and Lloyd 2014: 658, original emphasis). Theatre might be construed as just such an exercise, of and in 'explicit temporality', an artful re-proportioning of detail, through timing, in relation to the dominant and habitually accepted 'fabric of perception'. Theatre's phenomenological aspect might thus be identified as how it not only depicts but also demonstrates 'appearances as being resistant to enclosed borders and fixed points' (Trigg 2012: 47).[9] To redeploy a resonant phrase from Anne Carson's writing on the force of Eros: theatre reaches 'between known and unknown' for 'something else than the facts' (Carson 1998: 173).

Steve Taylor suggests time is often characterized as an enemy or adversary because our personal senses of its expansions and contractions frequently seem to work, perversely, against our wider inclinations: when enjoyable experiences may seem to 'shorten' and miserable or boring ordeals may seem to 'lengthen' in time (Taylor 2007: 5). Bachelard succinctly observes, 'we only find that time has *length* when we find it *too long*' (Bachelard 2000: 54). We can probably all recall theatrical, and other, experiences that we associate with these extremes: the resentful tedium that we experience when we feel insufficiently engaged by a performance (or film or television programme), or by company, and become annoyed by the *presumptions* on our taste, and our valuable time. On the other hand, engaging theatrical performances (or films or programmes) involve and reflect our capacities for taking an 'active role in crafting our perceptions of time' (Klein 2008: xix) with a consciously creative involvement of the will and imagination. These positively memorable events (like those spent in 'good' company) may seem surprisingly fast-moving (so that 'time flies') and yet simultaneously create an experience that is surprisingly resonant in the memory, so that its appeal to, and impact on, the subjective imagination seems (contrary to Bachelard's proposition above) out of proportion to its technical duration in clock-time. Such events involve a surprising *range* of imaginative experience, when a performance may, for example, appear to distil years to minutes, whilst generating a sense of implicit wider resonances. This is not only the case when we encounter what Matthew Wagner describes as overtly or specifically 'time-centred' plays: those 'stage works whose narrative, structural and theatrical preoccupations with time are particularly rich and evident' (Wagner 2012: 9: though we will consider some examples of these). Theatre, in its various manifestations, might be regarded as an immersive, prismatic and specifically designated space/time where actors, directors, scenographers and audience members are all differently involved, but jointly focused, in taking an active role in crafting perceptions of time: through an event of formalized physicality, arranged in space, which involves and demands an unusual fusion of imaginative attention and activity (all six of the temporal 'building blocks of time' identified by Rifkin). The process of this event will probably involve a lessening of attention to conventional quotidian (extramural?) time signals for audience members, with an extra-daily sense of *timing* operating for, and manifested by, the performers (the Deputy Stage Manager who has to cue effects of light and sound on specific occasions, for specific durations, may find herself alternating between – and synthesizing – several indicators of time).

Theatre also demands a designated duration of (various degrees of) sustained focused attention, to a designated space within a designated space. It does not permit the audience member to select briefer opportunities for attention, as we may when reading a novel or 'working our way' (as the colloquial phrase goes) through a DVD box set ('in the theatre we do not attend to Act I on Tuesday, Act II on Wednesday or Thursday, Act III perhaps the following week' [Priestley 1964: 116]). Bruce Wilshire observes:

> However strange or remote be the 'time' of the play's world, it can be enacted only within the time in which the actors and audience agree to be gathered together within the theatre's space, only within the world's time. 'Time' and time, 'world' and world, actors and audience, must intersect. This is the encounter which is theatre.
>
> (Wilshire 1982: 22)

Moreover, Wilshire claims 'two temporal dimensions' for (most) theatre events: its consciously finite duration and its repeatability from one performance to the next (when one-off single theatrical performances remain the exception rather than the rule [22]), contributing to the paradoxical sense of theatre as both 'ephemeral and enduring' (Wagner 2012: 21). This is just one of the ways that theatre characteristically 'plays in the space of "again"', and so 'troubles linearity with repetition' (Schneider 2014: 45). A further paradox of theatre is the way that its most enduring moments are experienced in terms that recall Priestley's observation on time, both 'intensely private yet also widely shared' (Priestley 1964: 276). We might identify such moments as occasions of explicit (or conscious) timing, disruptively located in a common fabric of cognitive perception. Jonathan Kalb acknowledges that it may be possible that theatre, on average, offers dramatic narratives that are 'no more socially edifying or provocative' than those available on some DVD box sets; however, few 'DVD marathon sessions are arranged for large groups,'[10] and 'the viewers rarely draw connections between their personal need for sustained experiences and the wider social need to question and challenge the mediated forces of compulsory abbreviation all around them':

> theatre at least *invites* greater social awareness (and potential activism) than media because it is watched less passively, attended in large groups where people are meaningfully present to one another, and requires more effort and expense to attend. Going to theatre is an active decision to seek out a communal encounter, and it usually signals a readiness to listen closely and engage alertly with complex and elaborate talk. Mediated performances

cannot accommodate challenging or extensive language, or serious meditations on time, as theatre can, and that difference is the small window of opportunity that the best marathon theatre exploits.

(Kalb 2011: 192, original emphasis)

Intensifying combinations: Theatrical time

Mike Pearson notes, 'Performance exists in and through time', as a '*time-based* art', but one that is usually specifically (even unrepeatably) scheduled in space and time, 'it demonstrates its nature by playing with time: slowing down, speeding up, attenuating and intensifying norms of social practice, in combinations of simultaneous, sequential, folded, suspended and discontinuous activity' (Pearson 2010: 159).

Matthew Wagner, in his brilliant book *Shakespeare, Theatre and Time*, considers the nature and details of such possible combinations:

> The theatre has a habit of abolishing clocks. Perhaps, more accurately, it dismantles and refigures them, making, in a god-like fashion, time in its own image [suggesting] that the clock is not equivalent to time. As in the Forest of Arden, something in the theatre severs or warps the ties that typically exist between clocks and time; and yet, the clock never fully disappears [...] What these stage moments embody, then, is not so much the destruction of one form of time (the clock) in favour of another (or, as it might be tempting to think, in favour of a kind of 'no time', an atemporality); rather they make manifest the juxtaposition of differing temporal schemes. They point up temporal dissonance as a key constitutive element of theatrical time. Perhaps even more significantly, the relegation of the clock to a different, less prominent position, changes the nature of the present moment: it restructures and redefines 'now'.

(Wagner 2012: 12)

Wagner offers – like Carroll – three identifications of different aspects of time, but here as encountered in theatre:

> temporal dissonance, or as Hamlet puts it so succinctly, time which is 'out of joint' (*Hamlet* I.5.189); temporal 'thickness', or that understanding of the present as being heavily weighed by the past and the future; and temporal materiality, the sense, especially prominent in Elizabethan England, of time being material, having a bodily presence in various forms.

(Wagner 2012: 2)

Wagner's sense of 'thick' time is here developed from Edmund Husserl (1859–1938), the German philosopher who drew a distinction between 'objective' (or 'cosmic') time (which is external to the immediacy of human experience, and which clocks attempt to measure in order to provide structures for negotiations of social activities) and what he variously termed 'subjective', 'inner' and 'phenomenological' time, which is experienced by an individual inconsistently, dependent on circumstances (Plato is the philosopher who originally distinguished between two domains, as the atemporal world of ideas and form, and the temporal world of phenomena, substance subject to change and perceived by the senses).

Wagner's characterization of 'theatrical time' suggests that theatre may not limit itself to entertaining and foregrounding ideas about time, but characteristically offers an experience of time by 'presenting an audience continually and inherently with dissonant time schemes', which gives unusual emphasis on 'the close proximity – indeed, the dimensional layering – of past, present and future' (6). Theatre provides 'a temporal experience wherein the present moment always bears the weight of past and future, and their extreme manifestations of beginning and end, birth and death', ensuring 'that what has been and what's to come are never far from view' (6). Wagner acknowledges:

> This of course raises the question of what the relationship between time and the theatre *is* governed by. At this stage, it might be tempting to align theatrical time with Husserl's phenomenological time [though even here there] exists a search for consistency and unity. It seems more appropriate to propose that temporally speaking, the theatre places us between phenomenological and objective time. It provides us a sharpened awareness of both, by shuttling us back and forth between each, and, most significantly, by not reconciling the one with the other or explaining one in terms of the other.
>
> (Wagner 2012: 18, original emphasis)

Thus, Wagner's argument implies that theatre dissolves the exclusivity of the *either/or* distinction, between objective time and subjective (or phenomenological) time, permitting the audience member to *entertain* more perspectives (*both/and*) than they might usually, and otherwise; 'the theatre heightens, in human experience (that of performers and audience alike), the temporal reality of inconsistency, mostly by producing differing, but equally [simultaneously] evident, time schemes' (Wagner 2012: 19) (ideas that I propose to extend, with reference to the theories of Gaston Bachelard and Barbara Adam). Schneider notes how Stanislavsky, in his theories of acting

> called for an actor to be in the *time* of the action, and whether the time of the action is set in the past or in the future, the time is to be 'now' for the naturalist actor – not a copy of now. Both now, then – and then, now. His system is brimful of ways to access one time in another time, newly each time, or to enclose one time within another like a 'circle of attention' that forms a kind of scrim between the time of the audience and the time of the actor's concentration [so that the actor's sense of time 'now' is not the same as the audience's sense of time 'now'] even as these 'now's and 'then's meet and bleed,

paradoxically, into a shared moment [enabling] what might be called a temporal slip, or crack, in any number of directions.

(Schneider 2014: 39–40)

Jerzy Limon goes further than Wilshire or Wagner, attempting a sub-categorization of eight forms of theatrical time.[11] These temporal dissonances offered by theatre have many different resonances and directions, as they briefly subvert linearity and exclusivity, and heighten senses of pressure and import. *As You Like It's* theatrical setting of the clockless Forest of Arden promises a suspension of conventional norms; Jez Butterworth's play *Jerusalem* (2009) dramatizes the various social appeals, claims and properties of different (and contradictory) senses of time, which 'thicken' increasingly[12]; Trevor Griffiths's *Comedians* (1975) stipulates the onstage presence of a real clock, in both locations of its fictional action, to heighten a coiled-spring sense of pressure, increasing tension and dramatic inevitability, as one character chooses actions, which are startlingly divergent from those of his fellows (and even his respected tutor) in conscious relation to his past and future. debbie tucker green's play *random* (2008) immerses character, performer and audience in a retrospectively thickened sense of (phenomenological) time, and the deceptive texture of apparent and so-called 'everyday' experience (objective time), struggling to comprehend, 'catch up with', and so avert an outcome – a fatal stabbing – which has already been completed. *random* then turns out the question: how and why can the events it depicts become 'everyday' experience?

Theatre's manifestations of temporal *inconsistency* demonstrate a plurality of claims on human consciousness, and human dealings. These effects mitigate any sense of a single, exclusive, ideological authority or perspective, often establishing one frame of reference in order to qualify or interrogate it by the introduction of another (which makes it a powerful medium for ethical enquiry, investigation and speculation), a process that links to what Barbara Adam envisages as a *layering* of different times (Adam 1990: 161–169), in terms we will address in closer detail later.

Melting clocks and snapped elastics

Many contending issues of time may not present themselves as such: though they be matters of common experience and concern, their forms and effects may be generally presented and accepted as matters of so-called 'common sense', that is unresponsive to (or a misplacement of) further enquiry. Carroll aptly observes that 'time is something we literally don't know how to live without' (Carroll 2010: 10), but Hoffman is also correct when she observes that patterns of temporality are 'largely created by culture – that system of visible customs and invisible assumptions, unwritten codes and subterranean values that structures, even if we are not aware of it, our perceptions and views of the world' (Hoffman 2009: 117). Adam notes how *differently* time is cited, appealed to and used, when theorists (and politicians, and theatre practitioners) may 'associate it with change, stability, order, control, and measurement or combinations of these'; and draws attention to one specific rhetorical slight-of-hand: 'in functionalist theories time is identified with change and sequence while stability and order are conceived as timeless' (Adam 1990: 11). However, Hopkins argues that time 'not only forms part of consciousness, it is the process by which consciousness develops and forms' (1982: 28–29). Adam extrapolates this, suggesting that what 'appears like a dualism of external and internal experience and consciousness of time' is shown by Hopkins to be 'a duality of mutual dependence where the created, external and shared aspects of time re-enter consciousness as constitutive features and vice versa' (Adam 1990: 17).

Theatre gathers semi-anonymous strangers in a given place at a given time to focus on an experience that suggests that there is always more than one way of looking at things, and that no single perspective on these matters can be presumed to be dominant (gathering to focus on them is itself indicative of a still-healthy social curiosity). However, this is not to decry or dismiss an element of the *mysterious* that is innately theatrical (and counter-scientific): an ultimate resistance to finite definition, which theatre shares with time.

Hoffman also notes how time is 'both the most intangible of entities and the most inexorable'; on the one hand, 'the great given, the category of reality which – outside fantasy or fable – cannot be changed, deconstructed or wished away' (14); but also time is, importantly, a 'relational and intersubjective' medium, a dimension of human reality that, like language, 'mediates between interior experience and the external world' (Hoffman 2009: 117) (Carroll points out that, according to researchers at the *Oxford English Dictionary*, '*time* is the most used noun in the English language', Carroll 2010: 1). It might appear excessive to borrow Hoffman's terms and claim for the similarly 'relational and intersubjective' medium of theatre, the status of 'one of the fundamental dimensions of human reality'; however, Augusto Boal has persuasively identified 'the essence of theatre' in 'the human being observing itself', proposing a model of reflexive human (self-)consciousness that has parallels with the imaginative work of a dramatist-director-scenographer who does indeed mediate between interior experience and the external world, to the degree that Boal suggests '*The Human being not only "makes" theatre: it "is" theatre*' (Boal 2005: 13, original emphasis).[13] As I have commented elsewhere, the lure of fantasy is conventionally viewed as a simplification of life's complexities, a melodrama of gratification; but it is also notable that imaginary fantasy, personal and staged, may incorporate or be based on elements that complicate rather than simplify quotidian surfaces (as in the case of tragedy) (Rabey 2002–2003: 69). The imagination characteristically rehearses scenarios in the individual's 'theatre of the mind', in order to anticipate and confront possibilities in the most resourceful way, sometimes involving alternative and provisional senses of the self, and of others. This also happens involuntarily, in the cases of dreams – 'those vast private theatres in which we are dramatists, directors, designers, actors and audience' (Priestley 1964: 297) – or nightmares, in which we seem to lose control over the images of our 'night life' (in *Titus Andronicus*, the protagonist expresses his horror with a temporal question regarding a manifest loss of control: 'When will this fearful slumber have an end?' Shakespeare 2007: 1648). Edward Bond claims we are 'naturally and necessarily self-dramatists because of the complexity of our experience and knowledge'; dramatization (including that of the self) is how we all 'combine unlike situations and disparate abilities into a liveable whole' (Bond 2014b: 1).

Bert O. States goes so far as to suggest that the theatrical performance offers a purging – not, as Aristotle proposed, of pity and fear – but of time: a resistance of nature's tendency to resolve its own tensions (States 1985: 50). This may recall the 'folding' that Pearson identifies, which incorporates theatrical performance's impulse towards suspension and discontinuity, as well as towards sequence and simultaneity. Using terms intriguingly reminiscent of the fertilization laboratory, States suggests the exposition of any play 'is really the surreptitious planting of an embryo future in a reported past and the sealing off of time in an inevitable space' – by which I think he means, a space of specifically pressurized but speculative possibility – 'in which the past, freed from the infinite contingencies of reality, now corners the future and eliminates it as a category of care' (States 1985: 48). This seems to ignore dystopian theatre, but indicates one way in which theatre can suggest that the normal, ostensibly 'natural', rules need not apply – whether in the speculative efforts of Augusto Boal's theatre, which opens up spaces in the tempo of normal social action for consideration of alternatives, or in Howard Barker's drama, which offers alternative mythic histories that offer artful re-visionings of normative familiarities: implying that this is possible outside the theatre, as well as inside the theatre, that (in Rifkin's phrase) the 'revaluation of time is a prerequisite to the revaluation of life' (Rifkin 1987: 197). Wagner suggests that the theatre is a designated space (a past, present or future 'which is another country') where the 'temporal characteristics of dissonance and thickness are given room to breathe'; the theatre 'clears a space for their emergence, as it were' (Wagner 2012: 13). Importantly, States suggests that that moments of suspension (which Barker might identify as the 'ecstasy of not knowing', Barker 2016: 30) are not achieved only by cessation of movement, 'the ubiquitous "freeze" of stage and film endings'; rather, this is just one of theatre's many forms of 'mysterious transformation of dramatic time into lyric space' (States 1985: 49). Schneider similarly suggests that theatre (and a theatrical sense of life) may be 'composed in the ambivalences', and displacements, of temporalities, where 'something that may have happened in one time reappears, sometimes radically disguised, in another time' (Schneider 2014: 85). All these perspectives suggest that the theatre event may be a 'spacetime' where we dis-locate in order to re-locate. Intriguingly, Barbara Adam uses a theatrical image, in her social analysis of time, described as a bid to 'make visible the assumptions that inform the western understanding of time'. She professes a desire to 'bring to the forefront the backcloth upon which descriptions are drawn' (Adam 1995: 31). Theatre also persistently develops ways of foregrounding (the one-dimensionality of) that which is drawn on what Adam terms 'the assumed backcloth' of 'our time' (33).

The second half of this study focuses on connections and intersections between dramatic texts and theatrical events that throw into relief the wider senses and processes of time, which are usually taken for granted in social life. Furthermore, it suggests how the associated presumptions of possibility are implicated in political power and social agency, but that these are not beyond interrogation and consequent re-visioning. Adam indicates what is at stake in the dynamics of images, by which we live:

> [...] clocks, computers [and] water are so powerful as metaphors precisely because they work on the basis of non-verbal imagery. They function as dynamic images that induce in us a non-linear understanding of systems and their principles, help us to grasp processually and holistically how things work, [facilitating] understanding of complex systems in their interactions. Metaphors as conceptual tools cease to serve their purpose and proper function, however, when they become naturalized, when they become absorbed into the phenomenon, and when we consequently no longer recognize them as metaphors, as aids to a specific conceptual task [as with] the machine metaphor of clock time.
>
> (Adam 1995: 164)

Wild mercury

J. T. Fraser observes how the human experience of time is simultaneously 'all pervasive, intimate and immediate', and so it 'follows that no single faculty of learning, in itself, is capable of accounting for the nature of time': itself a cause of intense 'concern and argumentation' (Fraser, introduction to Whitrow [1972] 2003: xi), which would seem to require necessarily inter-disciplinary forms of address.

This may be an apt juncture to anticipate another concern, expressed in another context (G. F. Waller's critique of Ricardo Quinones's *The Renaissance Discovery of Time*): if the mercurial nature of time prevents it being singly identifiable (so that time can be alternately described in terms of 'change' and 'unchangability'), then the category of time may become 'so unhelpfully vague, so much a conceptual imperialist, that it is extendable to include any matter of human concern in which the eager scholar chooses to be interested' (Waller 1976: 2). Wagner responds that, while Waller's concern is understandable, 'it is a bit like taking the ocean to task for being too wet' (Wagner 2012: 4). In other words, the fluidity of time and the diversity of its connotations constitute two of its principal attributes. Moreover, I suggest, the distinctive terms in which these attributes are imagined and presented, and the identifiability of the underlying principles, are nevertheless of potentially fundamental importance.

This attendant intensity of 'concern and argumentation' identified by Fraser is intensified by the intrinsically indefinite forms that any sustained focus on time will take, particularly when it approaches questions of potential pluralism on issues of reason, truth and law. Fraser identifies how inquiries into the nature of time are never emotionally neutral; positions of debate may tend to become parochial or dogmatically fundamentalist, because thinking about time mobilizes issues of 'passage and permanence in humans, animals and matter', not least the conflicts between the certainty of individual mortality and 'the fantasy of eternal life', in ways that will approach, but not fathom, a 'rational mystery about passage, rooted in the incompletability of nature' itself (Fraser, introduction to Whitrow [1972] 2003: xii–xiii).

However, nothing changes so irresistibly as time, or expires so regularly and thoroughly as 'truth'. Barbara Adam poses an important and persistently resonant question: 'if time is conceptualised as a socially constructed symbol then it is pertinent to inquire what is symbolically represented' (Adam 1990: 43). Phil MacNaghten and John Urry suggest that absolute notions of a linear time (by which to measure natural phenomena) still tend to dominate the social sciences, although twentieth- and twenty-first century science has moved towards a sense of nature, as being intrinsically temporal, and as having discernibly complex and dynamic non-linear qualities. MacNaghten and Urry also point out that 'there is no fixed time independent of the system to which it refers – time is thus a local, internal feature of the system of observation' (MacNaghten and Urry 1998: 145). Barbara Adam similarly identifies the intrinsic limitations of any single paradigm, single discipline, approach: if time is, in many ways, socially constructed, how then might we 'conceptualise the symbol and its multiple sources' if we insist on staying within a single disciplinary tradition? (Adam 1990: 43–44). Adam's work is salutary in alerting researchers to the fact that, prior to her work, no attempt at a comprehensive conceptualization of time had been attempted in social theory, 'since this would necessitate the transgression of social science perspectives and, worse still, a disregard for disciplinary boundaries'; however, as she notes, without such a 'deviation from the tradition', 'time can neither be grasped in its full complexity nor appropriately incorporated into social theory' (Adam 1990: 44).

Points of departure

Wiles notes that it is difficult to 'conceptualize time except through spatial metaphors'; however, linear metaphors, such as a road, entail notions of progress that may be 'consistent with the word "development"', but that may not be consistent with 'Buddhist or older European conceptions of time as cyclic': rather, a perspective that favours cyclicity might observe in theatre an 'alternation of phases of change' with 'phases of stability', and so 'unhook' a theatre event from the dominant 'ideology of "progress"' (Wiles 2014: 3).

Theatre is an event of shared, but differentiated, observational focus on issues precisely, but indefinitely, manifested by a rhythmic arrangement of bodies and forces in spacetime. As such, it might be a form and art particularly well suited to the study of human organisms in relation to their environment, conducted over and through time. Hawking explains the theory of relativity thus: 'Space and time are now dynamic quantities: when a body moves, or a force acts, it affects the curvature of time and space – and in turn the structure of space-time affects the way in which bodies move and forces act' (Hawking 1998: 38). *The dynamic interaction of forces and bodies over time* might provide a basis for thinking about theatre's forms and concerns (States notes how, of all the fictional and temporal arts, theatrical performance and dance are the only art forms that imitate 'human action, in the medium, one might say, of human action' [1985: 49]).

Intriguingly, Klein uses a theatrical image for his explanation of relativity: 'If the cosmos were a theatre, audience members would always see the play differently, depending on their seating, but the stage of time and space itself would not change' (Klein 2008: 245). In this image, people focus on the same thing from their different angles and subjective viewpoints, to try to discern patterns of cause and effect that give time its visible direction, which, again, also may provide us with a way of thinking about theatre. While it is true that, as Hoffman says, we cannot escape time as a dimension of experience, theatre can offer a creative (physical and imaginative) *dislocation* from daily rhythms, by manifesting variations in the forms of alternative responses: an overwhelming (and subversive) effect that Pearson likens to cutting a hole in time, causing a 'losing track' (Pearson 2010: 162); what Lefebvre calls 'a time that forgets time, during which time no longer counts (or is counted)', which 'arrives or emerges when an activity brings plenitude', and is thus distinct from the more familiar 'obligation or imposition come from without' (Lefebvre 2004: 76–77, again recalling our image of theatre as a defiantly, astonishingly plentiful 'waste of time'). Seremetakis writes of a 'still-act' (Seremetakis 1994: 12) that 'does not entail rigidity or morbidity' but rather 'requires a performance of suspension', a 'corporeally based interruption' of externally imposed models of the 'flow' of the 'present', in order to slow down and interrogate the linear (ostensibly 'progressive') terms of predominating economies of time (Lepecki 2006: 15). As well as decelerative effects, we will also consider accelerative effects in theatrical performance (as when the events of a lifetime, or several generations, are selectively condensed into the duration of a play, or the terms of a pregnancy into several minutes of performance); in both instances, this unusual regulation of durational time is usually intended to permit and intensify an imaginative exploration of (possible) *consequences*.

Similarly, States suggests how theatre's dis*location* of those involved from daily rhythms throws the texture of lives into new reliefs, which manifest unfamiliar meanings[14]:

> a play plucks human experience from time and offers an aesthetic completion to a process we know to be endless. The play imitates the timely in order to remove it from time, to give time a shape.
>
> (States 1985: 50)

Wagner offers a more detailed account of the processes that this 'shaping' may involve, in three proposals:

(1) that our understanding and experience of time inevitably oscillate between subjective and objective time; (2) that the difference and dissonance between disparate temporal schemes – of which subjective and objective temporality might be considered one of the most elementary – form a major part of the unique character of theatrical time; (3) that Heidegger's *'sum moribundus'* ['I am in dying', Heidegger's refashioning of Descartes's

cogito ergo sum to foreground an awareness of time and death in any substantial apprehension of human experience] lends a unique insight into the ways in which we experience the theatrical 'present'.

(Wagner 2012: 10)

We might deduce and summarize: the audience at a theatre event engages with the proceedings with an enhanced expectation and sense of experiential *finitude* and duration – it is that event's heightened sense of specific formal boundaries, temporal and otherwise, which alters their nature and quality of attention, and may intensify the reflexive process of seeking meaning.

Creative tension

As Wiles observes, it is difficult to 'inhabit a "now" without thinking both backwards in time and forwards in time', as this involves a decoupling from sequential patterns of meaning: if 'you isolate a single note of music, it ceases to be music' (Wiles 2014: 8). Nevertheless, a composer or performer may concentrate on achieving or refining a specific note, gesture or detail of performance in order to 'play against' and alter the dominant flow of sequence and terms of meaning, for self and audience. Bachelard goes further, proposing that the action of music is 'discontinuous: it is our emotional resonance that gives it consistency' (Bachelard 2000: 124). One might extend this to theatre: we can also analyse (and learn about) rehearsal processes and theatrical performances in terms of what Bachelard calls 'the accumulation of processes of atomisation' (124), focusing primarily on one aspect of the whole; however, we do so in order to appreciate how that which develops, may reverberate and consolidate.

Whitrow also notes the imaginative strain that accrues from the operation of what may be (or become) compulsive reflexes, in how time problematizes the terms of individual human meaning: 'The mental and emotional tension resulting from man's discovery that every living creature is born and dies, including himself, must have led him intuitively to seek some escape from the relentless flux of time' (Whitrow [1972] 2003: 3). A religious belief and ideology might indeed offer a transcendence of a frustratingly limited sense of mortal time. More secular forms and notions of 'escape' will present themselves for consideration later, but it is worth noting that Hoffman suggests the benefits of therapy and meditation are, correspondingly, principally *temporal*: ways to create a pocket of 'countertime', 'a sense of timelessness in the subjectivity, in the here and now' (Hoffman 2009: 163, 164).[15] Bachelard observes how the 'dialectic of joys and sorrows' is 'never so absorbing as when it accords with the dialectic of time': the moment of appraisal that it is 'time that takes and that gives', and the attendant knowledge that 'time will take from us again', so that it becomes impossible to 'attribute uniform continuity to time when we have had such a vivid premonition of the weakening and failing of being' (Bachelard 2000: 51).

To focus on an earlier word in Whitrow's sentence: (outside of the unusual promises of 'countertime') a consciousness of time involves *tension*, which the dictionary closest to my hand associates with tenseness, mental strain or excitement; and with a strained (political, social) state or relationship.[16] This sense of individuality contextualized follows through to Whitrow's observations that an 'enormous effort must have been required for man to overcome his natural tendency to live like the animals in a continuous present'; but that a 'vital factor' in the human intuition of, and response to, time was and is a sense of *rhythm*: if a 'highly developed sense of rhythm enabled a tribe to function with precision as a single unit both in war and in hunting', this sense of *periodicity* might also inform more *pacific* ends: the principal transitions from one phase of a man and/or woman's life to another 'were thought of as crises and as a result the community assisted' with appropriate rituals: a social reflection of how the principal transitions in nature were also regarded as occurring suddenly and *dramatically*' (Whitrow [1972] 2003: 4, emphasis added) in the change from nomadic to agricultural forms of social existence.

So what is 'rhythm' here? We might start by thinking about a specifically and precisely arranged sequence of actions, functions (such as notes, words or coloured lights) or events – arranged with a sense of duration, alternation or both. We might wish to refine our basic image of theatrical performance to: the dynamic interaction of forces and bodies over time, presented in a dialogic 'feedback loop': something which is mutually informative but also formally surprising in its distortions.[17]

Stretch and flow

Perhaps it's not too soon to start trying to build up a sense of what is at stake in theatre and performance in its relation to time. A first working model could be a rhythmically specific event, which identifies, physically responds to and *works through* transitions in time, with reference to different 'time schemes' of personal life and wider community and nature (thus manifesting a sense of theatre and performance) – not least by recognizing and acknowledging the tensions that the awareness of such differing claims and transitions generate (thus manifesting a sense of time). The relationship is like a *hinge*: it lets you swing from one plane to another (imaginative/physicalized, past/future) in a move *in and through* the present (which is redesignated and shown as pivotal).[18] This effort may be artificial, but also artful: may involve artifice and even aspire towards a distinctive realm of life: art. Whilst tension may sometimes involve, say, a narrative 'situation or condition of hostility or uneasiness', it does not always entail aggression or dominance; its other factor, 'suspense', may be pleasurable (consider the conscious approach of the God Jupiter in Shakespeare's play *Cymbeline*, who aims to 'make my gift / The more delayed, delighted' [Shakespeare 2007: 2307]), even erotic (the most vivid memory of my Philosophy classes turns out to be from a lecture on pleasure, in which the lecturer identified the values of creating a pleasurable tension, then relieving that tension pleasurably). 'Stretching' may involve some effort, but is not always unpleasant. Perhaps the ultimate objective here is a sense of *flow*[19]: suggesting a plunge into a moment and movement 'without excessive resistance or excessive strain', yielding the pleasure of engagement with something occurring within its own proper and remarkable tempo, 'neither too fast nor too slow' (Hoffman 2009: 182), and requiring, on more than one side, 'receptivity, rather than headlong forward determination' (Hoffman 2009: 185), with the effect of attention fully focused on the present, rather than subject to distracting concerns associated with the past or future (effects that Klein associates with 'intense mindfulness' or 'presence of mind' [2008: 97]).

But if the initial and possibly main objective of this focal event is to recognize and acknowledge the tensions which the awareness of transitions generate, you will inevitably come up against the questions: how exactly do you negotiate changes, in any specific occasion? On whose terms? And who will the terms ultimately favour?

Cause and effect

Whitrow makes an important observation that holds true for any creation myth, when he notes how the creation myth recited by the chief priest of ancient Babylon 'was not really regarded as a record of the *past*', rather it 'served the theologico-politico purpose' of securing the supremacy of a specific god 'in the *present*' (Whitrow [1972] 2003: 5), often through calendars devised so that religious ceremonies could be performed on specified dates (incidentally, the Babylonians first proposed and instigated the seven-day week, which was subsequently adopted by the Jews). John Milton's epic (and in some ways dramatic) poem *Paradise Lost* identifies its prime objectives at its outset: to 'assert eternal providence', and 'justify the ways of God to men' (Milton [1972]: 462). Milton's poem aims to show how Christianity's distinctively linear (as opposed to cyclical) emphasis on the non-repeatability of events can, from an admittedly unusual (initially non-human) perspective, divulge the surprising but identifiable consolation of fortunate patterning (the Fall of Man, expulsion from Eden and the Great Flood are offset, in the wider time scheme of things, by moments and achievements that reflect to the mutual glory of God and humanity). Thus, interpretations of the past are consequential: they identify a sense of cause and effect; they are used to justify the present, and propose a future (and, hence, any version of the providential is also political; I would like to nominate that as Rabey's Law).

Slaves to the rhythm

But if time is not cyclical or seasonal, but to be perceived as a sequence of unrepeatable moments – how do you offset a sense of inevitable irrevocable *loss* (the dominance of which might be one definition of melancholy)? One secular response was the ideology of discernibly linear and specifically man-made progress, as propagated in 1602 by Francis

Bacon, in an early work significantly titled *Masculus Partus Temporum/The Masculine Birth of Time*, and thereafter by philosophers Leibniz and Locke and the linear advancement propagated by the Enlightenment, positing such progressiveness as instinctive (to humans, or men) and inevitable (because linear) in its providence – though under the law identified at the end of the previous paragraph, this is at least as likely to reflect a sense of political (self-)justification as biological or social evolution. Jay Griffiths has traced how time has frequently been genderized, implicitly rather than explicitly: 'linear time is phallic, male in shape'; 'cyclical time is yonic and female in shape'; and significantly 'the way time is pictured, or described, in any age, mirrors remarkably closely the way the feminine is treated then'; masculine linear time tends to denigrate feminine alternatives (Griffiths 1999: 119). Julia Kristeva suggests that feminine subjectivity will be opposed to the symbolic denominator of distinctly masculine conceptions of linear temporality ('civilizational, obsessional'), not least in the ways that feminism has 'the enormous merit of rendering painful, that is productive of surprises and symbolic life,' in 'a civilization which, outside the stock exchange and wars', is 'bored to death' (Kristeva 1981: 18). Kristeva notes how female subjectivity 'would seem to provide a specific measure that essentially retains *repetition* and *eternity* from among the multiple modalities of time known through the history of civilizations' (16). This distinctly feminine temporal perspective also 'renders explicit a rupture, an expectation, or an anguish which other temporalities work to conceal' (17). I will argue later that theatre, like feminized time, heretically proposes and offers a *dissipative structure* – and hence its analogous denigration in some hegemonies.[20]

To backtrack for a moment: in an agricultural society, work patterns were identified through reference to a providential sense of a natural cycle of time, which informed biological rhythms: patterns proposing that 'day is for labour, night for repose, and the round of seasons is a sequence of warmth and cold, planting and harvest, life and death' (Landes 1983: 15). This changed with the emergence of alternative sense of rhythm and priorities, and a new form of measurement: the clock. David Landes has identified the impact of how the times of church services were designated and set in terms of clock hours, in deference to a new sense of objective in terms of communal rhythm (which you will remember we are identifying as a specifically and precisely arranged sequence of actions, functions or events, intended to negotiate changes). Christianity proposed not just the performance of religious ceremonies on specific dates, but the multiplication of simultaneous devotions on a daily basis, a synchronization of efforts by monks and general churchgoers, as 'the way of salvation for all', instilling both a need for regular time signals and 'a new and special kind of temporal servitude' (Landes 1983: 63). Again, this sense of divine providence had its political ramifications, not just nationally but globally. The European invention of the mechanical clock, and its social centralization by Christianity, gained international dominance over its principal world rival in the perception and negotiation of change: the Chinese water-based form of measuring time. Landes identifies how this was crucial amongst 'a number of advances that turned Europe from a weak, peripheral, highly vulnerable outpost of Mediterranean civilization into a hegemonic aggressor' for whom 'Time measurement was at once a sign of new-found creativity and an agent and catalyst in the use of knowledge for wealth and power' (Landes 1983: 12).[21] Lewis Mumford, the American historian of technology (of whom more later), has consequently argued that the clock, not the steam-engine, is the key-machine of the modern industrial age, but that it has crucially annexed and dissociated the concept of 'time' from the specifically human, partly subjective, view of events: mechanical processes were 'treated as more "objective" than organic behaviour'; so the model of the machine became a central image and 'criterion for scientific accuracy and adequacy even in dealing with subjectively conditioned organisms' (Mumford 1971: 392).

Morality and money

Is Mumford being overly (even impractically) protective of subjective perceptions here? As Landes points out, social and personal interaction 'works only because the member units have learned a common language of time measurement'; without this language, and without 'general access to instruments accurate enough to provide uniform indications of location in time', 'urban life and civilization as we know it would be impossible', because '[j]ust about everything we do depends in some way on going and coming, meeting and parting' (Landes 1983: 2). If the rhythms of medieval (largely innumerate as well as illiterate) society could be arranged principally on an almanac based on the year, this was less appropriate to those who worked in towns, for whom reference points based on specifics of the day and week would be more appropriate. The first clocks were installed on church towers in the fourteenth century, and expanded their duties from the summons to church service to proclaim the opening and closing of city gates, the beginning and end of market time. The fascination for timekeeping devices extended beyond the church's liturgy, into other contexts (man-made, but partly imitating the religious community) in which living by the clock became the promise of a rhythm for success, not in the afterlife but in the here and now: in royal and aristocratic courts, which demanded performances of duty within a precisely formalized hierarchy; and in the commercial and industrial day of the towns and cities, in which artificial time signals and technologies of illumination are devoted to the fulfilment of a specifically and precisely arranged sequence of actions, functions or events – arranged with a sense of duration and alternation in serial engagements, given the spatial compactness of the city; particularly in 'cities that were engaged in textile manufacture, the first and greatest of medieval industries', where 'the definition of working time was crucial to the profitability of enterprise' and the prosperity of the city (Landes 1983: 72).

 This leads us to the historical juncture where the observation of time changes from being the use of external timepieces to summon people for a given purpose of constitutive social activities (which Landes calls *time obedience*) to an individual internalization of the responsibility to consult the clock in order to make possible goals of productivity and performance (which Landes calls *time discipline*, 1983: 7): the relocation of the onus of clock-time from being objective and external, to subjective and internalized, with the effect of a socially organized impersonality entering (and, Mumford might suggest, mathematizing and colonizing) the individual consciousness. The enthusiasm of merchants and earliest industrialists for the clock was ratified further and more fundamentally by Puritan and Protestant religious ethics, which designated waste of time to be the deadliest of sins, so that 'time' was 'evolving from a measuring device into a moral barometer' (Klein 2008: 158). E. P. Thompson identifies an orientation to time rather than task or social activities as the principal characteristic of industrial capitalism (Thompson 1967), with the effect of emptying out of time, space and humanity until, in the memorable phrase of Marx and Engels, the human being is nothing but 'the carcase of time' (Marx and Engels [1976]: 127). Perhaps the most succinct example of capitalism's co-opting of clock-time is the generally uncontested acceptance of Benjamin Franklin's maxim that 'time is money'.

(Un)Doing the maths

This is not to say that Franklin's statement is uncontestable. MacNaghten and Urry gather several oppositional viewpoints, noting that Marx did not pursue how the dominance of clock-time (or foresee how the dominance of computer-time) would 'transform people's subjectivities' (McNaghten and Urry 1998: 136) (an observation that indicates tasks for our further consideration):

> in most senses time is in fact not like money. Time can be shared to a limited degree (in a babysitting circle, for example), time can be stored up and exchanged (in time-share holiday accommodation, for example), and people vary enormously in their capacity to use time effectively (hence the importance of 'time-management'). But these are very limited opportunities. Mostly time, unlike money, cannot be stored up or saved, whatever sense we are employing. Time constrains human activity more firmly than does money since it inevitably passes and subjects everyone and everything to its passage: humans, animals and other organisms cannot escape the movement of time. Indeed [Barbara] Adam suggests that rather than time being like money, money is time. In many cases having a lot of time is of little value to people without money, such as the poor, the unemployed and inmates of total institutions [...] What is important is access to money which enables time to be put to good use (even if it still inevitably passes).
>
> (McNaghten and Urry 1998: 137)

Indeed, Jay Griffiths pithily observes how 24-hour-society despots will repeat Franklin's mantra 'without somehow answering the question *whose* money is made from *whose* time?' (Griffiths 1999: 164). Barbara Adam observes how 'the wealthy can buy the labour, service and skills of others *as* time, while agents of state and persons in positions of authority have the right to time-structure the lives of those under their control' (Adam 1990: 114). George Lakoff and Mark Johnson, in *Metaphors We Live By*, identify further ways in which time is not money: 'I can *give you a lot of time*, but you can't give me back the same time, though you can *give me back the same amount of time*' (Lakoff and Johnson 1980: 13). A crucial part of what teachers give their students is *time*, in the sense of the offer of appointments of properly focused attention, from both sides (which have parallels with the performer-audience relation) – in the case of universities, for a specified tuition fee (rather than the theatrical ticket price). Nevertheless, the particularly complex demands of timetables in schools and universities require both students and staff to demonstrate sharply defined senses of time management and discipline, involving a reliance on watches and clocks in situations, such as lessons or exams, which can seem to shorten or lengthen notoriously in subjective terms. James Gleick observes 'Our modern economic life depends increasingly on the scarcity of time, the competition for time, the revaluing of time, and the redistribution of time' (Gleick 2000: 242); driving him to provide an incisive satiric response: 'With no irony the message comes through: you have too little time, and you are working too hard, so buy this – quick' (202). Barbara Adam notes how the perpetual circulation of money pre-eminently valourized by neoliberal economic systems is 'the economic equivalent of Newtonian particles in motion: abstract, decontextualized, de-temporalized', a vision of order (like that of Mumford's machine) in which the physical environment and processes of the natural world become external to a central overriding image (Adam 1998: 75–76).

Beating the bounds

Clocks made navigation possible for ships at sea, and train timetables required temporal consistency between various towns and punctuality to achieve both efficiency and safety. However, Gleick points out that 'if we pay attention to our watches', they can also teach us, in their most surprising moments, 'that lived time is different from clock time': that subjective temporality is variable, changing with our moods, age and degree of engagement, and this lesson can create and reflect an occasional but significant critical distance from the 'version of truth you wear on your wrist' (Gleick 2000: 41–42), an awareness of its limitations. A notable encouragement to our initiative is provided by the words of Mumford, in his critical consideration of the relationship between man and time in the age of the machine, systematic quantification and hence increasingly centralized power. In his 1971 book *The Myth of the Machine*, Mumford writes: 'Man's existence in all its dimensions is perhaps best understood in terms of the theatre', as he can posit no better paradigm or 'scientific analysis that does such justice to every aspect of human development': theatre, Mumford suggests, is an apt metaphor for human consciousness and endeavour because of its orchestration of specifically different elements of time and action: by themselves, 'none of the physical constituents, not even the human bodies, are important', but rather how they accumulate and form (Mumford 1971: 414–415). Mumford's principal dramatic examples from Shakespeare's plays, Lear and Prospero, are both characters who testify memorably to a conscious sense of human power contracting with time, to a sense of decline and expiry: the fearful 'tension' that Whitrow associates with a contemplation of the finite nature of human life. Significantly, Hoffman suggests that 'literature offers few portraits of contented old age'; rather, 'the last stages of life get relatively short shrift in literature, as if the old were narratively, no less than evolutionarily, dispensable, or at least less interesting' (Hoffman 2009: 53–54, though Mangan [2013] offers a considered study of how plays and performances, past and present, may inform our understanding of ageing). *King Lear* begins with a king and father trying to determine change: the breaking points between King Lear and his daughters occur when they question (and effectively deny) his attempted determinations of the *pace* of change, and his terms; alterations that are later significantly focused on Lear's wish/need for an entourage of knights to obey and manifest his entitlement and power ('What need you five-and-twenty, ten or five? ... What need one?': *King Lear* II. 2. 449, 452, Shakespeare 2007: 2039). Prospero's dominion has contracted (admittedly from his own neglect) from a dukedom to an island, where he has nevertheless achieved a magical mastery within specific circumscriptions of space and time (the island and theatre) for just so long as it takes to perform the play *The Tempest*: beyond these, he emphasizes his own mortal limitation (V.1.346, Shakespeare 2007: 50). However, Lear and Prospero are particularly remarkable as dramatic characters in and because of their attempts to 'make sense' of their worlds and their selves over time, and in relation to its crucially finite quality. Lear's structures for sense break down, tragically; Prospero is aware of the poignant spatial and temporal limitations of his discovered spacetime and consciously manufactured 'sense' – the comedic present – in relation to past and future. They provide uniquely memorable examples of what Hoffman identifies: 'The problem of time is inseparable from that of meaning. Time *is* the fundamental medium and condition of human meanings'; 'What are the uses of a finite life, and what uses do we want to make of it? (Hoffman 2009: 182).

On this occasion, our tracing of a delineation of time in relation to theatre might help us to a heightened appreciation of both, as joint means by which human beings perceive and actively (re)make meaning in the relationships between their selves and their environments. Artaud indicates what is at stake when he describes theatre as a 're-conquest of the signs of what exists' (Artaud 1958: 63).

Sean Carroll proposes:

The entwined subjects of time, entropy, information and complexity bring together an astonishing variety of intellectual disciplines: physics, mathematics, biology, psychology, computer science, the arts. It's about time that we took time seriously, and faced its challenges head-on.

(Carroll 2010: 375)

Barbara Adam observes how human beings characteristically 'create artefacts and technologies that constitute physical environments for themselves and others'; and how time is 'implicated in all these dimensions of our being but is expressed differently in each of them'; yet if 'the entire range of natural times is central to our existence it seems appropriate for us to explore and to explicate what would normally be considered outside the sphere' of a single disciplinary perspective (Adam 1990: 49). The ramifications are considerable:

> 'We' and 'our time' must therefore not be presupposed or left implicit. To make explicit what we know intimately at the non-discursive level requires a phenomenological attitude. It demands that we extricate ourselves from the natural attitude and take the position of the stranger [...] we must get to know that invisible time and recognize its fundamental role in the constitution of the lives and institutions of those we study.
>
> (Adam 1995: 41–42)

My primary (but not exclusive) reference here is to (inevitably selective) facets of a specific art, series of different physical environments, technologies and artefacts, all summarized under the term: theatre. I will be considering some of the ways in which it explores and expresses, explicates and implicates, time: its social symbolizations of individual experience. This cannot and should not be the last word on how these subjects are entwined (as Sean Carroll writes, when 'we aren't sure of the final answer, it behoves us to ask the question in as many ways as possible', Carroll, 2010: 4); but it's time to make a start.

Notes

1 Waters suggests that where 'towns become clone towns, and malls and gated communities from Rio to Rugby are identical', the very facts that theatre takes place at a specified time and 'in a unique setting', make it an act of resistance to the standardizing geography and temporality of globalization, 'whatever is staged' (Waters 2010: 58).

2 Patricia Schroeder remarks on how Keir Elam's *The Semiotics of Theatre and Drama* (London: Methuen, 1980) isolates 'four temporal levels' in drama, yet does so 'excluding actual performance time' and so 'neglects a unique and significant component of the drama's temporal dimension' (Schroeder 1989: 11–12). Elam identifies 'the fictional *now* proposed by the *dramatis personae*', 'discourse time'; 'the order in which events are shown and reported', 'plot time'; the temporal ordering of events inferred by the spectator, 'chronological time'; and the historical context of dramatic events, 'historical time' (Elam 1980: 117–119). These identifications offer ways of identifying co-ordinates in fictional dramatic time, but Elam does not explore the friction between the actor's 'now' and the audience's 'now', in the terms which Rebecca Schneider derives from Gertrude Stein, which might enable 'a temporal slip, or crack, in any number of directions' (Schneider 2014: 40). In contrast, Prigogine's work incorporates an additional consciousness of the observer's perspective and framework, when he insists that no analysis is 'without communication, time orientation, distinction between earlier and later states, past and future extension, historical embeddedness and contextual embodiment' (Adam 1998: 45).

3   Sierz and Ghilardi, in their introductory study *The Time Traveller's Guide to British Theatre*, choose to conduct their historical guidance from the perspectives of several fictional 'animateurs' representing each period, and in an active present narrative tense: a strategy reminiscent of a museum trying to 'improve' emphatically its 'visitor engagement'.

4   There is a link in the relationship and distinction between theatre and science which is comparable to Schneider's observation on the relationship and distinction between theatre and history: 'theatricality is in some senses the opposite of historicity, where "authenticity" and "accuracy" are the keystones of the concept, despite the facts that both "theatre" and "history", as words, bear traces in their definition of being both the representation of the thing and the thing itself' (Schneider 2014: 21) – as does science, with its promises of empiricist authority.

5   Comment attributed by Rob Young. Another noteworthy statement attributed to Waits is that which features in a 2011 interview with Andy Gill: 'You don't wanna be a prisoner of time. Otherwise, you're a goldfish in a plastic bag, and you've just been lowered into the aquarium, and told to stay in the bag' (Waits 2014: 109).

6   Kalb suggests that theatre, especially in its more deliberately measured and lengthy forms, may offer 'rare and precious experiences of sustained meditation', in contrast to 'the endemic "hurry sickness" of the media era, with its compulsive multitasking, 60-second sitcoms, pop-ups within pop-ups, and epidemic attention deficit disorder' which we suffer 'in screen-bound isolation', by generating 'an uncommon sense of public communion that transformed throngs of atomized consumers into congregations of skeptical co-religionists, or at least consciously commiserating co-sufferers' (Kalb 2011: 2).

7   Kalb notes the way that The Royal Shakespeare Company's marathon performances of David Edgar's adaptation of Dickens, *The Life and Adventures of Nicholas Nickleby* (1980) attempted to overwhelm the audience members' immediate considerations of physical discomfort (stiff legs, hunger), by affording 'the joyous sense' of 'an entire day and evening triumphantly and subversively stolen' from utilitarian authoritarians, and 'invested' rather in 'an astonishingly comprehensive imaginary world'; as well as 'the exhilaration of a day spent in the company of world-class, adrenaline-pumped actors sweeping a thousand people irresistibly along on their emotional tide while telling a dauntingly complicated story as if it were a dire personal mission for each one of them'; whilst a further exhilaration is 'the mutual pride felt by a cast and an audience experiencing shared exhaustion, weighing their interconnected feats of endurance, at a curtain call that, for all the hours invested, seems to come too soon' (Kalb 2011: 44).

8   Pearson's identification of main spatial questions for site-specific performance can usefully be extended to other forms of theatrical performance; see Pearson (2010: 156).

9   On the relations of memory, Trigg writes how the suggestion of personal continuity is implicit in 'the notion of memory as being stored for retrieval' (45), as the activation of memory involves 'questioning how the image relates to the past', but this synthesis involves 'a concurrent blending of presence and absence': a confluence which we might consider at least somewhat theatrical, in that it joins the process of remembering with that of imagining, bringing together and consciously foregrounding a 'past experience with a playful reworking of that past in the present' (46).

10   Intriguingly, in July 2015 National Theatre Wales promoted their production of *The Iliad*, directed by Mike Brookes and Mike Pearson and including a day marathon performance of all three sections, as 'Epic storytelling for the age of the box-set': http://www.theatre-wales. co.uk/news/newsdetail.asp?newsID=5695 accessed 28/07/2015. However, the spectator had no opportunity to pause the performance; so the headline seems to refer to the quality of the sustained attention, and therefore immersion, which the production might involve.

11   Limon makes his distinctions with reference to Patrice Pavis's *Dictionary of Theatrical Terms*:

- Fictional historical time, implied by the performance [...] Pavis calls this the extra-scenic time or dramatic time.
- The fictional (fabulous) time of the performance, including the time which passes (on the stage and beyond it) from a fictional moment x, in which the action begins (e.g., tea-time in the salon, Monday, the winter of 1825), until the moment of its end (say, a month later); Pavis does not differentiate this time from the time in point (1).
- The sum of scenic time, fictional (by which we understand the time of each scene of the performance [...] Pavis does not differentiate this time either [...].
- The fictional scenic time of particular scenes [...] also a category not mentioned by Pavis.
- The real time of the duration of particular scenes (i.e. biological time of the actors); Pavis calls this scenic time, although according to him this is a category, which includes the spectators as well.
- The real time of the duration of the performance as an event (with breaks between scenes, the entr'acte and so on); for Pavis this is also scenic time.
- The sum of the real time of duration of particular scenes.
- 'Systemic' or structural time – belonging to the dominating semiotic systems, which also has a temporal nature (for example, music in opera, or dance and music in ballet, verse in dialogues) (Limon 2010: 107).

12   On 'the clock and the forest', see Rabey (2015: 111ff).

13   The emphasis is in Boal's original text. I prefer Boal's formulation of this working model for jointly affective imaginative activity to Klein's assertion, 'The film of our lives originates in our heads and we are directors' (Klein 2008: xxi), which sits oddly with Klein's own observations on the dominant forms of electronic media entertainment which he claims are characterized, all too often, by a characteristic inconsequentiality, which deliberately involves no lasting purchase or extensive effect upon the memory: 'We might even say that electronic entertainment shortens our lives' (Klein, 'Machines that Kill Time', 2008: 131). I will consider aspects of the phenomena of live theatre screenings in the next chapter.

14   States's paraphrase of Brecht's statement on the watch – 'When it has told you the time, it has nothing more to say to you' (States 186) – is very much a paraphrase, though an interesting one, in its scepticism towards clock-time as consistently meaningful measurement. Brecht's argumentative trajectory, as translated by John Willett (1964) in *Brecht on Theatre* (London: Eyre Methuen: 144) is more focused on seeing the watch with an unusually astonished eye, appreciative of its intricacy.

15 Hoffman also suggests that the 'reversion to religious fundamentalism, so evident in various parts of the world', may be seen 'as an attempt to restore to time its dimensions and significance', 'in defence against the extreme pressurization, and the banality, of fast time', 166.

16 J. B. Sykes (ed.) (1984), *The Concise Oxford Dictionary,* 7th ed., Oxford: Clarendon, p. 1102.

17 The rehearsal exercise/game 'The antiquated telephone exchange' generates examples of this (Boal 2002: 144).

18 Since first writing this sentence, I recognize some affinities with Lepecki's sense of contraction, drawn from Bergson's philosophy: that which 'implies an understanding of the present as simultaneously and permanently splitting open towards the past in dilation and towards what-will-come in dilation' (Lepecki 2006: 86).

19 Klein attributes this deployment of the term to the psychologist Mihaly Csikszentmihalyi (Klein 2008: 96). Time (quick or sustained) and Flow (bound or free) are also two of the four "Efforts" (the others being Weight and Space), action drives identified by Rudolf Laban in his practical analyses of inner attitudes towards motion, reflecting his characteristic bid to explore and integrate ostensible polar oppositions and extremes (Bradley 2009: 41–43).

20 On the subject of gendered time, I would accord with Adam, who acknowledges that time is not gender-neutral, but professes that her purpose 'is not to establish new dualisms and dualities – male and female time, productive and reproductive time, quantitative and qualitative time, instrumental and expressive time, employment time and its shadows – rather it is to sensitize us to a complexity largely untheorized and left implicit' in analyses 'that focus on some aspects of time to the exclusion of others' (Adam 1995: 94). Adam argues that a sense of 'women's time does not replace but shifts the emphasis from time as finite, rationalized, decontextualized exchange value to time as historically embedded and embodied, to a generative temporality that is nevertheless socially evaluated through the mediating filter of commodified time'; simultaneously, she invites recognition that 'men, the prime architects of the decontextualized, rationalized, standardized time of employment relations, are not exempt from living and making time, not excluded from the capacity for creating life' (99). Adam is concerned that 'very important feminist deconstructions of social time are in danger of being reabsorbed into the very frameworks of analyses they make problematic as long as these alternatives are constructed along dualistic lines' (106).

21 For more on the Chinese methods of time measurement, see Landes, who furthermore suggests: clocks 'embodied far more than an argument for the validity of Christianity', and were moreover 'an assault on China's self-esteem' (Landes 1983: 49); and that China's subsequent 'depreciation of the clock, among other western mechanisms, was also a protective reaction, an effort to erase the discrepancy between self-perception and reality' (48).

Chapter 2

Theatre in Time

Starting the day

Good morning. How do you decide to start the day (orient yourself in time)?

Like most people, I have a routine. I shower, dress, breakfast. Either before travelling to work, or starting work at home, I open my computer and consult a series of websites. This routine offers me structured continuity, in order to consider change.

In the house in which I grew up, my parents arranged for a newspaper to be delivered to their letterbox every morning, until they decided that this was wasteful because they did not have time to read the newspaper in full. Some people start the day by consulting news as broadcast by television or radio, but I find the tempo (and often the tone) of these broadcasts invasive and presumptuous (however I subscribe to the British television and radio guide magazine, *Radio Times*, because I like a 'hard copy' to which I can return over a week, in order to alert me to programmes and to help me to plan viewings and recordings; and to two music magazines, to alert me through reviews, articles and interviews, to developments in styles and genres of music that interest me). So I prefer to look at two newspaper websites each morning: scanning the headlines for major developments, and identifying stories to which I will return, in order to read further details. My choice of the two newspaper websites reflects my choices of perspective: if I told you which ones they are, you would probably be able to guess two other newspaper websites that I actively avoid, on political grounds.

I then check my e-mail, in order to identify urgent tasks and developments, and briefly consider an order, and ways, in which to respond to these. Before I settle down to address these, if time permits I will 'take a breath' (and offer myself a brief reward for having got this far) by consulting another news website, the national website for the sport of speedway (Speedway Great Britain).

Interlude: Ways of speed

Speedway is the only form of sporting performance whose developments I follow on a daily basis, even though I have lived for some decades in an area too far from an active track for me to attend any matches in person (so I have to make do with watching it on television, and have a satellite subscription for several months a year primarily for this purpose). Speedway appeals to me because its team matches (as opposed to its individual tournaments, such as the Grand Prix, which have a different appeal) demand that two riders engage strategically with two other riders in each race. Although I can appreciate the individual prowess of a rider in an individual tournament (as I can that of a snooker or darts player in similar contexts), I prefer a speedway team match because my fascination is not just with competitive acceleration or overtaking (though these have their exhilarations) but also with the ways that two riders will 'team-ride' to achieve a joint, mutual and team advantage over their opponents. Through demonstrating quick reactions, performing together 'in the flow' in such a way as to combine, skilfully and gracefully, the complementary reflexes and initiatives of two minds, bodies and machine, two riders will prove to be unpredictable together: they will outwit their opponents, by working with their partner on a moment-by-moment basis, without verbal conferring. Speedway is aptly named: *speed* is only half of it – the decisive test is how to find a *way*, in combination with another. Interpersonal timing and a sense of spatial relations are actually more crucial than speed: it is possible for two slower riders to outwit and beat a faster one, if they are tactically attuned in time and space; the most impressive individual rider may nevertheless end the match on the losing side, if his teammates have failed to work closely together, in time and space. The sport rewards a joint orchestration of energies, achieved through practice, tactical planning, intuition, spatial awareness, timing and courage. It requires a capacity for temporal resolution in the millisecond range, in order to estimate the relative speed and orientation of an opponent, and distance to one's position, and adapt one's own timing and implementation of decisions accordingly. It has many contact points with theatre: for me, the most of any sport, which is probably part of why I enjoy it. Like many other sports, it takes place in a stadium that is, like a theatre, a 'crucible of anticipation'[1]: a space that waits for most of the day, for a sudden intense focus of interest and attention.

Starting the night

Ah yes, theatre. When I have done all of the above, I begin work. I teach people to pay attention to things: focusing more insistently, on more things, than they otherwise might; and teach them why this is important. I teach people to consider what *is* (apparently) (t)here; and what (apparently) isn't; to discern, anticipate and implement complex choices, and changes, accordingly. My colleague Richard Downing, lecturer in Scenographic Studies, often alerts people to 'mind the gaps': to look for, seek out, the gaps in habitual perception and official definition, in order to energize and activate the spaces and relations between things, to unusual and surprising effect. Working together, we think about Starting the Night (which is more often when theatre performances occur; and I prefer to associate them imaginatively with night rather than day). Starting the Night is somewhat different to Starting the Day, although it may similarly establish and build in principles of familiarity, methods and routine, at times (not least because duration perception, which generally fluctuates between early morning and late evening, becomes particularly elastic in the intensities of production week, as it does when falling in love, and one form of mysterious estrangement has been known to involve the other). We explore ways to present a distinctly different space in time, in which to consider things differently, together. This usually involves a specific arrangement of artificial light that subverts, and to some degree supplants, natural circadian and diurnal rhythms.

We experiment with *transforming contexts*: both as activity and phenomenon. These should not be confused with perceiving a change in frameworks, because that would imply some still point of objective authoritative focus and stability, trained on something that is contrastingly in flux; or with shifting our perspectives, on something that remains fixed and stable. Rather, we are interested in contexts (frameworks and perspectives), which change; on processes, which transform; and the imaginative friction between these phenomena, suggesting other ways of looking, and choosing to act in response: inside, but also perhaps, by implication and analogy, outside, of the space and time and event of the theatre. In theatre, we 'mind the gaps' in official and habitual definition: identify, activate, energize and embody these gaps, interactively. Weitz suggests that play is the 'behavioural mode that allows us to make the world what we want', however briefly; and that it achieves this by its power to 'set aside or otherwise redefine actual circumstances and their everyday meanings', by transposing something, fictionally and momentarily, to 'some imagined or alternative context' (Weitz 2016: 6). Here, the usual rules need not apply: we can imaginatively experience 'a cure for gravity' (Jackson 1999) and irreversibility. Weitz links this to Žižek's concept of the 'event', which offers a 'change of the very frame through which we perceive the world and engage in it' (Žižek, quoted by Weitz 2016: 73), and hence a re-imagining of what might constitute the 'real' (and the 'Real', and the 'realistic').

Theatre foregrounds the implicit temporal structuring of conscious (and subconscious) experience in self-reflection. Zarrilli describes the process of rehearsal in terms of 'time intended as space in which the participant begins to discover an alternative relationship to time *through the body*' (Zarrilli 2009: 31). In his different discipline, Marc Wittman suggests our subjective sense of time 'emerges through the existence of the self across time as an enduring and embodied entity' (512, a notion of form and context that, I suggest, the dramatist Samuel Beckett most wryly explores and subverts). Wittman proposes a tripartite structure of time: 'I become aware of what is happening now to me through memory of what happened (to me) and expectations of what might happen (to me)', through which a sense of self emerges (and is determined). Thus, 'the present experience is a *stage* where the self emerges through the retentional and protentional part of an experience', which means, the part that 'reflects what happened to me and what might come about for me' (Wittman 2014: 514, emphasis added).

So, I suggest that a theatrical performance is a specifically heightened and demonstrative awareness of time and change, and that theatre may yield the sense of a temporal consciousness that Lynne Segal identifies when she writes of how 'the time we feel most at one with the world is often when we are in a sense *least* our ordinary selves', when, paradoxically, 'being in time with time in these ways involves stepping outside of normal temporal patterns'

(Segal 2014: 181). These 'normal' (normative?) patterns are associated with unremitting demands of the social world, and our habitual and normal reflexes in relation to them, to maintain our usual sense of self (and relations to others).

The theatre that I will be considering principally does not offer a release from self/ consciousness in an anodyne way, but offers an occasion and arrangement – a time and space – for the refocusing of standard perspectives, of self in relation to others, embodied. Demands for the necessity of immediate responses are suspended, while we watch and listen to how events and consequences 'play out' (unless the theatre has some form of participatory structure eliciting audience response to determine consequences, though even then it will usually present some initial premise of problem that will require some considered and consequential form of active witnessing, involvement or specification of preference: subsequently to *something*, rather than immediately).

Theatre is an occasion for the simultaneous physical gathering of adjacent individuals, who – simultaneously but differently – accord their attention to some matter of collective interest and/or concern, the presentation of which is gradually unfolded, in ways that take time. As Hoffman observes in a non-theatrical context[2]:

> In order for disparate occurrences in the political space to coagulate into an 'event', we need to make connections between them, to reflect on their meanings, and to see their shape. Instead, as indiscriminate information keeps bombarding us from all sides, the happenings in the public realm remain just that: something that happens, and then disappears [...] in this perpetually created and perpetually vanishing present, there is no time to take stock, to consider relationships between occurrences, or link into the longer and deeper time of history.
>
> (Hoffman 2009: 171)

Time in theatre is not reversible, as is the running of a film (which, when played in reverse mode, can make a throw appear a catch, or poured water flow upwards). Theatre actors may *simulate* performing an action 'in reverse' (for example, walking backwards off a stage after they have walked on to it), but they and their actions will be different on some muscular and molecular levels, as they use different physiological initiatives, as will our perceptions of the actions. A play such as Harold Pinter's *Betrayal* (considered in more detail later) may employ a reverse chronology in the ways it selects events for presentation, but it does so in order to assemble a surprising and unusual temporal framework within which we are invited to consider the sequential resonances, tensions, ironies and poignancies of what might otherwise seem isolated and unremarkable events and details. However, this *reframing* process, through successive *spatial* exposures of different *temporal* levels, is not the same as the Newtonian idealization of 'reversible time'.[3] As Adam observes, there can be no 'un-living, un-knowing, un-thinking or un-doing' that involves literal and sustained human rejuvenation, or the separation of a baked apple pie back into its pre-cooked ingredients (Adam 1990: 169).

G. H. Mead has observed how it is customary to think of the past (or, I would add, the dead) as 'there' (in significantly *linear* terms), situated irrevocably and beyond change (Mead 1959: 11), in that we cannot change or undo events (or the consequential narrative details of a life) as they have happened. However, as Barbara Adam adds:

> In its meaning and the way it is preserved, evoked and selected, however, the past is revocable and as hypothetical as the future. The past is continuously recreated and reformulated into a different past from the standpoint of the emergent future. It has no status apart from its relation to the present.
>
> (Adam 1990: 39)

History plays reanimate and contextualize their subjects surprisingly, and hence dramatically. Shakespeare's *Henry V* trains a succession of perspectives on its protagonist: the dramatist self-consciously changes the frameworks for consideration right up until the last lines. In a spirit of extreme formal restlessness, Caryl Churchill's play *Heart's Desire* (the first half of her 1997 double bill, *Blue Heart*) specifies that performers should explore a series of scripted tangents from a given opening dramatic situation (parents awaiting the return of their daughter), and subsequent dramatic developments (an unexpected visitor), so that the scenario (and performers) appear to 'skitter' in time, behaving afresh as if the variant developments had not occurred. However, they *have* occurred, for the theatre audience, who are challenged, through witnessing the accumulation of incompletions, to revise their expectations of dramatic development and consequence accordingly (*Heart's Desire* is a pointedly impatient demonstration of how limited suburban family dramas usually are, given the possibilities of theatre for, say, a ten-foot tall bird to enter: as it does at one point, as a dramatic non sequitur).

A theatrical performance explores ways to spatialize time, to delineate time's motion in spatial terms: in order to imagine and consider it (in some ways) anew, by activating attention to transformative (external and internal) contexts for its estimation. A theatrical performance foregrounds the ways that time involves (sometimes even barely perceptible, or imperceptible) change, depicted through (even barely perceptible) spatial motion in (over a period of) duration. A theatrical performance is a specifically heightened and demonstrative awareness of time and change, an embodied field of estrangement involving action and emotion. It is an event when/where our multifaceted and mysteriously inconsistent capacities for subjective time judgements and alterations of perception are manifested and presented physically and spatially, scenographically and (usually) verbally (dance theatre will usually, characteristically, replace speech with soundscape).

An aside: there are, of course, notable exceptions to theatre where the dimension of spoken words is as prominently significant as the dimension of physical actions. This may be a distinctive feature of so-called 'physical theatre', although I dislike this categorization personally, as I find it hard to consider or identify meaningfully a *non*-physical theatre,[4] when the body is 'the functional anchor of phenomenological experience' (Wittman

2014: 512) and reaction to stimuli, including that of uttering and receiving speech. The 'physical' versus 'textual/implicitly non-physical' theatre binary sets up an unhelpful and unconvincing opposition that relegates speculative and formally experimental dramatic theatre, such as Samuel Beckett's *Acts Without Words* and *Breath* that depict in strikingly and unpredictably distilled forms, respectively, insistence of interpretative response and mortal process, over time; and Howard Barker's *The Forty* that depicts, amongst other things, the decay and transformation of an impulse, initially formulated as repeated gesture and/or brief utterance, over time.

People choose to go to the theatre for a variety of reasons, but those reasons will usually involve some search for a space and occasion that offer transformative frameworks. Even someone who makes successive visits to performances of a theatre production or play with which they are (perhaps intimately) familiar – such as Agatha Christie's *The Mousetrap* or a West End or Broadway mega-musical, or a Shakespeare play with which they studied or have seen before – is likely to enjoy some degree of recognition, of predetermined and reassuring familiarity in the occasion. However, they may also enjoy some minor degree of modulation, either in the occasion and timing of interpretative performance, or in their own degree and focus of attention to what is unfolding (the relish and appreciation of a detail or skill previously unremarked as significant). They may also enjoy the ways that the performance presents its perspective of difference from their habitual experiences outside of the theatre (the enjoyable suspension of habitual categorical definitions, values, pressures and powers that is, even briefly and tenuously, afforded, in different terms, by comic style and tragic speculation). They may even enjoy the setting of action in a distant or recent historical period, when such definitions, pressures and powers might at least be believed to be manifested and responded to *differently*, including differences of subjective emphasis and focus over time. For example, one may view and respond to aspects of a given Shakespeare play differently after gaining or losing a child, or lover, or leader of government. Re-encounters with familiar plays in different temporal contexts may constitute what Winnicott describes as a space of play for creative repetitions, renunciations and recuperations: 'varieties of playing, uses of illusion' that nevertheless form 'threads of continuity that enable us to differentiate and recapitulate past experiences' (quoted in Segal 2014: 25) as we negotiate the processes of ageing and deriving meaning.

People will also exercise choices in their perspective: as when I choose to read a particular newspaper website (rather than another), or to play (or read about) a particular style and genre of recorded music. Those who attend theatre are likely to be informed, at least to some degree, of the style and genre of the presentation, and perhaps the characteristics and style of the hosting theatre and/or the company (they will also have a preference about how close to the action they want to sit, in exchange for their money). However, I suggest that the importance of the second category above – recognition, based on an unusual degree of attention to an unusual variety and combination of things, onstage and off – is more of an insistent, even conscious, lure for theatregoers than it is for, say, someone choosing to watch a given film in a cinema for a second time. Admittedly, one may derive pleasures from a second cinematic screening of what remains a (de)finite electronic recording, when one's first individual subjective responses to this might be shown up as not (de)finite: one may change or deepen one's reaction to how details unfold, particularly if sharing it with (different) company, as one may on a second visit to a theatrical event. However, the stakes of repetition and difference are higher: the cinematic actor is not required to make renewed efforts each time a film is edited and screened. Depending on the theatre architecture and style of presentation (the action may be framed by a proscenium arch; or alternatively presented in-the-round, traverse, promenade or site-specific or immersive, or a combination thereof), it is possible for a returning theatregoer to choose a crucially different perspective on the action, and identify (principally subjective?) changes deriving, if not from narrative events or sequence, then from viewpoint. This choice of perspective is not available to the television or cinema viewer. Theatre involves, from audiences and performers (who, unlike filmed performers, operate 'in the moment' yet repeatedly), more intensive expenditure of energy in the cognitive and emotional processing of complex and novel and embodied stimuli, which dilate the subjective sense of duration. Indeed, action triggering emotion, in turn, triggers neural and psychophysical actions, in a dynamic interpersonal temporal resonance, a hyper-estimation of immediate time (through an acceleration of the internal clock of subjective time). However, this will probably not entirely, or lastingly, disrupt or disorganize an overarching perception of, and sensitivity to, continuation time: an expectation that the theatre event will conclude, and external rhythmic priorities be resumed.

The increased availability and popularity of live, or repeated, screenings of theatre performances is an interesting phenomenon. On the one hand, the cinema audience for a live screening (unlike the theatre audience before whom the performance most immediately unfolds) have no directly interactive or dialogic relationship with the performance. Waters observes that usually 'in cinema, what is screened has already been filmed and is located in the past tense', hence only 'in theatre is time so irreducibly centre stage' (Waters 2010: 71). However, I often find that the cinema audience for a screening of a live or repeated theatre or opera event follow their emotional and physical *interactive* impulse to applaud at the end of the performance, even though the actors and production team cannot hear their applause, as they are in a separate space (and, in the case of a repeat screening, in a different juncture of time). This may be for several reasons, or a combination thereof: the cinema audience may wish their own appreciation to be enfolded into that of the applauding theatre audience (who *are* present in the prime location of performance), following the theatrical 'cue' for its occasion, perhaps as a demonstration of distinctly theatrical manners; and/or they may wish to register their appreciation of the event to their immediate cohort, and/or to themselves (interacting with their immediately neighbouring audience members, as at the end of a demanding tragedy or theatre marathon, where there may be an element of congratulation not only of the performers' focus and endurance, but the audience's own focus and endurance: a collectively expressed respect for rediscovered individual dignity, which in tragedy is not smug, but more mindful of enhanced fragilities).[5] Barbara Adam identifies the important principle that, on some (micro-) level, 'no routine, tradition, or regular recurrence is ever the same in any of its repeats' (Adam 1990: 29). Adam's observation above also accounts for the possible fascination of observing closely a given production or performance on a second occasion: discerning how minimally (or otherwise) it may alter, or alter you, or those around, in combination. Actors and directors are, professionally, keenly aware of variations from one performance to the next, even as the production may promise minimal divergence from a specified level of excellence.

Chronos and *kairos*

'Immediacy' is a term that is often over-used with reference to theatre and its claims, as a vacuous non sequitur. However, we might venture a more precise reading of the word: a reminder, that Time is a resource of which we can never know how much we will be granted.

Priestley argues that 'Time cannot be reduced to mere change', but without the possibility of change 'there would be no Time'; so Time cannot be reduced to 'merely something happening, but unless something *is* happening, there can be no Time' (Priestley 1964: 64). Our physiological processes may be distinctly and identifiably rhythmic, and our social and cultural arrangements may establish further objective markers, measurements and co-ordinates to identify duration and location. However, despite our needs for points of reference and standards of comparison, our personal imaginations and memories remain subjective arrangements of past experiences and fiction, and capable of surprising and bewildering misjudgements in/of objective details. Hence Priestley's sense that the 'idea of Time as a combined joke-mystery is not to be despised' (Priestley 1964: 61); and the widespread sense of mingled wryness, frustration and yearning associated with the wish that one could have known, when one was younger, what one knows now.[6] The classical scientific concept of the 'arrow of time' posits linear movement, in one direction only, so that the future will always be different from the past. Nevertheless, Oscar Wilde's (often dramatized) story *The Picture of Dorian Gray* (1891) imagines a mysterious suspension of the rules of time: rather than an arrestment or reminder of the inevitability of human decay, Gray's uncanny portrait becomes, for a while, its repository, in defence of its subject (inexplicably but hauntingly).[7] *Groundhog Day* (originally a film, directed by Harold Ramis in 1993, scheduled for adaptation to theatre production in London 2016, at the time of writing) also imagines the single direction of 'the arrow of time' subverted, so that only the protagonist realizes he is arrested in a loop of recurring events. These events seem to offer the protagonist a range of possibilities to explore actively, but they actually constitute a fixed monotonous order: his actions are literally *inconsequential* and so time-less. The film/play depicts his struggle to discover some understanding and response that might free him from this cyclic rhythmic structure, where nothing can happen to make a lasting difference, into a more natural rhythm of seasonal change, notwithstanding the decay involved. The story of the film/play vindicates the protagonist's active consciousness and acceptance of, and commitment to, a limitation of possibilities and personal choices (associated with a resurgence of a more 'natural' temporal order and perspective that is reappraised as strangely, surprisingly redemptive). However, it does so by enabling us to imagine a situation where (somehow) the normal rules might not apply, and where the superficially intriguing attractions of this 'unnatural' situation are revealed to be mere *dis*tractions in a desert of inconsequentiality.

The aboriginal dreamwalker,[8] the industrial capitalist and the protagonist of *Groundhog Day* are nevertheless united in their sense that time holds, and therefore represents a sense of opportunity that should not be neglected. This is more finely delineated by the Greeks' use of two different words for time: *chronos*, the time of continuity and mutability (and the name of the most powerful God, who is also capable of eating his own children); and *kairos*, 'the temporality of the auspicious moment, of opportunity or crisis – the kind of heightened and irretrievable instant that we need to grab by the horns' (Hoffman 2009: 184–185). Jacques (1982) characterizes this distinction in terms of succession (clock-time/ *chronos*) and intent (*kairos*), two axes that stand in a necessary relation to each other, where the latter always incorporates the former, but never the other way around (Adam 1990: 17). Negri envisages *kairos* as the moment/event/passage of 'the arrow that has been released' (Negri 2013: 158), decisively and irreversibly linking one point of time (comparable to the point of the arrow) with (or extended into) that which is to come (the target struck): 'temporality augmented by expression' (162). Anne Bogart delineates the distinction further in the context of her theatrical practice as a director:

> *Chronos* is measured time. *Kairos* is unbound and unmeasured time. *Chronos* is quantitative while *kairos* is qualitative. *Chronos* is chronological time. The difference between *chronos* and *kairos* is the difference between time and timing […] Neither *chronos* nor *kairos* is time itself. *Chronos* is a particular way of understanding time by the clock. *Chronos* is chronology. *Kairos*, on the other hand, is timing or opportunity. Our current cultural moment of digital frenzy has obliged us as a culture to be super attentive to *chronos*.
>
> (Bogart 2014: 80)

Theatre, as a medium, courts and conducts *kairos*, the window of opportunity for favourable decisive action, 'on the edge of lived temporality' (Negri 2013: 169).[9] At best, theatre may present and foreground the moment/sense of *kairos* ('in production', in deed) as unconventionally valuable in contrast to the dominant claims of *chronos*. By 'courts', I mean that the process of theatre rehearsal is often principally an (informed but) open-ended exploration of possibilities and alternatives in search of the valuably unpremeditated, a hunting of invisible game. By 'conducts' I mean the director oversees and directs the experiments of the performers, mindful of when/how to instigate, when/how to hold back and permit potential to arise, when/how to intervene in order to inflect and select, facilitating 'the moment in which the arrangement of spatial and temporal issues begins to vibrate' (Bogart 2014: 83). Dufourmantelle's description of *kairos* as 'the here and now deployed absolutely' (Dufourmantelle 2007: 41) suggests an ideal of theatre's transforming contexts. Indeed, at best, it may be, in both form and content, a re-presentation of an 'occasion in human life when one makes a decisive choice, a commitment which gives a definite form to one's future and a retroactive meaning to one's past' (Dreyfus 1975: 151). By 'form and content', I mean that a notable performance of *fictional* 'pivotal events', such as those that often comprise the narrative of a drama, may potentially be perceived and become established as more widely significant pivotal events that define or extend or transform the professional career and associations of a given performer, director or scenographer – or open up and extend the personal emotions, thoughts and reflections of the spectator into unforeseen configurations. Bogart again:

> Readiness seems to be one of the keys to unlocking the experience of both spaciousness and *kairos* [...] *Kairos* is the alternative, the readiness to take advantage of changing circumstances. It is withheld from no one, but one must do the preparatory work in order to be in a position to perceive it. Because it is not 'our' time, we do not own it and as such it cannot be controlled; it happens when it happens. It is necessary to cooperate with *kairos* rather than force it [...] The best I can do is pay attention to the sort of things that lure it in my direction.
>
> (Bogart 2014: 81–82)

However, what remains culturally arguable is the nature of opportunity. Systems of hierarchical social organization characterize a self-legitimizing meaning through appeals to a sense of control, claiming to be uniquely discerning of, and responsive to, 'deep structures' within time, 'beyond the immediate confines of remembered generations experience' (Aveni in Lippincott 1999: 53): whether presented in the form of appeal to a sleeping god, or to the force of the national or global economic market (our current western cultural saturnine and superhuman presidencies to be appeased). Authorities (self-legitimizingly) claim that forces, which precede more immediate human intimations, must be appeased, in the terms that these authorities specify (because these authorities claim to find these forces not quite as unpredictable and inscrutable as we do: ultimately, the logic of the fatal forestalling, the pre-emptive strike). Theatre nevertheless offers a means – a time and space (depicting times and spaces) – of defamiliarization, calling into question assumptions regarding the 'deep structure of things' (Dahl, quoted by Gipson-King 2013: 148). In Rebecca Schneider's words, 'theatre can be called an art of time, and also an art of passage – the passing of one person, thing, or idea into another persona, thing or idea, where person, thing and idea are *in play*' (Schneider 2014: 69, original emphasis). I suggest it achieves this by mobilizing and foregrounding a multiplex variety and orchestration of different but compatible temporal frameworks and definitions, which constitute its transforming contexts.

How might *different* temporal frameworks be *compatible*? Arstila and Lloyd propose that the concept of subjective time might more appropriately be replaced by 'subjective *times*': 'the psychology and phenomenology of subjective time' could 'rest on mechanisms that operate at different scales, but that overlap at their edges' (Arstila and Lloyd 2014: 319–320) and so increase a density of experience and consequent sensed duration. Accordingly, I suggest theatre puts in play numerous variant temporal indicators (and 'fast' and 'slow' processes), simultaneously, as a continuous multiplicity of relations to construct a fictional (what William James termed a 'specious') present by processes that actually extend over a longer period (including rehearsal and performance): theatre presents the apparent (and actual) discovery of actions and words by performers *in the moment*, artfully concealing how far this moment is a result of previously instigated and co-ordinated processes and constituent contributory micro-events (such as a change in lighting). This contributes to an experience of succession (rather than what might be identified as a succession of experiences), fictional causality and consequence: flow.[10]

Thomas Fraps similarly notes how the conjuror's performance of a magic trick depends on a manipulation and misdirection of subjective temporality and sensed causality, the construction of a deceptive perceptual 'window' or framework, to achieve an effect comparable to M. C. Escher's paintings of impossible objects, where the observer perceives, momentarily, 'a "real impossibility"' rather than a painted one (Fraps 2014: 271; one might consider Caryl Churchill's play *Traps* as one deliberate theatrical instance of accumulating deliberately contradictory frameworks).

One such presentation of significant 'impossibilities' might be theatre's presentation of the incursion of ghosts, instances of what David Edgar characterizes as time operating 'on the plane of space' through figures 'embodying the past', who instigate a theatrical dialogue between past and present (Edgar adds, theatre's 'effectiveness in holding present failings and past errors to account is proved by Chairman Mao, who banned all plays with ghosts from the Chinese theatre', Edgar 2009: 188).

David Hume's famous proposal that 'the mind is a kind of theatre, where several perceptions successively make their appearance' (Hume 1739: 821) has been questioned by suggestions that 'both the locus and the subject of consciousness are divided into multiple processes that take place in various parts of the brain' (Mölder 2014: 22). But Hume's image was adapted by William James, who suggested 'the mind is at every stage a theatre of simultaneous possibilities' (James, cited in Arstila and Lloyd [1890] 2014: 10), perhaps implying that it potentially therefore tends towards intuitions of simultaneous inclusion more often than concepts of sequential exclusion. Furthermore, James elaborates his image: the 'relation of conceived to intuited time is just like that of the fictitious space pictured on the flat back-scene of a theatre to the actual space of the stage', where objects painted on the flat, '(trees, columns, houses in a receding street, etc.)', seemingly extend a series of objects 'solidly placed' on the stage space so that 'we think we see things in a continuous perspective, when we really thus see only a few of them and imagine that we see the rest' (19). This is a process of attention, a focalization and of consciousness that 'implies withdrawal from some things in order to deal effectively with others', a 'condition which has a real opposite in the confused, dazed, scatterbrained state which in French is called *distraction* and *Zerstreutheit* in German' (10).

Regarding the continuous visual (and usually aural) experience of cinematic and televisual narrative, Walton distinguishes film (from, say, photographs) as 'pictures whose temporal properties do contribute to their representational content' (quoted by Phillips 2014: 147) so that cinematic awareness might be characterized as 'mainly perceptual awareness of the scene present to us here and now' (Arstila and Lloyd 2014: 81), though the pictures and their edited sequence are *finite*. In theatrical performances, more variants are in play, the event is consciously less finite: a film actor cannot vary his recorded performance, or its angle of presentation. Whilst a theatrical performance is ubiquitously assumed to be constituted by its creators following a broadly or tightly agreed sequence of actions, its development is not entirely finite: nuances may vary, accidents might occur, heightening a sense that the future *is* unwritten. I suggest theatre offers a denser 'extensionalist' perspective than film, a 'thicker' spread of temporal awareness where 'immediate past and future join with the present in an extended temporal window of awareness' (Arstila and Lloyd 2014: 81): theatre seems to involve moments that cannot coexist temporally, yet *physically* cohabit the same space (or some designated portion of it). In theatrical performance, differing experiences and representations of time are manifested as discrepant, and yet cohabiting, inclusively rather than exclusively (a manifestation of *both/and* rather than *either/or*). This has wider imaginative implications for our habitual imagined boundaries of exclusion, not least of what the experienced present (and notional past and future) might be, and offer.

Jerzy Limon proposes a '*basic formula of theatre*' in terms of a framework of '*mutual agreement*' in which '*at least one person (the performer) pretends before another (the spectator) that what belongs to the past tense (or future) of the spectator is the former's temporal present; in most cases the one who pretends will also pretend to be someone else and at another location*' (Limon 2010: 37); furthermore, he adds, the experience of 'contradiction between different models of perceiving reality is deepened by the fact that time flows with a different tempo in each of the spheres, undermining what we know about physics and biology'; and that 'moreover in the fictional realm it reveals unique features; such as its elasticity and flexibility or ability to slow down, accelerate or even to stop completely' (37–38), in ways that one cannot ordain in the experiences we recognize and designate as 'real life'. Limon deduces that 'the creation of different time structures and the juxtaposition of different models of perceiving reality are the essential features of theatre as art', as the 'two incongruous models of perceiving reality can logically co-exist only if separated by time' (38).

David Edgar suggests that theatre proposes new forms of meaning 'by concentrating experience sufficiently to expose patterns and connections which audiences would otherwise miss' (Edgar 2009: 12): he thus characterizes a forensic and deductive process, reflecting his own theatrical processes.[11] Furthermore, he suggests how theatrical drama is well placed to reflect and provoke the dialectical dynamics of memory:

Drama's capacity to point up connections is one of the reasons it has – historically – been so successful in comparing and contrasting different worlds: the objective and the subjective, the individual and the collective, the personal and the political, the worlds of the family and the state. Drama can bridge the two great sources of our experience: our direct, lived, first-person experience and knowledge that is reported to us second- or third- hand. In doing so, it echoes the way our memory works.

(Edgar 2009: 10–11)

Bachelard and *The Dialectic of Duration*

Thus we have a basic model of theatre as a place that distinctively and consciously entertains and explores (apparent) contradictions. In the rest of this chapter, I will develop a sense of theatre, with reference to three theorists of time: Bachelard, Prigogine and Adam.

Henri Bergson (1859–1941) extended his philosophical speculations in counter-enlightenment directions, drawing attention to forces beyond the reach of principles of exclusive rationality (including change and memory), and was concerned with the fundamental differences in/between time and space. However, the French phenomenologist Gaston Bachelard (1884–1962) advanced a critique of Bergson's concept of duration, as something continuous and devoid of contradiction. Bachelard cited biology, molecular physics and radiation study to deduce that there is movement, rhythm and dialectic, a process of *becoming*, in all matter, so that, as Wiles observes, 'the separation of time from space was an impossibility' (Wiles 2014: 10). However, a closer inspection of Bachelard's arguments suggests ways in which his ideas may be more resonant for theatre, as a temporal/spatial crucible of exploration, than Wiles has time to pursue.

Firstly, Bachelard notes that the appeal of duration (like that of consistency) is limited, and that Bergson appears to have written nothing 'on and for' *risk*, addressing the curious appeal of *instability*: 'the strange emotional game that leads us to destroy our security, our happiness and our love, nor about the sense of exaltation that draws us to danger, newness, death and nothingness' (Bachelard 2000: 27). Bachelard's words resonate beyond their immediate context, figuring the attraction of speculative theatre, particularly tragedy, for the watchful theatre artist and spectator.

Secondly, Bachelard criticizes Bergson's notion of duration as immanently both immediate and deep, a form of plenitude largely impervious to external forces (such as language) and appearances. In contradistinction, Bachelard unfolds a series of images for creative consciousness that have several points of contact with processes of direction and rehearsal (as characterized by Bogart, Zarrilli, Barba and others). Bachelard begins this with the appealing direct observation on how space must be cleared, for constructive work to begin: whilst it is true to say that 'you can only empty what you first found full, it is just as accurate to say that you can only fill what you first found empty' (30). This, however, does not involve denial of what has gone before, but rather the conscious adoption of a willed perspective which relegates that which has been previous to the sidelines, deciding that normal terms need not apply: if 'it is objected that the positive experiences we have erased still subsist, we shall reply that they subsist without playing a part in our present knowledge' (36).

Hence, forms of consciousness are 'either realised or dissolved' in time (50): though Bachelard's own paradigms imply, rather, that both processes occur, dialectically. Bachelard's account of speculative intelligence and creative consciousness (which both 'creates and strengthens leisure', 18) is strikingly applicable to theatrical processes of rehearsal, and vice versa. He proposes that there 'is in fact no other way of analysing an action than by beginning it all over again', and that such beginning again involves 'disassembling' it: 'that is to say by enumerating and ordering the decisions which constitute it' (38), considering it as a series of subtle distinctions of the will that does not have its basis in continuous flow, but is more precisely perceived as a dialectical wave-motion, 'preceded by hesitation', and 'expected, deferred, provoked' in potentially separable impulses, informing physical manifestations (39).

In development from this, Bachelard approaches his distinctive characterization of time as pluralistic and dialectical rather than single, linear or absolute (Newtonian or Kantian). He proposes that time is 'continuous as possibility', but 'discontinuous as being'; this is illustrated by the way we may decide that, in a given instant, either something is happening, or nothing is happening: a value judgement of significance, based on temporal duality rather than unity, and on a subjective definition of function (44). This reflects Pierre Janet's characterization of time as either an obstacle (from which one should protect oneself) or a help (to be seized and realized) (Bachelard 2000: 50). However, Bachelard observes that the rhythm of (obvious) action and (relative) inaction is intrinsic to a sense of temporal progression: for any two successive events to be identified as fruitful or useful, an intervening juncture of the apparently useless (I suggest, perhaps better termed 'fallow') has to occur (54). Thus, Bachelard proposes a less superficial and accelerative emphasis on output and commodity, preferring to observe how a shifting and relative focus will involve either the realization or dissolution of a given state of consciousness, such as a singly specific perspective and definition of value (recalling, for me, one of my favourite descriptions of rehearsal, which admits the possibility of process of refinement even in an apparently barren occasion or period of fallowness: 'Imperceptible redefinitions occurred / Which at a later date may seem significant', Barker 1987: 37). Bachelard identifies the dialectic process of refinement as proceeding from 'an initial drama', an emotional memory created by surprise by opposites, in which a formerly exclusive polarization collapses. However, the sequencing of developments will form, and elicit, a montage of deductive meaning, which overrides and cancels the formerly apparent irrationality of their temporal conjunction, where/when audiences, if not performers, will create an emergent continuum of sequential and causal meaning from the formerly disjointed components, now gathered into a single identifiable composition: 'We show one phenomenon to be a cause and another to be an effect when we draw a line round each of them which defines and isolates them, giving each the unity of a name' (Bachelard 2000: 66; compare Booth's delineations of the dynamics of in/definition at work in tragedy, Booth 1983). Bachelard's emphasis on the importance of watchfulness in formulations of notable and surprising complexity again recalls the aforementioned processes of rehearsal, energetically quarrying or simply reiterating in order to admit *Kairos*:

a patience, with reference to which he proposes knowledge of time should be taught, and indeed expounded (49), through attention to specifics (Bachelard quotes Jacques Maratain: 'Distinguish in order to unite', Bachelard 2000: 88, and observes the 'better we teach, the more we shall differentiate', 72).

Bachelard's combined observations on how knowledge of time might be taught are both eminently salient to, and ideally exemplified by, the work of the theatre director in rehearsal, eliciting the preconditions for an emergence of creative consciousness, among practitioners and spectators. I suggest the process of rehearsal might be defined as *surprising knowledge of dialectical affect, which first emerges in temporal and spatial disconnectedness, subsequently integrated and developed by a process of consolidation.* Its objective is to discover and apply a new temporal *framework* (or series of frameworks) in which to (re)locate and (re)consider the prevalent (and otherwise generally accepted, available and imposed) terms of life.

Thirdly, Bachelard ascribes to time a potential for multidimensional density, a pluralistic spectrum of lacunae, of which I suggest theatre might constitute a uniquely formal(ized) manifestation (compatible with Limon's model, in different terms). He proceeds from Hönigswald's distinction between immanent, or vertical, time (subjective time, as sensed by the self) and transitive, or horizontal, time (objective time, as demarcated by the world at large); and provocatively defines 'reality' as grounds for agreement: reality 'makes what we see wait for what we say', confirmatory verbal definition resulting in that which is privileged as 'objectively coherent thought', though this might be considered more closely as a superimposition of transitive (horizontal, objective) time on immanent (vertical, subjective) time, in ways that are deemed mutually confirming, congruent and hence 'give an impression of objectivity' (108).

However, power is not an entirely colonialist one-way street in this negotiation: Bachelard claims that dreaming offers a subversive reversal of this process, disengaging the usually dominant order of superimposed but different time schemes, by foregrounding subjective associations (108).[12] I submit that the same claim might be made for speculative and interrogatory theatre.

Bachelard's enquiry leads him into areas that offer a further 'thickening' of pertinence, for the processes of theatre, when he outlines his active interest in *pretence*, which he also describes in terms of a 'temporal superimposition' (112): an 'artificial psychology' that is formalized through an artfully foregrounded and compulsive manifestation of a (subjective, immanent, vertical) sense of time. He suggests, if we are to 'pretend successfully, we must indeed make what is essentially discontinuous and disparate appear to be continuous' by increasing the 'density and regularity' of the 'temporal texture' of actions (113): the continuity of this performance of pretence does not need to appeal to the terms of continuity associated with 'natural feelings', but rather it establishes, and depends upon, its own distinctive and seductive tempo.

It is surprising that Bachelard himself does not extend the application of his terms to theatre and performance, as they provide such clear terms for analysing the interplay of differing temporal frames within a theatrical performance, and for the development, in rehearsal and performance, of charismatic performance (the skills that Barker, in particular, might hope to be manifested by his performers, portraying self-consciously performative characters who aspire to the achievements of 'perfect liars'[13]). Bachelard's ideas indicate ways in which we might consider theatre as an unpicking of the habitually privileged superimpositions, and power relations, between the claims and demands of different time schemes – instead, theatre takes *its* time, to unfold and consolidate *its* intellectual and emotional processes and associations – and confirms how we might identify the compelling performer as someone who takes, creates and develops *their* entirely distinctive and transformative sense of time.[14]

Finally, Bachelard's concept of *poetic causality* is germane to all sustained pretence and metaphor, but particularly salient to theatre, especially of the non-realistic, expressionistic and epic varieties. Bachelard states directly that being a poet 'means multiplying the temporal dialectic and refusing the easy continuity of sensation and deduction', in order that '*poetic causality* will appear, in all its disconnectedness': an imaginative synapse that 'reverberates for a long time from one centre to another, despite all intermediaries' (132). One might observe that this reverberation (implicitly if not explicitly) calls into question the primacy of exclusivity of any single 'centre', any purportedly exclusive, absolutist and systematic terms of definition, privileged perspective or centralized power.

Prigogine and theatre as dissipative structure

I will now turn to the development and resonances of the 1970s and 1980s work of Ilya Prigogine with Isabelle Stengers, including their coinage of the term 'dissipative structures': frameworks that incorporate the conjoined presences of both shape and flux (which would otherwise appear inherently contradictory opposites), in a state of stability that does not involve fixity, but rather permits – and indeed depends upon – fluctuation and variation. Fritjof Capra observes:

> The radical nature of Prigogine's vision is apparent from the fact that these fundamental ideas were rarely addressed in traditional science and were often given negative connotations. This is evident in the very language used to express them. *Non*equilibrium, *non*linearity, *in*stability, *in*determinacy, etc., are all negative formulations [...] Many of the key characteristics of dissipative structures – the sensitivity to small changes in the environment, the relevance of previous history at critical points of choice, the uncertainty and unpredictability of the future – are revolutionary new concepts from the point of view of classical science, but are an integral part of human experience.
>
> (quoted in Griffiths 1999: 135, original emphasis)

Griffiths takes the observation 'one step further': the nuancing of 'time's character, as revealed in the model of dissipative structures, has all the qualities which patriarchy has attributed to *women*, and has therefore devalued for so long' (Griffiths 2000: 135, original emphasis).

I also wish to take this 'one step further' from the non-linear dynamics and non-equilibrium thermodynamics that may entertain both linear and cyclical images of time: the qualities of non-equilibrium, non-linearity, instability and indeterminacy are also the affective exuberances of theatre, which at its best characteristically approaches bifurcation points, where structures break down, and indicate and/or form alternative possibilities in wild admissive variety – *pan*, rather than *mono*.

In Todd Haynes's 2007 film *I'm Not There* (a kaleidoscopic dramatic fragmentation of various *personae* associated with Bob Dylan[15]), the character Billy the Kid expresses his intense awareness of susceptibility to personal change on a daily basis: 'It's like you got yesterday, today and tomorrow, all in the same room. There's no telling what can happen'. Theatre can go one step further than even Haynes's artfully kaleidoscopic film or other screen-based dramatic media: it can *physically* manifest representatives of yesterday, today and tomorrow, all on the same stage, in the same room as the audience member, amplifying senses of significance and possibility, so that there's no telling what can happen.

If we turn directly to Prigogine's work with Stengers, we discover a theoretical model of time and chaos that has several contact points with theatre's dynamics, starting with Prigogine's enquiry placing emphasis less on *laws* than on '*events* that bring an element of radical novelty to the description of nature' and the expression of possibilities (Prigogine 1997: 5). Prigogine suggests that the 'top-down' classical scientific model of a centrally managing form of space–time, which unifies whatever it contains, and the associated deterministic, time-reversible description of nature, is less appropriate or admissive than a 'more dialectical view of nature' (Prigogine 1997: 182) based on 'dynamical instability' involving the 'conditions necessary to generate evolutionary patterns of nature': 'the dynamics at the root of complexity that are essential for self-organization and the emergence of life' (128). Indeed, though Prigogine does not linger on this, there are political ramifications for deductions, made by him and others (including Biebracher, Nicolis and Schuster) on how self-organizing systems of biological systems permit and demonstrate adaptation to the prevailing environment by forming 'complex products' 'with unsurpassed accuracy, efficiency and speed' (Prigogine 1997: 72). Thus, 'the creation of unpredictable novelty, where the possible is richer than the real' (72) is an intrinsic facet of nature as a chaotic system: an 'example of unstable motion because trajectories identified by distinct initial conditions, no matter how close, diverge exponentially over time', in amplification of chaos (the so-called 'butterfly effect') (30). Intriguingly, Prigogine notes how Freud wrote that 'the history of science is the history of alienation' (71): a word that might be most effectively (re)considered in the Brechtian theatrical sense of the *Verfremdungseffekt*, an estranging re-location of perspective and transformative framework (the resonant implications of which are, for example, followed through in Brecht's play *The Life of Galileo*). Prigogine proposes something further to the perspectives of Copernicus (who showed that the earth is not at the centre of the planetary system), Darwin (who deduced that we are one species of animal among many others) and Freud (who proved that our rational activity is only one part of human consciousness): 'human creativity and innovation can be understood as the amplification of laws of nature already present in physics and chemistry' (71).

It will be less abstracting, and more aptly dialectical, if we apply Prigogine's theories to specific pieces of theatre that work as self-organizing dissipative structures.

Theatre as diffusive resonance: green's *random*

Prigogine identifies two types of trajectories: 'nice' trajectories, associated with determinism, and 'random' trajectories, associated with erratic resonances. He observes how, 'when we increase the value of energy, we increase the regions where randomness prevails [and] chaos appears' so that 'the cloud of points generated by a trajectory leads to diffusion' (Prigogine 1997: 41). Diffusion challenges any 'approach to uniformity in our *future*', by delineating 'an irreversible process' (41) of entropy (which might here be associated less appropriately with an apparent loss of energy than with its transfer from one system to another, a transformative re-location, a changing of shape).

debbie tucker green's play *random* (2008) relates dramatically, in the present tense, the processes whereby several characters (members of a British Afro-Caribbean urban family household, who will be depicted by a single solo female performer) attempt to negotiate the events of a given (apparently ordinary, but ultimately extraordinary) work and school day and (re)orient themselves in time. The actions and rituals of the family members are observably particular but also *commonplace*, in space and time. The fundamental distinctiveness of this day is that it contains an emergent confrontation with irreversibility: the son of the household has been stabbed to death, in circumstances and for reasons never fully divulged. The murder will be reported as a local event, but green's play runs counter to the journalists' task by tracing and its amplifying *resonances* in time. Prigogine observes how resonances are 'not local events' (though they may *emerge* from local events): they are not limited to occur at a single given point or instant but rather 'imply a nonlocal description' and so instigate a '*diffusive* motion' of energy (Prigogine 1997: 42). Resonances invite attention to the observably 'persistent interactions' in these diffusive terms, suggesting that it is reductively meaningless to consider any detail of a given system in isolation (45). The amplification of diffusive resonances, and Prigogine's definition of a cornerstone of the formulation of quantum theory in terms of 'instability driven by resonances' (46), may also offer ways of looking at theatre.

The amplification of diffusive resonances is the driving theatrical process of *random*. The first speaker, Sister, begins by describing/enacting the process of trying to stare out/down a clock, 'which stares me right back'; even as she becomes aware of 'somethin in the air / in the room / in this day' that is ominous: 'shadow of a shadow feelin…/ off key' (green 2008: 3). No detail coheres into decisive meaning, in isolation, but usually unremarkable features combine to unsettle: 'Kitchen radio don't tune [in] right', 'something ketch me out today' (6). Mum remarks on a shared confusion in relation to a common factor, unseasonably chilly weather, which the young characteristically attempt to outface ('dress like iss summer / while spring still strugglin'), equating youth with invincibility rather than transience: a common misprision (Mum wryly reflects, her daughter 'still think she young ... / She like me. / She'll learn. / Like me', 7).

green's skilfully poetic structure of perceptions through resonance may be informed distinctively by her acknowledged inspirations from black music and performance poetry, as variously practised by Louise Bennett, Lauryn Hill, Beverley Knight and Jill Scott (Aston 2011: 183; and I would guess that bel hooks, Gil Scott-Heron and Dana Bryant may also be influential in their cadences). Aston notes how green's language is significantly 'elliptical', arranging lines that 'can often consist of a single word and are frequently punctuated by silences during which the meaning-making transfers to visual communication between the performers – the choreographies of gazing, or the beats and pauses in which characters physically convey their feelings for or attitudes towards each other'; and green's specification of what she describes as '*active silences*', where the names of the characters stand scored without accompanying dialogue, in order to 'cue silences as punctuating the verbal interactions', 'to produce a halting yet intensifying effect' (Aston 2011: 196). This is a prime characteristic of green's musicality as a dramatist, as is her constant specification of perceptual tempo, making her audiences suddenly mindful of the gaps between signs, things and people.

Prigogine points out how it is through the common experience of temporal irreversibility, an arrow of time, that we understand nature's two principal facets, of unity and diversity: 'unity, because the arrow of time is common to all parts of the universe' and provides the condition and basis of our communicative interaction with the physical world and our fellow human beings; 'diversity, as in the room where I write, because there is air, a mixture of gases', discernible as odours, specifically 'organized thanks to temporal, irreversible, nonequilibrium processes' (Prigogine 1997: 58).

green's character Mum provides engagingly witty observations on social impulses towards diversity and unity, which many are likely to find resonant with their own memories and observations, however specific these may be in other terms. On the one hand, Mum notes how school pupils demonstrate ingenuity in making a uniform look 'not like a uniform' (green 2008: 12), customizing it to express their intentions of originality; on the other hand, she observes the manifestations of 'posse / crew / pack' mentality on the street, a disinclination to walk in 'ones and twos', the aggressive effort in solidarity based on the 'same kinda different', 'tryin too hard – to look hard' (20). However, even family unity and agreed timing is fractured by the arrival of police and the realization: 'We already way too late. / ...And never even know it' (34).[16] At/in this time, there is 'no need to hurry' (34): no social efficacy in speed. Later, Sister will find herself, unusually, inhaling deeply in Brother's bedroom in an immersive bid to 'keep his stink in' (50), retain the highly organized mixture of gases which are specific to a person, room and time, even as they inevitably dissipate.

The events of *random* invite and involve a renewed focus on what is transient, from the perspectives of characters and audience members. They also pose questions of consequence, how and why Brother's life could be ended by a 'random' action, with no readily evident motivation or meaning, which is nevertheless so small, precise and terminal: 'Juss a small / deep / sorta / round / sorta / hole. / In him' (37) – an aptly double-negative shape that is 'Not no random' (37), but a specifically defined and located hole in definition and duration itself, which will not close up into legible, sensible consequences: the efforts of Victim Support officers 'makin no difference / to the difference we got now' (43).

random suggests that what is transient should not be dismissed, because, as Prigogine suggests, 'we are all transient', as he asks, is it 'not natural to be interested in our common human condition?' (Prigogine 1997: 62). *random* highlights common human experience of time, even as it slides into catastrophic time of grief and bereavement: irrevocable, specific yet sometime shared by all, in terms that nevertheless defy generalization. The final moments of the play may suggest how even the immediately traumatic and paralytic terms of confrontation may (have to) prove transient, and that Sister must somehow find a way to 'step out' (50) from this temporal framework: 'this' framework being a conflation of the familial, the social and the formally theatrical (we hear that the character of Mum is 'destroyed', sadly finite and capable of no such resurgence). Furthermore, the performer of Sister will step out of role, and prove herself fortunately capable of doing so. When she stands for applause, the audience applaud not only her skill, but their common relief at being similarly able to 'step out' of the characters' broken time, though mindful of what has briefly united them: the status of witness-communicants in an ordeal (which, within its fiction, can find no witnesses), the formal delineation of a nameless 'cycle of shit', a reductive determinism based on systematic thought and perception, which yields only meaninglessness – until the dominant senses of consequence and possibility, uniformity and diversity, can be re-visioned. *random* suggests how racial prejudice inflects the social narratives and mediations of probability, informing and congealing into systematic thought and presumption, both externalized and internalized, which can render everyone 'too late' in their human specifics; and how this is exacerbated by newspaper and television reporters 'soundbitin so-called "solutions" in seconds' (41), rather than – as in the theatre event – considering the surprising forms of common grief, and asking questions, on the basis of a shared encounter based on perceptual modification and dissemination: 'Random don't happen to everybody. / So. / How come / 'random' haveta happen to him?' (49).

Theatre as dissipative structure: Wesker's *The Kitchen*

Prigogine's (chemical) model of a dissipative structure involves two conditions: the identification of far-from-equilibrium situations defined by a critical distance; and catalytic steps that push the system farther into non-equilibrium, so that new bifurcations typical of chaotic behaviour may arise. He notes how neighbouring trajectories diverge exponentially to create what he terms 'deterministic chaos' (Prigogine 1997: 68), meaning a transformative and ultimately potentially constructive disruption of the predictive and pre-emptive determinism at the core of systematic structures (which are man-made rather than inclusively natural). Chaotic bifurcations involve a breaking of symmetry on which the *uniformity* of a system depends: they constitute 'the manifestation of an intrinsic differentiation between parts of the system itself and the system and its environment'; thus, 'once a dissipative structure is formed, the homogeneity of time [...] or space [...], or both, is broken' (69). Intrinsically chaotic in their tendencies towards a complex self-managing, 'bifurcations can be considered the source of diversification and innovation' (70).

Arnold Wesker's play *The Kitchen* (1959) assembles a theatrical event in which the eponymous kitchen provides an image of society regulated by the pressures of time management. Wesker's introduction and notes to the play specify that no real food should be cooked and served, but all preparation should be mimed meticulously by the chefs working alongside each other, with three stages of increasing speed, from 'brisk but slow' to 'fast and hectic' (Wesker 1976: 10), a far-from equilibrium situation building to a pace where the workers find 'no time for breathing here' (48). The international cross-section of kitchen workers oscillate between a deterministic acceptance of these conditions, configured to maximize profitability through uniformity ('The world chase [*sic*] money so you chase money too' [37]), and an awareness and expression of the environment's systematically dehumanizing effects ('when the world is filled with kitchens you get pigs' [53]). Denied time and 'a chance to dream' (in ways that the dominant regime would significantly dismiss as a 'waste' [52]), the workers become disobedient and violent (as one porter observes of the protagonist Peter, he wants to fight, in desperation 'to show he is a man some way' [20]). A performance of *The Kitchen* is likely to command an audience's attentive respect for the precision and speed of the choreographed interactive movement by which the performers mimic the processes, tasks and responses of trained kitchen staff, affording a view of what is produced and presented – and the time it takes – in terms that are conventionally denied by 'product'-orientated commodification, and by demarcated and separated senses of time. The diners at a restaurant will associate the location with ease, alleviation of domestic pressures, occasions for conversation and pleasurable 'flow' from one course to the next. Wesker's play in production exposes the temporal disjunction, and the way that the customer's expansive sense of time is bought at the expense of those usually behind the scenes: with implications for wider aspects of the service industry and social economy. One of the temperamentally calmer chefs reflects on the wider manifestations of impatience, and the status of time as political currency: how his neighbour, a bus driver, expresses a murderous contempt for those involved in a peace march, principally because the march held up traffic and 'the buses couldn't move so fast!' (54). This bus driver is enraged by anything that jeopardizes his own ability to fulfil the inflexible demands imposed by his employers, and so prove his own worth: a startling internalization of oppressive terms. As Adam observes, social organization 'within a time-grid of calendars and clocks facilitates precision', but it also potentially devalues and eliminates the dimension of human interpretation that is thrown into relief by any variation in viewpoint (Adam 1990: 107); its ultimate logical application extends towards the fundamental intolerance of totalitarianism. *The Kitchen* throws into relief how capitalist society segments time into decontextualized, disembodied, commodified, linear units, quantified for exchange. In response to the increasingly frenetic pace of work and ever-accelerating demands, neighbouring trajectories diverge: Peter strikes out at the machinery of the kitchen (realizing that this, rather than a fellow worker, represents *'the enemy'*), and so he transgresses the boundary of separation, stumbling into the dining area with bloodied hands. The restaurant owner accuses him, 'You have stopped my whole world', and expresses incomprehension at what anyone can want in this world, beyond payment for their labour: 'What is there more?' (71). These final words are repeated for emphasis, but also invite the audience to formulate an answer to this rhetorical question, in the time before the curtain call.

One answer might be: time as a resource, of limited personal supply, which becomes scarcer with age (Adam 1998: 66), which leads us into …

Theatre as chaotic map: Beckett's *Krapp's Last Tape*

Prigogine observes how maps represent a simplified form of dynamics (Prigogine 1997: 81): one sort charts simple periodic behaviour, the second (and I suggest the one which has more frequent affinity with theatre) charts 'deterministic chaos' (82), in which a trajectory, followed through numerical situations, becomes erratic and divergent. Following Prigogine, I suggest that theatre might offer a form of *chaotic map*, in which time is (re)determined to act at specific discrete intervals, counter to perceptual norms. Wesker's *The Kitchen* begins by re-presenting how capitalist monetarism valorizes periodic behaviour, but how this creates pressure and a build-up of increasingly erratic energy within neighbouring trajectories that seeks discharge; the titular kitchen, contrary to its industrial objectives, becomes something more theatrical: a dissipative structure. On the other hand, Samuel Beckett's play *Krapp's Last Tape* (1958) might be viewed as an exploratory manifestation of what Prigogine calls 'deterministic chaos', and how contrary impulses may be delineated in the selective form, as the 'chaotic map' of a life.

Krapp's Last Tape depicts a man who is an obsessive, but subjectively partial (as are we all), cartographer of his own life, who annually carves out a space/time for recording and reflection in order to make an ordered, even systematic, sense of the stages of his life, with conscious references to time, emotional cause and unforeseen (unforeseeable?) consequence. The observation of the psychoanalyst Adam Phillips seems appropriate here: on how life becomes 'progressively stranger as we get older' though 'we become increasingly frantic to keep it familiar, to keep it in order' (quoted in Segal 2014: 75). Krapp's first repeated sequence of acts – producing, contemplating and peeling a banana – suggest a mechanical, clownish insatiability only just held at bay. But he defers a second consumption, focusing with *'relish'* (Beckett 1986: 216) on details, of objects and words, smiling at their very *identifiability*: the ultimately pleasing congruence of signified and signifier, notwithstanding some superficial disarray. However, the uncoupling of word from remembered experience occurs, at first semi-comically: Krapp cannot recall a supposedly 'memorable' equinox, and baulks, puzzled, at the very phrase; and the specified turning of a page introduces a rhythmic beat in his reading of an old journal entry, which produces an audible lack of investment in the speaking of the last word in the phrase 'Farewell to – […] – love', precisely because it is unforeseen (217). Beckett's deployment of a full stop after the word 'love' steers the performer towards a suspended downbeat in vocal delivery (rather than, say, the further clownish effects that would accrue from an exclamation mark or question mark).

The recording of the birthday reflections of the 39-year-old Krapp informs us how he marked the occasion, ambivalently: loudly secure in the sense of his own prime, but finding 'awful' this indication of a potential tipping point; celebrating 'quietly' and meditatively (with closed eyes) in a public place that is deserted, then returning to his private 'den' and 'old rags' with relief (217). However, even the *'rather pompous'* Krapp-at-39 is not impervious in his sense of self: he acknowledges his own active sense of selection, 'separating the grain from the husks', which leads him (and perhaps, by implication, the audience) to question and imagine exactly what might constitute the 'grain', how he might (re)shape his life and values from his current perspective, in a recollection that is also a reinflection.

Eva Hoffman observes how, as far as we can tell, 'we are the only species capable of deliberately deciding to recollect the past; of reflecting on it, revising it and sometimes lying about it' (Hoffman 2009: 74), through construction and reconstruction of temporal consciousness: not necessarily by 'revising the facts' but by placing experiential information and details in new contexts, so that 'the past changes under the pressure of the present, as well as vice versa' as emotional memory entails acts of 'creative self-making' in and through time (Hoffman 2009: 108). The hippocampus is the name given to the part of the brain that orders experience, in a process by which the brain – no less than the mind – processes experience with a dynamism that an experience is 'dismantled into its component parts to enable our memory to stow and retrieve them' (Klein 2008: 109), an 'intrinsically plastic and constructive' process involving the 'transformation of short-term perception into long-term episodic memory of sequential events' (Hoffman 2009: 75). However, Bergson notes how in most cases mingled memories of various occasions 'supplant our actual perceptions, of which we then recall only a few hints', adding the 'convenience and rapidity of perception are bought at this price' (quoted in States 1985: 189). In *Krapp's Last Tape*, Beckett dramatizes questioningly the constructive *bricolage* of sequential memory, foregrounding its plasticity and the intentness of Krapp's varying bids to construct individual sequence, and, hence, rationale. Beckett achieves this by effectively assembling a layering/series of 'Krapps', recorded in his late twenties and late thirties, and now physically (re-)presented in his seventies (making what the title of Beckett's play tells us – from some unspecified vantage point of *future* time – will turn out to be his *last* recording, thus further 'thickening' the conscious awareness of temporality[17]). The play stages a friction between these various different perspectives in time, each of which Krapp experiences and would reduce, in recorded form, to a material presence (the properly and obediently categorized spool of tape); however, he (and we) discover a profound dissonance in the theatre of Krapp's memory. This is first encountered in comic terms: Krapp-at-39's determination to abstain from bananas, regularly and compulsively broken by his older self; and the resolution to drink less alcohol which Krapp-in-his-late twenties and Krapp-at-39 approach seriously, but which the present aged Krapp finds manifestly ludicrous.

To revisit and apply the terms that Wagner develops with reference to Shakespeare, *Krapp's Last Tape* sharpens our awareness of the sometimes vexatious and discrepant relationship between phenomenological and objective time, 'by shuttling us back and forth between each, and, most significantly, by not reconciling the one with the other or explaining one in terms of the other' (Wagner 2012: 18). This lack of reconciliation, and failure of convincing explanation, takes a less comic turn when Krapp-at-39 detects a 'False ring' (Beckett 1986: 218) in Krapp-in-his-late twenties sneering dismissively at the passage of his youth. After further alcoholic fortification (and/or anaesthetization), Krapp-in-his-seventies stumbles on the recording of Krapp-at-39 reflecting on the atomization of life to 'moments' – his moments, and those of his dying mother, the nurse and a dog – and then deriving from a 'year of profound gloom and indigence' the height of his personal conviction, a vision that suddenly permits a glimpse of 'the whole thing' in a 'light of understanding' that ignites a 'fire' of determination and professed dedication (220). This, however, gives way, in turn, to a contrasting aural sequence, which details the final encounter with the unnamed girl in a punt, to which Krapp-in-his-seventies listens with more intentness than to the account of the vision at the jetty, and the deduced mission. After further lubrication, Krapp embarks upon the recording of his present-day reflection, in which disbelief and disgust at his former pretensions leads him to a statement of relinquishment and relief – 'Thank God that's all done with anyway' – only to find himself drawn back into an echoing wave of reverie, 'The eyes she had' (222). His former senses of investment have issued in wry mockery: the principal index of a life's work attaining 'seventeen copies sold'; the former 'engrossing sexual life' diminished to a regular arrangement with a 'bony old ghost of a whore', barely 'better than a kick in the crutch' (222). However, when propped up in bed, alone in the dark, his imagination leads him to 'Be again' in specifically re-marked confluences of place and time, 'in the dingle on a Christmas Eve', and 'on Croghan on a Sunday morning' when he would 'stop and listen to the bells' (223). The exasperation at his own continuing reflections – 'Once wasn't enough for you' – gains a decisive answer in his recall of sensual detail and search for more, as he returns to the recording of the physical proximity of the punt scene, its resistant awareness of personal exclusion ('Let me in') and the poignantly contrapuntal sense of human physical inclusion in nature's rhythms ('under us all moved, and moved us' [223]). Finally, last-Krapp, and the audience, listen to Krapp-at-39 repudiating his 'best years' and the 'chance of happiness', with a reiteration that may question his certainty even then (223).

Krapp's Last Tape offers one of the most distilled ways in which 'the theatre heightens, in human experience (that of performers and audience alike), the temporal reality of inconsistency, mostly by producing differing, but equally [simultaneously] evident, time schemes' (Wagner 2012: 19). It does so by extending the principle of inconsistency to that of *character time*, as we watch and hear Krapp (a dramatic fiction) re-viewing his former selves, and realizing the extent to which they are (often unconvincing) dramatic fictions in their delineations and deductions of significance. Beckett's play is, amongst other things, a striking theatrical manifestation of Klein's observation of how the 'twin gauges' of this inner time, 'movement and memory', combine to form a conscious sense of an event, and how 'we experience time exclusively against a background of events' (Klein 2008: 53, 55) in our constructions of subjective time. Indeed, the process of the play stages a questioning reversal of the usual activity associated with the hippocampus. Krapp, who has characteristically sought to weave details into the sense of a finite and providential linear narrative that would render him a subject and source of (distinctly and defiantly) individual meaning, and constitute a definite self, now begins compulsively unpicking the sequence, rendering his experiences back into vivid fragments: the sensual, destructuring, delimiting qualia of eroticism. Last-Krapp's movements – so determinate in his (and Beckett's) co-ordinates – nevertheless provide a bathetic, undercutting accompaniment to the narratives he has self-consciously developed from the registration of his memories; his sense of a precise, familiar routine barely keeps at bay the incursive sense of personal disintegration. However, the play does not keep us at an ironic arm's-length from its protagonist, notwithstanding the staged recollections of his most smugly distant and sanctimonious moments. Rather, the final movement of the play *collapses* distance between character and audience, as the audience are enveloped in the compulsion to revisit physical sensual erotic memory in preference to more remorselessly 'rational' deduction, categorization and strategic game-plan. *Krapp's Last Tape* finally turns outwards the question/statement 'Once wasn't enough for you' and raises the spectre that our own identifiable former selves are similarly (if extra-theatrical) 'dramatic fictions', designed to vindicate our own delineations of significance. Krapp's meticulously significant (and significantly flawed) ritual is an externalized projection, and extrapolation, of the ongoing negotiations with former selves, and experiences of temporal dissonance, which we all pursue in the theatres of our consciousness, where time becomes alternately and dialectically fragmented and (re)unified.

If, as Prigogine suggests, we consider 'dynamics as a *history of correlations*' (122), then the correlations involved in dynamical processes are resonances, akin to those which similarly couple harmonics in music (122–123) and challenge exclusively linear and symmetrical terms of literal temporal and physical proximity. Prigogine notes how the processes of resonances couple the creation and destruction of correlations, leading to redistributive collisions that 'have a dramatic effect on dynamics because they break time symmetry' (124). Theatre such as the plays to which I refer to for consideration may suggest how symmetry (despite its formal attractions) may be merely fearful, as an exclusive principle. Contrastingly, theatre uses the physical presence and proximity (of bodies ageing together in time and space, which is, to some degree, shared) in order to ground and earth its destructive and constructive elaborations of dissipation: drawing chaotic maps in the air between performers and audience.

Barbara Adam and quantum theatrics

The developing work of Barbara Adam, which seeks to reposition and reformulate time within social theory and life, will be central to my third analysis, and to ensuing discussions. In her first major work, *Time and Social Theory*, Adam notes how 'an explicit focus on time requires us to reassess our assumptions and to find a way through uncharted ground time' by bringing together 'what we tend to separate and dichotomise in our social analyses', including the compartmentalizing divisions of knowledge into academic disciplines (Adam 1990: 18). Adam points out how in 'Newtonian science time is not studied in its own right but used purely operationally as the measure of things and events', as 'unit', like 'space (length) and matter (mass)' (50). However, Einstein's theories question this pseudo-objectivity by demonstrating that 'simultaneity and instantaneousness can only be defined in relation to a particular frame of reference': 'two events which may be simultaneous in one frame may occur at different times in another' (55), which shows time to be '*a local, internal feature of the system of observation, dependent on observers and their measurements*' (56, original emphasis). I would add to this that theatre offers a framework of observation that foregrounds the processes and (often unacknowledged) reference points of how observers negotiate, structure and restructure their temporal perceptions of events, forces and actions.

It might even be appropriate to think of theatre as a 'quantum' art form, if one takes the term 'quantum' as a 'unit of action which contains energy and time', and quanta as 'dynamic patterns of activities', 'based on the realisation that matter cannot be separated from its activities'. If 'both action and the very notion of pattern are fundamentally temporal', theatre presents and explores a 'quantum world' that 'displays a temporality which is different' from that of our predominant daily experience, because time and space 'lose their conventional meaning where action seems to happen instantaneously' across what is usually perceived as distance between places and moments (Adam 1990: 59). Adam's summary of quantum theory strikes me as eminently applicable to theatre: a place where time as distance is reformulated in terms of relationships, action, and 'the "trying out" of possibilities before actualisation' (59).

Adam goes on to describe Prigogine's fundamental changes in scientific law, by virtue of his re-characterization and re-establishment of the laws of nature in terms of irreversibility, directionality and an essential difference between past and future (where 'reversibility, far from being the primary and most fundamental aspect of nature, is agreed to be a product of the consciousness of human observers', Adam 1990: 65); in summary, '*events occur in time* in classical physics whilst *time is in action and events* in thermodynamics and the work of Prigogine' (68, original emphasis). Prigogine's paradigm again seems closer to theatrical focus, process and relations than the traditionally linear and dualistic associations of Newtonian systems of exchange that conceptualize transfers of energy in terms of waste. Instead, Prigogine's concept of dissipative structures characterizes 'unpredictable, non-linear, flowing, irreversible connectedness' as a source of order and creativity (Adam 2004: 33).

I suggest that theatre might constitute for itself a new theoretical 'double', not in terms of Artaud's image of the plague, but in the dissipative structure. In contrast to the Newtonian paradigm of the efficient machine, which operates with the minimum of energy exchange to maintain consistency (and minimize surprising deviations), a dissipative structure is open to the flow and use of energy generated and emitted from one system as the energy source for another, an interactive ecological exchange system in which 'time becomes internal to the event' of a 'system-specific process' (as opposed to the Newtonian principles of linear, time-reversible 'abstract motion') (Adam 2004: 33). Theatre is a medium of highly specific *timefullness*.

Adam suggests that, to replace exclusive 'either/or' binaries and dualities (which resist implication and resonance), negotiations of contemporary life might identify and theorize a multitude of times involved in existence, in terms of the descriptive metaphor of different levels; and that this must involve any 'tendency to reify the levels, to conceptualise them hierarchically, and to postulate clear cut-off points between them' (Adam 1990: 161). The conceptual paradigm of levels of time might permit and emphasize connection and implication in ways that resist any hierarchically fundamental or exclusive claim to be attached to any one mode of being.

I have noted elsewhere how theatre may, at its most demanding, distinctively offer effects of conscious personation, with implications of wider simultaneity and non-exclusivity in values ('both/and') and ethical responses when encountering what is normally constituted as 'otherness' (Rabey 1997: 1–14ff). One definition of 'play' is that which has a power 'to make what is impossible at the empirical level of existence possible at a symbolic level' (Levi-Strauss, quoted in Kearney 1988: 364).

Adam's concluding claim, that a focus on time 'helps us to see the invisible' (1990: 169), is developed into the departure point for her next book *Timewatch* (1995). Here she argues that 'the market economy depends on a standardized, decontextualized, commodified time' (Adam 1995: 8). In consequence, 'the institutional structures and practices of Western-style education work to socialize, habituate and train' young people to valorize clock-time in ways that devalue other modes of time, such as temporality – the focus on processes that permit 'the times of consciousness, memory and anticipation' come to the fore: possible sources of alternative consequentiality that 'are rarely discussed with reference to situations dominated by schedules and deadlines' (12). Whilst time (re)presents 'constraint, discipline, control and structure', it may also be invoked and explored in myriad ways and experiential contexts not limited to 'abstraction, reduction and objective observation', in order to 'bring the taken-for-granted to the forefront of our attention', and so 'the spell of clock-time is broken' (6). Adam suggests that multiplicity, simultaneity and implication might be 'key features' of this work (11), which might demonstrate that/how there is 'no single time, only a multitude of times which interpenetrate and permeate our daily lives' (12). If in mechanical clock-time the future is 'finite because it excludes becoming' (52), then in temporality the future is precisely a process of emergence and becoming.

In line with Adam's proposal, I suggest it might be not only possible but appropriate to characterize theatre and theatrical performance, in all the temporal complexities of simultaneity, multiplicity and implication that it involves, as an event of invested and shared *time focus* that (re-)presents a *physicalized accumulation and emergence of different temporal levels*. I would add that theatre distinctively physicalizes and materializes what might otherwise be literally invisible: through physicalized metaphors and similes, which allow us to understand 'one domain of experience in terms of another' (Lakoff and Johnson 1980: 193), theatre calls forth (presents and invites) a constitutive, formalized focus on time. Theatre constitutes an event, process and occasion to imagine *otherwise*: to re-vision the habitual (a pocket of what Hoffman calls 'countertime') in ways that manifest what Adam identifies as 'both the continuities and the irreducible aspects of our social time'. It thus positions itself strongly to facilitate perceptual and imaginative connections 'between the creation of time and its control, and between the reifications of clock-time and relations of power' (Adam 1990: 164–165), and to focus on processes that suggest how the physical and artefactual aspects of human creations might connect with, or disconnect from, our social theories and political objectives. This might well involve the manifestation of an otherwise unavailable or invisible link 'between the reifications of clock-time and relations of power'; and how 'the dead things which are so conscientiously excluded from social analyses are not only implicated in our daily existence but constitute our social theories' (1990: 169) (as when the staged ghost of a dead father instructs 'Remember me' …). Again, there is some overlap with (which I would prefer to construe as support for) my argument, in the model of theatrical performance recently articulated by Jerzy Limon, which proposes a unique but reverberative structure for unforeseeable juxtapositions, synthesizing what conventional perception and conduct tend to separate and dichotomize:

performance is by no means limited to dialogue only and consists of multifarious material components, or the *signalling matter*, composed of live and inanimate substances, movements and gestures, words, light and sound, creating all sorts of relationships with each other in innumerable proportions and combinations. These become the material vehicles of signs; since they are composed of sundry substances, often in striking, occasionally shocking, combinations, the spectators try to bring logic and sense to what they see and hear. Thus we begin to realize that everything on the stage means more than just itself: it also begins to mean something that is not visible or audible, something we can only imagine […] each of these systems in isolation, such as language, dance, music, painting, film, poetry, video, scenography, installations, can be recognized and described, but during the performance they intermingle and coalesce, creating compound configurations, heterogeneous conglomerations, amalgams of higher order, unique for the particular production. Through this, they generate new relationships, hence meanings; they undergo transmutation, evading formal classification and description […] thus creating configurations not to be found outside theatre.

(Limon 2010: 6, original emphasis)

I am briefly tempted to identify the 'countertime' of theatre with the 'counterclockwise', except that this would suggest a principal emphasis on mechanical reversibility in motion which is inappropriate. Adam, like Prigogine, identifies reversibility as a Newtonian abstraction and idealization inapplicable to human social life; rather, Adam and Prigogine insist on irreversible unidirectionality, an arrow of time which indicates that we cannot reverse the processes of the living and material world: there can be 'no rejuvenation, no unknowing, no reconstitution of pollution back into aeroplane fuel' (Adam 1995: 18). However, Elias suggests (quoted in Adam 1990: 28–29) that it is the property of the symbol to represent as repeatable that which is irreversible and unrepeatable (for example, death).

Consider, for example, the way that green's play *random* engages us by introducing us to an identifiable sense of a daily routine (however much its specifics may differ from ours), based on consciousness, experience, knowledge and the execution of the tasks, but it does so in order to involve us in a confrontation of, and encounter with, irreversibility. As Adam observes, 'it is not time but events and tasks which are endlessly repeated': attending school or work, 'tending the animals, organizing the food for the family and washing the dishes could classify as recurring, repetitive, habit-infused activities, but this makes neither them, nor the time in which they occur, reversible since there can be no un-going to work, no un-tending the animals, no un-washing up' that restores things precisely to their former condition (Adam 1995: 39). By the end of *random*, we appreciate in a deeper ethical context how time can neither stand still nor go backwards: Brother's fatal stabbing cannot be undone, and neither he nor any of the characters – nor audience members – can be restored to their original condition.

However, there is a difference, which is made narratively and in performance. We are clearly informed how the fictional characters of Sister and Mum are (differently) changed by events; and it is unlikely that audience members attending a performance of *random* will forget it; more likely it will re-emerge as a personal association (through the media of dramatic fiction and performance) in some future encounter, such as the report of a 'random' murder. It has provided an encounter, from which the character Sister can try to 'step out', as the audience can do more surely and literally (though shaken in their certainties, and perhaps with increased curiosity about what might be habitually unquestioned). The event of performance foregrounds compulsion, including that to persistence: how 'it is within the power of the human mind to visit past events, to re-invent them, create alternative versions and plan a multitude of futures', to 'imagine the world in a projected future-present upon which we can reflect and make our choices' (Adam 1995: 18), which might be one definition of culture – the time of relative freedom for self-controlled reflection and planning.

One might return to the quantum imagery, as deployed by Gwyneth Lewis, in her collection of lectures published under the title, *Quantum Poetics*. A 'quantum' is a unit of action that contains energy and time (Capra, quoted in Adam 2004: 63). Lewis describes poetry as a rhythmically conscious and affective 'time-based form which uses its medium to defy chronology' (Lewis 2015: 39): terms that we might extend to the medium of theatre. Like poetry, theatre considers one thing in terms of another, through metaphor: which is, in theatre's case, *embodied*. Like poetry, theatre shows how apparently 'solid' words 'alter in response to their neighbours' (Lewis 2015: 47), but extends this process to bodies, objects, light and all facets of scenography, in line with quantum theory's holographic shift of focus from a collection of disparate physical objects to the complex web of relations between the various parts: in the estranging transfer of energy from one state (or framework, or context) to another. Holography emphasizes 'parts being implicated in the whole and vice versa', meaning arising from interconnectivity and interaction, 'on multiple perspectivity and on the centralising of that which is not visible' (Adam 1998: 51–52). Quantum physics *admits* the principles of temporality, relativity and reflexivity: the very terms that theatre deals in, even more actively and variously than poetry, in its physicalized interactive reorientations, and intersubjective emergences in materialized expression.

Chronos v. *kairos*: Thomas's *Flowers of the Dead Red Sea*: 'THE WHOLE FUCKING SHIT PALACE FALLS ON OUR HEADS'

Ed Thomas's theatre is surreal rather than absurdist, with its distinctive and repeated emphasis on pluralistic possibilities, which transcend and defy the fundamentalist absurdities of authoritative finalities and dualities. Thomas's *Flowers of the Dead Red Sea* (1991), like Wesker's *The Kitchen*, depicts characters 'under the spell and pressure of the time economy of the clock', 'because they are embedded in a market economy organized to the principles of commodified time' as 'finite, rationalized, decontextualized exchange value' (in the terms of Adam 1995: 87, 99). Thomas situates the action of his play at an earlier stage of the consumerist 'food chain' to that in Wesker's *The Kitchen*.[18] Mock and Joe are slaughtermen, rising to work at the sound of an alarm, in (not so much a designated abattoir as) an acutely present *'world of chains, knives, steel, blood and falling objects'* (Thomas 1994: 103), but crucially distanced from their external hierarchical influences that tightly determine their time economy. Mock holds on to his personal craftsman's knowledge that for him to kill more beasts than his 'daily capacity' of 'Forty a day' will involve a loss of dignity, 'shame' for both man and beasts when his knife becomes blunt. Thomas moreover suggests that the passivity of the beasts – for whom the audience members, counted at the outset by Mock, 'stand in' – implicates them in the potential systematic degradation ('There is not a bone of revolt in their bodies': 'They would rather starve in a crowded pen than revolt', 108–109). The situation and stakes are intensified by the erosion of Mock and Joe's personal senses of temporality: their working and living conditions of standardization insist that they experience time as separation from content and context; the dominant commodification of time has reduced it to an abstract exchange value, a universalized and non-specific unit in the calculation of profit and efficiency, which can only be translated into money *if* neutralized and standardized, decontextualized from events and disembodied. *Flowers* goes further than Wesker's *The Kitchen* in its increasingly surreal depiction of how, under this regime and logic of control and exclusively economic resource, time has become deracinated from temporality and specific events. Thomas ingeniously spatializes the compression of Mock and Joe's time, when their definitions of space are overwhelmed, as tidal water encroaches audibly on their workplace, turning it into an island. Like other Thomas (and Beckett) characters, Mock and Joe are amnesiac (though Thomas, unlike Beckett, identifies this as a matter of social and political consequence), but like other Thomas protagonists, Mock holds on, in defiance of the prevailing circumstances, to a belief in human life involving the interaction of memory and anticipation, perception and desire. Unlike the increasingly mechanistic Joe, Mock at least has the 'sickness' of intimations of a memory that has become detached and decayed, in a world where people (and beasts) have become controllable (and in Joe's case, controlled and oblivious to his own ridiculousness) by the orientation of social and personal life to one single and specific kind of time. Their unseen taskmaster, Cragg, has the power to impose his temporal logic and structure as norm: time as money and power, and, so, time as measure, both 'as quantifiable resource and as a parameter within which working lives take place' (Adam 1990: 91). Mock cannot remember his own father, so is pathetically grateful for fragmentary (and possibly specious) narratives offered by Joe, who may even be Mock's brother, in this system of economically constructed competitive *chronos* that demands that one character's sense of time (and therefore power) is driven to deny that of the other, even as various items associated with consumerist domesticity crash from the skies around them: 'cooker, washing machine, frozen chicken, hair drier, microwave', pram (Thomas 1994: 120). These are technological fetishes of promised security, a fiscally tamed and ordered future, turned nightmarishly threatening. Mock expresses and acts on intimations of a 'shadow time' beyond what is more widely assumed to be time per se, which he senses (and mocks as) a decontextualized and disembodied, rationalized and commodified time ('THE ANGRY STALLION OF PROGRESS', Thomas 1994: 122), and which is purposefully dismissive of the culture invoked by the female artist whom Mock dimly recalls or imagines (135). Nevertheless, Mock holds to her inspiration by trying to make problematic what Joe is assuming to be necessary, rational, natural and inevitable for the sake of a dominant discourse (intrinsically tied to economic productivity), predicated on notional security and the marshalling bugle of the personified 'General Good' (160), about whom even Joe is residually sceptical in his defeated fatalism. Mock challenges what Adam identifies as the 'validity and value of existing appropriations of clock-time to the denial of all other times' (Adam 1990: 105), by struggling to trace and read an *embodied* time through his agency in his own dreams, the marks on his body, erotic encounters and family relationships, which might provide a basis for persistence and challenge. Mock opposes Joe's sense of finality, 'THE END' and 'OBLIVION', with 'CATASTROPHE' and 'METAPHOR'. Significantly, Joe dismisses metaphor – the imagination's yoking and synthesizing of material from different orders, places and times – as 'AVOIDANCE, EVASION, SHEER ORNAMENTATION [...] IN THE HEAD'. However, Mock regards metaphor as 'THE START OF THE SOLUTION', towards a defiantly subjective sense of knowledge and power that might yet separate him from the shameful herd. Joe's insistence, based on his reports of Mock's shameful reflexes, that Mock is, in fact, 'THE SAME AS EVERYONE ELSE', seems to reduce Mock to exhausted submission (Thomas 1994: 162–165). Significantly, Joe professes his dutiful pliability to

Cragg (and claims a subordinate's tenuous authority by way of antagonistic displacement of another: 'I'm main man now') in terms of an upsurge in processing the beasts-as-products, 'as many as you like', as merely economic resources and externalized outcomes to accumulate wealth, 'as if there was no tomorrow' (166). Nevertheless, Mock suddenly '*stops JOE in his tracks*' by insisting 'I AM STILL HERE' (166): a powerfully surprising claim and kairological demonstration of the importance of persistence in both creative uniqueness and embedded contextuality, even (or particularly) in the discontinuities of chaotic catastrophe.[19] In Negri's terms, Mock compulsively re-presents a perspective that tries to re-vision time from being a quantitative measure of exploitation, to being a qualitative measure of alternative and change (Negri 2013: 21). Mock's respect for a 'mystery' finds echoes in other Thomas plays, which locate surprising chaotic power and possibility in what is latent, immanent and hidden from view (not least, the power and possibility *to* surprise), over the terms of being that would be dictated by Newtonian principles of decontextualization and predictability, which accentuate divisions in space and time.[20]

Theatrical timescapes

I return to the important theories on time of Barbara Adam, and their application in/to theatre. In her study *Timescapes of Modernity* Adam develops her concept of the timescape: a perspective that embodies and re-presents practical approaches to time, acknowledging temporal aspects of consciousness and activity, so that 'contextual temporal practices become tangible' (Adam 1998: 11). She distinguishes this perspective from that of Newtonian science, which is primarily 'tied to the measure of motion' and implies 'atemporal time, a time unaffected by the transformations it describes' because it 'recognizes no contextually based differences in rhythm and intensity, no contextual timing or tempo, duration or change, no times inherent in process and phenomena' (40). However, Adam proposes that Prigogine's theories have established irreversible, unidirectional, internal temporality as a law of nature, whilst incorporating the (space *and* time) location of the scientist's framework of observation in the terms of analysis[21]; this provides points of departure for further terms of analysis that can 'move towards recognising multiple temporalities, irreversibility, indeterminacy and the centrality of the invisible' (50).

This observation deserves development, in (at least) two directions. Firstly, the identification of multiple temporalities is more clearly expressed by Adam in her subsequent book, *Time*: 'in everyday life, the relative temporality of past, present and future and the objective time of calendars and clocks are not chosen on an either-or basis'; rather, they 'co-exist, interpenetrate and mutually implicate each other': we move between these claims in daily activities, notwithstanding their 'conceptual and logical incompatibility' (Adam 2004: 69). However, a theatrical delineation of the definitional boundaries and relations in social practice (which habitually remain invisible) might refocus a questioning attention on temporal frameworks, contexts, processes and possibilities: dissolving polarities and distinguishing the terms and relations of conventional associations, in line with Adam's objective, to render 'the distant close and the strange familiar' (151), so that 'each move can be interpreted within this expanded frame of reference' (152) that recognizes and posits a variety of relations to time.

Secondly, Adam's mindfulness of the invisible (and imagined) as significant feature(s) in a timescape might constitute one of the important intersections between timescape and theatre. As McAuley points out:

> What is presented in performance is always both real and not real, and there is constant interplay between the two potentialities, neither of which is ever completely realized. The tension between the two is always present, and, indeed, it can be argued that it is precisely the dual presence of the real and not real, that is constitutive of theatre.
>
> (McAuley 2000: 127)

Jez Butterworth similarly and succinctly identifies what he considers 'the first and best trick of the theatre': 'the real juice lies in the tension between what's onstage and what's off'; 'It's what's left *off* that ignites what's *on*' (Butterworth 1998: 147, original emphasis). The idea of an evocative, constitutive absence also occurs in Adam's model of the timescape, which seeks to 'gather up sources of knowledge from both material and "immaterial", visible and invisible sources' (Adam 1998: 54):

> From the point of view of the observer, of course, a landscape can never be an objective absolute, since what observers can see depends on their prior knowledge, their power of deduction and their imagination [...] A landscape is a record of constitutive activity. It includes absences [...] It is relative to the eye of the beholder [...] With the idea of the timescape, I seek to achieve an extension of the landscape perspective, that is, to develop an analogous receptiveness to temporal interdependencies and absences [...].
>
> (Adam 1998: 54)

I submit that *theatre* actualizes and physicalizes Adam's paradigm, by providing an *embodied timescape* that throws into estranging relief temporal interdependencies and consequences, presences and absences, through its selective presentation and orchestration of multiple temporal perspectives in physical and imagined forms. As such, it affords a medium particularly suited to *open-ended* enquiry and speculation, regarding the complexity of the existential demands and challenges that we all face in considering, disrupting, revaluing and reformulating the terms of 'common humanity'. Adam identifies how a timescape perspective effectively counters dominant presumptions:

> A timescape perspective [...] allows us to move from single and dualistic approaches and abstract, functional perspectives to knowledge that emphasizes inclusiveness, connectivity, and implication. It promotes understanding that acknowledges the relativity

of position and framework of observation whilst stressing our inescapable implication in the subject matter and acknowledging personal and collective responsibility. It explicitly incorporates absences, latencies and immanent forces, thus helping us to move away from the futile insistence on proof and certainty for situations characterised by indeterminacy, time-lags of unspecified durations and open dispersal in time and space.

(Adam 1998: 55)

In the second half of this study, I will focus on selected plays that specifically foreground multiple time schemes, and selected dramatists who are characteristic and notable in their complications of conventionally single and dualistic approaches to time. My selection of references and case studies is personal (predominantly, but not exclusively, British and modern), and aims to encourage the reader to extend the field of enquiry on the basis of their own knowledge.

Notes

1 Owen Sheers, 2/12/2014: Penrallt Bookshop, Machynlleth.
2 However, Hoffman makes one of several occasional allusions to theatre in commenting on how the title words (and I would add, the events) of Mark Ravenhill's play, *Shopping and Fucking*, provide an astute distillation of the sense of the loss of time as a continuum, reflected by late-capitalist culture's 'segmentation of experience, loss of shared ethics and emphasis on immediate satisfaction of impulse and desire' (102).
3 If I may be permitted observation of a particularly Puckish reframing of reversible screen-based drama: the subversive YouTube series *Arson Sam* plays back in reverse the events of the children's television series *Fireman Sam* and adds subtitles and amended theme tune lyrics, which together suggest that the principal characters are deliberately and gleefully starting, rather than putting out, fires.
4 Audio dramatic place-prints, such as those by David Rudkin that are considered later, work on the sensed 'layering' of the audience member's physical presence, with an imagined former temporal presence, in a specific space; radio plays appeal to the audience's aural sense to create and subvert expectations in ways that have physiological manifestations, and film and television do the same, with added visual stimuli, even though the performers are not physically present in the same room as the audience except through the means of electronic recording and playback.
5 Priestley identified a feeling of immediacy that he associated with theatrical performance rather than film: 'When I watch a play I feel I am looking at something that is happening', 'all in the present tense', compared with a film (where 'I feel I am looking at something that has already happened' – as, indeed, the performances, production and post-production have). However, he also foresees at least some of the properties and pleasures of live theatrical screenings when he suggests 'it is not difficult to imagine enormous television theatres in which audiences are able to watch, projected in full colour on an equally enormous screen, performances taking place in the same building' – or another, on the other side of the

world – 'thereby enabling audiences and players to respond to each other as they do in the theatre' (Priestley 1964: 121), at least to *some* extent. This was thrown into relief when, in 2014, I watched, alongside my partner, a *repeat* screening of the Royal National Theatre's production of *War Horse*, adapted by Nick Stafford from Michael Morpurgo's novel. When the protagonist horse was climactically threatened with death, my partner involuntarily raised her arms and murmured 'No!': notwithstanding the facts that the enacted events were occurring at a temporal and spatial remove, that the narrative expectations generated were clearly redemptive (though fraught) and that the threatened fictional animal was portrayed by a puppet (strictly speaking, inanimate, though masterfully animated). My partner's intervention was a bid for *intersubjectivity* that the cinematic mediation of the narrative did not permit, though a theatrical performance would also have ignored her initiative at this juncture. Edward Bond provides a scathing critique of the one-way direction of screened interaction: as a fundamentally commercial predication whereby the 'eyes on the screen cannot look at you – they are blind. So you are blind when you look at them'. Bond identifies one of the instances of the corruption of the modern stage as being 'parasitic on the blindness of the screens': 'When it looks at the audience the blind are winking at each other': Edward Bond, 'Four Little Essays on Drama', http://www.edwardbond.org/Theory/theory.html accessed 21/10/2014.

6 A sentiment succinctly expressed by the protagonist of the song 'Ooh La La', written by Ronnie Lane and Ronnie Wood.

7 Dorian Gray is most recently re-visioned as a regular central character in John Logan's Showtime television drama series *Penny Dreadful* (2014–2016).

8 The term 'aborigine' derives from *ab origine,* 'true to the beginning' (Adam 2004: 77).

9 Negri's somewhat compressed account of *kairos* in action may conceivably be extendable to theatre: 'through the body the common name finds itself in the materialist field without losing any of its power to throw a net of knowledge over the *to-come*. And so through the body, reflection, which is hoisted up to a point that it is always situated on the edge of time, has the capacity to seize the materialist field, and to illuminate it with passion' (177–178).

10 Jerzy Limon approaches similar observations from his own trajectory of enquiry, which describes theatre as an art that requires 'the articulation of at least two different modes of perceiving reality', in that it simultaneously manifests 'two spheres governed by different laws of physics, and that includes geometry (space) and – most importantly – time', so that:

> time in performance becomes split: it is the real time of the performer, who is a live human being, and the created fictional time of the figure (which may occasionally seem to overlap). In fact, we are dealing with not only split time, but two presents: one is the present time of the live performer and the audience, the other is the present time of the fictional world, which might be labelled *agreed or transferred present*.
>
> (Limon 2010: 18, original emphasis)

11 I agree with Edgar's observation that theatre permits no 'marking the page, falling asleep and picking it up again tomorrow', but I am wary of his insistences that a dramatist can, individually, 'control the tempo of a play's consumption' and so 'guarantee that connections are perceptible to the audience' (Edgar 2009: 10). A dramatist may suggest (though cannot

ultimately control) relative duration, but cannot legislate for the spectators' ongoing imaginative dialogue with what they perceive, its tempo during or after performance.

12   Matt Fraction and Chip Zdarsky's ongoing graphic novel series, *Sex Criminals* (Fraction and Zdarsky 2014, 2015), imagines the brief subversive powers enjoyed by two protagonists who discover that, in the immediate aftermath of the *Kairos* of sexual intercourse, the surrounding sense of *chronos* is suspended around them: one might say, their personally vertical (immanent, subjective, associative) time becomes a lacuna for significantly transformative interventions into their society's frameworks for horizontal (transitive, objective) time schemes, which constitute the usually dominant order, terms and values of their surroundings.

13   Such characters include Placida in *Ursula: Fear of the Estuary* (who is identified in these very terms).

14   Hammer (2008) and Read (2003) consider Bachelard's theories in relation to theatre, but concentrate on his study *The Poetics of Space* rather than *The Dialectic of Duration*.

15   Dylan, incidentally, has recently offered the intriguing observation: 'Life has its ups and downs, and time has to be your partner, you know? Really, time is your soul mate'. http://www.independent.co.uk/arts-entertainment/music/features/bob-dylan-interview-passion-is-a-young-mans-game-older-people-gotta-be-wise-10029328.html accessed 16/10/2015.

16   This line always reminds me of the pathos of Lear's 'too late' address to the corpse of Cordelia, 'I killed the slave who was a-hanging thee', as if the strenuousness and ultimate success of his effort could wrest the action of hanging back from a terminally finite neck-breaking instant to a reversible process of interruptible duration.

17   As E. Brater puts it, Krapp is defying time, 'but soon undone by it', even as he winds his tape back and back again (Brater 2011: 109).

18   Thanks to Isabel Rabey for this observation.

19   Negri's characterizations of *chronos* v. *kairos* may be pertinent to the opposition of Joe and Mock, respectively. Joe becomes a figure of what Hardt and Negri call 'dead labour' (Negri 2013: 6), literally labouring in and maximizing death, displacing and excluding subjectivity; Mock becomes a restless figure of 'living labour' in search of what is '*to-come*' (179), in resistance to the limit of materialism. Mock favours and invokes a sense of 'propitious or *kairological* time', reconstructing the past (though not dependent on it) by reference to several associations of *kairos*: 'opportune moment, appointed time, appropriate measure and timing, unpredictable arrival', 'ethical context for persuasion, breakthrough, rupture, and revolutionary time' (Ryan 2015: 179).

20   Interestingly, Thomas has expressed a wish to direct a future production of *Flowers* that would reunite the original performers and add an additional palimpsest of video recordings of them performing the play at its time of premiere, to create a 'layering' of echoes similar to that practised by Kantor (Carlson 2003: 108). This might incorporate an overt sense of timescape within the production, through the ageing processes manifested by the performers, adding poignancy and renewed urgency to a play in which the characters seek definite senses and deductions of temporal and cultural consequence.

21   Elam's semiotics of theatre and drama (1980) similarly draw attention to time orientation, distinction between earlier and later states; however, Prigogine's analysis incorporates the additional awareness of the observer's perspective as a factor.

Interval: A Hole in the Night

Gaston Bachelard was not primarily considering the theatre interval when he wrote about intervals in his study *The Dialectic of Duration*, but his words are pertinent to this phenomenon (and to other aspects of theatre): he noted how if 'the continuity of a temporal movement is to be truly reliable', then the '*intervals* must be properly *organised*' (Bachelard 2000: 96, original emphasis).

The context of Bachelard's statement is his consideration of how we might view time as a series of alternating *instants* and *intervals*, designations that we might also recognize as 'transforming contexts', that which might be categorized broadly as time we appear to use, and time we appear to refuse (not solely theatrically): in Bachelard's distinction, time that is 'cohered, organised and consolidated into duration', versus time that is 'ineffective, scattered in a cloud of disparate elements' (91). In the larger context of *The Dialectic of Duration*, Bachelard evokes this distinction in order to interrogate its functionalism: he suggests that, in order to know and 'fill' time well, some juncture of non-acceleration must occur in a complementary rhythm of work and repose. Thus, he develops a critique of the utilitarian valorization of constant and determinable 'function', in favour of a more dialectical approach:

> there is nothing more normal or more necessary than going to the limit and establishing the relaxation of function, the repose of function, the non-functioning of function, since function must obviously often stop functioning [to be identifiable as such] [...] there is a fundamental heterogeneity at the very heart of lived, active, creative duration [and] in order to use time well we must activate the rhythm of creation and destruction, of work and repose (29).

Bachelard's characterizations of instant and intervals are widely pertinent to exploratory activity, but are readily applicable to rehearsal and theatrical performance (Howard Barker may repudiate functionality in his style of theatre *as a whole*, but might not when directorially designating the objectives of a specific day or half-day's rehearsal, or in deciding to incorporate an interval or curtain call). As Matthew Wagner observes, a theatrical interval, which is a 'temporal phenomenon in its very nature', 'bears pronounced marks of temporal contradiction – it both refutes and extends the time of the theatre, interrupting the temporality of the performance while lengthening the overall theatrical event' (Wagner 2012: 122).

In Bachelard's terms, the performance is the time most readily designated and activated as recognizably 'used' by performers, scenographers and audiences ('cohered, organised and consolidated into duration'), whereas the interval appears on its surface to be time 'refused', 'ineffective' in terms of narrative, dramatic, performative development, in favour of a juncture when external claims may reassert their primacy and distractions. However, if an interval provides a hiatus of time where the consciousness of those presenting and attending is relatively 'scattered in a cloud of disparate elements', this should not imply that it is necessarily time wasted.

An interval (itself a transforming context) permits an opportunity for physical relief and imaginative reflection when it inserts a hiatus in the theatrical action; the suspension of this action will, moreover, often be heightened by an increase in narrative tension and emotional *suspense* (registered by the characters, expressed by the actors, extended to and evoked within the audience). Narratively, the interval is usually positioned to complement formally the narrative development of pressure, extending (rather than deflating) the sense that something or someone is approaching or being pushed to, or has reached, breaking point; and creating curiosity and amplifying expectancy as to what courses subsequent events might take, in consequence; even as it offers a 'breathing space' to reflect on what has led up to this point in the process, on the energies that have been activated, and to speculate on the developments that they may further determine and transform.

Our surviving forms of Shakespeare's playtexts stipulate no definite junctures for intervals, though their narrative shapes carry strong implications: it would be an unusual, and probably unwise, directorial decision *not* to begin the second half of *The Winter's Tale* with the self-conscious appearance and speech of the figure of Time in Act Four, scene one. The development of events in *Love's Labour's Lost* seems to imply and call for an interval break after Act Four, scene three, when the tensions of the scholar's vows, and Berowne's performance of moral superiority, have arrived at breaking point, and renewed initiatives, of courtship, are proposed.[1] Similarly, *Titus Andronicus* seems to suggest an interval break at Lucius's determination to defect to the Goths, partly to enable the audience to assimilate the shattering momentum of events that have enveloped Titus's wider family (though my 1987 production ended on the image of Aaron alone onstage, laughing in triumph, my bid to extend the tension, even perhaps create expectation of, and appetite for, a responsive counterforce, which would be ostensibly 'morally justified', but prove – appropriately – complexly troubling and darkly ironic).

Alternatively, as a director, I have also found some structural and experiential effects to be felicitous, in terms of opening up space/time for reflection and building tension, by adopting two intervals, rather than one, in productions of Shakespeare plays: positioning first, then briefer second, intermissions in *Coriolanus* (at the ends of II.1 and IV.2) and *Antony and Cleopatra* (at the end of the galley scene, II.7, as is usual, but also after IV.9, the death of Enobarbus). I was informed in these decisions, at least to some degree, by directorial engagements with Bernard Shaw's *Heartbreak House* and John Whiting's *Saint's Day*, which both indicate, if not specify, two intervals. The second interval in *Heartbreak*

House is particularly effective as it permits a reconfiguration of stage space (and, in my 1999 production, the audience's spatial relations to the action) for events to escape the confinements of the house, and occur in the astonishingly different and 'licensed' terms of the garden at night – terms that extend to a sense of the immanence of potential destruction (which some characters pronounce prospectively thrilling, if specifically targeted). *Saint's Day* builds its mounting sense of apocalyptic strangeness to almost surreal levels, by admitting previously unseen characters from the surrounding village *into* the doom-laden house for its third section, even as the unleashed destruction reportedly extends, appallingly, throughout the surrounding English rural peacetime landscape. More recently, Jez Butterworth's *Jerusalem* deploys two specified intervals to accrue a gradually but definitely and variously amassing sense of darkness building in and around its pivotal location of a rough mobile-homestead in a forest clearing.

Directions for single intervals intrinsically throw a more definite emphasis on an identifiable principal point of tension. In John Osborne's *Look Back in Anger*, Alison's silent scream forms a differently expressive 'breaking point' to Jimmy's garrulously regular, deliberately offensive detonations, and establishes their relationship as the principal focus of tangled resentment and attraction. The interval point in Howard Barker's *The Castle* is both ominously and unpredictably fraught, as it is approached through characters' discrepant senses of time and strategy: the witch Skinner has just previously experienced an epiphany of militarized masculine bloodlust through and across various historical ages (a reach that can be reflected by the chronologically variant costuming of the combative knights whom the audience glimpse, through permitted access to the embodied terms of her prophetic vision); she then surprisingly and uncharacteristically admits the advances of the castle builder, Holiday, who finds it hard to believe his luck. The audience may also reflect on how it may be unwise to take Skinner's invitation at face value, and then have this deduction confirmed when they learn, in the second scene of the second half, that Skinner has (perhaps not unsympathetically, for some) staved in Holiday's skull with a brick.

Unusually, Gregory Doran's 2008 production of *Hamlet* for the Royal Shakespeare Company positioned the interval at a point of *Hamlet*, behind Claudius, raising his blade in readiness to strike a fatal revenging blow. As Wagner observes, the theatre interval's 'meeting of time and "time"' would seem to strengthen 'the already powerful position of objective clock-time', cueing the audience to 'reset their internal clocks, aligning them with the clock in the foyer' (2012: 122) and permitting temporal space for reflection, not only on the theatrical event, but on the details and pressures of the wider world (which may prove otherwise invasive, even in theatrical presentations of tumultuous events, despite these theatrical events being distantly situated in space and/or time; or else because of the theatrical actions' repercussive resonances with, or direct references to, external tensions and events). Most of Shakespeare's original audiences may have expected *Hamlet* to conform to the developmental form of the revenge tragedy rather than opt for further deferral by Hamlet; however, most of the present-day audience for Doran's production were likely to *know* that further deferral by Hamlet would ensue after the interval, though perhaps not on the level of consciousness that was uppermost, before the interval. Doran thus created a 'cliff-hanger' moment, amplifying suspense for those unfamiliar with the play's narrative development, and providing a surprising *degree* of tension for those who presumed (but probably, momentarily, sought to check) their own familiarity.

However, the interval's suspension (rather than expansion) of time in this way for me lends force to Wagner's observation on how an interval, perhaps counter-intuitively, generates a sense of 'the time of the theatre intruding on the time of the world, rather than vice versa: a resistance to the strength of the objective clock', particularly when it is set against the 'measure of the thickness of the theatrical present that is built into Shakespearean dramaturgy' (2012: 123). Theatrical time is framed, shaped and multidimensionally intensified, foregrounding process in ways that may make the *terms* of daily life seem the more limited, and limiting. If an interval resembles a conjuror's 'reveal', exposing the means by which a trick is executed, it does not diminish the wonder, surprise and curiosity generated by a successful performance of the trick, which may even render the 'reveal' disappointingly prosaic. Similarly, theatre is capable of throwing into relief the extent to which our dominant senses of (day)time are prosaic (and limiting), rather than poetic (multilayered, associative and expansive). In Howard Brenton's *Magnificence*, a character recalls the disruptive effect on a film's power to sustain engagement and faith when a hole is ripped in a cinema screen (an observation recalling William S. Burroughs's initiatives to disrupt projections of dominant hegemony, which he termed 'the reality film' [Burroughs, 1968: 151]). Similarly, theatre may rip a hole in the night: notwithstanding, or even because of, an interval (which can provide a further demonstration of the surprising fragility of regular temporal co-ordinates). Theatre can expose an unexpected fluidity in time, and terms. The theatrical interval may constitute a narrative, dramatic and performative hiatus, but it also points up the way that the surrounding action of the theatre weakens (briefly but significantly) the effects and strength of our habitual temporal indicators, and our associated evaluations.

Note

1   I saw a production of this play, in 2000 at Schauspielhaus Bochum, in which the scholars marked this change in impulse and narrative direction with unusual definiteness, by performing a rap and stripping to their underwear as ostentatious expressions of *macho* self-confidence, which prompted appreciative shouts and applause, not least for the aplomb of the actors' delivery of the direction.

Part II

Time in Theatre

Chapter 3

Shapes of Time

Everything must change

For time, as for theatre, Aristotle provided a provocative starting point: he claimed 'time is the calculable measure of motion with respect to before and afterness'; in other words, 'the precise measure of an ordered succession of states' (Aristotle, *Physics* IV, 11, 219, b1; quoted by Eco in Lippincott et al. 1999: 10). He suggested the primary indicators of change, to and from the perspective of human perception, were the Sun (which appeared to move and vanish, but rather intensified and faded in its brightness) and the Moon and stars which, in their movement and return, provided a 'constant periodical appearance' (Lippincott et al. 1999: 10), cyclical as well as directional and linear, marking the progression of days, nights and months.

But civilizations, cultures and individuals define, experience and characterize time differently (if not uniquely), at different moments and in different contexts. Our bodies are 'bone clocks' (to use the phrase of David Mitchell 2014), testifying to a process of maturation, ageing and decay that is essentially irreversible. However, in Maori and Aboriginal Australian cultures, the past may often be perceived as something that exists side by side with the present, as 'an active principle that explains why things are how they are' (Lippincott 1999: 27): a benign informing, prompting respectful appreciation of self in relation to others, encapsulated in the Aboriginal concept of *dreamtime*. This characterization contrasts fundamentally with that of the significantly Faustian slogan chosen by a chief of the portable computer division of Hitachi to accelerate his workers: 'Speed is God, and time is the devil' (Gleick 1999: 75). Malign time is usually depicted in terms of hostility, deceptive transience, and irrevocable, inescapable destruction. A similar note of destructive jealousy, and the association of inconstancy with criminality, is sounded by Ogden Nash's lyrics for Kurt Weill's 1943 song, 'Speak Low', which identifies love with gold, and Time as a thief. Both demonizations appear to reflect Thomas Pynchon's suggestion that 'all investigations of Time, however sophisticated or abstract, have at their true base the human fear of mortality' (Pynchon 2006: 553). 'Let's make time an ally rather than a thief', says a character in one of my plays (subverting Nash), when she surrenders to the seduction of another (Rabey 2004: 115), conscious that she is swimming against the tide of conventional presumptions (including her own) about her character.

This presumption of Time's hostility – expressed as a fearsome *loss of shape* – relates to the Second Law of Thermodynamics, often imagined in the appropriately irreversible image, 'The Arrow of Time': the sense that the order and structure associated with familiar and conventional terms of life are primarily subject to the disordering, dissipative force of entropy (the gradual 'running down' of the universe to the eventually terminal heat death of the cosmos). Disarray increases, inexorably: ensuring the future will be different to the past. However, Sean Carroll cites how a more appropriate, if difficult, overview of the process (identified in cosmologically impish terms as 'Maxwell's Demon') would observe how life creates entropy somewhere, 'in order to maintain structure and organization somewhere else' (Carroll 2010: 197). A castle will erode with time, and its constituent elements will reconfigure as a wind-shaped mound of earth or sand: a less fearful prospect.

In the seventeenth century, Leibniz challenged Newton's concept that time was a force independent of the universe. Anticipating Einstein, Leibniz's view of events in time was *relational*, suggesting that the human mind derives a sense of time (one aspect of the universe, rather than something independent of it) from its perception of events and not the other way round. From the end of the nineteenth century, several theorists – Einstein and phenomenonologists such as Husserl, Bergson, Merleau-Ponty and Heidegger – furthered challenges to the hitherto accepted and classical imaginings of time by emphasizing how human subjectivity constructs images and perceptions of time as a function of consciousness, rather than construing time as an external, objective absolute. However, phenomenology also suggests that the determination of time by human beings is not merely passive and receptive, but dialogic and dialectic, in that perceptions of time will inform initiatives and transformative interaction.

Whitrow suggests that the essence and ultimate significance of time may be found in 'its transitional nature',[1] which leads on to his claim that 'without the fact of transience there could be no significance' (Whitrow [1972] 2003: 139).[2] This significance of time's 'transitional nature' is nevertheless most frequently interpreted in directional terms: for example, H. F. Blum claims it is 'difficult to deny that the over-all effect of evolution is irreversible; the Ammonites, the Dinosaur and Lepidodendron are gone beyond recall' (Blum, quoted in Whitrow [1972] 2003: 116–117); it is however *imaginable*, though *unlikely*, that some cyclic aspect of time might recreate the preconditions for the return of apparently extinct species.[3]

Jay Gipson-King observes how 'the day-to-day experience of time is the result of multiple layers of functionality' (Gipson-King 2013: 148; a similar observation to those of Adam 1990–2004). He also succinctly recapitulates observations that will be important for this chapter:

Western cultures tend to perceive time as *directional, irreversible* and *continuous* – in other words, as *linear*. This model is tied up with Christian cosmology, which moves in a straight line from creation to Armageddon, and with the Industrial Revolution, which segmented time into discrete, linear units in order to increase productivity in the factory.

(149, original emphasis)

It may be pertinent to add here an identification of the late eighteenth and nineteenth centuries' 'shift of focus from quantity and timeless laws to change, growth, and evolution occurred almost simultaneously in physics, biology, astronomy, philosophy, and the arts'; in 'the social sciences this change of emphasis is exemplified by Marx's theories and the evolutionism of Spencer, and in physical sciences by thermodynamics' (Adam 1990: 61). I would propose that, in theatre, this was exemplified by the emergences of naturalism (in relation to evolutionism) and epic theatre (in relation to Marx).

Distinctions in time

Sean Carroll's ensuing statement might seem self-evident: 'Time has a direction and space doesn't'; time points or flows from the past towards the future (Carroll 2010: 21). However, this apparently clear-cut distinction between time and space was complicated by the seventeenth-century mathematician Isaac Barrow, who observed: 'Time denotes not an actual existence but a certain capacity or possibility for a continuity of existence; just as space denotes a capacity for intervening length' (Barrow quoted in Whitrow [1972] 2003: 75). Barrow's notion of time's capacity (redolent of space) seems closer to Pearson's model of theatrical performance as establishing an aporia of spacetime for the 'slowing down, speeding up, attenuating and intensifying norms of social practice, in combinations of simultaneous, sequential, folded, suspended and discontinuous activity' (Pearson 2010: 159); and also of the crucial importance and capacity of a spatial environment in envisaging time, if, as Klein suggests, 'we experience time exclusively against a background of events'(Klein 2008: 55). A theatrical example is provided by Beckett's *Waiting for Godot*: the budding of a single leaf on the central tree testifies to a sense of transition that the characters cannot independently establish, through their inability to recall details or events. Whitrow suggests: 'it is not time itself but what goes on in time that produces effects'; time is 'not a simple sensation but depends on processes of mental organization uniting thought and action' (Whitrow [1972] 2003: 27). I would make the same claim for theatre: it is a complex imaginative response to time, refocusing our attention to processes of organization (both personal and social) uniting thought and action – both in the moment of the performance event, and with resonant implications for our wider tendencies and capacities for ordering and renegotiating priorities, beyond the theatre.

Theatre is one means, using motion in space, by which we create and present images, and unusual effects, of time. This chapter will consider some ways in which theatre, itself a dialectical activity, has generated notably and specifically dialectical images of time and consciousness.

Models of theatrical time: A survey

In considering time in relation to theatre, specifically Shakespeare, Wagner acknowledges the ideas of Ricardo Quinones, who proposed 'three basic conceptions of Time' emergent in Shakespeare's plays and sonnets: these are 'augmentative time, contracted time, and extended time' (Wagner 2012: 2–3; Quinones 1965: 328).[4] However, Wagner observes that Quinones proposes this tripartite analysis as '"concepts", either moral or psychological – however accurate, they are of the text and the context, not of the stage'; the 'time of the theatre' – 'performative activity' – is, rather, 'an anchor for the time of the character, and it is the material, experiential buoy for the concepts or views of time that may emerge in the staging of a play' (Wagner 2012: 3).

Richard Schechner has indicated three distinct ways by which theatre configures time:

In *event time* the activity takes as long as is required for completion: application without fixed duration.

In *set time* all the activity has to be completed in a given time: a fixed duration that may lead to a different sense of urgency and quality of energetic engagement.

In *symbolic time* one span represents another duration.

(Schechner 1969: 87–88, original emphasis)

Mike Pearson aptly notes how a given theatre performance conventionally 'runs in *event time*', all activities being completed in 'narrative order, until the story is told', though this may also include phases of *symbolic time*, where three days elapse between one scene and the next; however, all three senses of time operate as '*organizing principles, structuring devices and operating principles*' in what Pearson identifies as 'site-specific performance' (Pearson 2010: 160). However, my conjecture (and, presumably, Schechner's) would be that this sense of multiple apparent temporalities, 'informing and enfusing performance' (Pearson 2010: 161), is true of many forms of theatre, including what Pearson identifies *specifically* as both performance and theatre: 'the superimposition and subtle interaction of a range of time frames and scales, containing the juxtaposition of short-term events and long-term elaborations of theme and dramatic development' (Pearson 2010: 160). States suggests that the distinctive compressive swiftness of theatre is not to do with either clock-time or the suspense of the plot, but with the performer's sense of distillation, 'the swiftness of condensation, of life raised to an intense power of temporal and spatial density' (States 1985: 154). I have more questions about the distinctions proposed by Hans-Thies Lehmann, in his demarcations of a so-called 'postdramatic theatre' than I have time to undertake fully here. If Lehmann is suggesting that the most notable theatre of any age alerts spectators to the dominant social and temporal frameworks of their lives, by opening up a time/space for analytic distance, I would agree. His contention that this is a new development, constituting a binary opposition to 'dramatic' theatre, is less convincing (when set against all of the 'drama' I consider herein, from *Everyman*, *Henry V*, *Love's Labour's Lost* to *The Skin of Our Teeth*, random).[5] When Steve Waters attempts to identify 'what is substituted for conventional scenes in works that have been characterised as "post-dramatic"', he deduces that in plays by Sarah Kane, or the later plays of Martin Crimp, 'the action often has a suspended, imagistic quality'. However, Waters specifies that 'time, and therefore change, is still at work': so, even if 'no one in the text changes', as in Crimp's *Attempts on her Life* (1997), Waters claims 'the audience is transformed' (Waters 2010: 16). It may be more precise to say that the contexts, in and by which the audience perceive unfolding events, prove transformative.

Gipson-King offers another tripartite paradigm, a framework based on Audience Time, Dramatic Time and Narrative Time, which deserves quotation in full:

> *Audience time*, as I define it, is time as experienced by a spectator sitting in the house. This includes the duration of the performance, the number and spacing of intermissions and each spectator's personal absorption or boredom within the performance as the case may be. *Dramatic time* refers to the progression of the plot or dramatic action. Does the story proceed from beginning to middle to end in Aristotelian fashion? Does the action move backwards from the climax to the inciting incident, as in Harold Pinter's *Betrayal*? Or is the dramatic action more diffuse, as in the repetitions and revisions of Suzan-Lori Parks? Lastly, *narrative time* is the fictional time experienced by the *characters* within the story. In some cases narrative time can be synchronous with real time, as in Molière's *The Impromptu at Versailles*, or it can stretch over days, months or years as in Shakespeare. Combined, these three types of time create what I call a play's temporal shape, or form. Phenomenologically speaking, form is the *container* that holds the content of the actual story. Like all containers, its *shape* alters the observer's perception of the object contained. Temporal shape, therefore, becomes a vital part of the overall experience and meaning of any play.
>
> (Gipson-King 2013: 149–150, original emphasis)

Waters further observes that 'in cinema, what is screened has already been filmed and is located in the past tense'; theatre is the medium that places time 'irreducibly centre stage' (71), creating 'something that unfolds in time, that creates a sense of time's movement', but according to the tempo of its own formal framework (72). However, Edgar points out how

> Plays which disrupt or dislocate time mount a challenge to the overwhelming dominance of narrative in popular drama, and contribute to an extensive body of work [...] of which the subject is the reliability or otherwise of narrative itself [...] Plays which put together two or three apparently unrelated narratives and invite the audience to connect them – as happens in three of Sarah Kane's five plays – [...] imply or even insist that making cause-and-effect connections is harder than it used to be, but they also assert the overwhelming human urge to do so, however unpropitious the *Zeitgeist*.
>
> (Edgar 2009: 115)

Waters suggests that four forms of duration may be identified in theatre plays: duration of story, scene, moment and activity; he moreover characterizes theatrical time by reference to six (overlapping and simultaneously operating) social forms (calendrical, festive, functional, ludic, biographical and historical 'times') (Waters 2010: 73–76). As noted earlier, Limon goes into further distinctions by proposing an eightfold classification of time in theatre (2010: 107).

However, in this section I will principally consider various theatrical bids to observe (what Gipson-King artfully designates) shapes of time, in passage and in play.

Temporal 'thickness' in morality plays

Whitrow identifies the terms of one such moment of transition in the temporal terms of authority:

> Throughout the whole medieval period the cyclic and the linear concepts of time were in conflict. Scientists and scholars, influenced by astronomy and astrology, tended to emphasize the cyclic concept. The linear concept was fostered by the mercantile class and the rise of a money economy. For as long as power was concentrated in the ownership of land, time was felt to be plentiful and was associated with the unchanging cycle of the soil. But with the circulation of money the emphasis was on mobility. The tempo of life was increased, and time was now regarded as something valuable that was felt to be slipping away continually: after the fourteenth century public clocks in Italian cities struck all twenty-four hours of the day.
>
> (Whitrow [1972] 2003: 9)

Cawley notes how little remains from the secular drama of the early English Middle Ages, though pagan seasonal festivities and ritual folk-plays often contained motifs of symbolic death and resurrection that paralleled (and could be mapped onto) Christian myths, and this 'coalescence of religious and secular' traditions produced a fifteenth-century 'vernacular religious drama with a strong infusion of humorous and popular elements' (Cawley 1977: viii–ix). From one perspective, these plays present (re)inscriptions of deterministic principles: Prigogine observes how the paradigm of the Christian God as an omnipotent superhuman contributed to the development of a deterministic vision of nature, which aimed to bring human scientific knowledge closer to a divine and therefore 'atemporal point of view' (Prigogine 1997: 12). In contrast to this divine state of atemporality, human transgression in the Garden of Eden was considered to have admitted mortal transience and seasonal variation, fear and toil in the face of the fall from bliss to loss, birth to death, growth to decay, imposing a shameful debt to be 'worked off' in fractional (but insufficient) mitigation, and so the 'battle with time commenced' (Adam 2004: 11).

However, medieval morality plays also testify to a strong sense of temporal 'thickness', which in Wagner's sense of the present is 'heavily weighted by the past and future' (Wagner 2012: 2), in ways that transcend the merely annual-seasonal. They aim to re-present a spiritual perspective that is, tellingly, beyond the limiting boundaries and distractions associated with human mortal time: an ordered regulating (and potentially restorative) structure behind distinct and irreversible events. Schroeder is precise in her observations on British medieval forms, the Corpus Christi cycles of pageant and mystery plays, and morality plays: how the Corpus Christi plays located the resurrection of Christ within broader historical contexts, depicting 'two sorts of temporal relationships at once: the historical sequence of God's creation and the coexistence of all events in God's mind' (Schroeder 1989: 15). She further notes how morality plays also reflected the vision of time as 'both concurrent and sequential: by weaving together two distinct yet parallel plots, the morality plays typically suggested the interconnectedness of all events', whilst also focusing on 'psychological conflicts', developing a dramatic need for means to give 'dramatic expression to idiosyncratic versions of both past and present', thus providing the basis for Elizabethan stage conventions (such as prologues, inductions, dumb shows, asides, soliloquies and plays-within-plays) 'constructing and exploring alternative connections between past and present' through possibilities of stage time freed from the observation of an exclusively linear causality (15–16). Kalb suggests these plays might manifest entwined needs for both (i) play that subverts limitations (including those associated with human mortality and ageing, which a divine perspective alone may transcend) and (ii) reassurance of boundaries: through an immersive experience whereby medieval Christians 'could imagine *themselves* as players in the grand historical drama of man' (Kalb 2011: 12).

The morality play *Everyman* (circa 1508) begins with a prologue concerned to mark its difference from subversively irreverent seasonal revels such as May Day and the Feast of Fools. The Messenger entreats the audience to give all their attention to hear a 'moral play' with proper 'reverence', that 'of our lives and ending shows / How transitory we be all day', and he crucially (re)focuses attention on long-term rather than short-term reckonings ('The story saith: Man, in the beginning / Look well, and take good heed to the ending', Cawley 1977: 207). Everyman, threatened by Death, confronts his innate isolation ('Now I have no manner of company / To help me in my journey, and me to keep') that impels him to appeal to God (reacknowledged as almighty). Everyman has to render account of all his days spent ('In my time, sith life was me lent', Cawley 1977: 216), and in the process discovers the unenduring nature of the comforts he has sought. He reflexively seeks to reassure himself, 'it is said ever among / That money maketh all right that is wrong', and perversely tries to 'clean and purify' his reckoning by appeal to Goods, who unequivocally states 'my love is contrary to the love everlasting'. However, Goods adds a reminder that money need not be corrupting in all its deployments: 'But if thou had me loved moderately during, / As to the poor to give part of me, Then shouldst thou not in this dolour be' (Cawley 1977: 219) (this may latterly recall the observations by Derrida [1992: 41] on how a gift, above all, offers *time* …). When Everyman perceives and locates the only enduring value in the crucially counter-worldly Good Deeds, he finds his only support in making a 'crystal-clear' reckoning before God, within the significant timeframe: 'after death amends no man can make' (Cawley 1977: 233).

Carol Ann Duffy prepared a new version of the text of *Everyman* for Rufus Norris's inaugural production as artistic director of the Royal National Theatre of England in 2015. In an interview preface to the 16 July 2015 live screening, Norris explained how the play was 'about someone running away from death – which [*sic*] is all of us'. This production presented Everyman as an initially secure city hedonist, convinced the world was his to spend, in flight from durable commitments (memorably exemplified by his exceptional visit to his ageing parents and his sister, their carer, during which scene a clock ticked loudly; and his dependent mother thanked him for 'finding time' for them, while his father, bewildered, constantly quoted the words of others). Having claimed Everyman, Death finally scanned the audience and asked 'Who's next?'.[6]

Everyman's realizations develop those of the titular protagonist in the earlier play *Mankind* (circa 1470), the abilities to perceive and value that which lies beyond modish distractions (which are presented and embodied in the lures of the characters New Guise, Now-a-Days and Naught). However, this could be viewed as one form of *kairos*, the importance of, and readiness in, the moment: Mankind learns to seek and maintain a responsiveness and atonement in the identifiable present rather than trust to repentance in the later hour of death – an awareness of prescience that recalls Saint Augustine's definitions, 'the present concerning the past is memory, the present considering the present is immediate awareness, the present considering the future is expectation' (Augustine 1998: 235). The emphasis of the play *Mankind* is on the present moment, as a (conventionally obscured) window to eternal life.

To return to Schechner's terms: the narrative event (and performance) of Everyman's (and Mankind's) life/time is a *set time* in which all the (symbolic) activity has to be completed in a given period: 'a fixed duration' that transpires to imply and demand 'a different sense of urgency and quality of energetic engagement' to the materialism that is socially dominant. These dramatically multiple temporalities are early but urgently demarcated and distinguished theatrical examples of what Pearson identifies as 'the juxtaposition of short-term events and long-term elaborations of theme and dramatic development' (Pearson 2010: 160).

We might even dwell (fleetingly) on the designation, 'morality play'. Priestley observes that the 'root idea' of the moralist, 'that in Time there is opportunity, which sooner or later must be taken if we do not want to live with regret', is 'a sound one' (Priestley 1964: 60). We might paraphrase this: how to distinguish the possibility of *kairos* within *chronos*? The two Greek terms offer a direction out of the apparent human paradox that Priestley applies to the reclusive mystic and the extravagant hedonist alike: both 'must use his time to try to free himself from Time' (Priestley's rendering offers an intriguing distinction, through capitalization). However, the means and terms of freedom will crucially vary: for 'who is to decide when [time] is being saved, when apparently squandered?' (60). Variations in perspective, tempo and causality are crucial in Marlowe's theatrical developments.

Dr Faustus: 'The double motion of the planets'

The contrasting appeals of the short-term and the long-term are keynotes for Christopher Marlowe's tragic development of the morality tradition, *Dr Faustus* (circa 1592). Like other plays by Marlowe, *Dr Faustus* artfully negotiates a tightrope that stretches between the morality play's demonstration of the futility of worldly power and the heroic poeticization of post-Medieval human aspiration beyond the confinements of conventional mor(t)ality and, in this case, knowledge. On his first appearance, Faustus expresses frustration with his human and professional temporal restrictions, located in an acute sense of the injustice of mortality, and seeks to be eternalized:

> Yet art thou still but Faustus and a man.
> Couldst thou make men to live eternally,
> Or being dead, raise them to life again,
> Then this profession were to be esteemed.

(Marlowe 1969: 266)

This incorporates a witty theatrical slight-of-hand, in that it is Marlowe's skill in the (often suspect outsider's) speculative art and profession of theatre that is enabling the 'dead' scientist-scholar Faustus to be reanimated on successive occasions of performance, which extend, if not eternally, then to the present distant century. Marlowe's Faustus furthers his ambitions, having obtained the diabolical services of Mephistophilis, to self-aggrandizing and remorseless fantasies of disrupting natural lunar and tidal rhythms – 'to make the moon drop from her sphere / Or the ocean to overwhelm the earth' (Marlowe 1969: 274) – to the degree of wreaking global catastrophes, by wrecking time's cyclical rhythms of measure and regeneration. To return to the terms of Whitrow's account of the social transitions from medieval cyclical time to mercantile linear time, Faustus places his hopes in superhuman (or Promethean?) mobility and tempo, and significantly fantasizes about destroying astronomy and astrology (the Eden he would desecrate, in Satanic terms). In counterpoint, Mephistophilis admits his damnation resides in his experience that the so-called 'eternal joys of heaven' can actually be revoked as penalty for mutiny, so that time becomes a searing and mocking awareness of the deprivation of, and irrevocable severance from, 'everlasting bliss' (Marlowe 1969: 275). However, Mephistophilis warns Faustus that the merely human perspective is easily overwhelmed by plenitude of choice, and shrinks to grab the first options of 'frivolous demands'; indeed, Faustus only considers more fundamental alternatives when he senses that the apparent temporal liberations of his bargain are, when seen from a larger perspective, more poignant in their temporal restrictions. Matthew Wagner astutely notes how Marlowe's play

> is explicitly drawing attention to temporal discordance, both within a singular time frame (the fictive world of Wittenberg, where time in Faustus's study is at odds with time in the rest of the world), and between time frames (the variable speed of time on stage compared to the consistent speed of time in the audience's world).

(Wagner 2012: 17)

I would add that this is not only an effect of the play's penultimate scene, but a consistent feature and motif within its dual perspectives on protagonist, world and theme. Mangan notes how Marlowe dramatizes 'a revulsion of nature' against Faustus's contract with the devil, and this is expressed in terms of biological rhythm, pulse and cycle in a further dramatic irony of dual perspective: the circulation of Faustus's blood stops, in order to give him a chance to save his own life; however, as soon as his blood flows again, 'his death-warrant is signed (literally)' and his licensed term of power for 'twenty-four years begins to tick away' (Mangan [1987] 1989: 48).[7]

The issue of time in relation to spatial perspective is amplified to cosmic proportions, with implications for human knowledge and perceptions, in Faustus's questions about the movements of the planets ('have they all one motion, both *situ et tempore*?', Marlowe 1969: 286). Mephistophilis explains that all planets move directionally and regularly, but at different speeds; the one authoritative perspective is God's empyrium, beyond which further heavens are empty 'fables': however, Faustus maintains that this is no great revelation.[8] Mephistophilis's refusal to divulge a first cause in that Universe also implies the limitations of what that human perspective can accomplish in topographical comprehension. Faustus may claim to 'know' empirically 'the double motion of the planets' and be able to profess a unified (objective) perspective; however, his dizzying experiences, and those of the theatre audience watching his story in Marlowe's dramatic context, problematize and confound all senses of unity and measure with regard to time, perspective and speed of movement. Astronomy and astrology retain a fascination for Faustus, who seeks to find out their secrets, but does so by fantastic and magical means: he scales Olympus 'in a chariot burning bright', and goes to 'prove Cosmography', mounted on a 'dragon's back' (Marlowe 1969: 292–293), thus manifesting the terms of the cartographer's superstitious admonition, 'here be dragons', in deed.

In a further magical dissolution of former limits, Faustus astonishes the Duke of Vanholt with his ability to procure ripe grapes, out of local season, from a different hemisphere (anticipating the aseasonal and decontextualized cornucopia of year-round availability of internationally sourced food promised by supermarket globalization![9]). However, the Old Man provides a reminder of prescience (telling Faustus, 'thine hour is almost come'), urging a renewed sense of the implications of temporal processes, recall of human limitations, unattended relationships and latent dangers: Mephistophilis counters with a distraction that can be performed 'in twinkling of an eye', the reanimation of Helen. The Second Scholar seeks to remind Faustus that mercy is 'infinite' (Marlowe 1969: 333); however, the infinite is crucially *that which is beyond human imagination*: the most challenging and distant alternative to mortal perception. The Good Angel paradoxically poeticizes Faustus's loss in teasingly immeasurable terms, 'Pleasures unspeakable, bliss without end': the Angels' words are semantic containers by which one may approach, glimpse or sense the possibility of infinite delimitation, but not fathom it. Once more, Faustus bids to achieve the impossible: 'Stand still, you ever-moving spheres of heaven, / That time may cease and midnight never come' (Marlowe 1969: 336).[10]

However, *Dr Faustus* raises a question of cause and effect, in the connections of past to present (and future), when Mephistophilis boasts that he directed Faustus's readings towards the most tempting occult texts. Marlowe's play has selected particular shaping events from the past of his lead character to demonstrate their determining consequences: the process of condensation that dramatists (and other artists) apply (given a theoretically infinite chain of prior causality). The audience will conventionally assume that the dramatic events of *Dr Faustus* began with Faustus's crucial choice, a matter of will and control. But what if determining factors of Faustus's story began *before* protagonist or audience recognized – or *were able* to recognize – them? Mephistophilis's boast exposes Faustus as unreliable in his determination of the spectators' temporal understanding of what has happened in the play.

Matthew Wagner's aforementioned reading of the discordant time frames of this scene finds the play's most foregrounded counterpoint between the (sonic, if not physical) presence of the clock and its unnatural acceleration of stage-time in contrast to Faustus's self-consciously poetic attempts to arrest it:

> The theatre allows for the clock (objective time, materialized in the form of the clock striking on stage) to be present and forward in the auditorium, but also to be notably *directed* by subjective experience. Clearly, what matters in the scene is not that something might be wrong with the clocks in the Faustus household, but that those clocks are deferring to a more powerful experience of time for both character and audience. And each temporal experience – the objective and the subjective – is required to be palpable for the moment on stage to be theatrically effective.
>
> (Wagner 2012: 18, original emphasis)

Thus, *Dr Faustus* offers a startling example of what Adam describes as multiple time-schemes, and their identifiably discrepant claims and appeals. We might also consider Schechner's terms here: Faustus's *set time* is becoming rendered, alarmingly, in terms of *symbolic time* that eludes his control. Furthermore, Mangan observes how Faustus's attempts to escape his fate are increasingly 'predicated on the idea of *space*', the supposition of a physical aporia that might offer security; and, from there, he seeks to set a limit on eternity ('Let Faustus live in hell a thousand years, / A hundred thousand, and at last be saved'), but again finds that his language has the opposite effect to that intended, 'expanding' time 'into infinity' ('no end is limited to damned souls') (Mangan [1987] 1989: 91). This foreshadows Barrow's seventeenth-century sense of time as capacity (for a continuity of existence), redolent of space (denoting a capacity, here for intervening security). Whitrow's observation provides an appropriately definite check, when applied to Faustus's predicament: 'In the final count, time is a fundamental property of the relationship between the universe and the observer which cannot be reduced to anything else' (Whitrow [1972] 2003: 127); in this instance, try as he might. In divergence from the Christian myth of the morality play, Faustus's tragically symbolic death remains just that: death, with no chance of resurrection.

Marlowe's tragedy ends with a Latin epigram, translatable as 'The hour ends the day, the author ends his work' (Marlowe 1969: 339). On the one hand, the lunar cycle seems to have re-established its authority, prompting a corresponding termination and conclusion. The limits of human knowledge may appear to be recircumscribed, and we might agree with the deduction of Hector Berlioz, 'Time is a great teacher, but unfortunately it kills all its pupils' (quoted in Carroll 2010: 287). On the other hand, one might argue that Faustus has made a lasting claim on our imaginations, remembered (literally so, in this fictional theatrical manifestation: we see him regrow severed limbs) for exploration of 'unlawful things' and 'deepness' that may nevertheless give the 'wise' occasion for 'wonder' and entice 'such forward wits / to practice more than heavenly power permits' (Marlowe 1969: 339), raising the metaphysical question of what might be 'more than heavenly power permits', and why. Some of the boundless fascination and questing spirit he represents is detectable in Sean Carroll's injunction: if our lives are 'brief and undirected, at least we can take pride in our mutual courage as we struggle to understand things much greater than ourselves' (Carroll 2010: 374). However, Faustus's chosen course involves a significant lack of mutuality, from outset to end, tending towards a self-defining isolation. Marlowe's play is a haunting dramatization of what Klein identifies as 'the intensified fear of death' that can accrue from a separate sense of self: 'If you live in a state of increased separateness, your existence is now more valuable and important to you, and you fear its end more', prompting a denial of death, a pretence that it will not occur (Klein 2008: 122). However, there is a sense in which Faustus lives forever. If not literally or dramatically resurrected, he has the potential for reanimation as folk devil, akin to Guy Fawkes; he bequeaths the adjective 'Faustian' for application in other contexts, a form of 'afterlife': his story is replayed and disseminated because of Marlowe's ingeniously paradoxical and provocatively indefinite theatricality. The play, like the planets, demonstrates a 'double motion', where perspective is relative, and crucially informed by speed of movement.

Shakespeare: Too long for a play

Shakespeare compulsively explores and experiments with problems of formal definition: genre, shape, containment, duration and play.[11] *The Comedy of Errors* (1594) pivots on the limit (and provides the aporia) of a single pressurized day in which to resolve some tension of disproportion and consequent injustice (so will *The Tempest*). Specifically, *The Comedy of Errors* plays with a market town economy's reliance on social designations of junctures in time and location, in order to resolve the dislocations of 33 years in a single hour, partly by showing how words and names, such as 'Antipholus' and 'Dromio', can refer to distinctly separate (though associated) things and people, which nevertheless refuse to stay within their designated limits and appointed times. Shakespeare apparently follows the triumphantly chaotic, benevolent formalism of *The Comedy of Errors* with his pointedly inconclusive experiment with comic form, *Love's Labour's Lost* (1598?), in which time is associated with separation, notably in its final lines for both characters and audience: 'You that way: we this way' (Shakespeare 2007: 363). The formally promised artifice of romantic reconciliation between male and female characters is deferred, on point of conditions of penance, patience and strained imaginations:

BEROWNE:	Our wooing doth not end like an old play:
	Jack hath not Jill. These ladies' courtesy
	Might have made our sport a comedy.
KING:	Come, sir, it wants a twelvemonth and a day,
	And then 'twill end.
BEROWNE:	That's too long for a play.

(Shakespeare 2007: 362)

Anne Righter observes how the year of penances, to which the male characters are consigned, 'lies, as Berowne ruefully points out, beyond the scope of artifice' (Righter 1967: 101): artifice that *Love's Labour's Lost* overtly associates with theatrical (character) time. Jonathan Bate describes the play as 'a great feast of linguistic sophistication on the theme of the inadequacy of linguistic sophistication' (Bate in Shakespeare 2007: 305); indeed, in *Love's Labour's Lost*, words promise reliable numeration, and try to measure, shape and limit time, but fail. The King of Navarre begins the play by describing his men's principal initiative of reclusive study as a bid to transcend 'cormorant devouring time'. They initially vow to adopt the principles of self-separation and deferral (retrospectively, a notable irony), with the hubristically Faustian superhuman objective of becoming 'heirs of all eternity' (309), based on the preservation of oaths of scholarship over a 'mere' three-year period. Instead, their calibrations and characterizations of the promises of time are refuted, and reinvented in directions associated with literary pronouncements of courtly love – with all the over-confident hyperbole which literary conceit can also assume regarding the accelerative powers ('swift as thought' [340]) of lover and beloved ('A withered hermit, fivescore winters worn, / Might shake off fifty, looking in her eye' [338]). The men determine to 'solace' the objects of their affections with 'some strange pastime', 'Such as the shortness of the time can shape' (341). That latter phrase suggests, whatever might be agreed and accomplished within urgent limits. However, it is also associated with (and applied to) the negotiated arrangement and presentation of a theatrical performance; which is shaped and defined precisely by the pressures of its brief duration, yet has the capacity to surprise and subvert habitual definition, with its 'strangeness'. However, the Princess and her women refute 'measure', in senses of both calibration ('Ask them how many inches is in one mile. If they have measured many, the measure then of one is easily told' [348]) and compliance in the formal rhythms of dance. Berowne complains that the women's mockery of the men, when they appear in their 'own shapes', is a refusal of seasonal licence: the women have determined to 'dash' the proffered 'merriment' 'like a Christmas comedy' (354).

It then reflects badly upon the men that they vent their frustrations through harsher and repeated mockery of the festive Pageant of the Nine Worthies, presaging more instances of performances grinding to a halt because of the audience's refusal to evaluate events and behaviour from the usual complicit perspective. In *Love's Labour's Lost*, the characters demonstrate a compulsive tendency to 'talk it to death', to use a modern phrase highly evocative of the play. Then Marcade's interruption of artifice takes everything, uncomfortably, *further*. He disrupts dramatic action and formal generic expectations with his news of the Princess's father's death, signalling the extrapolation of action and potential conclusion beyond the usual temporal capacities and shape of a theatrical comedy.[12] Rather, imagined action and potential conclusion are extended and relocated to barely imaginable challenges for comic wit ('To move wild laughter in the throat of death' [361], addressing the patients confined to a hospital, where time passes in unpleasantly particular ways) to be conducted over an imposed ritual period of 'twelve months and a day'. Thus, the men are required to adopt and refine their initial principles of self-separation and deferral, not in their former individualistically focused terms, but in active social consideration of others. *Love's Labour's Lost* thus pivots between senses and expectations of specifically focused, limited and concentrated, festive and generous time (of which comic theatre is one example), and the extended temporal perspective that *interrupts* and perforates such comic suspension. *Love's Labour's Lost* does not permit the selectivity and contrivance of comic shaping artifice (but rather includes and confronts illness, pain and death); instead, the play deliberately and pointedly includes a sense of time that, as Berowne exclaims, renders it 'too long for a play'. It, therefore, does not end like 'an old play' or even a 'comedy', but insists on pointing towards the challenging dissipation of (either brief or irrevocable) separations. *Love's Labour's Lost* at least *partly* incorporates imaginative reference towards that which comedy cannot readily incorporate: an artful confusion of (inclusive) form and (extensive) content, with particular regard to time. *Love's Labour's Lost* infuses comic form with a pointedly excessive and non-comic sense of the paradoxical relativism of perspectives in and on time.

This prefigures some of the qualities that are apparent in many Shakespeare plays: the dramatist experiments with stories (and characters) that strain to extend their duration beyond the comfortable generic limits of the play in which they are placed, as if in search of what might constitute a breaking point. *The Taming of the Shrew* pursues its anti-romantic investigation of shrewdness in game-playing one scene beyond the traditional comic conclusion of marriage, to examine consequences of (in)compatibility. *The Two Gentlemen of Verona* shows a character wilfully entangled in the abstractions and signifiers of courtly love, who suddenly impatiently threatens rape. *The Merchant of Venice* extends its tension beyond the defeat of Shylock, to the examination of men's post-marital loyalties offered by the intrigue of the rings. *Twelfth Night*, like *Love's Labour's Lost*, ends with a song that reminds the audience of the rigours of deepest wintertime drawing in, but adds further references to experiencing indignity and failure with increasing age, after a punishing humiliation that seems over-extended, and a consequent threat of vengeance. *All's Well that Ends Well* and *Measure for Measure* interrogate the neat closures of their own titles by presenting events that extend tortuously beyond the will of many and even the complete control of their instigators (as in *Measure for Measure* when Barnardine refuses his allotted part in the Duke's plan, insisting he will go on living, as will Parolles and Lucio); these dark (tragi?) comedies end on a note of possibility, rather than certainty: the tensions, questions and problems of changes, which are consciously wrought under temporal condensations and spatial confinements, become the central focus of *The Tempest*.

Booth (1983) identifies how the tragedies *King Lear* and *Macbeth* work to release their audiences from dependence on usual limits, and involve confrontations with conventionally antipathetic experiences: the plays' discernible patterns (forms, limits, fabrics) are themselves made of disjunctive elements. This is also true of *The Tempest*: Prospero finally consigns his magic book to be swept away by the tides he has formerly commanded. He emphasizes the ephemerality of his tightly focused endeavours (and perhaps of his accomplishments): having claimed the power to readdress historical injustices, freeze action, and even open graves and reanimate the dead, he now claims that his 'every third thought' (Shakespeare 2007: 50) shall be focused on his own grave, and that 'the baseless fabric' of the vision he has conjured shall 'dissolve' to 'Leave not a rack behind' (41).

Pericles (1608), attributed to Shakespeare and George Wilkins, initially echoes the morality play's choric form of introduction, as present in *Mankind* and *Everyman*, but assumes an importantly different tone. *Mankind* begins with the character of Mercy insisting (rather mercilessly) that God is the 'Founder and Beginner of our first creation', deserving 'to be magnified' by 'us sinful wretches', not least for his lack of 'indignation' when his 'own Son' was 'torn and crucified' (Wickham 1976: 7). The self-consciously anachronistic and resurrected figure of Gower introduces the story of Pericles by setting up this latest imaginative framing and theatrical performance of his 'story/song' as a continuance of its festive folk performance tradition ('It hath been sung at festivals, / On ember eves and holidays'), its effects almost magically medicinal ('lords and ladies in their lives / Have read it for restoratives') and its focus distinctly worldly rather than divine ('Its purchase is to make men glorious', words probably by Wilkins, but collected in Shakespeare 2007: 2327). Two of the most notable aspects of *Pericles* are its identification of itself in relation to earlier performance traditions, and its distinctly Shakespearean capacity for surprising developments, with specific reference to time. The stories of Pericles, Thaisa and Marina involve apparent resurrection, leading to a cumulative sense that time's cycles and delineations can prove restorative if the human perspective can discern and trust to that possibility. Aptly, its events and revivals are accompanied by the rhythmic sounds of tidal water and music, moving through apparent discord to resolution, insisting that the present moment only yields its full significance within a definite sense and sequence of past and future moments. Shakespeare's late romances *Pericles, Cymbeline* and *The Tempest* seem directed towards sensing and presenting a musical shaping of time, where the temporal and spatial intensifications of theatre are focused on depicting and ordering aspects and dimensions of both measurable external time and subjective lived temporality. Shakespeare's *extent* of this seems to strive to reflect and challenge, theatrically, music's claim to be the art form that works 'most directly with time, both as its subject and material' (Hoffman 2009:

183), in the bid to present meaningfully ordered tensions. Favorini identifies the terms of what may be Shakespeare's sense of a dialectic exploration: as 'memory-suffused works', *Hamlet* and *Pericles* are a pair, 'one driven by the injunction to remember and the other by the injunction to forget, so long as we recognize and accept the paradox that the members of this binary infuse and are indispensable to each other' (Favorini 2008: 30).

However, *The Winter's Tale*, the Shakespeare play that permits the most overt and direct expression of time (as a dramatic character, Time), is also the romance that is most overshadowed by dissonance of time and space. Wagner shrewdly observes how the opening scene presages a series of disjunctions in both spheres: it manifests a stark, irreconcilable variance when Leontes erupts into his jealous commentary on the relations between Hermione and Polixenes:

> Whatever Hermione and Polixenes are doing during these 40 lines, they are doing it in a separate space and a separate time from Leontes [...] All this adds up to stage action which effectively forms a radical disjuncture, starkly separating the time before this moment from that which will inevitably follow it, and just as starkly separating the characters onstage, to the point where they may be said to be occupying two different and utterly distinct moments in time [...] The time is decidedly out of joint after this moment, and it is not set right until the end of the play [when] again one time stops (the out-of-joint time) and another begins, where the characters are both spatially and temporally united.
> (Wagner 2012: 102)

Accordingly, the personification of Time remains consciously conditional, rather than ultimately (if surprisingly) restorative as in *Pericles*. *The Winter's Tale* seems to present 'time as agent and object – containable within the human mind and governable by human faculties while also ever outside the reach of both' (Wagner 2012: 106), emergent from the play rather than framing it like Gower in *Pericles*, and moreover suggesting discontinuity and paradox. This reflects back on the importance of the terms of what Leontes *chooses to see* occurring in the space(s) between his wife and his friend: the play as a whole suggests, it is crucially a matter of individual perspective, location within a position and time, whether you behold and discern 'things dying' or 'things newborn' (Shakespeare 2007: 734). *Henry V* also offers an artful confusion of (inclusive) form and (extensive) content, with particular regard to time, in ways that I discuss towards the end of this chapter.

Antony and Cleopatra presents images of, and attitudes to, time, very different to those in *Pericles*, although *Antony and Cleopatra* is a play similarly dominated by a sense of tidal rhythms. This extends beyond the verbal aquatic references, to *Antony and Cleopatra*'s unusual structuring in a series of brief and inconclusive scenes, presenting what Emrys Jones describes as the 'teasingly discontinuous movement' of 'a world awash with the tide of merely human opinion', 'profoundly diverse' and lacking 'discernible unity' as it extends and changes through space and time (Jones 1977: 12). The eroticism and generosity practised by the protagonists reminds me of Anne Dufourmantelle's characterization of the promise of sex as a 'magnificent, essential power to forget' (Dufourmantelle 2007: 99): to shed preoccupations, external worldly claims, past grievances and chronological time, like snakeskins. If *Antony and Cleopatra* is 'structured upon a series of oppositions' (Bate in Shakespeare 2007: 2158), as are all of Shakespeare plays, one of its principal oppositions is that between different and contending senses and claims of time.

Antony and Cleopatra attempt to forsake and defy *chronos*, associated with Roman time, in favour of *kairos*, associated with Egyptian time: *kairos* as 'the here and now deployed absolutely' (Dufourmantelle 2007: 41), as in Antony's proclamation and accompanying action, 'The nobleness of life / Is to do thus'(kissing and/or embracing Cleopatra); and his insistence: 'Let's not confound the time with conference harsh: / There's not a minute of our time should stretch / Without some pleasure now' (Shakespeare 2007: 2163). This slowing of time to a succession of intensely present (but more largely discontinuous) moments of *kairos* characterizes and constitutes Antony and Cleopatra's repeated and ostentatious refutations of the more linear and directional terms of Roman *chronos*: prudent investment and predictable consequence, represented and characterized by Octavius Caesar's purposeful valorization of control; Antony and Cleopatra, contrastingly, determine to 'mock the midnight bell' (2212) and 'burn this night with torches' (2214). Cleopatra's proclamation 'My oblivion is a very Antony / And I am all forgotten' (2170) offers a memorable dramatic expression for Dufourmantelle's description of eroticism as 'a practice of oblivion' that seeks 'a constantly reiterated first time' (Dufourmantelle 2007: 100) of plenitude, merging and forgetting.[13] Similarly, Enobarbus notes how Cleopatra 'makes hungry where most she satisfies'[14] (Shakespeare 2007: 2182).

The subject of acting and theatre is the place, and pace, of the body: in time, and in space; and *Antony and Cleopatra* is a sustained consideration of how its principal characters *act*, and perform intending to have definite effects on others, but with varying degrees, tempos and extents of successful completion. The play also demonstrates the force of Carson's observation: the 'experience of *eros* is a study in the ambiguities of time', and issues of control (not least control of self: its loss, its exercise) (Carson 1998: 117, 121–122). Many episodes in the play reflect processes of waiting, one protagonist for the other: dis/junctures of elaboration both painful and pleasurable, recalling Carson's proposals that, from one viewpoint, desire seems to the lover to 'demolish' prevalent temporal perspectives and consequences, 'to gather all other moments into itself in unimportance'; yet 'simultaneously, the lover perceives more sharply than anyone else the difference between the "now" of his desire and all the other moments called "then" that line up before and after it' (117), which here threaten the protagonists' own valued senses of presenting an impressive and controlling self. Together and separated, Antony and Cleopatra re-present aesthetic perspectives that try to control (slow, arrest) time, only to find that the vertiginous anxieties associated with the physical present cannot be kept at bay, and threaten to control them, ultimately. For example, Antony contemplates dissolution: the way the dissipating 'rack' of clouds 'dislimns and makes it indistinct / As water is in water', so he 'cannot hold this visible shape' of Antony (Shakespeare 2007: 2222). However, he is granted no such graceful disintegration: his death is delayed, first by the reluctance of Eros to strike a deathblow as commanded, second by his own hand's inability to hit the fatal bull's eye, consigning him to undignified terms of continued, painfully extended existence. A bleakly ironic comic incredulity may erupt through the strained vocal pitch of Antony's questions to Diomedes when the latter brings news that Cleopatra, whose reported death prompted Antony's suicide attempt, is still alive. Antony asks when and whence Cleopatra sent Diomedes to him, and discovers (possibly with more exasperation than relief) that her existence is extended beyond its reported bounds.

Cleopatra's determination on 'resolution and the briefest end' (2228) after Antony's death is intended to render 'paltry' Caesar's accomplishments, by her own tragicomic performance (successfully focused in time and space, avoiding the extensive pitfalls experienced by Antony) of 'that thing that ends all other deeds, / Which shackles accidents and bolts up change' (2230), which achieves and demonstrates self-definition on her own terms. However, the encounters with Proculeius, Dolabella, Caesar and the Clown extend, refine and sometimes question this process, maintaining elements of uncertainty regarding Cleopatra's strategy and timing. We learn that she has kept back a portion of her treasure, which sits strangely with her professed intention to make 'the briefest end'; it may be that she is 'playing for time, lulling [Caesar] into a false sense of security until she can seize her opportunity' (Wilcher 2010: 40–41), in a renewed sense and moment of *kairos*. Her increasingly dreamlike responses to Dolabella may even suggest Cleopatra's intimation of, or conscious performative appeal to, another sense of time, as she idealizes Antony. As Bridget Escolme points out, one production choice might involve Cleopatra addressing her speeches, not to the characters in the immediate space/time of the stage, but definitely and insistently to the audience:

We have, throughout the play, been her assumed admirers, occasionally thrown a defiant glance when our faithlessness has been in doubt. Here, Cleopatra can be seen to acknowledge us as part of a world outside her fiction – mysterious figures that just might understand Antony as she does.

(Escolme 2006: 87–88)

Cleopatra observes how Caesar 'words' her with assurances to distract her from what might make her 'noble' to herself, whilst Iras urges haste towards completion and finitude: 'Finish, good lady, the bright day is done / And we are for the dark' (2234), which presages another attempted acceleration of tempo, endorsed by Dolabella's brief re-entry to confirm that Caesar intends that Cleopatra and her children should begin their journey to humiliation and public parody within three days. Even now the interlude of the Clown contains a series of 'false exits', moments when all signs suggest his conversation with Cleopatra has (over) reached a proper end, only for it to resume, in a resonantly *impertinent* application of comic rhythms to the serious matter of means of death by the oddly inscrutable yet knowing character of the Clown, outstaying his welcome. However, Cleopatra resumes control over the tempo of events and directs all performances, including her own, with determined and defining confidence, which will monumentalize both Antony and herself and open a portal to eternal afterlife, for which she is impatient, not least to prevent Iras from claiming the first kiss. This is a *definite* contrast to Propero's attempted conclusion of his process, which emphasizes its own ephemerality and limits. Cleopatra finally emphasizes the release of tension, applying the asp as if homeopathically untying 'this knot intrinsicate / Of life' (2237), permitting escape from (and refutation of) Caesar's chronic control, as confirmed by his final affirmation of historical renown, their abiding heroic and romantic self-definition, both in and beyond the world ('No grave upon the earth shall clip in it / A pair so famous' [2238]). To adapt the terms of our previous deduction about *Love's Labour's Lost*, we might observe that *Antony and Cleopatra* infuses tragic form with a pointedly excessive and non-tragic sense of the paradoxical relativism of perspectives in and on time.

Dislocations in dreamtime

I now propose to consider a series of plays in which theatre time is indeed, in Wagner's words, 'the material, experiential buoy' for the concepts or views of Time that emerge, overtly and self-consciously, in the staging of the play (Wagner 2012: 3); and to consider further, how these plays use theatrical compressions to present and inflect their chosen theme.

Few plays of the early twentieth century direct attention to their self-conscious dramatizations of time as overtly and centrally as those of Thornton Wilder (in America) and J. B. Priestley (in Britain). Indeed, as my citations of his provocations already testify, Priestley was compulsively fascinated and speculative (not only theatrically) about time, and the fullest ranges of its manifestations and images. Priestley's development of his sequence of 'time plays' was partly inspired by the ideas of P. D. Ouspensky (who developed his own distinctive ideas of self-development whilst in the midst of life from those of George Gurdjieff) and J. W. Dunne (whose 1927 publication *An Experiment with Time* argued for the viability of unusual perspectives on, and through, time). In a 2014 BBC4 radio documentary reconsidering Dunne's ideas in the context of Priestley's drama, Francis Spufford observed how Dunne's background, as an aircraft designer and pilot, may have informed his development of time in the image of a map: the aerial view of a landscape, as seen from the speed and vantage point of a plane (by a cloudless night), is crucially different from that of infantrymen creeping blindly forward (by a fogbound day).[15] Dunne suggested that a more holistic sense of what future time would unfold was briefly but significantly available through the imagery of dreams, which were based on a mixture of an individual subject's past and forthcoming experiences; hence, dreams briefly and partly offered a nocturnal dissolution of daytime barriers to perceptions of the future that might prove informative, suggesting the possibility of an eternal (godlike) perspective on human consciousness in action. As Spufford observed, Dunne's theory avoids the symbolic or metaphorical complexities (and id-based sexual impulses and contradictions) of Freud's interpretations of dreams, proposing a clearly literal, linear and programmatic basis for potentially informed perception and procedure. Nevertheless, his ideas gained some currency in the culture of the 1930s, provoking the imaginations not only of Priestley but also of T. S. Eliot – who proposed in his 1935 poem 'Burnt Norton' that all time might be 'eternally present' (including the enfolding of the future in the past and present) yet predetermined ('unredeemable', Eliot 1975: 189) – and of other writers.[16] This initiative seems particularly provoked by the post-war impulse, to discover a knowable possibility of stability and renewable sense of human agency, in a world traumatically characterized by catastrophic transience.

J. M. Barrie's play *Dear Brutus* (staged 1918, first printed 1922) should be acknowledged as an attempt, preceding the ideas of Dunne and the plays of Wilder and Priestley, to suggest and dramatize the possibilities of an informatively non-linear view of time – albeit with strangely self-limiting effect. In *Dear Brutus* a Puckish and eerily ageless yet childlike character, Lob, presides over the Midsummer Eve night-time estrangements of a number of guests at his house, and in the neighbouring wood, where they encounter strange transformations of their selves and others. Lob suggests at one point that the uncannily engrossing forest offers 'what nearly everybody here is longing for', 'a second chance' (Barrie 1931: 52). However, the subsequent experiences are more complex than this promised miracle, which might recall *A Winter's Tale*. The characters find themselves in what more recent science fiction, fantasy and comic book scenarios have established as the premise of an alternative timeline, in which a series of 'what-if?' divergent possibilities displace the prevalent consequences. Most notably, the central couple, who are childless, and tellingly named the Dearths, meet as strangers. Mr Dearth is here 'father and mother both' to a daughter, Margaret, whereas Alice (in the principal timeline his wife, and the play's most spirited and formidable female character) has married another suitor, and later becomes a vagrant. Margaret's relationship with her father is dramatized in strangely demanding and profoundly unsettling terms of possessive intimacy (as when Dearth and Margaret fantasize about killing her future suitors by strangulation, to preserve their own closeness). When her 'father' steps away from the forest towards resumption of his daytime life, Margaret calls to him '*out of the impalpable that is carrying her away*': 'Daddy, come back; I don't want to be a might-have-been' (Barrie 1931: 98). The effect is not so much one of plaintive pathos, as something chillingly, *viciously* sentimental: as if the traditionally infanticidal mythic figure of the Erl King were *displaced* to a childlike and feminized form, as a diabolical cuckoo seeking to supplant and override any rivals for parental affection.

The other characters in *Dear Brutus* conclude, with a resignation that seems reminiscent of a regression to inertia, that their specifically limited Dionysian experiences of the wood have taught them that their lives are ruled, not by accident, but by fate, and that (rather contemplate the substantial promise and demands of a 'second chance') they will not lastingly consider or embrace alternatives. Rather, they conclude 'something makes us go on doing the same sort of fool things, however many chances we get' (111), in line with a generally fatalistic reading of the Shakespeare lines, 'The fault, dear Brutus, is not in our stars, / But in ourselves'. Though the wood offers a 'useful' warning (113), only the minority with the necessary 'grit' (112) have the powers to shape themselves, substantially anew (for example, an unfaithful servant reverts to criminal behaviour even when fleetingly granted more social opportunities: he goes on to financial embezzlement of the Working Women's Bank). Barrie's characters speculate self-consciously on their presence in a 'strange experiment' and whether or not it will have 'any permanent effect': even the most corrupt character deduces it will 'not often', but concedes that it might, 'once in a while'. Barrie's stage directions specify that there is '*hope in this for the brave ones*', and that – somehow – '*If we could wait long enough we might see the Dearths breasting their way into the light*' (140). However, it seems that '*we*', or Barrie, cannot '*wait long enough*': we do *not* see (or hear) this onstage, and only the reader of Barrie's play text can strive to imagine what forms this action, and '*light*', might take. It *might* possibly take forms that suggest or demonstrate a full and unembittered acceptance of their childlessness; however, the theatre audience, unapprised of this stage direction, might as well be left with the sense that the Dearths, and their relationship, remain between two worlds: one dead, one powerless to be born. Barrie's *Dear Brutus* is simultaneously overdetermined and crucially (regarding the Dearths) vague; however, it notably attempts a forward projection, from a complacent present to – for some – a complicating and bitter future, and briefly raises questions of agency, even as the dominant self-congratulatory and sentimental self-restrictions of the present resume. The notion is broached in *Dear Brutus*, that despite the prevalent presumptions that human beings have no meaningful choice, an unconventionally expanded sense of time may provide a moral challenge: the possibility that one can resist the determinism supposedly inscribed in one's character, and behave more courageously, and so less restrictively and damagingly, to self and others.

Wilder: Stygian perspectives on the passing world

Patricia Schroeder's study, *The Presence of the Past in Modern American Drama* (1989), offers a valuable and resonant contextualization of the plays of Eugene O'Neill, Thornton Wilder, Arthur Miller and Tennessee Williams, with particular focus on their variant theatrical treatments of time. Schroeder observes how the typical nineteenth-century American character is often depicted as self-consciously without a past or tradition 'forced to survive through wits and willpower in a hostile, untamed world'; lacking 'a sense of either a meaningful personal history or a place in the nation's annals', these characters create 'mythic identities for themselves to compensate for their often debilitating alienation from the past' (Schroeder 1989: 23; processes of defiant dramatic self-fashioning that can be observed subsequently and still in the popular forms and appeals of two distinctly American genres: the western and the superhero adventure[17]). In America, as elsewhere, into the twentieth century, repercussions of the industrial age, and subsequent theories of psychology (Freud and Jung) and political sociology (Marx), generated contending narrative and analyses of causality and consequence. New uncertainties emerged through the gaps in, or clashes between, ideologies, and new experiences of isolation and alienation (such as those expressed in Eliot's *The Waste Land*) qualified or replaced the promises of self-reliance.

Schroeder notes how the American dramatists under her scrutiny are informed, to varyingly evident degrees, by two traditions: Ibsen's realistic forensic investigations into what haunting causal secrets the past may hold; and the expressionist drama (as practised by Strindberg, Kaiser, Toller) that attended to a more subjective (often character-based) conception of the past and present, with dreamlike symbolism, condensations and displacements, and episodic and emotionally associative (rather than linear) structures providing a 'method for revealing interior reality' and postulating 'alternative visions of the past' (Schroeder 1989: 26). However, all four American dramatists present searches through the past, as action by which to understand the present (28). Arthur Miller may be the principal American dramatist in a consciously Ibsenite tradition of dramatizing processes of disclosure and responsibility (though the title and associative structure of Miller's 1987 autobiography, *Timebends*, testify to his abiding sense of the capacity of time to *surprise* and defy predictable logic, as does Miller's sense of the perpetual *immanence* of times past[18]). Schroeder describes O'Neill as exploring his characters' 'understandings of the past' (rather than 'an objective sequence of preceding events'), though in his later plays the characters 'become so obsessed with understanding the past that they are incapable of purposeful present action' (27). Williams presents a 'double view of time', in that his plays depict time passing in a fictional present but also remaining 'frozen' in the narrative memories of the characters, who 'attempt to control the present by controlling the accepted version of the past', with apparent causal dramatic structures 'disrupted by the anti-mimetically depicted memories of his characters' (28), as in Williams's *The Two-Character Play* (1967, revised 1975).

Thornton Wilder, who may be presumed to be the least radical of these dramatists, is nevertheless the most consistently, consciously and overtly experimental in addressing the problem of developing theatrical forms that might permit differing theatrical embodiments of contending (and conflicting) visions of character and audience time. Wilder dramatizes this by what Schroeder terms the 'overlapping of temporal contexts', personal present and historically recorded past (27), in ways that evoke earlier British theatrical forms, and shapes, of time. The celebrated and widely performed play *Our Town* (1938), with which Wilder is predominantly associated, may superficially appear archaic and self-congratulatory in its characters' professions of folksy optimism and 'cracker-barrel wisdom'.[19] This impression should not obscure the drastic and discomfiting condensations of time, which are Wilder's principal formal and contextual experiments, in producing effects of unusual acceleration and distance. Wilder criticized the literalism of conventional realistic theatre's tendency to fix and narrow the action to 'one moment in time and place' (Wilder 2007: 684); indeed he objected to how a dominant concentration on *place* in theatre tended to 'limit and drag down and harness time' to a single specific location that 'thrust the action back into the past time' of fictional distance and exclusive particularity, as opposed to the 'now', the textures and reverberations of moment-by-moment experience (685). Wilder claimed that dramatic action as a theatrical representation 'is inseparable from forward movement, from action' (700), and observed how, whilst this will inevitably involve some identifications of 'repetitive patterns', it also constitutes a definite and distinctive sense of theatrical 'power', which was 'precisely what nineteenth-century audiences did not – dare not – confront', in preferring to load the stage with 'specific objects', with devitalizing effects (685). Contrastingly, Wilder was concerned to 'raise' the action 'from the specific to the general' (701) of collective experiences and concerns, through a directive and heightened attention to the present moment as part of a process:

> The novel is a past reported in the present. On the stage it is always now [...]
>
> *A play is what takes place.*
>
> *A novel is what one person tells us took place.*
>
> (702)

Writing just after the emergence of J. W. Dunne's theories, Wilder seems similarly concerned to discern an identifiable and consolingly definite temporal order in post-war social existence, but (as in Priestley's work) the foreshadowings of a second world war provide both a critical perspective on characters' refusals to learn from traumatic social mistakes, and a poignant sense of their destiny to drift towards further crushing disappointments of their hopes. In a telling stage direction, Wilder identifies a character as being both *'serene and didactic'* in *'surveying the passing world'* (Wilder 2007: 138): a precisely significant critical indication of how social beings can be both limited and limiting (and how dramatic characters can be simultaneously comic and oppressive, as in the plays of Ayckbourn), as well as sometimes courageously persistent, in continuing their 'business' without understanding 'why' (142).

Wilder's 1931 one-act play *The Long Christmas Dinner* (which also formed the basis of the libretto for an opera by Paul Hindemith, performed at the Juilliard School of Music in New York in 1963) is a notable experiment in theatrical time. *The Long Christmas Dinner* compresses 90 years of family life and character time into approximately 30 minutes of stage time focused on seasonal festivities: Wilder's script stipulates that the actors should indicate the increase in their characters' ages principally through their acting, with some few indicative props, as they eat imaginary food with imaginary cutlery to maintain the tempo of action and focus on character development (a device that foreshadows the one used in Wesker's *The Kitchen*). The accelerated tempo is relentless: the action begins when Roderick and Lucia Bayard hold their first Christmas dinner in their new house (Wilder 2007: 61), then moves to five years hence (63), to the birth of their first child Charles (64) and then to the arrival of his sister Genevieve when Charles is aged 12 (65), all within a space of four pages of the script. Furthermore, major transitions are rendered spatially and symbolically: the characters emerge from a portal on one side of the stage, associated with birth, and approach and exit through another, representing death. When the adult Genevieve suffers the death of one of her own young children, Lucia seeks to reassure her, 'only the passing of time can help in these things', before Lucia herself exits through the death portal '*serenely*', bidding 'Don't grieve' (70), and indeed, these losses are promptly offset by the arrival of twins. The characters also alter significantly with an ageing that is portrayed with extremely heightened rapidity, as when Genevieve laments her own sensed loss of purpose and the '*corners of her mouth become fixed*' as she '*becomes a forthright and slightly disillusioned spinster*', while her brother Charles '*becomes the plain business man and a little pompous*' (72). Distinctions in the characters' senses of time serve to characterize their age and social perspective further: Mother Bayard alone remembers (and so reminds the audience of) the former presence of native Americans in their social vicinity; Charles's association of speed with progress, 'Time certainly goes very fast in a great country like this', is countered as subjective and partial; the women are more aware that, in Europe, 'time must be passing very slowly' because of a war that does not yet impinge directly on the Bayards' circumstances (73) or Charles's concerns (he maintains it may even be a healthy purgative for societies). The discrepancy in perception, of sensed and wished tempo, is also dramatized across generations: Charles's son, named Roderick after his grandfather, behaves rebelliously, and claims 'Time passes so slowly here that it stands still', a reason for his deduction 'you gotta get drunk in this town to forget how dull it is' (75). But the absence of the younger generation, however impatient and volatile, soon changes the perceived atmosphere: Charles remarks, 'How slowly time passes without any young people in the house' (77). Thus, Wilder highlights the *relativity* of perceptions of time and social upheaval, depending on age and social position, and how different company and contexts can seem to alter the tempo of events, to extend or accelerate duration through activity. Additionally, Wilder, like Barrie in *Dear Brutus*, shows his characters to be haunted by the sense of alternative possibilities and consequences: Genevieve remarks that it is not only soot from the family's factories that permeate and seep through the walls of their once-pristine house, but also 'the thought of what has been and what might have been' (77). The death of young Roderick's brother provides an ironic riposte to Charles's formerly casual attitude to war; Charles professes an intention to write his remaining son a letter of apology and reconciliation, but he exits through the dark portal before he can do so. Charles's wife Leonora leaves the house to go to 'stay with the young people' for Christmas, leaving her cousin Ermengarde there alone: Ermengarde '*grows from very old to immensely old*' in her solitude (79).

Wilder's use of repeated verbal motifs points up the accruing parallels between characters and their elders and forebears, in ways that may be irritating but also capture some of the repetitiousness which may characterize formalized family events as well as individual processes of ageing. The extreme brevity of the play's dramatic tempo works against the exchanges becoming too grating, though it may also generate difficulties for any one character to become deeply engaging, such is their rapid turnover. Eric Specian pertinently identifies a key question: is the play 'about progress and optimism, or is it about decay and entropy'?[20] Here and elsewhere in Wilder's theatre of *time taking place*, there is an artful potential for ambiguity in his images and directions (like the famous image of a drawing that might be alternately perceived as a duck, or as a rabbit, even by the same viewer).

Wilder seems concerned here, as elsewhere, to present a non-realistic illustration of universality: the surprising and ironic recurrence of concerns and characteristics throughout generations, in terms that are nevertheless focused on (and principally confined to) the cultural specifics of an American moneyed or middle-class setting. In this respect, his theatrical writing is perhaps not so far as he might have wished from the nineteenth-century theatre that he criticized. However, *The Long Christmas Dinner* shows how edifice and inhabitants are not immured from specifically social change and context, and the play generates irony from the character's reversions to type, as well as presenting compassionately the disappointments of their hopes. Charles's senses of progress and optimism are grounded in political priorities that are forcibly qualified by the events and frameworks that Wilder selects, providing a critical perspective on his assessments, but we also see how even Charles can finally try to admit personal fault and attempt change. The brevity of *The Long Christmas Dinner* has a theatrical deftness and sense of telling nuance which ensures that even its depictions of generally cyclical behaviour are never entirely predictable in their outcomes, nor inconsequential. Having established a distancing 'reverse-telescope' effect upon his characters through his use of time, which intrinsically limits their opportunities for reflection, Wilder brings them suddenly and surprisingly closer to the audience precisely in his delineations of their disappointments, and in the conscious identifications of changing senses of *character time*, highlighting the limits and partiality of individual perspective, which may provide a point of contact with the audience's own senses and experiences of time's surprising elasticity.

The Long Christmas Dinner depicts the erosion of its characters' hopes and certainties, and even individualities, in terms that do not, and perhaps should not, entirely negate the uniqueness and significance of their moments of joy. But Wilder shows the audience clearly the degree to which the characters' experiences, and the senses that they try to make out of them (predicated on continuity), are informed – and perhaps determined – by their upbringing, their position in a family, their social class and (lack of) mobility, and their inhabitation of a specific place and time in global history: with the wider implication, that these are factors that may feature similarly, if in somewhat different terms, in the lives of the audience members.[21] The play may thus skilfully – and remarkably rapidly – erode the ironic distance from the characters that the audience may presume and entertain. Characters and audiences share the activity of discerning the consequences of the passing of time, and so 'grow old together', but at markedly and extremely different tempos, with the audience permitted opportunities for reflection (principally, after the duration of the performance, which may increase the play's capacity to *haunt* the audience's imaginations) on the possible consequences of actions (the characters', and, at one remove, their own). These chances, (different) spaces and times for reflection are conspicuously denied the characters (theatrical effects that will be developed, in a specifically English temporal and geographical context, by Priestley in *Time and the Conways*).

In contrast to the acceleration of time's passage in *The Long Christmas Dinner*, Wilder's short play *Pullman Car Hiawatha* (1932) dilates and expands one specific moment in time: the moment of death of one character. The character of the Stage Manager addresses the audience to engage and direct their imaginative co-operation (similarly to how the Chorus in Shakespeare's *Henry V* operates) as he delineates a railway carriage in chalk lines. He regularly and abruptly shifts the focus of audience attention to the varying perspectives of other passengers in the train, and the circumstances around it, and then he introduces an array of personified co-ordinates – geographical, temporal and 'theological' – in their conjunction for 'December twenty-first, 1930'. He explains '*helpfully*': 'The minutes are gossips; the hours are philosophers; the years are theologians' (Wilder 2007: 102) – cueing a tableau of female figures, each representing an hour by repeating the observations of a given philosopher. Subsequently, the Stage Manager orchestrates a (primarily sonic) representation of the configuration of planets, again personified, and finally the incursion of 'archangels' (104) to remove the soul of the dead woman, Harriet.

Within the frameworks established by the Stage Manager, *Pullman Car Hiawatha* foregrounds the perspectives of two characters. An 'Insane Woman' is the only character, apart from the Stage Manager, who gazes out towards the audience; she seems to be the one who is most changed by the presence of death, overcoming her fear of impending incarceration with a (somewhat Beckettian) resignation to 'waiting', less haunted by an old and terrible 'story', but still significantly disengaged from the limiting perspectives associated with sanity ('At last I understand myself perfectly, but no one else understands a thing I say'; 'everyone is so childish, so absurd [...] like children; they have never suffered', 104–105). The dying woman, Harriet, is permitted a briefly intense and expansive 'out-of-body' expression of subjective time, in which to say goodbye. The intrinsic limitations of this perspective expressed by Harriet as she reluctantly relinquishes her role in the world is not satirized or ironized; rather, the purportedly forensic, yet anti-mimetic, proliferation of time perspectives in the play prevents any one point of view from seeming ultimately authoritative. Harriet's individually specific, expressionistically expressed perspective on personal temporal and emotional accumulation (perhaps impossible, except at this Stygian boundary, of transition out of life) provides one of the two most haunting senses of character time; the Insane Woman provides the other, as she emphasizes the denial and limitation inherent in the selectivity of what counts for sanity.

The devices of briskly functional anti-illusionistic scenography, and a briefly expansive epiphany in death, are further developed by Wilder in *Our Town* (1938). Again, a 'Stage Manager' chorus character presents a focus (with a sense that 'time is limited' [159]) on what seems an unremarkable town, and time, and their mutually supportive elision: the general designations of 'our town' and 'our time' initially appear to proceed, principally unquestioned. Nevertheless, the inhabitants demonstrate conscious awareness of perspective: one observes that 'once in your life before you die you ought to see a country where they don't talk in English and don't even want to' (138); others provide statistical data on the town, its co-ordinates, politics and culture, details that can be incorporated into a time capsule, placed in the cornerstone of a bank, to be opened in the future. The Stage Manager even plans to include 'a copy of this play' to inform people thousands of years hence, mindful that 'even in Greece and Rome, all we know about the *real* life of people is what we can piece together out of the joking poems and the comedies they wrote for the theatre back then' (166). As dusk falls and the day begins 'running down like a tired clock' (166), the presence of the moon further emphasizes the relativity of perspective: characters describe it differently (and some alternately) as 'wonderful', 'terrible' and threatening, and some are mindful that it is simultaneously shining on other continents over half the world (171–172). A central section of the play, on marriage, depicts a relationship in flashback and acceleration, emphasizing the desperation and imperfection of the wedding, which is dogged by the bridegroom's briefly admitted fear of ageing. The final third of the play, which focuses on death, is set in 1913, identifying depicting gradual changes (such as increased fearfulness) as war approaches, its future reach unknowable to the characters. Act III also manifests on stage the commenting presences of characters formerly alive, now dead. The Stage Manager acknowledges the impulse to believe that '*something*' in each human being is eternal; however, he is also careful to suggest how the dead experience and represent a detachment from prevalent human temporal values: they 'don't stay interested in us living people for very long' but gradually 'lose hold of the earth', including associated ambitions, pleasures, sufferings and loves, as they are 'weaned away' to a point of indifference:

> Some of the things they're going to say maybe'll hurt your feelings – but that's the way it is: mother' n daughter … husband' n wife … enemy' n enemy … money' n miser… all those terribly important things kind of grow pale around here. And what's left when memory's gone, and your identity, Mrs Smith? (*He looks at the audience a minute, then turns to the stage*).
>
> (197)

This Stygian perspective is a (paradoxically) vital ingredient in *Our Town*, which *may* be presented in a predominantly resolutely optimistic production, just as *Henry V* can be presented principally in heroic and patriotic terms. However, *Henry V* may also be performed in a style that is cool and ironic about the limitations of power, in human time: limits both natural and forcibly, politically imposed. *Our Town* might also be presented in ways that amplify its expressionist shadings rather than its reassurances,[22] and the liminal awareness expressed by Emily, a departing spirit, of 'how in the dark live people are': 'sort of shut up in little boxes, aren't they?' (201). Like Harriet in *Pullman Car Hiawatha*, Emily is granted the valedictory opportunity to relive and amplify one given juncture of her life, selecting her twelfth birthday in 1899, when she and her family are happy and together, 'just for a moment' (206). If Emily's choice of episode seems a sentimental, childish or *kitsch* juncture with which to end her story, Wilder's play raises the question as to what might provide an alternative choice, for each audience member, to offset the otherwise abiding sense of human 'ignorance and blindness' (208) in failing to realize 'every minute' of life 'while they live it' (207). *Our*

Town depicts and foregrounds how the daily 'directional cycle simultaneously constitutes a *time-frame* within which we organize, plan and regulate our daily existence: night and day, the seasons, birth and death' but also how '*tempo* and *intensity* make up further "components" of the meaning-complex of Western time' and 'surround us at every level: we know that a birthday tomorrow can feel like an eternity to a little child whilst a birthday a year ago can seem like only yesterday to an old person' (Adam 1995: 23, original emphasis).[23]

Wilder's play and its explicitly reflexive approach to time may thus raise questions about dualistic models of what separates 'our town' (and 'our time') from those of others. The Stage Manager's final speech accordingly emphasizes the strain of becoming: which is in itself exhausting, though in terms ubiquitous but often unremarked, or undramatized.

Wilder's *The Skin of Our Teeth* (1942) constitutes a further overlapping of temporal contexts, in which the historically recorded past is superimposed on a personal present, intending to present, in Wilder's words, 'two times at once' (687), in ways that he acknowledges to be consciously influenced by James Joyce. Wilder imposes a concentrated and accelerated version of human history, from the Stone Age to post-revolutionary fervour, onto the primarily domestic perspectives of a contemporary suburban American 'hunter-gatherer', Mr Antrobus, and his family members. Sabina, their maid, presents a parodic exposition, which skitters on the line of tenuous relief, 'we came through the depression by the skin of our teeth' (Wilder 2007: 216), providing a cue that is (supposedly) unanswered, disrupting (supposedly) intended clear theatrical consequences. The resulting absurdist comedy resembles the chronological reach of Bernard Shaw's *Back to Methuselah* colliding with the fourth-wall-breaking 1938 comic review *Hellzapoppin'* (which inspired a 1941 film): its absurdly disrupted domesticity looks forward to N. F. Simpson's *A Resounding Tinkle* (1957, 1959); and its transference of suburban commuter concerns to a Stone Age setting, where extinct animals are pets, may have provided an influence on the 1960s television Hanna-Barbera cartoon series, *The Flintstones*.[24]

The Skin of Our Teeth requires a production of considerable momentum in order to be consistently engaging, but various moments deliberately dramatize a forcible strain on the predominating performances of superficial cheerfulness, and an awareness of what it almost keeps at bay, in ways satirically resonant before, during or after war, or other social crises (Wilder recollects post-war productions in Germany and Warsaw, Wilder 2007: 687). Sabine assures the audience energetically that the world is *not* about to end, that no one will actually starve ('you can always eat grass or something') and that those who did in times past were only 'savages' ('Savages don't love their families – not like we do!' [Wilder 2007: 231]). The first act ends when it becomes apparent that insufficient protection is afforded to the characters by multiplication tables and scripture learnt by rote, or even the determined singing of 'Jingle Bells': the characters issue a request for the audience to hand up their chairs, in order to start a fire to 'save the human race' (239).

Act Two of *The Skin of Our Teeth* transposes Antrobus and family onto the story of Noah and the Flood, with Babylonian excess represented by a fair. The catastrophes of former ages have been replaced by a time of self-satisfaction (from which some recalled former friends and relatives have been fatally excluded by infections, disaster and 'differences of opinion', 241), and Mrs Antrobus notes some 'backsliding' from female rights established by the institution of marriage. In a section that permits less ironic distance, a Fortune Teller identifies a member of the audience inside whom 'the watchsprings will crumple up' next year, resulting in death 'by regret' (246); she further refers to the Antrobuses, blithely two-dimensional at best, as 'Your hope. Your despair. Your selves' (247) (a perspective that seems close to that of the God Ra, addressing the audience in Shaw's *Caesar and Cleopatra*). The third act set in an indeterminate idealistic post-war period (bravely, given the play's time of premiere in 1942) reprises (more arbitrarily) the personifications of the hours and planets from *Pullman Car Hiawatha*, with characters conscious of the pressure, 'now that the war's over we'll all have to settle down and be perfect' (269), notwithstanding extremely limited resources and extensive deaths: Sabina replies to an order to continue in her work, 'I'll go on just out of *habit*, but I won't believe in it' (275). This sense of disillusionment is most powerfully expressed through the dramatization of a generational schism between Antrobus and his son Henry, who both express a sense of 'hollowness' and resentment derived from the paradigms of masculinity they have felt required to adopt: for Henry, the militarized frustration that suggests to him that 'you have to kill somebody else so as not to end up killing yourself' (278); for Antrobus, the adoption and internalization of a work ethic: 'work, work, work – that's all I do. I've ceased to *live*' (279). This extends to Antrobus's sense that he has lost the desire to begin again, to renew and rebuild. He recovers his momentum, in the company of his family, as they consult books for remembered philosophical encouragement, and the Stage Manager assures the audience that the cycle is resuming, even as he notes the precarious terms of persistence (his observation, 'why the house hasn't fallen down around our ears long ago is a miracle to me' [284], seems an echo of Bernard Shaw's similarly allegorical *Heartbreak House*[25]). As in *Our Town*, the specifics of a given production will determine which keynotes within the play are amplified to most resonant effect. Wilder's invocations of cyclical redemptive time, associated with the temporal scheme of the morality play, are offset by notable expressions of dislocation, pain and confusion, evidence of a substantial dialectic within his theatre, focused by discrepant experiences of time: important qualifications of the terms of idealism that his plays might seem to privilege.

Priestley: Hinges in time

Significantly, Priestley acknowledges his awareness of both *Dear Brutus* and Wilder's *The Long Christmas Dinner* in his book *Man and Time* (Priestley 1964: 133–134), as precursors to his own theatrical 'experiments with time'. Priestley shares and develops Wilder's sense of specifically *social* nature of power and perspective in the details and matter of individual experience; however, Priestley also develops Barrie's sense of a mysterious existential crossroads that offers a glimpse of alternatives, and a challenge to moral growth (absent from Dunne's more linear and predetermined sense of temporal delineation), to inform and expand the conventional terms of pragmatism. If a strictly linear view of time implies determinism and predestination, then human free will, and therefore the assumption of responsibility for actions, are severely limited in their possibilities. Contrastingly, a sense of non-linear or circular time, which constitutes a heightened awareness of the past and the present as decisive portals into variant futures, 'allows for an avoidance of disasters' (Gale 2008: 91). Priestley aims to encourage an active attitude towards 'the caused, the actual and the potential', which permits what Adam describes as 'a conscious act of living unto the future', 'an achievement of pre-emptiveness, anticipation and creativity' (Adam 1995: 37, who adds the dichotomous perception of linearity or circularity 'depends fundamentally on the framework of observation and interpretation' [38]).

Time and the Conways foregrounds the dramatic principle of the framing of events, and operations of selectivity in presenting details, by counterpointing (in what might be likened to musical terms[26]) a selection of exchanges in an English family home one evening in 1919, in the immediate wake of war, then dissolving the usual temporal barriers to glimpse most of the characters in '*present day [1937]*' when another war looms (Priestley 1969: 34); and finally returning to them in 1919, providing an overtly formal resolution to the play that adds poignancy to their hopes, which (as in Wilder's *The Long Christmas Dinner*) we know to be subsequently compromised or disappointed (that with one war over, people will be 'sensible' again and that certain characters will remain 'quite safe'). If the characters initially seem juvenile, frivolous and complacent in their games of charades and sense of social buoyancy (which they think affords them 'plenty of time'), a modern-day sense of moral (and political) ironic superiority and impatience should be tempered by an appreciation of social context: these consciously representative characters express an elation at incredible survival amidst incomprehensible slaughter, as part of a traumatically fractured, but apparently fortunately vindicated, nation. Priestley's social realism also takes care to suggest that the characters' experiences have led them to new valorizations of time, and what might constitute its waste: for example, Kay has abandoned and burnt her first attempt at a novel, which the materialistic Joan dismisses as a 'waste of time' (Priestley 1969: 21) rather than a necessary experimentation and honing of skill, but which Kay's brother Alan contrasts to wider more conventional wastes of time, in an increasingly hastening, utilitarian culture. In Act Two and 1937, Kay will prove surprisingly dismissive of her own novelist's ambitions, as she attempts to reconcile others (and, we may sense, herself) to her regular professional output of hack celebrity journalism. The characters have arrived at (in the context of the surrounding acts, jarringly) revised senses of what Madge calls 'real life': pragmatic social expectations and appropriate personal investments, which Kay nevertheless realizes, are frequently underpinned by intimations of shame, however strenuously denied (Priestley 1969: 39), and/or a conventionally denied but surprisingly immanent despair, such as is manifested when their apparently ever-cheerful maid attempts suicide ('she'd had enough of *everything*, she said' [Priestley 1969: 41, original emphasis]). This obscure(d) sense of shame turns out to be a rhetorical weapon that the characters use against each other, and against which none prove invulnerable. The youngest and most optimistic daughter of the family, Carol, has (unaccountably) died, contributing to the others' bewilderment about their personal terms of survival. Madge wryly mocks earlier hopes, which she shared, for socialism, peace and universal brotherhood, in the light of later (and present) developments, and the family matriarch is witheringly scornful of her children's personal contractions, which she designates failures, in her own (conventionally materialistic) terms. Shaken by this, Kay testifies most directly to a disintegratory, destructive sense of time:

> Remember what we once were and what we thought we'd be. And now this. And it's all we have, Alan, it's *us*. Every step we've taken – every tick of the clock – making everything worse. If this is all life is, what's the use? Better to die, like Carol, before you find it out, before Time gets to work on you. I've felt it before, Alan, but never as I've done tonight. There's a great devil in the universe, and we call it Time.
>
> (Priestley 1969: 60, original emphasis)

However, her despair is tempered by Alan's response, a quotation of a Blake poem which maintains that 'Man is made for joy and woe', and that an acceptance of the inevitability of such entwinements is a precondition for courage, persistence and a sense of adventure, as opposed to the prevalent fearfulness. Alan suggests that time is a dream, not a destroyer: 'half our trouble now is because we think Time's ticking our lives away' and that is 'why we snatch and grab and hurt each other'; Kay adds 'As if we were all in panic on a sinking ship' (61).

In the third and final act's return to 1919, Madge resolutely expresses just such a sense of adventure, striving to characterize the aftermath of World War I as an opportunity for renewal, her determination expressed by her quotation of Blake's 'Jerusalem'; however, the '*generous mood*' is shattered by her dismissive mother. Kay's idealistic avowal to write only 'what I want to write, what I feel is true to me, deep down', and not 'just to please silly people or just to make money' (78) is also contextualized ironically by the audience, but probably with more compassion than the characters express (her mother asks 'You're sure you're not over-tired, Kay?' [78]); an effect developed to its fullest by Carol's poignant youthful enthusiasm for a life in theatre, bohemian friendships, uncompromising and multiple possibilities: 'I'm *going to live*' (80), when the audience, *strangely* together yet alone in the theatre, know(s) otherwise. The play ends with the reprise of a musical theme and provides a sense of intimation which the characters may sense, but cannot completely express: their faces fade in moonlight until '*the Conways have gone*' (82): inevitably and irrevocably, this suggests, unless in the audience's memories.

Priestley's dramatic and theatrical paradigm here seems to be the work of Chekhov, and its elements that have dominated English dramatic realism from the 1930s onwards: an elegiac demonstration of what Katharine Worth identifies as the ways that 'commonplace detail can be used to bring out the complexity and pathos of ordinary lives' and 'the almost unbearable sadness of time's effects upon them' (Worth 1972: 7–8). Specifically, Chekhov's *The Cherry Orchard* has identifiable resonances in several detail of *Time and the Conways*: a family estate that must be sold because of a complacent matriarch's lack of worldliness, a promising opportunity for contact between two fervent young people that fails and becomes a fateful road not taken, and a social outsider who is nevertheless ascendant (Chekhov's Lopakhin, Priestley's Ernest). However, Priestley's sense of time is different to Chekhov's. States describes the central activity in Chekhov's plays as 'accommodation to boredom', where 'Time is an old condition, like rheumatism or arthritis, that one tolerates' (States 1985: 72), revealing principally 'the ironic nonresponse of the world' (78) to human habit.

In Quinones's terms, *Time and the Conways* might at first seem to offer a sense of 'augmentative time' that he associated with bringing destruction and succession. However, Priestley's vision of time, and his theatrical form, does not resemble a one-way arrow towards entropy and shapeless disorder, nor Dunne's sense of an irrevocably predetermined map (the extreme logic of which would seem to threaten the sense of human agency, and perhaps morality, altogether). *Time and the Conways* contains a definite flavour of elegiac melancholy: an awareness of irrevocable loss, most strikingly represented theatrically – though crucially not directly expressed – by Carol's presence and words: the sense of devastation is precisely not in what Carol says or does, intrinsically (she is boundlessly optimistic), but in how this is contextualized and *framed* by the play. However, this sense of waste, premature severance and loss is offset by the subsidiary patternings in the play, and their resolution into a wry awareness of limitations and ironies that the audience perceives fully through the sequencing of the play's events, and which some characters, Kay and Alan, seem teasingly on the verge of being able to glimpse or intuit. Priestley's unusually pronounced sense of time's 'thickness' is more complex than the delineation of entropy: his characters repeatedly express some inchoate sense of embryonic dimensions of future possibilities to which they might break through, through dreams, visions or uncanny interventions, and so break the deadening force of habit and self-defeating accommodation to objectification (Priestley's experimentations with discerning and formalizing a musical form to his characters' concerns is most overtly represented by his 1939 play, *Music at Night*). Kay's phrase 'we can't be anything but what we are *now*' (60, original emphasis) encapsulates the delicate balance of Priestley's play; on the one hand, it suggests a socio-historical dramatic analysis that is deterministic but compassionate; on the other hand, it suggests that each moment and juncture of experience should be given its full due (even if it only represents a momentary cross-section of personal potential), but in order to inform future choices and developments in actively informed ways, which may challenge social drifts towards inertia and regression.

Priestley's *Johnson Over Jordan* (1939) and *Ever Since Paradise* (1947) continue his stylistic experiments in the dissolutions of conventional temporal boundaries to reveal and present a multiplicity of time schemes, part of his professed project to move dramatic action from 'the surface of the mind to deeper and deeper levels of consciousness' (quoted in Evans 1964: 137). If Time is a less overt or dominant theme in Priestley's subsequent play, *The Linden Tree* (1947), it nevertheless demonstrates and vindicates an active, curious and indefatigable attitude to time, which is different to the deliberate self-anaesthesia of the work ethic of Chekhov's characters. *The Linden Tree* has a more sympathetic protagonist – a nonconformist university professor, opposed to a 'mass-production and conveyor-belt system of education'

(261) – who comes under pressure to retire from his institution. The play testifies to a sense of *erosion*, in which old forms, shapes, styles and values are being gradually but steadily replaced by new ones – more often than not, more sharply, myopically polarized forms, of generalizing instrumentalism – but Linden's (somewhat Shavian) spirit persists despite them, opposing the more spurious aspects of a self-proclaiming, self-validating 'modernity'. Time is imagined and dramatized most directly, and dialectically, in Priestley's other 'time plays'. *Dangerous Corner* (1932), *I Have Been Here Before* (1937) and *An Inspector Calls* (1946) emphasize how a dominant concept of self, based on the conceptually structured recollection of experiences, can be unsettled by an amplified sense of '*déjà vu*: a sense of false familiarity that occasionally characterizes our awareness of the present so that we have the uncanny feeling that we have experienced long ago what is actually happening now' (Whitrow [1972] 2003: 28).

An Inspector Calls gathers members of a representative conventionally successful household in 1912, around the eruptive disclosure of a young woman's despairing suicide (which harks back to the offstage event in *Time and the Conways*, the maid's attempt at suicide, but presents this image of fatal desperation as a more determining factor in the drama). Like the other Priestley plays in this group, *An Inspector Calls* suggests that a social disinclination to *admit* something (particularly in the more privileged echelons of society) has led to an individual and collective sense of malaise; that when forcibly reminded of their oversight, the self-righteous rich may still backslide into attempted denial; but that an effort of the will can ultimately break cycles of destructive behaviour, renounce attachment to ideological encumbrances and provide preconditions for renewal. Birling, the ostensibly 'self-made' industrialist prides himself on the conviction that war is unlikely, and that the interests of capital must be protected at all cost to ensure immanent prosperity; however, Priestley's play suggests how (then and subsequently) the establishment and maintenance of a market economy in a socially decontextualized position of fundamentalist infallibility displaces all other human ethical values. Each privileged member of the household has exercised their power over a young (every) woman, who has been effectively and systematically designated a member of the 'deviant' poor, and thus they have contributed to the social exclusion that systematically identifies 'winners', who can only profit at the expense of 'losers', who are consigned to isolation and despair. In *I Have Been Here Before*, the industrialist Ormund personifies a similar top-down style of Taylorist management (he tells an employee on the phone: 'Holidays are for boys and girls, not men ... I know all about your children, but they can get on without you' [Priestley 1969: 100]) that is crucially self-defeating. He acknowledges that work and alcoholism offer him brief but futile escapes from a sense of meaninglessness and despair, based on images of life and time that he has 'settled for' and that, Dr Görtler forces him to admit, are 'tragic' (Priestley 1969–77: 114). Görtler later challenges other characters' formulations of time as a merely destructive enemy, notwithstanding his own personal sense of loss, arguing that time is 'not single and universal', that instead of experiencing it 'successively' we might experience it 'spatially' (Priestley 1969–77: 123). Ormund's wife Janet is attracted to a man who contrastingly suggests that history is not something 'dead and done with', but a matter for active construction: 'we're making it all the time' (107). Görtler – referring to theories for which Priestley acknowledges his debt to Ouspensky – proposes to Ormund a starker image of actively selecting a 'new time track' that, though difficult, breaks away from 'the old dark circle of existence', through glimpses of alternatives: Ormund is accordingly inspired, in terms that recognize and appreciate the repeatability and refinement of the theatre event:

ORMUND: […] Why should this poor improvisation be our whole existence? Why should this great theatre of suns and moons and starlight have been created for the first pitiful charade we can contrive?

DR GÖRTLER: It was not. We must play our parts until the drama is perfect.

ORMUND: I think what I've resented most is that the only wisdom we have is wisdom after the event. We learn, but always too late. When I was no longer a boy, I knew at last what sort of a boy I ought to have been. By the time we are forty, we know how to behave at twenty. Always too late. So that the little wisdom we get is useless to us.

(Priestley 1969: 152–153)

Ormund's decision to live more positively but less conventionally with regard to time and social expectations – even if it involves relinquishing a former partner – is paralleled by the decision of the protagonist in Priestley's more mature, less theoretical and schematic play, *The Linden Tree*. Priestley's earlier plays can seem so programmatic as to forestall fully complex characterization; nevertheless, they aim to offer provocative and educative examinations of how the choice of terms, by which time is valued, has a social and moral dimension for self in relation to others, and how it is never too late to reverse the conformist social drift into docile mechanical instrumentalism, a 'grey chilly hollowness inside', at the expense of possibility, 'gaiety, colour, warmth, vision' (Priestley 1969: 300). In several cases, supporting characters (who lack Shaw's sense of idiosyncrasy) are (otherwise similarly) rather apparently designed to vindicate the perspective of a protagonist, and this leads to an instructional tone in Priestley's drama. At his best, however, Priestley attempts to discern and express a sense of music in time: a pattern of potential and resolution that is conventionally obscured by dominant short-termism, but available through an exercise of free will, a human ability to change an otherwise materialistically predetermined future. Though they discern and testify to a tendency to erosion, Priestley's chronologically looping plays also suggest that one of the things eroded by time is *certainty*: as the constituents of the present cannot entirely predict or define the future; in Layzer's words, 'The future grows from the past as a plant grows from a seed, yet it contains more than the past' (quoted by Whitrow [1972] 2003: 126). Priestley is attempting to formulate theatrically an identifiably English form of *dreamtime* (where, as noted at the start of this chapter, a potential coexistence of different moments may prompt an informative and unusually respectful appreciation of self in relation to others). The sense of future time in *Time and the Conways* seems the most fixed and determined, and a matter for some melancholic resignation. Priestley's other time plays contrastingly attempt dynamically informative indications of multiversal possibilities, decisive 'hinge moments' where an exercise of human will in an unusual response may disclose options, beyond a prevalent conscious accommodation to cumulative damage and loss. His concerns, to delineate a surprisingly interactive web of human relations in an underlying unified field (time), and to discern the resonances and implications of different fractal possibilities, suggest and reflect a quantum (rather than linear) dimensionality in the shape of time.

Wesker: Disillusion and dynamism

Priestley's depiction of an ongoing struggle between neoliberal social conceptual structures and a more dynamic image of time is notably developed by Arnold Wesker, in ways that this excerpt from Wesker's *Chips With Everything* deftly summarizes:

HILL: You always need leaders. […]

PIP: Always, always, always! Your great-great-grandfather said there'll always be horses, your great-grandfather said there'll always be slaves, your grandfather said there'll always be poverty and your father said there'll always be wars. Each time you say 'always' the world takes two steps backwards and stops bothering.

(Wesker 1980: 46–47)

It is, however, significant that, subsequent to this avowal, Pip will revert to social type and take his hereditary place in the officer class of the military hierarchy that the play offers as a microcosm of wider British society. Wesker's plays are keenly and repeatedly mindful of the pressures to compromise, and the erosion of youthful idealism emerges as a persistent and identifiably melancholic *leitmotif* in his dramas of active tension, where physical action acts as a frequent counterpoint to verbal explication in ways that, as I have noted elsewhere, are 'simultaneously realistic, representational and thematic' (Rabey 2003: 37). We have considered in Chapter 2 how Wesker's *The Kitchen* (1959) provides a good example of this.

The Four Seasons (1965) adopts what Wesker terms a stylized form, an overt counterpoint of seasonal settings, in order 'to explore the essentials of a relationship' between the characters Adam and Beatrice 'with deliberately little recourse to explanation or background' or social realist style, whilst simultaneously resisting allegory or symbol (Wesker 1976: 123) (Gwenlyn Parry's 1978 play, *Y Tŵr/The Tower*, similarly charts stages in a relationship, mapped onto ascent of an architectural structure). The first scene, 'Winter', seems a time of disintegration and dismissal, with Beatrice refusing to speak to Adam. 'Spring' thaws their relationship into gestures of love and play to repair a wintry sense of damage and self-enclosure, but does not entirely dispel a tendency to generalized and self-preoccupied behaviour on both sides.

Adam suggests that they embark on a conscious resistance to determinism: 'Let's see how long we can stay away from morbidity' (89). In 'Summer', Beatrice issues the testing demand that she be central to Adam's existence: 'Every second you shall give me' (98); however, they cannot remain synchronized in their responses to experience, which Beatrice formulates in terms of making her a third-hand bruised and damaged clock. This clock 'wheezes and whirrs' and strikes 'midnight when the hour is only six', and yet 'the hands always point to the right time' (105). They both seem unable to transcend previous experiences, patterns and memories of behaviour, or to accept their pasts in order to permit regeneration. Adam's 'real-time' summer preparation of an apple strudel provides a characteristic Wesker image, of personal time invested patiently and skilfully in preparing food, as a means to intimate companionship. However, 'Autumn' ends on an image of dead, damp leaves that will not light or burn. Adam's recollections of his father's death remind him that 'time passes and time passing reminds me of sadness and waste and neglect and suffering', and that 'all those lovely moments of youth will not return' (121). Although Adam claims that this melancholy awareness brings a spirit of forgiveness, Beatrice seems beyond his reach, withdrawing into a personal sense of coldness that he cannot alleviate by igniting the leaves. The play's motif of single-year seasonal progression does not permit the sense of a second Spring: its progress of disillusionment seems linear (rather than cyclical), tending towards 'the essentials of a' – or at least, this – 'relationship' being characterized as involving an erosion of trust and sensed possibility, and an inevitable, irrevocable separateness.

This sense of time as an arrow of disillusionment, where momentarily perceived spatial and physical, verbal and imaginative congruencies only point up sad ironies, also pervades Wesker's play *Their Very Own and Golden City* (1966), which follows the life, hopes and career of an architect, Andrew Cobham. Wesker refers to the construction of the play as being in the form of a 'flash-forward' as opposed to 'flash-back' (Wesker 1976: 134) as it covers the period 1927–1990, in which two groups of actors might be required to play four friends in their youthful and older forms; however, he also acknowledges how one set of actors might play the characters, at all ages, young and old (with particular implications for the ending). The youthful optimism of Andy's early career success in 1933 is first shadowed by a presentiment of how 'the cities will fall' amidst bombs, killing and destruction (145), and he aims to design splendid building co-operatives that will present both social and aesthetic alternatives. His political mentor, Jake, observes how many invocations of so-called 'realism' tend towards timidity: '"The time isn't ripe!" [...] The sort of answer we all give when we don't do the things we feel are right'; rather than compromise, Jake advocates boldness, which risks defeat, but he maintains 'in the long run all defeat is temporary', when the principles of action will be more accurately recognized, judged and appreciated by the citizens of the future rather than those of the present (150). Jake is one of Wesker's revolutionaries who have a sense of responsibility to the past as well as the future, rather than rebels who would dismiss the past. In Act One, scene seven, the youthful versions of the friends express their political and social idealism with a recital of Blake's 'Jerusalem' (which may, for some theatregoers, recall Priestley's dramatic use of the same words to suggest a mood of determination and generosity in *Time and the Conways*).[27] Andy subsequently opposes Jake in local political debate, arguing that 'old men should stand down' (163), but admits to a growing sense of 'waste' occluding and defying his wife's assurance that their experience is 'all a time of growing' (165). Defeated, Jake warns Andy to be careful of his idealized cities, when he too will, in time, incur the wrath of rebels: 'One day you're old and you say right things – but it's all too late' (168). In 1947, Andy arraigns the Labour Council for their faint-hearted terms of post-war slum clearance, and meets the dismissive objection 'You're asking us to change our whole society' (172), as well as the allegation that his own civic plans might be another form of 'patchwork', 'a little bit of order in the midst of chaos', attractive but superficial and merely decorous. Andy still blames the objections on a deterministic cynicism, a failure of imagination, and a lack of vision over time, at the heart of the national English spirit:

> Whether you stonewall, whether you legislate, whether you lobby, argue, deceive or apply your lovely reasonable sanity, the end is the same. A cheapskate dreariness, a dull caution that kills the spirit of all movements and betrays us all – from plumber to poet. Not even the gods forgive that.
>
> (172)

Nevertheless, in another context Andy feels driven to admit that 'There – is – no – revolutionary – situation' (179) to drive fundamental change, but he begins building, mindful that something at least must nevertheless be attempted, as partial reform. Though he denounces caution as a kind of fear, and apathy as a kind of cancer, Andy is increasingly isolated, in apparent vindication of another character's assertion that 'those of us who build the Golden City can never live in it' (185); words that – like Andy's provocations, which extend to repeating Jake's pronouncements on the importance of principled decisions for future generations – seem to have more resonance (at least without the benefit of properly astonishing achievements of scenography) than Wesker's (admirably challenging, if indefinite) stage directions: '*now, visually, we must see and feel the magic and excitement of a city growing*' (199). The final view of Andy, now 'Sir Andrew', in 1990, finds him disillusioned and resigned, deducing from his context and experiences: 'I don't suppose there's such a thing as democracy, really, only a democratic way of manipulating power', and, in lieu of equality, the only possibility remains 'a gracious way of accepting inequality' (203). The play concludes with the younger Andy's expression of idealism. Wesker adds in a note, if one set of actors play the friends at different ages, Andy should remain alone; if two sets of actors play the roles, Old Andy should be surrounded by the youthful characters/ performers as he speaks the words, '*creating a dreamlike effect: the "flash-forward" will have become a "flash-back"*'; but Wesker stipulates unequivocally: '*in either case Old Andy must deliver Young Andy's lines wearily in contrast with the gaiety of the others, to retain the sad irony*' (206). Wesker's principal identification of the play in terms of a 'flash-forward' would seem to suggest a particularly substantial qualification of youthful optimism by extending speculation into a prospective future (the 1990s, in a play written and first staged in the 1970s) that is as yet unlived by characters, dramatist and audience: raising the question, to what extent does this prediction of disillusionment itself risk becoming a form of deterministic foreclosure?[28] The idea of a 'flash-back' to poignantly recalled idealism would formally link *Their Very Own and Golden City* more closely to David Hare's play *Plenty* (1976), and at least weight compromise with experience and (significantly limited) achievements. Though a single evening's drama rather than a theatre marathon, Wesker's play exemplifies what Kalb calls 'the mayfly effect: the illusion of living a lifetime within the span of a single day' in a theatrical journey 'so extensive, adventurous, varied, and marvellously circuitous' it may '*seem* to compress the incomprehensibly messy, bewilderingly ramified whole of life between their opening and closing curtains' (Kalb 2011: 49). Returning to Wagner's comments on *Dr Faustus*, we may note how Wesker's play, like Marlowe's, 'is explicitly drawing attention to temporal discordance, both within a singular time frame' (the fictive world of Andy, where his personal time is at odds with that of others) and between time frames ('the variable speed of time on stage compared to the consistent speed of time in the audience's world') (Wagner 2012: 17).

Wesker's dramatizations of separation and isolation and a search for meaningful shape in time continue in *The Friends* (1970), where the death of a woman throws into relief the lives of her friends, their remaining possibilities and probabilities (and potentially invites the audience to consider their own, correspondingly). *The Friends* reprises and develops the distinction broached in *Their Very Own and Golden City* between rebels and revolutionaries (the latter believe that the past is 'too rich with human suffering and achievement to be dismissed' [Wesker 1980: 124]). Moreover, it suggests a diagnosis of the personal 'mess' associated with disappointment, erosion and entropy, such as that encountered by Andy Cobham and by Adam and Beatrice in *The Four Seasons*: a 'confusion' based on 'the silly things we've added to the world: easy achievements, ephemeral success', and 'little damages we've done each other', which together accrue in a 'once and only life more than half over' becoming increasingly coloured by 'a terrible sense of defeat and time passing and appetites fading and intellect softening' (Wesker 1980: 125). However, one character in *The Friends* insists that whilst this sense of erosion and entropy might not be entirely ignored, it is not a rationale for despair: their dying friend wanted to *live*, nonetheless, and they have opportunities that she was denied. Wesker's most haunting dramatization of separation, isolation and withdrawal through dedication to an ideal may be *Caritas* (1981), in which a young woman literally materializes a sense of temporal framework, in a bid for self-transcendence: she elects to be walled up as an anchoress in the name of her religion.[29] The play shows how, in her bid to transcend the short-termism and erosion associated with the scales of human time, she also places herself beyond the human complications and consolations of contact and interaction, and this leads her into the involution of madness. Wesker's finest dramatic address to the rigours of time, and its varying facets of quantifications, chaos and contradictions, is *The Old Ones* (1972/3), in which two ageing brothers, Manny and Boomy, watch over the fortunes and misfortunes of their family household, issuing philosophical proclamations and quotations of optimism and pessimism – or, more precisely, regenerative and erosive senses of time – respectively. Manny finds the dialectic of provocation, to counter Boomy's preoccupation with human vanity, absurdity, futility and decay, paradoxically vivifying: 'With his philosophy of doom he keeps me alive' (Wesker 1980: 135). Wilcher has observed how *The Old Ones* seems possibly to be in part a theatrical response to a theme identified by Wesker in a journal, how 'ageing involves being less cheered by goodness than one is tormented by evil' (Wilcher 1991: 91); yet it also sets this intimation within a collage of different forms in which characters, of varying ages, fight to survive, remain fully alive and interact meaningfully and constructively with others, overcoming fearful cynicism.

The tensions and problems encountered by the characters of *The Old Ones* permit no simple resolution, and the generational differences in perceptions of time and the past constitute a particular tension. Rosa, the daughter of Manny and Boomy's sister Sarah, quotes the maxim that it is inappropriate to measure life quantitatively, 'It is not the number of years but rather the quality that determines whether life is transient or permanent' (138); nevertheless, she admits to her mother that she fears death as irrevocable loss (172). As a teacher, Rosa struggles to instil a sense of conscious temporal perspective into a school class:

What you decide now can affect your whole life. I can't understand why you don't care about that. *(Noises of mock surprise.)* You're sixteen now. How many of you have friends of fourteen? You're different from them, aren't you? They're almost like kids to you. And at fourteen were you the same as you were at ten? And so, can't you imagine yourselves being different in the future? When you're twenty, twenty-five, thirty-five, fifty? Can't you imagine that you'll feel differently, think differently, have different needs? That's got to be prepared for, hasn't it? Can't you project yourself forward, with your imagination. Can't you use your imagination to put yourselves into another situation? *(Noise)* No, I don't suppose you can. I must be bloody mad. *(Crescendo of noise, mock applause.)*

(Wesker 1980: 156)

The breakdown of imaginative sympathy between generations is most chillingly dramatized in *The Old Ones* when Manny's wife Gerda is mocked, then mugged, by a gang of youths, and Jack (Sarah's eccentric neighbour who seems a contemporary East End version of Shakespeare's Feste and Poor Tom both) rings his bell and sings his eccentric litany/fool's refrain of remorseless seasonal succession: 'the young folk is living, Jack is a-dying, the young folk is coming, the devil is in me' (165). At this point in the play, Boomy has just revealed that it is a disagreement between what should be transmitted from one generation to the next that fuelled his quarrel with his brother: Manny threw away a bag of diamonds representing their father's hard work to pay for their education, because of Manny's personal disagreement with the principle of inherited wealth. More reflectively, Boomy tells Gerda he is 'not very good at being old' because he feels defenceless, missing the favourite time of his youth when 'I had strength, I could fight' (163–164); now he feels like 'a senile Doctor Faustus', with a son who is a revolutionary, not from love but from what he interprets as oedipal hatred: which would make him a rebel rather than a revolutionary, in Wesker's terms.

However, images of disintegration and breakdown are theatrically counterpointed by the physical and scenographic action of the characters building a *Succah* – a symbolic tent partly roofed with branches – on the balcony of Sarah's council flat, preparing for a festive meal and celebration based on traditional Jewish forms, but which she intends and envisages in secular terms, 'to declare the glory of man' rather than God (137), a reinvention of a ritual intended to bring young and old characters together. The second half of the play assembles various dogged forms of personal and community interactive resistance to circumstances and forces that might be dispiriting. Rosa tells her class that books represent informative centuries of 'other people's knowledge, experience' that they can add to their own and use to measure their own, as means to 'freedom and happiness' (179). However, there is also a suggestion that other people's ideas can only take you so far: Manny's self-proclaimed victory over Boomy occurs when (like Beaty in Wesker's *Roots*) he can reply in his own words of personal testimony rather than relying on quoting others. In the final festive celebration, there is a suggestion that Boomy is the rebel, who would associate the past with transience, failure and futility, dismissing the endurance and significance of human achievements; and Manny is the revolutionary, in his insistence that the abandonment of work and knowledge, particularly in the face of destruction, is a discouraged capitulation to evil and foolishness, and an abnegation of human potential. For Manny, the past is 'too rich with human suffering *and* achievement to be dismissed', to add a crucial word of emphasis to the earlier line in *The Friends*. Though Boomy finally persists in his pronouncements that 'time and judgment' will characteristically provide limits to human purpose, his very dismissal of human power is drowned out and interrupted by the festive laughter, dancing and singing of the other characters, young and old, from which he has chosen to withdraw his participation. *The Old Ones* offers a notably and fruitfully complex series of dramatic images of ageing and the active exercise of informed *distinction* – considering and choosing what should be discarded, retained and developed from the past – to demonstrate and recreate active spirits of family and community (despite the dismissive contempt of some for what they do, or prefer, not to understand).

Rosa's challenge to her rowdy 16-year-old pupils to project themselves forward, imagine themselves ageing in decades and discovering changing needs, embryonically anticipates Wesker's one-young-woman play, *Letter to Myself* (2004). From another perspective, *Letter to Myself* offers a riposte to Wesker's earlier play, *Letter to a Daughter* (1990), in which a professional singer formulates a letter to the daughter from whom she is separated by her professional itinerary and wider personal choices. *Letter to Myself* depicts that 13-year-old daughter Marike, apparently alone but initiating a dialogue with her own present and future selves, writing a letter that she intends to help her 18-year-old self remember and realize what it was like to be 13 (thus facing the conscious challenge of articulating to herself, in the present, what it is like to be 13). As she expresses her current dislike of boys, their fearful conformity and smell, she questions herself as to what might make her likings, and hopes, change: 'Who can tell what forever will bring?'. Marike reviews the ten points of advice that her mother has sent her in a letter when Marike was aged 11; 13-year-old Marike interrogates the presumptions of some points (why can she not 'grab knowledge' but also grab her chances while she may?), and defers some to her 18-year-old self ('Love has nothing to do with anything you dream, or plan, or decide'), while developing a sense of how her mother is similar, inconsistent and clever. While Marike finds some of her mother's precepts too sweeping and generalized (including her refutations of dogma and blame), she acknowledges that some of her peers have already abandoned a sense of responsibility for their selves, and pre-emptively assumed a deterministically narrowed sense of potential and possibilities:

> There are girls in my school who are going to be victims all their lives. You can see it. Even now aged thirteen. Nothing is ever going to be their fault. *(Beat)* Why does that make me want to cry?
>
> (Wesker 2004)

So, Marike's observation proves to her that, even at 13, what you accept as probable and imagine as possible is not only significant but formative: perhaps decisive. Like the characters in *The Old Ones* and other Wesker plays, Marike is (already, at her younger age) actively involved in the process of distinction, sifting through the pronouncements and prescriptions of those older, questioning their conclusions and measuring the knowledge of others against her own, whilst developing a mindfulness of her own inevitable changes in situation and needs, for which she must also try to prepare. To further this preparation, she continues with her 'time-capsule' letter to her future self:

> Dear Marike aged eighteen. I hope this has been of some use to you. I'll write another one next year – Marike aged fourteen to Marike aged nineteen. And perhaps one the year after – from Marike aged fifteen to Marike aged twenty. And perhaps that's how we'll stay in touch with ourselves, you and me, spend our lives together until Marike aged seventy-five is writing to Marike aged eighty. *(Beat)* Who may not be around to receive it! *(Beat)* Oh, my God! Who may not be around.
>
> (Wesker 2004)

Marike '*thinks deeply about this sudden confrontation with death*', then looks into the mirror and (re)assures herself about her own present beauty (with a touch of defensive vanity). But there is a poignancy, growth and something that glimpses and approaches the essential terms of being human in the young woman's first projection of herself into so many rigorously imagined times, envisioning herself successively different, and then brushing against the startling prospect of the world in her eventual absence. Her newly concentrated and formalized attempts to achieve an imaginative sympathy with her future and her past (and even with her mother) may inform and affect her future, decisively.

Although a dramatic miniature, *Letter to Myself* offers a notable development of Wesker's exploration of a theatrical effect of 'flash-forward', and also an intriguing riposte to Beckett's *Krapp's Last Tape* (1958), in which the aged protagonist embarks on what will apparently be his final ritualized review: of the diminishing returns of his present, and encounters with his past rationalizations. Krapp looks back, ultimately questioning his middle-aged self who repudiates the value of the sensuality and companionship he has (he maintains, purposefully) forsaken. Beckett's theatrical framing of Krapp's experience and paraphernalia offers a bleak cosmic joke at the expense of his protagonist's former certainties and pretensions (exemplifying Beckett's development of what States identifies in Chekhov: 'Suddenly, you can hear the ticking of the objects and the ceaseless flow of future into past', revealing 'the ironic nonresponse of the world' [States 1985: 73, 78]). Wesker's Marike *looks forward* with a sense of possibility befitting (and perhaps unique to) a 13-year-old, and collides with a startling form of insight into the unpredictabilities and alterations and final remorselessness that the individual consciousness will inevitably at some stage associate with the succession of selves, in (and finally out of) *time*: its different facets, paradoxes and – ultimately, literally – unimaginable properties. In *Krapp's Last Tape*, Beckett wryly discovers a tragic subjectivity at the terminal stage of life, whereas in *Letter to Myself*, Wesker contrastingly foregrounds (against the relief of death's shadow) youthful enthusiasm and energy, as Marike begins her own re-evaluations of values, in the dialectic of narrated and unforeseeable history.

Thus Wesker's plays testify to the inextricable presence (even the prevalence for some) of disappointment over the time of a fully engaged life, but also to a resurgent spirit of assent (more akin to the kernel image glimpsed at the end of Beckett's *That Time* than to *Krapp's Last Tape*) that flies in the face of cynicism. As Caitlin Moran observes in her novel *How to Build a Girl*, cynicism is an armour against disappointment, which fearfully, pre-emptively and paralytically reduces the dynamism of the future: 'When you keep saying "No" all that's left is what other people said "Yes" to before you were born' (Moran 2014: 262). Wesker takes care not to ignore or dismiss the recurrence of disappointment (and how it may be informative), but is persistently exploring, in his theatre, how even this might *build* a girl, and a boy.

Comical-historical-tragical

Alan Ayckbourn disarmingly suggests 'I once coined a phrase (I think it was me) that tragedy was merely comedy interrupted. Or vice versa' (Ayckbourn 2002: 26). This playfully draws attention to the importance of the dramatist's time decisions: where to start, and where to end, in the selection of events for presentation. Ayckbourn, a masterful comic dramatist, expresses a general personal preference for condensation of action, 'in how *short* a time can I tell my story?' (in both fictional time and audience time); this may assist in lending credibility to the confusion by giving the characters 'less time to think about things' (21). Comic (and *tragi*comic) characters usually begin engagingly, and may be particularly sympathetic in their considerable and serious dilemmas (as at the outsets of *A Midsummer Night's Dream* and *Twelfth Night*). However, in their reactions to developments, they become more rhythmically mechanistic: they lose what Bergson identifies as 'their consciousness of duration, the essence of being alive and endowed with free will' (Wiles 2014: 28). Ayckbourn further observes that the more closely 'stage time equates to real (theatre foyer) time, the closer to the action we appear to get', with the effect of giving minutiae of stage details and action considerably more significance, bringing awkward silences, for example, 'sharply into focus' (Ayckbourn 2002: 22).

Ayckbourn's proffered example of this from his own work is *Absent Friends* (1974); however, we might apply this to the opening and momentum of Jez Butterworth's tragicomedy *Mojo* (1995), which begins with two 'wide boys', Sweets and Potts, considering their ambitions over teapot, tray and three incongruously pretty cups, as they speculate hyperbolically about their prospects of advancement. Sweets and (particularly) Potts will become more desperately, comically, frenzied and mechanistic in their reactions when events spiral out of their control, whereas Butterworth's protagonist, Baby, characteristically *slows down* the action, or else accelerates it suddenly and unpredictably, stretching and complicating the initially dominant rhythms of comedy of desperation to their breaking point. This occurs most startlingly, when Baby shoots a character, Skinny, who takes a gruellingly and disturbingly long time to die (as opposed to the swift cancellation of a character that a pistol shot may conventionally evoke), and he even consciously explores the minutiae of his own death.

What Ayckbourn identifies as 'the sharp focus' of 'real time' is also at play in many works by Harold Pinter, in which the attentions of all involved are irritably, discrepantly and ominously focused on immediate or recalled, but disputed, details (*The Dumb Waiter, The Homecoming, No Man's Land, Ashes to Ashes*). This demonstrates that the intensification of sharp focus is a technique not confined to the remit of comedies of manners (but explains why Pinter's plays may initially or occasionally recall comedies of manners that turn increasingly sinister and claustrophobic). In contrast, Ayckbourn claims that a play which takes place over a greater arc of fictional time (he nominates his own *Joking Apart*) involves events being 'seen from a greater distance' (Ayckbourn 2002: 22), which would *suggest* more detachment. However, this does not always follow: Priestley's *Time and the Conways* seeks, in its switchback final act and final moments, to subvert the irony and detachment that its Olympian perspective might have seemed to offer. Ayckbourn's own conscious 'expeditions' into the genre of time plays (Ayckbourn 2002: 20) also involve foregrounded subversions of conventional time-schemes: *Time of my Life* (1992) begins at an awkward family celebration, then follows the younger couple backwards in time, and the older couple forwards in time (a complex structure that Ayckbourn selects to serve both plot and theme, interestingly describing his technique in cinematic terms: 'shooting' various angles of a single moment in time, allowing 'before, during and after to be seen in long shot, medium and close-up' [24]); and *Communicating Doors* (1994) mobilizes the science-fiction fantasy of racing back in time to change historical consequence through averting a pivotal event. In both cases, however, Ayckbourn's 'conclusion' is that more care should 'perhaps' be applied to valuing the present moment (25), the terms of its particularity and its implications.

It is difficult to think of an effective play that involves events being 'seen from a greater distance', and hence detachment. Bernard Shaw's *Back to Methuselah* (1921) is a notable experiment in this direction, in which Shaw invites a radically sceptical perspective on prevalent contemporary political short-sightedness, sentimental romanticism and self-satisfaction in herd-instinct conformity. This incisive satirical spirit of social and evolutionary impatience with what is characterized as a prevalent childishness is also discernible in the preface to Shaw's *Caesar and Cleopatra* (1898), *Man and Superman* (1905), *Heartbreak House* (1919) and the tragic conflict of *Saint Joan* (1924). *Back to Methuselah* develops Shaw's critical perspective with particular reference to the unfortunately dominant, human but all too limitingly human, frameworks of time perception and life expectancy. He suggests that it is only through an extended imaginative development of skills, wisdom and perspective and a commitment to long-term solutions that political leaders and their properly discerning electorate might avert disasters (depending also on the deceleration of physical deterioration through ageing, and even, in the last section of *Back to Methuselah*, the apparent transcendence of physicality by consciousness). Shaw's theatrical 'metabiological pentateuch' combines a fundamentally educational initiative with rhetorical satire and utopian science fantasy through a series of scenes that are more presentational and demonstrative of their thesis than tensely dramatic.

Back to Methuselah has the form of a dramatic quest, in which the sole enduringly formidable obstacle or adversary is the imaginative limitation that it challenges the audience to reject – even as it satirizes the probable inability of contemporary humans to achieve this. The perspective of critical distance and detachment from the limitations of one's own point in species evolution is a difficult one to sustain or apply (though comic books and films in Marvel's *X-Men* series might, with their varying degrees of skill, nonetheless constitute notable dramatic examples of a critical impatience with the dominant fearful and intolerant reflexes of *homo sapiens* and a sympathetic association with representative of a hypothetical 'next stage' in human evolution). However, my impressions on watching the Royal Shakespeare Company's 2000 revival of *Back to Methuselah* at The Other Place theatre were of theatrical (if not always consistently dramatic) vitality, with the performative and scenographic energies harnessed by David Fielding's production demonstrating theatre's refreshing (and literally limitless) strengths in embodying imaginatively challenging speculation (a strong tradition incorporating *Dr Faustus*, Caryl Churchill's *Far Away* and Philip Ridley's *Mercury Fur*), in contrast to how theatre is often required to remain within the confines of conventional literalism. *Back to Methuselah* is Shaw's strenuous (and sometimes strained) bid to reverse the prevalent direction of time's arrow from disorder (dystopia) to order (utopia), imagining (in the section 'Tragedy of an Elderly Gentleman') various reactions to the terms of a future Arcadia (of which more, in relation to Stoppard). However, the audience's capacities for *choices* in reaction to Shaw's speculations remain unclear, beyond the dramatist's encouragement of a healthy impatience with complicity in political infantilization and short-termism. In this respect, *Back to Methuselah* resembles the Medieval Morality Play, with its significant and educative dramatic process of detachment from the immediate 'worldly' terms and baits of time squandered, uneasily and impatiently comic from a cosmic perspective: indicating what fools these (short-living) mortals can be.

Rather than consistently dramatize events 'from a distance' of detachment, theatre more often (as in the instances specified by Priestley and Ayckbourn) speculates, hypothesizes and questions predominant assumptions through the subversion of linear temporal sequence. Shakespeare's *Henry V* constitutes a startling example of this, in how the play's action is consciously recalled from the past and animated in the immediate present by the narration of the Chorus ('jumping o'er times / Turning th'accomplishment of many years / Into an hourglass' [Shakespeare 2007: 1033]). Exeter's intimidating assurance to the French King that the formerly reckless Henry has learnt to weigh time 'even to the utmost grain' (1054) is, however, likely to be qualified (like so much of what is spoken in this play) by what is shown and seen. Whilst it is *possible* to portray Henry V as efficiently calculating, even chillingly mechanical, a performer's characterization of the protagonist is likely to be *more* engaging, the *less* Henry seems to calculate masterfully, and the *more* he seems to be initially uncertain, off-balance, and at odds in his personal 'tempo' with those around him, actively struggling to learn to 'weigh time' and act appropriately, which is more resonant with common experiences of engaging with complexities. This sense of responsive action 'in-the-moment' may also contribute to Henry's (and his performer's) arrivals at performances of assurance and decisiveness: a matter of process and emergence, both theatrical and (apparently) personal (in terms of 'character time'). Notwithstanding this, *Henry V* encompasses, in its final third, sharply complicating and often *awkwardly* intensifying points of focus on minutiae of stage details and action, and their significant consequences: the British infantrymen's imagining 'all those arms and legs and heads, chopped off in a battle', joining and crying out in 'heavy reckoning' (1071); the peevish international negotiations; Henry's strenuously 'comic' wooing of Katharine, intended disarmingly; and the Chorus's astonishing final speech that reverses the telescope. This final speech, somewhat *deflatingly*, if perhaps also poignantly (depending on the tone of the production), relocates the figure of Henry (who has been actively, surprisingly dilated and contextualized during the previous two hours' theatre) into the deterministically finite pageant of historical sequence, which, we are reminded, involves the loss of France and presages the further bleeding of England. The 'jolt' that is created by Shakespeare's sudden transition from one time scheme to another, from sharp focus to long focus, offers a forceful reminder on both the importance *and* the selectivity of perspective – whether personal or historical – and how this may prove a matter of life and death. Rebecca Schneider makes a wider point about how theatre shows everything as being open to question, in ways that are eminently applicable to *Henry V*:

> If the historian's aim is to untangle the forgetting from the remembering, or distinguish the fake from the real to get at a true story, and the theatre (or politician's) aim is to confuse the borders again to truly tell a story, the best way to do *either* might be to acknowledge

the ways in which the theatrical and the historical are, at all moments, profoundly and fundamentally co-constitutive.

(Schneider 2014: 76–77, original emphasis)

The historical perspective formalized in *Henry V* serves as a corrective to the dying Hotspur in Shakespeare's *1 Henry IV*, and his proclamation: 'thought's the slave of life, and life, time's fool; / And time that takes survey of all the world / Must have a stop' (Shakespeare 2007: 958). Hotspur's subjective temporality may reach its mortal limit, but his pronouncement is 'historically inaccurate', a moment in theatrical history (re-presenting historical time) that reminds us that time, as historical continuity, will proceed 'with or without the perceiving subject' (Wagner, who further observes how the character Hotspur here mistakes '*his* time' for '*all* time', when the wider theatrical context directs our attention beyond such subjective limits [Wagner 2012: 77, original emphasis]). Phyllis Rackin goes further than these commentators, in arguing for *Henry V*'s radical relativism: its presentation of two disparate accounts (not just interpretations) of the action (provided by the discourse of the Chorus and the events staged in dramatic representation) not only emphasizes differences, but also insists on 'each other's inadequacies', antithetically 'directing our attention to the abyss at the centre of the historiographic project' – the 'impossibility of recovering the past or of getting beyond the historiographic text (whether that text be a written record or a dramatic representation) to discover the always postulated and never graspable fiction called historical truth' (Rackin 1991: 69). This suggests that time, which takes survey of all the world, is protean: politically so (on which, more in Chapter 5).

Sean Carroll notes how Tom Stoppard's *Arcadia* (1993) uses the arrow of time as a central organizing metaphor (Carroll 2010: 29): the idea of irreversible processes that happen in a specific sequence in a progression from order to disorder. *Arcadia* combines 'two plots from two distinct time schemes', presented alternately in a shared space, so that 'humour stems from the temporal paradox' by which 'the same material substance of the production' (specifically, set and props) 'is shown as belonging to two different time streams, which overlap and appear in one sequence' (Limon 2010: 121, 123). The play opens in 1809 in Sidley Park, a country house where the prodigy Thomasina considers, to her tutor Septimus, how you can stir jam into rice pudding, but not dissociate the two things by stirring in reverse (Carroll adds the example: we can turn eggs into omelettes, but not omelettes into eggs, 2010: 30). As the play progresses, scenes from 1809 are interwoven with scenes, occurring in the same house and room, in a contemporary setting, where two scholars, Hannah and Bernard, seek to piece together how events unfolded in 1809, to which the audience are made privy. Thus, the audience are not initially omniscient, but have the pleasure of being the best informed detectives in the attempted reconstruction, and becoming ironically aware of when the 'modern' characters jump to erroneous conclusions, in their 'snakes-and-ladders' game of deductive processes (the apparently disorderly detritus of which is represented by a steady accumulation of objects on the table, half of which remain invisible to the characters who do not share their time scheme:

only the audience can unite and appreciate the processes by which these accrue). The play's title, and one juncture of conversation, both refer to the artistic premise, in the paintings of Poussin and others, of the shadowy presence of Death even in the most idealized, apparent temporal suspense of pastoral circumstances. The modern characters are holding an outdoor dance, involving dressing up in period costume, which further scrambles chronological signifiers (and recalls the innocent masquerading frivolity of Priestley's Conways).

Hannah is researching the presence and identity of the former inhabitant of the estate's deliberately landscaped hermitage: someone who withdrew from life, assuming his place in an artificial formal pattern, a 'garden ornament' akin to 'a pottery gnome' (Stoppard 1993: 27). The hermit is a figure whose personal sense of melancholy was apparently confirmed by the second thermodynamic law of entropy and final heat-death ('it was Frenchified mathematick that brought him to the melancholy certitude of a world without light or life', 65). This sense of inevitable linearity is offset by the sense of surprise and unpredictability that a contemporary character, Chloe, associates with the wilful chaos of sexual attraction: though the universe is 'trying to be' deterministic, 'the only thing going wrong is people fancying people who aren't supposed to be in that part of the plan' (73–74). This extends to various arguably inappropriate liaisons, in both time periods of Stoppard's play, and the dawning awareness of poignance, that Thomasina died in a fire on the eve of her seventeenth birthday, which impelled Septimus to take up residency on the estate as the hermit. We see Thomasina working her own way towards formulating the law of entropy (the 'frenchified mathematick'), yet also emboldened by another scholar's intimation of 'the attraction that Newton left out' (74), encouraging her own sense of a hidden cause – 'The action of bodies in heat' (84) – which may suggest an incompletion within determinism. However, all that remains from Thomasina's writings and calculations, in the present day, are her formulations of the arrow of time; only the audience are able to witness her resolve to dance, and how it combines with her unsuspecting of her preordained doom. The present-day characters interpret her writings as glimpsing the irreversibility of time; however, this is counterpointed by the more historically distant characters' sense that the scientific goal of 'nothing less than a complete description of the universe we live in' (Hawking 1988: 15) might itself constitute a further sense of limitation: 'When we have found all the meanings and lost all the mysteries, we will be alone, on an empty shore' (Stoppard 1993: 94).

Accordingly, the final temporally overlaid images of the play are Thomasina and Septimus waltzing with increasing fluency, while in the present day Hannah and a young aristocrat start to dance, '*rather awkwardly*' (97). Stoppard's theatrical strategy of dissolving temporal barriers between the occupants of a specific space, for the sole awareness of his audience, permits a paradoxical imaginative coexistence of what would normally be incompatible and impossible according to the laws of physics and biology (permitting a perspective that encompasses *both/and* rather than affording *either/or*). Moreover, it permits him, and the audience, some ironic wit at the expense of the characters' presumptions to full knowledge – particularly those of the self-consciously 'enlightened' modern researchers, as their traffic across the stage becomes more apparently chaotic (to them) but actually tightly managed and orchestrated (to us, the audience) for maximum comedic effects.[30] This provides the opportunity for Stoppard to play on the apparent spatial limitation and restriction of a single locale, as identified by States: the movement of stage props, 'lying in wait', into new layers of significance gives the play much of its 'optical and temporal interest', which nevertheless issues in a 'spatial fatality' (States 1985: 68, 69). Stoppard's theatrical emphasis is finally on the *partiality* of human knowledge: the ways that people understandably but foolishly assume things are knowable and entirely known, and how little this may account for human fascination, danger and decision (the female characters seem more aware of the appeal of the unpredictable; the male characters seem more linear and reductive in their deductions). *Arcadia* stages both the scientific difficulty and the theatrical possibility of reconstructing the past from the present; the latter being theatrically possible, thanks to the information that only Stoppard's imagination is shown to be able to conserve. The play appears to be a comic fantasia on Einstein's theory of relativity that leads us to regard time in terms of the relationship between the universe and the observer.[31] *Arcadia* is thus skilful, but tellingly selective (even idiosyncratic) in where it locates its imaginative power of reversibility (associated with the redemptive but significantly vague possibility of an anti-continental 'good English algebra', which proves beyond the reach of Septimus). Stoppard's *Arcadia* is contrasted to Howard Barker's *Ego in Arcadia* (1992) in the next chapter.

In full development of an allusion in the preceding paragraph, I turn to Stephen Booth's definitions of comedy and tragedy as a means to further consideration and characterization of dramatic (and, indeed, artistic) genres:

> Comedy operates from – and demonstrates – the proposition that there is a way things are and fools forget what it is. Regrettably, however, no one is always or altogether immune from occasional fits of foolish forgetfulness.

> Tragedy operates from – and demonstrates – the proposition that there is a way things are and that fools assume it is knowable and known. Regrettably, however, no one is or can be exempt from the moment-to-moment, day-by-day necessity of assuming that the ways of things are as previous experience leads us to expect them to be.

> (Booth 1983: 78)

One might, for our immediate purposes of enquiry and exploration, extend Booth's striking formulations by substituting above, for the words 'way things are', the words: 'shape of time'.

Notes

1 For example, Shakespeare's dramatic poem *The Rape of Lucrece* contains a sustained meditation on the divergent aspects of Time by the distraught Lucrece. She first blames 'injurious, shifting Time' for her catastrophic reversal of fortunes: more precisely, 'Misshapen

Time, copesmate of ugly Night', 'Eater of youth, false slave to false delight'. Then, she complains that Time has been crucially and degeneratively wrong-footed by Opportunity, Time's rightful servant, who has proved unfaithful, leading Time to stray from his rightful, ultimately benign path, which befits his 'office' ('To eat up errors by opinion bred') and his 'glory' ('To unmask falsehood and bring truth to light'), which reconciles, brings seasonal fecundity and mocks 'the subtle in themselves beguiled' (Shakespeare 2007: 2422). Thus the poem sustains a (rather strained) sense of what Quinones would term 'augmentative time' (Quinones 1965: 328): not intrinsically malign, but mercilessly transitional.

2   The context of Whitrow's observations is as follows: 'although our perception of time has many subjective and even sociological features, it is based on an objective factor that provides an external control for the timing of our physiological processes'; this objective factor 'is what we call physical time', 'which cannot be reduced to anything else'; however, 'this does not mean that it exists in its own right: it is an aspect of phenomena' (Whitrow [1972] 2003: 139).

3   The premise of the *Jurassic Park* movie franchise (1993–2015) speculates that human experimentation might instigate such resurgences of previously extinct species.

4   Quinones's distinctions might be further identified, respectively: augmentative time is Time the destroyer, but also Time as process of succession; contracted time involves a conscious, tragic confrontation and acknowledgement of the impossibility of defeating Time, and hence 'the limitations of the successful and the strengths of the doomed'(Quinones 1965: 336); extended time is 'rife in the late Romances', and operates as a 'kind of harmonization of the conflicting tensions of the other two' (328).

5   Lehmann's assertions seem to equate the 'dramatic' (and the dramatic imagination) with conventional structurings perhaps associated with (neo-)classical and social realist theatre, whereas I argue that theatrical drama, such as that considered here, is frequently demonstrably unconstrained by confinements to interpersonal relationships and narrative closure. I would suggest that Lehmann's example of *L'Age d'Or* is a successful, but not 'remarkable', theatre event, in that it potentially creates a situation whereby, for some spectators, 'the "other time" of staging had asserted itself against the reality of people's inner clock' (Lehmann 2006: 153); that a 'time of intersubjectivity' is not necessarily 'a homogeneous time' (154). Moreover, I contend dramatic theatre may continue to activate 'the dynamic capacity of the gaze to produce processes, combinations and rhythms on the basis of the data provided by the stage' and transform 'temporal events into *images for contemplation*' by the dynamizing of 'durational stasis' (157, original emphasis): whether through the images of Noh theatre and Butoh, or those of Hamlet's ghost and Macbeth's dagger, or the speech and actions of Barker's Gertrude. A 'dramaturgy of leaps in time that point to human reality and behaviour as discontinuous' (158) is not the exclusive province of epic theatre: I propose that a selective approach in designating a chronological framework is discernible in all theatre, and dramatic characters are always contradictory and complicating when well written and well performed.

6   Duffy and Norris's characterization of Good Deeds as 'ill', with faith in herself broken, reminded me of the disingenuously pitiful penultimate self-presentation of the eponymous character in Churchill's *The Skriker*.

7 Indeed, Mangan goes on to note further instances of distortions of time (such as the discrepant and anomalous, yet precisely specified, timings of the events of Faustus's orbiting of the globe, and Robin and Dick's alehouse trickery), and observes 'it is dramatically totally appropriate that Faustus and Mephistophilis should operate on a time-scale which is different from that of the real world, that time should take on a relativistic quality for them, and that they should seem to be outside the kinds of temporal rules which govern the rest of humanity' (Mangan [1987] 1989: 65).

8 Mangan observes that it represents a confirmation of an already-existing world view, 'the familiar Universe of the fifteenth- and sixteenth-century pre-Copernican scientist' (Mangan [1987] 1989: 56).

9 Wiles notes how Faustus's experience 'anticipates that of many beneficiaries of consumer society, able to take advantage of so many opportunities that they feel bereft of time because time is so finite' (Wiles 2014: 57). On the scientific relation to nature as a 'Faustian bargain', and the similar resonances of Mary Shelley's *Frankenstein* story (adapted for the stage for England's Royal National Theatre by Nick Dear in 2011), see Sheldrake (1990: 289–290).

10 This bid for suspension is, as Mangan notes, significantly 'unreal': 'an attempt to escape eternity by compressing it into the eternal moment of the present', followed by a request for the sun to rise, time to reverse and stand still, and his own subjective consciousness to be sustained and extended while the world and the devil freeze around him: 'but what the verse enacts is the very opposite of what Faustus is consciously praying for'; as he asks for his sense of an hour to be extended, 'we hear time contracting' in a span that diminishes imaginatively as he speaks the words: 'A year, a month, a week, a natural day' (Mangan [1987] 1989: 89).

11 As Booth observes, this is identifiable at the level of individual words in which Shakespeare recurrently demonstrates a playful interest: terms (like *cleave*) that have one meaning in one context, and an opposite meaning in another, and words (like *dear* or *care*) that have good or bad connotations depending on context or perspective (Booth 1983: 37).

12 Booth observes, '*Love's Labour's Lost* seems not only inconsequential but doggedly determined to maintain its inconsequence', even as it 'persistently beckons its audience up dark mental alleys ordinarily hidden from audiences moving, carefree, along the gracefully cut paths of situation comedy' (Booth 1983: 75).

13 Dufourmantelle further observes how sex may (at least seem) to offer a suspension of time, at least for the duration of a conjunction of the bodies of two people who feel they have, 'at that instant, no more accounts to render to time' (Dufourmantelle 2007: 18): 'sex answers to our anguish at being in time through the rediscovered grace of instants miraculously spared from any duration' (38).

14 Dufourmantelle again offers resonant considerations on love, desire, hunger and oblivion (81).

15 'I Have Been Here Before': a documentary presented by Francis Spufford and directed by Mark Burman, first broadcast by BBC Radio 4 on 14 September 2014. Dunne was also a keen fly-fisher of river trout – like the protagonist of Jez Butterworth's *The River*, a play which is discussed later.

16 Eliot also argued that his employers, the publishers Faber and Faber, should republish Dunne's work. Spufford suggests, in the aforementioned documentary, that Dunne's

theories may also have been inspirational to H. G. Wells, W. H. Auden, Rumer Godden, Flann O'Brien and J. L. Borges.

17 Arthur Miller's play *The American Clock* features a witty observation from one character who is a staff writer of Superman comics; she observes how the fantasy of the superhero represents a possibility of justice beyond the terms of the current society: 'You can't have justice under capitalism, so the implications are terrific' (Miller 1983: 63).

18 Miller states that the germination of his play *Death of a Salesman* was the concept that 'nothing in life comes "next", but that everything exists together and at the same time within us; that there is no past to be "brought forward" in a human being, but that he is his past at every moment and that the present is merely that which his past is capable of noticing and smelling and reacting to' (Miller 1981: 24).

19 As Billington observes, the Stage Manager's philosophical tone may now seem 'uncomfortably like George W. Bush', or Ronald Reagan before him (Billington 2004).

20 Specian, E., 'Critical Analysis', http://www.twildersociety.org/works/the-long-christmas-dinner/ accessed 25/09/2014.

21 Favorini notes how the time scheme(s) of Wilder's play is not simply sequential but complex and 'recombinative' in a way that reflects both heredity and environment (Favorini 2008: 131).

22 For example, the Stage Manager might present the achievements of Mrs Gibbs and Mrs Webb, focused for decades on washing, cleaning a house and bringing up children, with '*never a nervous breakdown*' (Wilder 2007: 175) in a way that is not ironic about their avoidance of such a susceptibility, but finds it genuinely remarkable.

23 The birthday is itself a phenomenon that calls forth (usually, to some degree, as a matter of wider social focus) a personal 'structure of interlocking memories', to use a phrase from Carlson, which leads into his discussion of 'ghosting' in Tadeusz Kantor's 'poignantly entitled' final theatrical work, *Today is my Birthday* (1990), a work containing self-consciously retrospective qualities (Carlson 2001: 104–105). The birthday's associations of an occasion for personal intensity of self-consciousness, and usually socially recognized, contribute to its particular resonances as a dramatic occasion for the unconventionally solitary events depicted in Beckett's *Krapp's Last Tape*.

24 More recently analogues or echoes of *The Skin of our Teeth* might be the scenery deconstructed around the protagonist in Anthony Neilson's *Realism* (2006), and the skittering on a line, which turns into multiple explored possibilities, in the 'Heart's Desire' section of Caryl Churchill's *Blue Heart* (1997).

25 Wilder unfolds his (mixed) feelings about Shaw in an essay, Wilder 2007: 725–730.

26 Priestley's play *Music at Night* (written 1938) develops more overtly musical analogies, and specifications of tempo, in its dramatic orchestrations of characters' soliloquies.

27 If *Their Very Own and Golden City* were to be performed in Britain now, some of its lines would contain ironies not foreseeable at the time of its premiere in 1976. I am thinking particularly of Act One, scene eight, and Andy's scorn for 'New Labour' – which echoes the rebranding campaign undertaken by the British Labour Party from the mid-1990s to the early 2000s under the leaderships of Tony Blair and Gordon Brown, involving the party's embrace of market economics and movement to the right. Andy promptly

dismisses the immediate achievements as 'patchwork', a criticism that echoes those of various critics of the New Labour governments, from Jimmy Reid to Andrew Giddings, with particular reference to their international, educational, health and environmental policies.

28   Wilcher sees a more balanced counterpoint in the play, preserved if the 'frame' of the cathedral remains onstage throughout the performance: 'The return to 1926 twice in each act then affords a powerful dramatic realization of two contradictory perspectives on time as the matrix of human endeavour: time as linear progression and time as generational cycle'; Wilcher goes on to quote Michael Anderson's observation derived from this theatrical juncture: 'While the clock of history cannot be turned back, youth, maturity and age is a pattern that repeats itself in every individual. One man's past is another man's future' (Wilcher 1991: 69).

Wesker's strategy of projecting a narrative that starts in the past, into a future, has some notable successors in the final volumes of two trilogies of novels: William Golding's 1989 novel *Fire Down Below*, the last sentence of which artfully connects apparently distant events to the reader's genealogy and present; and Cormac McCarthy's 1998 *Cities of the Plain*, which disorientatingly extends the events of a story that begins in 1952 into 2002: a future that was, at its time of publication, beyond the lived experience of its first readers, as it traced the decline in fortunes but physical survival of a principal character, implicitly challenging the 1998 reader to consider their own, as yet unknown and unknowable, parallel possibilities. Another closing instalment of a fictional trilogy, Roddy Doyle's *The Dead Republic* (2010), achieves a surprising concluding note by revealing that its narrator, born in 1901, is still alive in a contemporaneous present, 2009, at the age of 108. The promised and prospective arc of the historical trilogy evidently constitutes an attractive milieu for such projections of startlingly *extensive* time and possibilities.

29   Negri presents his own interpretation of *caritas* as a (limited) principle in Negri 2013: 217.

30   Alan Ayckbourn's 1969 play, *How the Other Half Loves*, stages two dinner parties simultaneously on the same space/set, a farcical instance of alternating rapidly between one contextualizing time frame and another.

31   Stoppard's joke about Saint Sebastian dying of fright in his play *Jumpers* might be seen as a play on the idea of Einstein's theory that space is continuous and infinitely divisible, and McTaggart's argument that the transitional aspect of time is purely subjective (Stoppard 1986).

Interlude 1

'Why don't you all just f-f-fade away'?: Further Thoughts on Staging Ageing

Mangan, in *Staging Ageing*, considers how ageing and becoming old are matters that defy generalization, even as they raise issues of value, politics and meaning. In this, ageing and becoming old are like time, of which they are indexical, and explorations of the process and discrepant perceptions of ageing are inevitably and significantly recurrent in the examples of theatre that I have selected for our focus. Social, cultural and material factors – along with aspects such as race and gender – are crucially specific determinants in the experiences and narratives of ageing (Mangan 2013: 19). For example, wealth may buy healthcare, and in some countries this is an even more pressing concern than in others. However, not even wealth can entirely circumvent the crucial limitations (including limitations of choice, and of the promise of increasing wealth) associated with ageing. This may be a factor in increased anxiety in later life, particularly for those who have placed their faith in the insulations of wealth. Hence, anxiety may not diminish with age, in all respects – *au contraire* in many cases. This raises the question: does ageing bring a sense of 'the interconnectedness of things' (as suggested in Plato's *Republic*, quoted in Mangan 2013: 19) – or is ageing a matter of *dis*connections, including from other versions of the self, in at least some instances? Ian Stuart-Hamilton has presented the questions of old age in terms of a binary: 'heroic summation of all that has passed, or as an agonizing brooding on all that has been lost?' (Stuart-Hamilton 2011: 17). This foregrounds a radical search for meaning, albeit in polarized and apparently exclusive 'either-or' terms. Segal similarly notes the prevalent binary of two cultural narratives: ageing well and ageing badly (Segal 2014: 17), and observes how it might, rather, be more appropriate to think less in terms of an essential core self and more in terms of 'multiple continuities over time', involving both memory and fantasy, where the self is not reflected by its present manifestations only (25). A principal challenge here, and elsewhere, is summarized by Adam: 'how to theorize the temporal discontinuity wrought by the social relations of clock time in the context of embodied continuity' (Adam 2004: 116).

Mangan notes how the stock figure of the old man commonly embodies various negative associations of age with an inappropriateness that is nevertheless integral to much comic theatre: *senex iratus*, the repressive and dominating father-figure who would block romantic resolution, and *senex amans*, the besotted and/or predatory ageing suitor to a much younger woman (Mangan 2013: 179–180). The old man as (legitimated) object of ridicule is fiercely dramatized in Ben Jonson's *Epicoene* (1609) with the character significantly named Morose.[1] Comedy at the expense of the *senex* exemplifies what Weitz describes as the farcical note that wages 'comic war against pretence, rigidity and civilised thought cut off from its corporeal basics' (Weitz 2016: 29). Weitz further notes Davis's distillation that characterizes farce as confrontation with 'the inescapable facts that all human dignity is at the mercy of the human body and its appetites and needs; and that those bodies themselves are imprisoned by the space/time continuum' (Davis 2003: 3).

We might also note how some more recent theatre has subverted the associations of the *senex*, including inherent comic potential and the frequent principal characteristic of impairment of memory: notably, Beckett's *Krapp* (though Pinter, Thomas and Ridley will also depict failures and discrepancies of memory occurring for the young and middle-aged, to particularly disturbing effects, distinct from the generously pardoning principle of forgetting that is dramatized in *Antony and Cleopatra*). Wesker's *Shylock* (1976) purposefully complicates the relationship between a (historically informed and aware) representative of one generation and those of another, who presume their 'enlightened' superiority but demonstrate insensitive philistinism. Barker's *The Twelfth Battle of Isonzo* (2001) brings persistently surprising, poignant and unsettling depths to the premise of betrothal of old man to young woman.

Mangan briefly considers an unsettling modern device for 'play-acting' the process of ageing: prosthetic 'empathy suits', which were designed to give younger people a foretaste of obstructed agilities (Mangan 2013: 51–52). Fortunately, physical changes and limitations associated with age (which suits and computer 'apps' offer to simulate[2]), and even the disorienting loss of memory, do not constitute the 'whole story' of ageing. The prosthetic suit omits (and cannot provide a simulation of) wisdom, acceptance, wry humour, self-knowledge, the ability to make connections, see through contemporary cant and offer a more informed (and often less materialistic) perspective, support, advice, guidance on the basis of experience and deduction and developed interests, which might, even at the 'last ditch', permit an ultimate, but authentic, self-willed reinvention. *Oedipus at Colonus* by Sophocles establishes the tragic template for the dramatization of the older citizen who would prefer a dignified withdrawal, but finds that modern *realpolitik*, and the injurious dismissiveness of its top-down 'management', draw him back to active intervention: one may discern the resonances of this protagonist in Priestley's *The Linden Tree*, Bond's *Lear* (1971) and Rudkin's *Merlin Unchained* (2009). In *Merlin Unchained* the protagonist, often heroically idealized, initially struggles to remember: precisely because he considers his achievements in unusually existentially harrowing terms, comparable to those of Stuart-Hamilton's binary, above. However, Rudkin's play (considered in more detail in the next chapter) also dramatizes a sense of (inter)personal connection and ultimate existential obligation, in relation to which, a further observation by Mangan is particularly resonant: to 'remember the past is, whether we like it or not, to perform a creative act in the present' (Mangan 2013: 124). The template of *Oedipus at Colonus* is also visible, in both homage and wry subversive projection, in Rudkin and Barker's simultaneously written plays about the last days of Euripedes: *Macedonia* (2015) and *Dog Death in Macedonia* (2015).

If ageing brings opportunities for late-stage instances of both connection with and disconnection from others, manifestations of dementia and memory stage a disconnective subjectivity (likened to the discourse of *Godot* as part of a wider account by Kiper 2015), at worst a 'crime against time', which erodes and reduces yet repeatedly stages 'death with the living' (Lewis 2010: 113). Florian Zeller's *The Father* (2014) and Nicola Wilson's *Plaques and Tangles* (2015) are recent plays that offer theatrical explorations of the discomforting manifestations of (sensed and prospective) discontinuity between a subject's own past and present selves. A notable recent tragicomedy of discontinuity is *Clockwork* (2012) by Laura Poliakoff, whose theatrical career itself represents a succession of generations. *Clockwork* takes place in a care home in 2065, where two characters who might represent today's apparent careless youth find themselves considering whether to extend their principally joyless proximity (no longer even relieved by recourse to sexual fantasies on the virtual reality headsets, which are broken) or to decide on disconnection, represented by visit to a euthanasia clinic. *Clockwork* updates the image of state care home, and its professed benevolence, as metaphor for the wider erosion of social values[3]: we learn from the 'senile delinquent' inmate Carl, and his long-suffering lifetime companion Mikey, how many pensioners have turned to crime, in a dystopian future characterized by (breezily unconcerned) disintegration. Though Carl is fiercely unsentimental ('Dignity's over-rated') in his resistances of a narrative of inevitable decline, even he baulks at the idea of an organized 'party' when the term has degenerated, from denoting 'a piss-up, a rave, or an orgy', to licensing at best 'a bunch of cripples eating cake' (Poliakoff 2012: 23). Poliakoff's stage directions are constantly important in modulating the tragicomedy of the play (mindful of 'the mixed experiences of old age, in which beauty, pain, resilience and resistance intermingle, while time appears more fluid' [Segal 2014: 173]). Characters react to disclosures with shock and embarrassment, struggling to maintain bravado as their confidence in their own memories (and, therefore, their personal narratives) is persistently, increasingly contradicted and eroded. Mikey finally tells Carl that he is leaving the home, to live with the daughter who Carl thinks is his. Mikey reveals that Carl has developed a brain tumour from implanting a 'memory clip' that holds comforting fabrications of events, including transpositions of other people's experiences and relationships. Carl wishes to deny this, but is increasingly disoriented by dimly emergent recollections that unsettle his convictions, and suggest that he has sought to transform his observations of others into his experiences: this revelation points to his increasing and irrevocable separation from others. Carl's final release into a posthumous fantasy involves a reunion with the ('live', or disappointingly animatronic?) figure of his revered ex-girlfriend (shared with Mikey): a wry, fragile, fantastic subversion of the increasingly dominant narrative of isolation and decline, and of the final scene of *A Winter's Tale*.

Kaite O'Reilly's *Cosy* (2016) is a blithely comic theatrical exploration of the potential impulse and right to assisted suicide, in the context of family manners and politics. Despite her family's assurances of her likely longevity, the protagonist Rose insists that a principal feature of existence being bearable is 'the certainty it's finite' (O'Reilly 2016: 244). Indeed, even as her daughter Camille professes indefatigable idealism and care, she acknowledges that her own experiences of social interaction suggest that 'The older and wiser I get, the less substantial my opinion becomes. I'm invisible' (233). Rose decides to reject the constantly 'moving line' of reconciliation to persistence, insisting 'Life means so much to me, I will not settle for anything else and I will not accept this living death as a substitute' (296). O'Reilly's play identifies losing heart with despair, and death with neither. Rather, death may offer a decisive resistance of 'the cowardice of flesh' that hangs on 'to repetition as if it were hope' (Rabey 2004: 43).

Notes

1 Constraints of time and space oblige me to leave analysis of the figure of the old woman in theatre to someone else: Noah's Wife and The Witch of Edmonton might figure in the early stages of this.

2 Playfully transformative computer 'apps' (such as the significantly titled Facebook) interestingly tend to concentrate on the 'face' (the principal focus of the mobile phone and 'selfie'), although the rest of the body would follow in implication: something perhaps too horrible (and insufficiently 'fun') to contemplate? Mangan includes no reference to 'body-ageing apps': maybe that is the point at which the 'empathy' is principally 'aborted' and the intended point of the 'empathy suit'.

3 One might identify, in this tradition, David Storey's Home (1970), in which a Beckettian sense of personal drift and disconnection is to some degree naturalized to a social realist context; Dale Wasserman's 1963 stage adaptation of Ken Kesey's 1962 novel, One Flew Over the Cuckoo's Nest (filmed by Milōs Forman in 1975); Peter Weiss's Marat/Sade (1963); and Peter Flannery's Singer (1989), in which the care-home is extended into logically projected economic terminus of the Conservative state. The offering of an animatronic dog as a surrogate companion in Clockwise may recall for some a similar if less expressive item amongst Hamm's gathered props in Endgame.

Chapter 4

Principles of Uncertainty

My title refers to Heisenberg's theory of uncertainty, which suggests that the more precisely a position is determined, the less precisely its momentum is known at this instant; or the more accurately we measure its momentum, the less precisely we can know its position. However, instead of position and momentum, the principle can also be expressed with reference to the ultimate indeterminability of both energy and time: 'the more constrained the one variable is, the less constrained the other is' (Jha 2013). Wesker's play *The Friends* (1970) refers to this theory explicitly, as a principle that shifts the dominant paradigm of the world from 'an *exact and predictable* pattern into a *blur of probabilities*'; this subsequently informs theories of quantum mechanics which suggest that descriptions of processes in space and time can never be completely definitive, because the observation is another event that those processes undergo (Wesker 1980: 103, original emphasis), which, of course, has further ethical implications. *The Friends* dramatizes attempts by fictional characters to overcome fear in their '*knowledge of death*' (126) and make senses of their (notional) pasts, presents and futures, creating a space and time where audience members may similarly reflect on how their pasts, present and futures may intersect (one might here recall Saint Augustine's useful offer of distinctions: 'The present considering the past is memory, the present considering the present is immediate awareness, the present considering the future is expectation' [Augustine 1998: 235]).

The drama and theatre of Beckett, Pinter, Barker and others considered in this chapter offer less immediately representational, but more directly disorientating, experiences of uncertainty, which forestall the usual direct and immediate terms of conceptual reflection (by characters and audiences, though several characters seem compelled to *attempt* this, and fail, engagingly). Beckett, Pinter and Barker present dramatic situations that are, physically and verbally, extremely spatially and rhythmically precise but, with regard to setting, temporally indeterminate: dislocations from contextual familiarity in which the characters express and explore the exacerbation of their own sense of *character time*, which heightens and extends a *strangely* absorbing and elastic consciousness of *audience time*, in which onstage events re-present identifiable experiences and associations of time (lassitude, impatience, the defensive rigidities of routine, attempted self-orientations in the topography of our existence) in extreme (and, paradoxically, strangely energized) forms, like reflections in a distorting mirror. For example, our processes of memory are selective: in *Waiting for Godot*, Estragon and Vladimir try to maintain a sense of purposeful decision (even a suicidal one) but their senses of resolution and consequence are undermined by their difficulties in remembering which day it is, or the events of yesterday; whereas in various Pinter plays, in the words of Chris Megson, 'memories are weaponised', in deliberate and conscious choices and (sometimes lethally) precise selections of the unsettling 'artillery of relentless interpersonal combat' (Megson 2014: 223). The rhythms of action – in which I include speech – are also sharpened in performances of both introspection and interaction. Indeed, musicality of language is an integral feature of the dramatic writing of Beckett, Pinter, Barker, Thomas and green, beyond the forms of sound: rhythms, silences, metre and cadences delineate a character's impulses, both manifest and subdued, reflecting patterns of thought and emotion. These dramatists assemble rigorously precise and detailed rhythmic scaffoldings by which to approach experiences of startling indeterminacy, by presenting theatrical spatial metaphors for simultaneous fixity and uncertainty, explored and reinforced through cadences of verbal repetition and hiatus. The work of the dramatists principally considered in this chapter also counters what Juliet Stevenson has identified as a central problem for the older female theatre performer (and, by extension, spectator): 'As you go through life it gets more and more interesting and complex, but the parts offered get more and more simple, and less complicated' (quoted in Segal 2014: 38).[1]

Beckett: Marking time/shoring up the debris

We wait in the anticipation of (and based on the consistency of) what we know. Early on in Beckett's *Waiting for Godot*, the script directs Vladimir to look '*wildly about*', '*as though the date was inscribed in the landscape*'; tellingly, he perceives and describes the audience as a 'bog' of indeterminate liquidity, capable of confirming nothing (Beckett 1986: 15). This contains a knowing element of metatheatrical comedy, which may (depending on the playing) permit the audience a wry chuckle, but it also disarmingly suggests that the audience might surrender faith and presumption in their own superiority and reliability as temporal co-ordinates. Vladimir begins the play reunited with Estragon, on one of two dramatized evenings (so there is potential license for a lighting design to lengthen shadows and fade brightness during the action of each half): Estragon is proclaimed 'there' again (though not 'here' – he represents an unshared perspective external to the viewer, Vladimir), though thought 'gone forever' (10). The duo try to draw reassurance from the actions and pronouncements of Pozzo with Lucky, establishing identifiable notions and circumstances that, 'So long as one knows', need not cause worry; 'One can bide one's time', knowing what to expect (36): ironically, Pozzo's first major speech seems to associate the regular fall of night with the unforeseeable nature and reach of global catastrophe. A disorientating sense of protean temporal relativity, allied with the requirement to persist, seems the principal identifiable characteristics of the *Godot* world: the first encounter with Pozzo and Lucky is deemed by Vladimir to have 'passed the time'; Estragon sardonically observes, 'It would have passed in any case', and Vladimir agrees, with a vestige of gratitude, but adds 'not so rapidly' (45). Vladimir also remarks on how Pozzo and Lucky have 'changed', though does not specify how; the audience cannot discern the terms of this change on the basis of a first encounter, and Estragon cannot confirm this on the basis of his lack of memory, though adding its probability: 'They all change. Only we can't' (48). Vladimir and Estragon seem required to mark time, in the two distinct senses of that idiom: from the original context of a military command, maintaining a rhythm through action, but without moving in any direction in the usual meaningful ways, a prescribed motion that frustrates and mocks the usual associations of 'progress'; and from the civilian context, the transferred and amended sense of occupying oneself with some relatively superficial preoccupation, whilst waiting for something more decisive (usually beyond one's immediate control) to occur, such as the opportunity for interaction with someone of superior power.

When Act Two opens, Beckett's stage directions specify '*Next Day. Same Time. Same Place*' and that '*The tree has four or five leaves*' (54). This remarkably accelerated burgeoning suggests a naturally resurgent seasonal cycle. Vladimir's song of the transgressive dog establishes a different keynote: a cycle of narrative, like a wheel spinning without traction, which generates its own insistent persistence, but in which perspective multiplies and closure recedes even as the singer persists in the tale of dogs trying to lay one of their numbers to rest. Estragon sees nothing remarkable in the tree when Vladimir directs attention to it, and cannot recall their suicidal initiative to hang themselves from it. Their subsequent dialogue seeks to establish common ground in what Estragon may remember. Vladimir subsequently reflects on how a sense of time levies a pressure to derive meaning (Beckett 1986: 47). He suggests that the passage of time demands reflexive actions and processes that tend towards habit, itself a bid to maintain reason through a thought or action repeated to a point of fixity, an automatic response to context that would seem in itself ultimately to occlude reason; however, it is only by an appeal to 'follow my reasoning' that Vladimir can even *seek* to establish a perspective or co-ordinate (intrinsically flawed and subjective, given the worst scenario) on the continuing viability of their shared sense of 'reason', which Vladimir's continuing reflections give him causes to doubt.[2] Again, there is a cyclical quality to Vladimir's argument, which offers neither confirmation nor regeneration. Indeed, it suggests that a part of the self may have been 'straying in the night' with a disturbing, splintered, inscrutable autonomy (presaging the central activity and unsettling turn of Beckett's 1955 novel *Molloy*, in which the stone-sucking vagrant who is tracked by a compulsively orderly private detective seems increasingly to be a facet of the detective's own personality in degeneration). Estragon is more phlegmatic, dispensing with any pretention to authoritative perspective: 'We all are born mad. Some remain so' (74).

When Pozzo reappears, he is further adrift through loss of sight, incapable of judging (con)sequence: 'The blind have no notion of time' (79) (Vladimir's immediate aside, 'I could have sworn it was the opposite', evokes the theatrical trope of the tragic insight of the blinded seer, such as Oedipus, only to reveal it debunked). Furthermore, Lucky has gone dumb. Vladimir asks, 'Since when?' (the answer to which would seem to be, since what was designated 'yesterday', apparently, in terms of character time), which vexes Pozzo further, driving him to plead for an end to this torment 'with your accursed time' (82). Pozzo has lost all sense of consequence beyond that of entropic decline, which occurs with a foreclosing rapidity so startling as to mock any pretention to wider significance: the birth and death of each individual effectively occuring 'the same day, the same second', with life an instant's 'gleam' before 'night once more' (82). However, this description of a sudden tempo does not generally accord with the theatrical configurations (I hesitate to say, 'processes', which may be more appropriate to what is left to the audience, in reflection on theatrical experience) of the actions in *Waiting for Godot*. Vladimir consciously recasts Pozzo's image of the birth astride a grave in terms of a gradual incongruity yoking the natal and the terminal: 'lingeringly, the grave-digger puts on the forceps' (83) (an image strangely redolent of a war hospital in its laconic response to the collapsing categories of emergencies). Vladimir re-visions the apparent dispensation: 'We have time to grow old'; and if 'the air is full of our cries' there is apparently (and appallingly) nothing to which you cannot become accustomed and indifferent – 'habit is a great deadener' (83). Even then, he experiences a desperate surge into feverish activity of attempted, failed consequence, exclaiming 'I can't go on!', then immediately asking 'What have I said?' (83). Their meeting with Godot is deferred again, and Vladimir claims 'Everything's dead but the tree'. Finally (?) they agree and determine to 'go', only to remain dutifully at post, marking time in deference to an inconsistent (despotically vague and/or wilful?) authority. Barbara Adam observes that the process of waiting, by which one demonstrates one's maturity through patience and compliance, nevertheless 'affirms that time is not exhausted by its symbolic formation and expression', and that any 'shared meanings', in the knowledge on which the activity of waiting purports to be based, are 'not necessarily available to us at a discursive level of consciousness' (Adam 1990: 126). *Waiting for Godot* gives theatrical expression to these very intimations.

Beckett's *Endgame* (1958) focuses on the desirability and difficulty of the end of a time – and the promise of cessation and closure – from its first lines: 'Finished, it's finished, nearly finished, it must be nearly finished' (Beckett 1986: 93). However, when Hamm asks what the time is, Clov offers only the bleak prolongation of an infernally eternal, fundamentally unchanging, present: the time is the 'same as usual' (94), though Clov has 'had enough' of the indeterminate 'thing' – a process of winding down which may, or may not, end (94); but the sense that 'this has gone on long enough' is precisely what makes it 'a day like any other day' (114). In the wasteland over which Hamm presides, nature is detectable only in terms of decay, entropy and disillusion (the loss of hair, teeth, bloom and ideals), and the erosive passage and navigation of time ('getting on' [99]) is wryly and overtly acknowledged as 'slow work' (97), given the characters' spatial, physical and consequential restrictions, eased only by diminishing supplies of painkiller that might blunt the calibrations of consciousness. Hamm has intimations of a process in his '*anguished*' sense of sliding, barely perceptible occurrence, described by Clov as the beginning of an end of 'Something', which is 'taking its course' (98). However, even this may be a feverish and deluded bid to elude the still point of nihilism and a loss of significance in time, 'To think perhaps it won't all have been for nothing!' (108). Clov's impatience with 'the same inanities' (114) is contradicted, and extrapolated, by Hamm's fearful retentiveness of his own contracting power that he nevertheless associates with his own remaining attributes of identity and performance (in his repeated cadence, 'Me to play'). It is this ludicrously misplaced sense of defiant tragic stature that nevertheless seems to assist Hamm to a sense of an ending when he tells Clov 'I don't need you any more' (131); Clov, despite his professions of impatience, seems incapable of significant personal independence, which may be involved in suffering 'better' (132). The glimpse of the child in the wasteland outside their shelter represents 'the moment' Hamm may have been waiting for: a possible logic of natural succession that may convince him to 'Discard' attempts at control, renounce the activity of his will and release his own narrative into an arc of dissolution, which is nevertheless consciously shaped and accepted – 'Moments for nothing, now as always, time was never and time is over, reckoning closed and story ended' (133) – performed until only the theatrical props and postures (the 'old stancher', the physical configurations and dress of the characters in '*tableau*') remain. *Endgame* depicts a process by which the trappings and figures of tragedy ('Old endgame lost of old') are rendered by Beckett as arthritically rusted clockwork automata (mechanically and reflexively re-presenting hubristic king, impatient retainer) running down: theatrical jetsam, postures and proclamations hollowed out to pure form, vestigial means towards their own evacuation ('play and lose and have done with losing' [132]), and the still point of activity ceased, uncertainty ended, apparently.

Beckett's *That Time* (1976) depicts an immobilized Listener, and three externalized voices recalling former junctures of his life: their incantations circle around a last visit to a 'ruin where you hid as a child' (Beckett 1986: 388), where the former trams have disappeared but the rusted rails remain; the respite of rest and contemplation in a dry, warm but almost deserted Portrait Gallery, until 'on to hell out of there' (388); a lover's vow on rock resembling a millstone. The recollections overlap as if in three separate waves of tidal rhythm that, though separate in their source, call forth and cue each other: for example, the action of peering at a portrait in oils of a famous prince or princess now 'black with age and dirt' recalls another active peering, at the face of the lover, the memory of whom can prompt 'tears without fail till they dried up altogether' (390). The Listener and his voices are seeking to establish 'something you could never be the same after' (390), notably dramatic events, in a process consciously redolent of the fictions that inform even intricacies of childhood play: the vividness of narrative self-fragmentation and dramatization, imaginative actions of 'making it all up' in conversations 'now one voice now another', which is often abandoned into adulthood. The voices recognize their own activities as attempts at shoring up the debris (the fragments of a life, what Krapp would call 'my dust') to 'keep out the void' and 'shroud' (390): an acknowledgement that presages a ten-second silence of audible breath before the Listener's eyes close in pursuit of an enquiry. Though compulsively identifying 'turning points' ('that was a great word with you'), which were decisive, 'the one the first and last', the confluence of space and time that left the subject 'making it up from there' (390), Listener recalls even an abandonment of professed self-knowledge, 'you started not knowing who you were from Adam', and 'trying how that would work for a change'; though this, in turn, yields to a reminder of how even the faces in the portrait gallery were considerately marked with temporal co-ordinates: the frames dating their subjects 'in case you might get the century wrong' (391); and the scrupulous observance of physical distance between himself and his lover on the sunlit rock, 'always space between if only an inch no pawing', creating a tension of abstinence or deferral that was frustrating if perhaps painfully enlivening, suggested by the artfully elliptical phrase: 'if it wasn't for the vows' (391). He even seems to have attempted, 'for a change', a complete abandonment of self, 'how never having been would work' (391), embracing a vagrancy until limbs and head 'dried up' or 'gave up' (392), but memory proves irrepressible: 'scene float up and there you were' (392). Destitution and age seem to bring in a time of 'always winter then', slipping into the refuges of public spaces/buildings such as libraries and post offices, but the drift, when 'huddled on the doorstep', towards an imminent terminal state – suggested by another ten-second pause (392) – is averted by a re-visioning of the 'same scenes', 'making it up that way to keep it going' (393), like the child talking to himself, 'breaking up' talk into 'two or more' and 'being together that way' (393). The Listener seems to appreciate that all the instants involved in 'making yourself up for the millionth time', even (or especially) where fact and fiction might prove inextricable ('hard to believe you even you made up that bit'), constitute times 'when you were never the same after' (394): no single point in time proves decisive, it is the compulsive succession of moments (in and out of sequence) that forms a sense of self. Even in a series of attempted relinquishments in different contexts – 'gave up for good and let it in' (394), 'away to hell out of it and never come back' (395), a sudden awareness of nothing but 'dust' (395) – no single event can be proved decisive: until what *perhaps* may be an external, heard voice proclaims the brevity of life and death ('come and gone in no time' [395]). The Listener's surprising smile, *'toothless for preference'* (395), suggests an unpredictably resurgent acceptance of ageing and self through time(s), or at least a spirit of non-avoidance: a riposte to Krapp's (self-)restrictions to 'sour cud' and twilight regret – a dwelling on, even delight in, the debris.

If *That Time* partly interrogates and reverses the conclusions of *Krapp's Last Tape*, *Footfalls* (1976) provides a sympathetic dramatization of how and why the compulsive process of 'making up' the self in time might reflexively prefer displacement in time and space, rather than the unlikely, defiant reconciliation that ends *That Time*. In *Footfalls*, the sense of a personal 'turning point', which initially impelled the hunt of *That Time's* Listener, has shrunken to a physical pacing, a doubling-back in *'clearly audible rhythmic tread'*, a more specifically contextualized marking of time than the scenes of estranged abstraction, arrested dynamism and co-dependence in *Waiting for Godot* and *Endgame*. *Footfalls* traces the exhausted dreamlike perception of a bedridden nonagenarian mother (disembodied on stage, fictionally imprisoned within a degenerating body in her terminally prolonged character time), and the daughter (in her forties) who tends to her, to the point of her own somnambulant exhaustion. Time in the 'intensive care' of Beckett's theatre increasingly resembles, even reflects, the personal specificity associated with terminal illness: the way that night-time dismisses the distractions of the day, and becomes 'a reaffirmation of everything that is internalized', enforcing a 'one-to-one relationship' between the subject and their conscience, consciousness, unconsciousness and reality: wearyingly when the body needs sleep whereas the mind needs to reflect (Adam 1995: 55). In performance, *Footfalls* maintains a relentless focus on the rhythmic physical activity of May's pacing, her dutiful self-sacrifice and deferral of wider initiative (domestically immured and 'not out since girlhood' [401]), which will prove irrevocable: formally *apparently* compassionate, May nevertheless extends no statement of forgiveness to her mother when she requests it (whether for her own infirmity or for May's birth, these seem elided). May is also relentlessly (and even perhaps terminally?) reflective, pointedly 'revolving it all' in her 'poor mind' (400), in ways that her movements seem to indicate, reflect and demonstrate to her mother. Her mother provides commentary on May's compulsive action, which requires sound as well as motion, and her bid to 'tell how it was' (401). However, the mother's voice and May's steps cease. Beckett repositions May so that the audience experience a crucially different perspective for her own narrative commentary: on how a similarly 'most strange girl, though scarcely a girl any more' (402) slips away by night to a personal vigil at a church, pacing unto a sensed point of personal 'vanishing', into the vision of a 'semblance' of tangled 'tatters' (402). In what seems to be a compulsive fictional self-displacement, May revolves the letters of her name (and its indication of potential) into the dramatic character of 'Amy', who disavows her own presence when her mother recalls a 'strange' thing at Evensong. Yet even this attempted process/scenario of self-displacement gives way and returns May to the same activity of pacing, marking time and 'revolving it all' in her 'poor head', perhaps because the fictionally resurgent figure of the mother, and her perspective, seems to occlude those of the daughter, 'Necessarily' (402). Finally there is a precise fade until *No trace of MAY* and a further ten seconds before fade out of lights (403), a stage direction that seems a thoroughgoing extension, more precisely realized in stage time and sound (Beckett specifies *'Pause for echoes'* [403]), of J. B. Priestley's concluding stage direction that *'the Conways have gone'* at the end of *Time and the Conways* (Priestley 1969: 82). It may be that time ultimately achieves an effacement of the residual May, in ways that she herself cannot, unaided. Her own testimony and ritually repeated actions seem to be her bid to shore up the debris of her life into narrative meaning; however, the immersive focus on her pacing, which ends in the thoroughness of her final vanishing, foregrounds the bleaker sense that she has been marking time.

Rockaby (1981) continues the investigation of what Krapp calls 'last fancies' (Beckett 1986: 222), terminal siftings and (ironically restless) reflexes of seeking meaning in closure. *Rockaby* depicts an isolated Woman ritually dressed, like a funereal Miss Haversham, in 'best black', which we are told recalls her mother's garb, designed to catch the light and eyes of others even as it suggests consignment. The Woman also cues, as if to *try on*, a narrative by that which is discernibly *'Her recorded voice'*, positing a decisive moment identified in a repeated and differently inflected (and perhaps paced) phrase: 'time she stopped/*time she stopped*' (Beckett 1986: 435, original emphasis). The reiteration insists on a deepening of engagement with the potential resonances of the words, a recognition that it is the apt time to cease activity, and on a sudden uncanny sense of temporal suspension. The voice suggests that the activity in question ('going to and fro', 'high and low') has been intended and performed for 'another creature like herself', or at least the prospect of one 'a little like' (435), until this founders on a scepticism regarding the possibility of this witness, 'whom else'? (436). Like Hamm in *Endgame*, she looks out through her window ('all eyes'), 'facing other windows', for evidence of 'another living soul', until finally sighting two significant alterations that defy presumptions: 'a blind up like hers/a little like', but also 'one blind up no more' (439). This sense of an audience, discernible if dwindling, seems to impel her to rock in her mother's chair 'till her end came/in the end came' ([440], a phrase that tellingly extrapolates even the prospective occurrence of cessation and adds an artful echo of '*Endgame*'), until sensing an unfamiliar sense of direction – 'time she went right down' – and audience/purpose: 'was her own other/own other living soul' (441). This leads into resolution provided, or at least marked, by new notes of relinquishment in her rhythmic litany of self-propulsion: 'done with that', 'fuck life' (442). Speech and action cease and decay into '*echo*' and '*coming to rest of rock*', then '*slow fade out*' (442), presenting and demanding an unusually insistent focus on sonic and physical entropy, as something that is nevertheless self-willed, promising relief, detachment.

Rockaby characteristically enfolds character(s?), performer and spectator in a characteristically Beckettian heightened awareness of the irreconcilable senses of *character time*, as well as a heightened and implicating awareness of *performance time*: how can the character and performer find the right inflections of a specifically restricted range of words and actions to 'go right down' and stop (time)? Is the spectator 'standing in' for the 'one other living soul' that might provide witness, and meaning, for the character's performance? If so, is their own time figured and reflected back as a blind 'coming up' or 'going down'? How much time does *s/he* have? An intently directed attunement to time, such as may be experienced both in moments of anxious emergency, and in concentrated focus on consciously heightened theatricality, transforms, distorts and distends subjective experiences of time, slowing down pace in sharper and deeper perceptions of detail. In a near-echo of *Rockaby*, Zarrilli writes of the actor's body becoming 'all eyes'[3]; this also extends to when spectators become 'all eyes' and ears, in an appreciation of an unusually high-level, or rare event, performance (theatrically, the anticipation and pleasure of watching a masterful actor seizing the challenge of in a highly demanding role), in terms delineated by Klein: when the 'realization that sublime moments never last makes them seem far more precious', a conscious recognition of 'the value of the moment we are experiencing' makes us 'try to savour every aspect of it'; hence 'the very awareness that time is fleeting serves to extend time' (Klein 2008: 69).

Beckett explores anxiety most keenly in *Play* (1963) and *Not I* (1972), where time becomes relentlessly and hellishly extrapolated. *Play*'s depiction of an infernal triangle stipulates a repeat rendering of the text, which 'may be an exact replica of the first statement' or 'may present an element of variation' (Beckett 1986: 320). In practice, any attempt to repeat a word or gesture will be dynamic (a sense of activated theatricality emerging through what Schneider calls 'the seeming gap between sameness and difference', where, if what happens once is not the same as what happens again, but 'not necessarily entirely *different* either', [Schneider 2014: 68, original emphasis]). From the perspective of the performer, Zarrilli defines acting as 'the dynamic embodied/enactive psychophysical process by which a (theatrical) world is made available at the moment of its appearance/experience for both the actors and audience', where what is conjured from imagination and/or memory – including the minutiae of timing – 'has not been reduced to a single possibility, but rather falls within *a range of appropriate possibilities* triggered by [the performer's] engagement with reading/ hearing/speaking the sentence at the moment of its saying/hearing' (Zarrilli, Daboo and Loukes 2013: 22, original emphasis). The art of performing indeterminacy is also described by Jonathan Kalb, referring to Billie Whitelaw performing Beckett in a way 'both purposeful and profound': she 'makes definite decisions that lead to confident actions onstage, but none of them resolves important ambiguities in the text' (Kalb 1989: 21) regarding identity, situation and time (I would suggest that Victoria Wicks's performances of Barker's work exemplify similar qualities). Even when an action or statement is directed to be repeated, members of the audience will also see and hear and imagine different things at different moments. For example, they will hear (and/or find imaginatively) different nuances in *Rockaby*'s refrain-couplet, 'time she stopped / *time she stopped*', when experienced both separately and sequentially, and in relation to *Play*'s reiteration, where the audience's apprehension of repetition becomes, in itself, a surprising, disturbing and intensifying moment, when instigating a process of attention by which at least some details (for example, of fixity, insistence and possible significance) will be (re)perceived anew.

Not I presents a relentless focus on, and immersion in, a thunderstruck dissociative sensibility that is traumatically fixed in a reflex of displacement, refusing to assume the first person ('no!..she!' [Beckett 1986: 382]) and thereby refusing any alteration to the rhythmic drive towards a persistent self-narration that aspires to be unique, finite and fundamentally unchanging. However, as Schneider observes, whenever citation or repetition is 'in play – as it inevitably is with gestures, stances and words – something akin to theatre' is taking place; the use of a word or gesture 'teems with other times', and couples with other uses, feelings, times and places (Schneider 2014: 7). *Not I* frames the central activity of creating a personal history in a way that shows how this history, like all histories, can be called into question, not least by exposing its overly insistent, desperately frenetic repetition. In contrast, *Ohio Impromptu* (1981) centres on a 'sad tale the last time told' and seems to end with the achievement of closure of both book and narrative process, a process of performance that permits a shared bleed of 'then' into 'now' (Schneider 2014: 40), for characters as well as audience. In *Endgame*, Hamm achieves this by active practices of resignation, occurring in the character's 'now' of performance; in *Ohio Impromptu*, it is the tracing, recounting and repetition of a history that permit the present to be enfolded into the past.

What Where (1983) is, I suggest, a Beckett play which is haunting in terms that are unique within his *oeuvre*. The dominant voice/perspective recounts a cyclical process whereby 'Time passes' through all four seasons. However, the rhythms of seasonal dormancy and regeneration have been overlaid by a man-made and systematically ordained circuit of self-vindicating suspicion, surveillance and torture, where a failure to evince the desired information results in the assumed complicity, and torture, of the torturer. The presiding despot insists on a code of consequence (in terms that have points of contact with the philosophical analysis of despotism undertaken by Lingis 2000: 42–45); he concludes 'Time passes. / That is all. / Make sense who may' (Beckett 1986: 476). This pronouncement of inscrutability fixes direction, sequence and meaning, repeatedly identifying an enemy within, to be excluded, as a means of consequential self-validation and sacrificial (but always ephemeral) security: a rationale of attention, anxiety, abjection, defacement, voraciousness and fixity, crystallized and anatomized in Beckett's most searchingly, resonantly political play.

Alphonso Lingis's description of attending the dying contains, for me, further resonances with Beckett's theatre, specifically with staged encounters with 'a time disconnected from the time of the world', and how these encounters nevertheless indicate what we must all sometime endure: the ways in which the process of dying 'takes time', extending 'a strange time that undermines the time one anticipates, a time without a future, without possibilities, where there is nothing to do but endure the presence of time' (Lingis 1994a: 173–174). Beckett's theatre manifests junctures where the approach and sensed finitude of death 'is not locatable across the succession of moments each of which presents the possibility of the next one' (Lingis 1994b: 233), *except*, perhaps, through moments in Beckett's highly distinctive theatre.

Pinter: In search of lost time

Harold Pinter's plays explore the ways that identifiable senses of time momentarily constitute or challenge senses of identity, possibility, power and relationships, through the dynamics of shared or discrepant memories: personal co-ordinates in time and space that sometimes compete with those of other individuals to establish immediate authority, even as they elude ultimate verifiability. Moreover, this is not only an interpersonal form of conflict, but also one that occurs in the terms of subjectivity. In the course of life, over a period of time, each individual will experience a series of conflicting perceptions that refuse to resolve themselves into a simple unity; as Frayn observes, 'we all reorganise our recollections, consciously or unconsciously, as time goes by, to fit our changed perceptions of a situation' (Frayn 1998: 118).[4] Pinter remarked in 1971, 'What it all comes down to is time [...] The whole question of time and all its reverberations and possible meanings really does seem to absorb me more and more' (Pinter, quoted in Megson 2014: 215). In 1972, Pinter worked on a screenplay adaptation (unmade, but published in 1978) of Marcel Proust's novel *À la recherché du temps perdu/In Search of Lost Time* (published 1913–1927) that may well have furthered and informed Pinter's sense of the present as subject to irruptions from, and portals into, the past, and the possibility of recapturing the past: not least strategically. Kristeva identifies a distinctly 'Proustian notion of temporal duration' as enabling 'us to name the irreconcilable fragments of time that are pulling us in all directions more fervently and dramatically than ever before' (Kristeva 1996: 168), which also works as a description of the dramatic process of a Pinter play.

The role of time in Pinter's plays of the 1970s is incisively considered by Chris Megson, who observes how in these plays identity is not only 'performative' and 'fluid' but also intrinsically time-based, because it is bound up with 'memory, which is conceived as a complex mode of self-presentation where emotions and expedients intersect, moment by moment, to exert control of the present' (Megson 2014: 218). These concerns are also present in Pinter's wider work: strikingly, in his early 1960 radio and television play, *A Night Out*, in which a repressed son challenges his mother's constraints of predictable order (such as the appointed time for dinner and their regular Friday night card game) with his stumbling forays into the wider social world; when she berates him, he goes to strike her with the household's audibly and relentlessly ticking clock. He later similarly threatens a girl whom he meets,[5] and recounts his memory of triumph over his mother: 'I finished the conversation … I finished it … I finished her … With this clock!' (Pinter 1991a: 371). However, he drops the clock and returns home, where his mother forgives him (his threat of violence was not, in fact, carried through), and '*His body freezes*' into a resumption of their former relations, cemented by the prospect of 'a holiday in a fortnight' (374). The frustration of sustained agency (Pinter's refinement of a Chekhovian effect) and the disintegration of consequence (which might otherwise be expressed dynamically in terms of claiming territory) are regular components in Pinter's depictions of infernal recurrence, where the defeated character is confined to regression and/or abjection (*The Birthday Party*, *The Dumb Waiter*, *A Slight Ache*; and *The Caretaker*, in which the most vulnerable character complains 'what I need is a clock in here, in this room, and then I would stand a bit of a chance. But he don't give me one', Pinter 1991b: 60). Pinter also mines discrepant memory and the conditionality of identity for comic effects in *The Lover* ([1963] in which eroticism is figured as a form of the 'forgetting' and redramatization of identity, at carefully appointed times) and the crystalline sketch 'Last to Go' ([1959] which pivots on two men's discomfortingly discrepant memories of location in space and time, and the identity and characteristics of a supposed mutual friend, but these are resolved by their mutually supportive agreement to subside into agreeing comfortably on simple instances of identifiability and predictability, such as the sense of consequence definitely confirmed by the remaining newspaper left for sale, which can therefore be designated and identified confidently as today's 'last to go').

The Homecoming (1965) shows Pinter's drama at its most tensile and pugnacious, where combative self-definition is crucially a matter of not only narrative recall but also performative *timing*. The superficial realism of the characters' linguistic and social exchanges – for example, a request for a cigarette – becomes imbued with an unusual definiteness and intent resonance (not casually 'thrown away') as characters try to establish the authority of their own perceptions, beliefs and presences, over and/or at the expense of others (for example, Max's professed expertise about horses [Pinter 1997: 18]). In this theatrical world, a commonplace phrase, such as 'Well, I'll see you at breakfast', can be freighted with an unnervingly threatening, or seductive, intentness. In terms of rhythm and pace, Harry Burton draws an important distinction in Pinter's dramatic notation, observing that the direction '*pause*' serves to 'indicate a moment's breath or pause', whereas '*Silence*' indicates 'some (potentially deep) uncertainty as to how to deal with what has just happened'; language is deployed as a raising of the stakes and strategic shifting of terms, where words are 'presented, lifted, inflated, stylised, relished, embodied and released' (Burton 2014: 206–205) (Pinter's plays, like Barker's, respond well to one of my own favoured directorial analogies in the rehearsal room: that actors/characters should seem to seek a phrase like the appropriate dart, select it from their personal arsenal, weigh it, aim it, launch it and look for its effect when it has struck home).

The Homecoming layers further tensions in its capacity as a conduit for conflicting interpretations of characters departed and unseen (who therefore remain inscrutable subjects of indefinite speculation: Jessie, Mac, the woman Lenny almost kills) and their former activities and relationships (which remain resonantly, uncomfortably unverifiable, such as the circumstances of Lenny's conception, and ambivalent, as in Max's statement: 'I've never had a whore under this roof before. Ever since your mother died' [50]). All the male characters prove vulnerably insecure: even Lenny, the most assured young male, admits to restless sleep because of the clock that ticks in his room, which he realizes must be addressed, perhaps stifled somehow. Max just about maintains an unstable dominance of the household through his switchback redefinitions and redramatizations of the past: his sentimental reminiscences when he claims Jessie taught their sons their morality, was 'the backbone to this family [...] with a will of iron, a heart of gold and a mind' (54) promptly gives way to a contradictory memory and moral designation of 'a crippled family, three bastard sons, a slutbitch of a wife' (55). A further question opens up, as to how exactly Ruth 'was different' when she met Teddy (58): she seems to reclaim some power associated with her former time as a model to command attention to the significance of the present moment as dramatized precisely by her self-conscious physicality (her orders to Lenny [42], her direction of the men's attentions to the moving of her leg [60–61], her refusal over two hours to let Joey go 'all the way' [74]). This proves more tactically effective than the men's invocations of the past. Ruth bids farewell to Teddy with the colloquial injunction, 'Don't become a stranger' (88); indeed, the power in the household has seemed to reside in the men's bids to estrange others, to render them subhuman and instrumentalized. However, Ruth demonstrates the power to estrange herself from their definitions, and manipulate them, in turn. Her recall of her modelling session at the edge of the lake, and her approach to the house (65–66), is crucially incomplete and indefinite, activating speculation but deliberately remaining ultimately unknowable. Even within the combative immediacy of its events, *The Homecoming* identifies a crucial strategic edge in who can most effectively characterize times past, and so draw power, with which to determine consequences. The household situation returns to the conflictingly defined but frequently recalled lost time of a central female presence, with Max attempting (abjectly and, most productions suggest, unsuccessfully) to deny his age might be an obstacle to Ruth's affections: 'I'm not an old man [...] Kiss me' (89–90).

Landscape (radio broadcast 1968, staged 1969) begins a sequence of Pinter plays most directly focused on what Megson describes as formally ambitious anatomizations of 'the vortex of memory' (Megson 2014: 231). *Landscape* presents two parallel but contesting reveries, in which the two characters appear not to hear each other; though Duff addresses Beth directly, she seems unreachable. The play traces how the two characters are at pains to situate themselves in space and time, in a series of landscapes, but differently and separately, like the two figures that Beth draws in the sand, close but 'not touching' and finally, literally inconsequential: 'They didn't look like anything' (Pinter 1997: 178). The reveries may recall the brief vivid recollections of Beckett's *Krapp's Last Tape*, not least because of the reported presence of a dog, the absence of any other 'soul', the final reference to rhythms of water in counterpoint to human intimacy.[6] However, the process of recall, of bringing past and present together, seems to presage the collapse of Krapp's rationalizations and fictions concerning his earlier life, in the face of the irreducibility of instantaneous and momentary sensuality. In *Landscape*, Beth seems to be separating herself, diverging and escaping into a landscape of increasingly fictionalized and romanticized sensuality, leaving Duff chasing after her, like the frenetic, well-meaning but ultimately uncomprehending dog, unsuccessfully.

Silence (1969) is an underrated short play by Pinter, with a stealthily estranging musicality in its dramatic treatment of time. Ellen, specified to be a girl in her twenties, seems to occupy a pivotal (and pivoting) relationship between two older lovers – Rumsey (who is 40) and Bates (in his mid-thirties). The characters are isolated in three separated areas for narrative of their personal perspectives, but brief interactions occur, in apparently significant flashback episodes. Mark Taylor-Batty observes how Pinter again brings 'past and present together' but in recollections that not only 'interact' but also 'interfere with each other', so that, whilst memory appears 'the hinge between past and present on stage', it also raises questions of precise relative location and verifiability, particularly in theatre:

> Typical cinematic discourses usually do not involve needing to warn of or clarify for an audience any leap backward or forward in time (or across an art/life divide), as this can quickly be adduced by a series of visual indicators, not least the visual age of the characters, their clothing and their environments. A different set of conventions dictate how we read staged material, however, and leaps between times need to be clearly marked verbally as well as visually (or textually, in an interruptive Brechtian mode).
>
> (Taylor-Batty 2014: 98)

In *Silence*, Pinter's precise calls for 'visual indicators' of age are pointedly at odds with what the characters say: Ellen's narrative incorporates reports of meeting an elderly drinking companion, to whom she, 'old', refuses to disclose details of 'the sexual part' of her youth (Pinter 1997: 194). Bates recounts his impatience with noisy neighbours who dismissively refer to him as 'Grandad' (193) and his landlady's imputation that he has reduced himself to a solitary 'childish old man', no apparent 'loveliness' to be recalled from his life (201). The characters appear visually as they would have done at the junctures of their significant interactions, earlier in their lives. Their speech oscillates between (what seems) historical immediately sensed detail, self-conscious recall from a position of age, and a sense of the silence that interrupts apparent (con)sequence (as when Rumsey breaks off his reverie, 204), and permits Ellen to hear herself (201) and contemplate the indefinite: the shapes in the trees, shadows 'looking at us' (198). However, Ellen also admits that 'I'm never sure that what I remember is of today or of yesterday or of a long time ago', an acknowledgement of subjectivity that is then abruptly and disorientatingly sharpened:

> My drinking companion for the hundredth time asked me if I'd ever been married. This time I told her I had. Yes, I told her I had. Certainly. I can remember the wedding.
>
> *Silence*

(Pinter 1997: 204)

The character, who appears in her twenties, seems to be consciously (though resiliently) negotiating the occlusion of memory associated with age and, in advanced forms, also with senile dementia or Alzheimer's disease (where her memories of the lovers of her twenties seem more definite to her than those of her own wedding). These words recur as her last. *Silence* is perhaps Pinter's most lyrical play in its detailed evocation of a rural landscape, on the edge of a town, and the characters' recollections finally dissolve into repeated phrases, like musical motifs, 'half things, beginnings of things', shadows and shapes in what Rumsey calls 'the folding light' (205): the play's layering of imagery of light and shadow suggests how not only dusk but memory may produce a sense of time as an internally 'folding light', glimpsing dim shapes and surprising shadows, on the way to '*Silence*'.

Dennis Potter's play *Blue Remembered Hills* (televised 1979 and subsequently adapted for the stage) generates unsettling comedy from its use of adult performers in the roles of children. Pinter's *Silence* reverses this effect, placing aged reflections in the mouths of actors in their twenties and thirties, lending a shade and poignancy to be deduced from the discrepancy between what is seen and what is spoken, suggesting the coexistence across time, in memory, of both the startling vividness of natural detail around personally significant periods, encounters and 'hinge moments', as well as a possible disintegration into increasingly free-floating images and echoes: a time/place when Ellen says 'I sometimes wonder if I think' (194); and Rumsey observes how his recall of encounters turns from sharp to 'smudged', then 'glimpsed again', 'then gone' (198), in a silence that yields no echo.

Old Times (1971) seems to give a face and a voice to one version of this glimpsed shadow. Kate appears to be present in the room, even as the married couple Anna and Deeley anticipate her arrival: a friend, whom Anna claims to have 'almost totally forgotten' (Pinter 1997: 250). Pinter's short play *Night* (1969) depicts a couple delineating their shared territory of the past, contentedly accepting minor discrepancies in their memories of their first encounter, until the final uses of a plural ('men') raise questions about the woman's sexual partners: their number and terms of possession. *Old Times* develops these briefly ambiguous nuances into a tensile power struggle (more reminiscent of a smaller-scale version of *The Homecoming*), in which Kate (who might initially seem a jointly constructed imaginary presence) suddenly intervenes to fight her corner in a fluctuating battleground of space/time, as 'the play develops through interaction with the past developed in the present moment', conducted by characters who are nevertheless 'susceptible to deliberate narrative collapse' (Taylor-Batty 2014: 109, 113). Deeley is resentfully alert to Kate's possible effect on Anna: 'I'll be watching you [...] To see if she's the same person' (Pinter 1997: 249–250). Kate confidently maintains the primacy in Anna's history of their time together: 'I came here not to disrupt but to celebrate [...] something that was forged between us long before you knew of our existence' (306). Pinter is characteristically fascinated by the sense of sudden slippage in temporal co-ordinates that provide unpredictable dislocations for his characters: Anna recalls Kate apparently losing track of which day it was, though Kate maintains she was correct (263). Anna and Deeley sing a succession of classic popular 'catalogue' songs, stopping just short of completing the refrain of Eric Maschwitz and Jack Strachey's song 'These Foolish Things' ('remind me of you'). Later they sing the Gershwins' song 'They Can't Take That Away From Me': ironically when *Old Times* suggests that power and security in memory can indeed be 'taken away' from the less adept player in this game.[7] Anna claims 'There are things I remember which may never have happened but as I recall them so they take place' (270); evidently it is not only the angles of the currently separated beds that are 'susceptible to any amount of permutation' (286). Anna offers to run a bath for Kate, but Kate claims she will run it herself 'tonight' (284): that telling word resonates into the interval, suggesting that Anna was in the habit of running Kate's bath for her, and indeed Kate later confirms that Anna is accustomed to placing the towel on her shoulders when she emerges naked afterwards (292). The ultimate tactic seems to be an effective consignment to death, the potential of which Kate warily detects earlier (272–273), then deploys against Anna ('I remember you lying dead' [309]), in a constructed narrative that suggests Deeley subsequently took her place, but in perfunctory and inconsequential terms – 'he suggested a wedding instead, and a change of environment' (311) – which impels the trio into a final harshly lit tableau of distanced and discarded time(s), fundamentally separated, disposed adjacently rather than together, as if hollowed out: 'old' times as former states, now expired, rather than memories shared.

Old Times shows how jealousy instigates a discourse of suspicion and a feverish attitude of (over)interpretation, not just in a theatre. Pinter's play involves the audience in a process of scrutiny, interrogation and speculation analogous to that of the characters, where everything becomes 'a potential target' in the urge to discover and ascribe meaning, even a *particularly* 'warped' and weaponized meaning, in a jealousy's 'hate-induced reorientation of desire' that ultimately preserves only 'the envious side of desire and the depressive side of hatred' (Kristeva 1996: 28–27). Hence the play's enervated, enervating cessation, where/when energy seems evaporated to aridity by swelling, inquisitional, feverish light (foreshadowing that at the end of Kane's *Cleansed* and *Crave*, in which the light may also seem to suggest or promise a possibly violent portal to transmutation or self-transcendence: a transubstantial 'grace', which is never apparent, or even sensed as a possibility, in Pinter's theatre). The sense that lost time cannot be stabilized, preserved, possessed exclusively (as in a photograph album) or even recovered in anything but highly subjective terms extends into Pinter's *No Man's Land* (1975), which suggests that, for its characters, memory may be the contentious and indeterminate zone of the title, 'both dead weight and galvanizing force' (Megson 2014: 226) that permits no lasting purchase.

An ultimate sense of separation is also detectable in *Moonlight* (1993), which initially presents the character Bridget as a devoted carer (to her father) and consciously fragile residue of life (recalling May in Beckett's *Footfalls*), who may also be a remembered dead young daughter whose absence (like that of Carol in Priestley's *Time and the Conways*) forms a central fragmentation in a family polarized, its relationships frozen in time by traumatic loss. The final image is Bridget, recalling a time when she was poised in deferral and anticipation, on the edge of the mysteries of adult experience.

Pinter addresses the sense of lost time with an unusual directness in *A Kind of Alaska* (1982), which depicts a woman, Deborah, awakening from a 29-year coma, her subjective senses of duration and behavioural patterns severely arrested (Taylor 2007: 60), paradoxically 'still young, but older' (Pinter 1998: 155). *Silence* achieved dislocatory effects by ascribing the words of elderly recollection to visibly relatively youthful characters; *A Kind of Alaska* considers the extreme disorientation and existential pathos of a relatively youthful sensibility emerging from the consignment of a surprisingly aged body (where a woman in her forties refers to her mummy and daddy, believing herself to be 15), her sense of time extremely destructured. Deborah's plight throws into stark relief the *irretrievability* of lost time (which mocks her hopeful sense that 'I've got all the world before me' [169], and renders her anomalous, 'childish' and 'Out of [...] tune' [161]). Deborah speaks of her sensed constriction in spatial terms, comparable to Lewis Carroll's Alice in a limbo *nebenwelt*, 'dancing in very narrow spaces' (173), and the vice-like closing in of mirrored walls (188–189). However, the play also depicts the suffering involved for those around Deborah, who simultaneously and nauseously embodies past and present, death and life (Taylor-Batty 2014: 144): they have been more keenly aware of the passage of time (hers, theirs), while she has been 'nowhere, absent, indifferent' [Pinter 1998: 184]), her realizations and disappointments deferred until waking. Deborah carefully professes 'no intention of looking into a mirror' (189) as she gamely bids to bring the flood of estrangingly intense perceptions and unfamiliar consequentiality into 'proportion' (190). Her first attempts to recognize her existence over time suggest one extreme form of what it might be to be denied what Richard Dawkins has described as 'the anaesthetic of familiarity' (quoted by Taylor 2007: 55). The play also suggests how her abject status as a living ghost and potential revenant has strained others immediately around her, by perforating their sense of progression and wounding normal forms of faith in time. The end of the play represents Deborah's uncertain beginning.

Betrayal (1978) gives artfully heightened dramatic form to the sense of how we 'live forwards, but we understand backwards' (Hoffman 2009: 107), how events acquire more meaning and significance through retrospection. The play begins with Jerry and Emma meeting, two years after their affair, and moves backwards in time, finally to the scene of Jerry's initial expression of the passion that instigated their liaison. This refocuses audience attention on nuances of interaction (verbal strategies and disclosures and body language), not least because it relieves the pressure of conventional exposition, and 'disallows the ordinary attachment to motivation, and to cause and effect', as there is not the usual 'tension about any dramatic outcome' (Taylor-Batty 2014: 133). In their first theatrical scene (but last in terms of linear chronology), Emma seems concerned to try to put Jerry, and her feelings for him, in some 'proper' (temporal) place, even as she admits a brief compulsion to revisit other times ('I thought of you the other day [...] Well it's nice, sometimes, to think back' [Pinter 1998: 5]), even as his surprise seems too over-performed to be convincingly nonchalant. The former lovers are also concerned to navigate their children's memories and impressions through potentially damaging straits (Emma assures Jerry that her daughter just remembers him 'as an old friend' [12]); however, Emma reports her confession to her husband, Robert, and emphasizes the irrevocable loss of times: perhaps even the futility of what has been attempted, and recollected: 'It's all gone', 'It's all all over' (22–23). However, in scene two (which, in character time, occurs the next day), Robert tells Jerry that Emma confessed the affair to him (not the previous night, but) four years ago. This knowledge, which the audience henceforth share with Emma and Robert, informs responses to subsequent scenes: scene three, two years earlier, when Emma and Robert meet in their rented flat and she decides to end the affair, claiming that the flat has become an alternative to them using their imagination for nocturnal assignations: she is impatiently dismissive of its (and their) functionality, he is tepid in response ('I don't think we don't love each other' [44]), she indicates the time pressure of her gallery's Thursday afternoon closing in which to end the arrangement. Scene four, set one year earlier in Emma and Robert's house, depicts a visit from Jerry and extends the subtextual irony and tension arising from Robert's knowledge. Scene five, set one year earlier, presents Emma's disclosure of the affair, and dramatizes how events and memories can suddenly be illuminated, and viewed, from a crucially different perspective, not least the issue of paternity:

ROBERT:	How long?
EMMA:	Some time.
ROBERT:	Yes, but how long exactly?
EMMA:	Five years.
ROBERT:	*Five years?*
	Pause.
	Ned is one year old.

(Pinter 1998: 71)

Emma confirms Robert is the father of their son: scene eight shows Emma's report of her pregnancy to Jerry (who has deemed it 'impossible' to change the arrangements of his life fundamentally), who tries to be graciously accommodating, perhaps too well. *Betrayal* also shows Pinter mining the slippage of detail in memory: it is a moot and disputed point, in whose kitchen Jerry threw and caught Emma's daughter; Jerry recalls Emma 'in white' at her wedding to Robert, perhaps in order to heighten his transgressive fantasy of her desecration by him. The ironies of *Betrayal* accrue, but in ways that are unlikely to increase any lofty superiority that the audience might harbour in relation to the characters; rather, empathy may increase, as we discover more of their hopes, which we know will be disappointed: an effect that might, theoretically and apparently, be likened to the last act of Priestley's *Time and the Conways*. However, Priestley's play locates the audience in a semi-divine position of historical hindsight; Pinter bypasses the theatrical power relations (of historical hindsight, distance and detachment) implicit in the more conventional ironies and pathos of *Time and the Conways*. *Betrayal* is crucially different in terms of these power relations: it explores deceptions and self-deceptions in ways in/to which the audience may feel an increasing and uncomfortable potential proximity. Over the course of the scenes, Pinter complicates, enlarges and dilates his dramatic characters (who, like Deborah in *A Kind of Alaska*, seem concerned to avoid the abyss of sentiment and self-pity, however brittle they may feel) by showing how they may appear to accrue, and act upon, more levels of temporal awareness: as the audience might hope to do (contrastingly, Priestley shows the intrinsically mortal limitations of his characters, and dissolves those of the audience). Consequently the characters in *Betrayal* are depicted as consciously re-viewing and struggling to come to terms with the retrospective, contradictory, agonizing and mysterious significances of details of past and present interpersonal interaction, and tracing the implied or identifiable consequences of pain and loss. This is analogous to the activities of the theatre audience: considering and reconsidering the central (and peripheral) relationships from varying perspectives, which destabilize and disrupt any consistent imaginative superiority.

Ashes to Ashes (1996) appears to show a man, Devlin, attending to his partner Rebecca, in what initially seems a therapeutic role, as she recounts memories based on scenarios of refugees and genocide into which she seems compelled to insinuate herself, either out of a pathological empathy with the victimized, or for purposes of erotic fantasies of submission, or both. Devlin also seems drawn into the postures of one of her scenarios, but the echo that elongates her words into a reverberation implies a confirmation of Rebecca's imaginings, located somewhere *beyond* the here and now, and seems to locate her beyond the reach of what is immediately visible, also (the script specifies the darkening of lights in the comfortable, gardened house in the country, and the separating intensification of two lamps). From one perspective, *Ashes to Ashes* reminds me of Beckett's *Not I*, in which an attendant therapist or confessor figure is forced to acknowledge his inability to halt the intensifying momentum of a woman's compulsive self-displacement. However, Rebecca's compulsion seems not to deny her own subjectivity (as is that of Beckett's Mouth), but to interpolate herself repeatedly into traumatic narratives of twentieth-century European history (through imagery that may be drawn from contemporary films: Taylor-Batty 2014: 185–186), so that her own uncontrollable and unending 'splitting' constitutes an idiosyncratic response to a political history of atrocity, which she may not have experienced first-hand, but which inescapably overshadows and interrogates her own attempts at life, love and ageing (in a way that reminds me, further, of Clive James's lyric to Pete Atkin's 2003 song, 'A Hill of Little Shoes').[8] Rebecca seems to be (wilfully) lost inside a compulsive, unending temporal cycle of systematic loss, which collapses the distinctions of past and present, public and private, subjective and objective, political and erotic[9]: distinctions that theatre is intrinsically and formally well placed to problematize, compulsively.

Barker: 'The sheer suspension of not knowing'

If Stoppard's *Arcadia* stops short of 'exploring whether sexual attraction helps us wriggle free of the iron grip of determinism' (Carroll 2010: 121), this might be identified appropriately as one of the principal themes of Howard Barker's theatre, alongside effects of surprisingly (and appallingly) thorough demonstrations of reversibility in terms of power. Another hallmark is the 'sheer suspension of not knowing' (Barker 2016: 30) which Barker offers the audience in place of the flattery of ironic superiority. Senses of temporal suspension, length, rhythm and deliberation are key features in the uncanny, haunting musicality of Barker's theatrical poetics. David Wiles claims that a 'shared experience of time', 'everyone seeing and feeling the same thing at the same moment', was a theatrical objective characterized by Vladimir Nemirovich-Danchenko as 'atmosphere', and by Konstantin Stanislavski as 'mood' (Wiles 2014: 4); however, 'everyone seeing and feeling the same thing at the same moment' suggests (beyond even the Victorian melodrama) the moral terms and rhythm of the Hollywood movie. Suspicious of what makes people fall into step with others, aesthetically and (therefore) politically, Barker experiments relentlessly with radical dramatic forms that are precisely (dis)ordered disruptions of all systems; his plays and productions are dissipative structures, in which the principal structures are provided by very highly and consciously structured rhythm (in movement or utterance), but these operate estrangingly rather than contagiously. In Barker's theatre of dynamic bifurcations, his plays and productions foreground the ways in which the terms of spectacle and the active exercise of the gaze can separate both characters and audience members. Barker's impulses may be postmodernist, in that he resists the imposed totalizations and unifications of public time and historical chronology, preferring to affirm (both dramatically and theatrically) the contingencies of an event-based time that emphasizes elusiveness, indeterminacy and irresolution of the problematic (terms I draw from Adam 1995: 155). On the other hand, Barker is defiantly modernist, particularly as a director, in his precisely measured evocations and orchestrations of combined and contrapuntal verbal, physical and scenographic effects, which could be described as subversively valorizing the 'fractured difference of embedded and embodied times *at the expense* of the constitutive power of that totalizing and standardizing time' (Adam 1995: 156, original emphasis). Thus he avoids the dualistic, binary and exclusive position and mode of *either* postmodernism *or* modernism.

Jay Gipson-King poses salient questions with salutary directness:

What are the politics of time? Can ruptures in time be used to affect the viewing experience? Can temporal shape be used to repoliticise myth? And can form alone, without reference to topical politics, create a subversive political system? Howard Barker proves that the answers to all of these questions is 'yes'.

(Gipson-King 2013: 148)

Gipson-King goes on to discuss these propositions with central reference to Barker's play *The Bite of the Night* (written 1985, staged 1988), how Barker's development of a radical dramatic form 'manipulates *time* at multiple levels of the theatrical experience in order to upset conventional habits of viewing and attack the political-moral system embedded within linear realism' by a threefold manipulation of 'narrative time, audience time and dramatic time' to create a 'theatrical-political system that empowers its spectators' (148, original emphasis). *The Bite of the Night* depicts the odysseys of the last lecturer and his last student in the (near-future?) '*ruins of a university*', when their unusual forms of imaginative persistence permit them to tear through their own (dystopic but apparently partly contemporary) time-space continuum into a version of the Trojan War's aftermath, a time frame more fractured (and fracturing) than classical. *The Bite* might retrospectively be identified as the first of Barker's experimentations with what Jonathan Kalb calls 'great lengths' (Kalb 2011), with a playing time of between four and a half and five hours. Barker goes on to write two other longer plays that contain even more extreme ranges and duration, *Rome* (written in 1989, published 1993, still awaiting a full professional production) and *The Ecstatic Bible* (written 1993–1994, staged in Adelaide, Australia, 2000), which similarly subject characters (in narrative time) and audience (in audience time) alike to an overwhelming plethora of experience, unfurling a dramatic time encompassing remarkable reversals of fortune, power and destabilizing desire. In these and other plays, Barker re-visions foundational mythic and historical narratives in such ways that challenge notional inevitabilities and present, instead, a provocative range of moral alternatives and perspectives.

Gipson-King notes how Barker deliberately fashions a challenging temporal shape for his plays, a conscious 'affront' to popular and media attitudes of 'flash consumption and easy meaning that surrounds and seeks to contain' the theatrical event; Barker achieves this partly through the anachronisms that permeate his *narrative time* to 'deny a stable landscape where spectators can ground the action', a diffusion of events that 'deny the cohesion of a linear *dramatic time* or the predictability of rising and falling action', and a 'proliferation of disturbing imagery, combined with the excessive length of the play', which 'create an *audience time* that overwhelms traditional methods of viewing and that shatters theatrical conventions' (Gipson-King 2013: 153–154, original emphasis). Thus Barker defamiliarizes 'not just the content' but the entire temporal 'experience of the historio-literary myth', to 'reveal the myth *as* myth – something invented and therefore open to change', and thus reactivate its questions and 'political potential' (154). Barker is also refining an 'art of theatre' consciously designed 'to resist the maddening, ubiquitous, and nearly irresistible' cultural pressures elsewhere, 'to reduce, abbreviate and trivialize' (Kalb 2011: 16), indeed to approach and present itself in contextual *terms which are not its own*. In some respects, Barker's deliberately plethoric theatre reaches back to nineteenth-century undertakings by Goethe, Byron, Shelley and Ibsen's *Peer Gynt* (as does Rudkin's, in different ways) to 'declare imaginative liberation' from the limitations of the age, by incorporating and presenting practically what might at first be considered 'defiant impracticality: fantastic settings, impossible stage directions, uninhibited shifts of time and space, and blurred boundaries between interior and exterior experience' (Kalb 2011: 13–14).

Wiles observes that the linearity of modern cosmopolitan time is 'predicated on the inevitability of progress, not the inevitability of death' (Wiles 2014: 23). Barker's radically sceptical counter-enlightenment drama interrogates traditionally linear narratives of development, partly through Barker's re-presentations of death (offering 'profound emotional experiences' that 'serve to increase resistance to social coercion' by obliging the observer to 'include death' in her/his 'categories of thought', Barker 2005: 14).

The Bite of the Night thus excavates and estranges the cultural associations of 'Troy', and *Rome* similarly finds surprising forms for that which its inhabitants seek to invest in city and empire, and a contrasting 'barbarity'. At some stages, Rome is identified with the shamelessness of the female protagonist Beatrice, at others with the very action of 'Wanting' (Barker 1993: 288), and with a systematically ruined pope whose actions are ascribed with meaning by his devotees, including Smith, who blinds herself to emulate and approach the man she adores. The final scene of *Rome* occurs at a water's edge, which suggests an oceanic and specifically *inhuman* rhythm of steady regularity and detachment, to counterpoint the frenetic human action and fixation: for some characters, the sea offers death, for others playfulness, for Smith a perfect solitude. Barker's evocation of tidal rhythms and water's effects are neglected but often significant elements in his dramatic palette (for example, in his plays *Seven Lears*, [*Uncle*] *Vanya*, *Defilo*, *Ursula*, *The Swing at Night* and the filmscript *An Eloquence* – and the final decelerating and decaying underwater words of the protagonist of the opera *Stalingrad*). Perhaps the most striking example of this is in *The Ecstatic Bible*, where the pace of the action is uniquely slowed in the section entitled 'A Pair of Scales': the pivotal figure of the Priest is thrown in a river, where he floats in a scene of *'tranquility'* (notwithstanding his personal misfortune), encountering the *'pensive'* indifference of fishermen, who then throw stones to weigh down his body:

They unhurriedly pile the PRIEST with stones.

He begins to sink among the reeds.

A passer-by enters, and made curious by the scene, stops to watch. After a short while he bends to pick up a stone, and adds its weight to the rest … the three continue with this activity until, with a bored air, the passer-by resumes his journey.

A buzzing of insects.

(Barker 2004a: 202)

This is a particularly striking episode in *The Ecstatic Bible* because of its uncharacteristically slow tempo (which might acquire its own mesmeric rhythm, even in its tragicomic portrayal of detachment). Elsewhere, *The Ecstatic Bible* provides Barker's most extreme and extensive odyssey (even by his considerable standards), with its 29 scenes, 84 characters and an estimated playing time of at least seven hours, over which its almost incessantly pregnant protagonist Gollancz gives birth to a succession of characters, even as she is pursued by the Priest and others for whom she becomes the subject of devotion. Barker himself describes *The Ecstatic Bible* as 'a testament to endurance, not suffered without meaning, but never *redeemed* (there is nothing Christian here) and unencumbered with any fatuous effort to *comprehend* [...]', Barker 2004a: 8, original emphasis). A character who is a baby in one scene appears in the immediately subsequent scene as 15 years old (Barker 2004a: 36); seven scenes later, she will herself be tortured and killed by her own daughter, who is later depicted wheelchair bound, with consciously greying hair (163). We are told that the Priest's agonized pursuit of Gollancz has endured for 40 years, a quarter of the way into the play (87) – and it will endure until the last page of the script. Barker again (but to an unprecedented degree) unfurls a length and intensity of experience that rolls over all generic markers of theatrical time like an avalanche, presenting a range of experiences in character time that encompass a dizzying succession of reversals and transferences (discussed in detail in Rabey 2009: 145–155).

One might identify other, less deliberately and literally prolonged, plays by Barker that nevertheless also activate a sense of catastrophic time (in terms that I have developed from Lingis: Rabey 2009: 15–17). Some of Barker's plays – such as *The Castle* (staged 1985), *Hated Nightfall* (staged 1994), *He Stumbled* (staged 2000) – present relentless events and surprising developments with which the characters and audience struggle to keep up. However, others – such as *Und* (staged 1999), *A House of Correction* (staged 2001), *Dead Hands* (staged 2004) – depict characters who speculate and deliberate compulsively, and the action seems to slow down as in a dreadful accident, in which characters experience an arrested dynamism, which I have elsewhere identified as a 'combination of frozen momentum, delirious insistence, dreamlike space and misplaced hopes' (Rabey 2009: 118). In both sets of scenarios, there is a sense that conventional and habitual certainties are forcibly suspended, both for characters and audience members, and the literal audience time of the performance may seem to extend to a remarkably intensive and extended scope of experience – even in the cases of relatively brief plays such as *Und, Dead Hands, The Brilliance of the Servant* (published 2001), *The Twelfth Battle of Isonzo* (staged 2001) and *Slowly* (staged 2010), which have a playing duration of between 30 minutes and two hours, but should be performed without interval division to maintain the senses of pressure and relentlessness. Barker himself reflects on this sense of temporal aporia, as exemplified in *A House of Correction*:

The characters assess, agonizingly, almost to the point of their own destruction: whether what occurs to them has been invited by their own collaboration or whether it's imposed on them; whether they will their own destruction, collaborate in it, or whether it arrives from outside. This struggle to make sense of the arbitrary preoccupies them, leads to their quarrels and makes them, perhaps heroically, try to fathom the nature of their existence.

(Barker, in Rabey 2009: 117)

Barker's play *Ego in Arcadia* (1992) challenges ideals more fundamentally than Stoppard's *Arcadia* (1993). Barker's imagined Arcadia is a place manifestly *not* idealized and abstracted – tempestuous, plane-scoured, a *'landscape of dereliction'* that contains bickering mobs and *'the detritus of heroic cultures'* (Barker 1996: 269) – but an apparent posthumous limbo in which various anti-heroic characters fetch up, alongside the painter Poussin (inspired by the historical artist who painted two separate artworks with the title 'Et in Arcadia Ego', depicting the incursion of Death into the pastoral idyll). This idea of the terminal 'waiting room', a juncture of space/time that precedes a full release into death, is most strongly associated with, and exemplified by, Jean-Paul Sartre's 1944 play *Huis Clos* (translated variously as *No Exit* and *In Camera*), and subsequently Samuel Beckett's *Play* (1962). Barker's catastrophic Arcadia proceeds from the sense that hell might be intensified, if constituted, by other people, and the painfully dependent entanglements of desire; this Arcadia is described by one character as a place 'where nothing lives but love' and so it is consequently 'a place of infinite suffering' (Barker 1996: 271). Applying Bachelard's terms, we might say Barker's Arcadia represents a claustrophobically idealized time, which is consistent without having continuity (Bachelard 1994: 118) ('in Utopia, everyone is a policeman' [Barker 2014b: 10]). Barker's characters, political flotsam, experience various challenges to their autonomy, pride and *self*-love as generated by relentless reconfigurations of appalling and frequently murderous desire, but they are also compelled to recover from any apparently or usually fatal attack: they are refugees denied relief. Their only way out is to humour the presiding figure of Tocsin, Arcadia's slowly discriminating but bathetically lowbrow figure of Death, by competing in a song contest, for which the prize is the promise of oblivion.

Ego in Arcadia offers a painfully and wryly comic existential repudiation of that cliché of 'anaemic kindness', **'Time heals all wounds'** (Barker 1996: 279). Rather, the characters find that the pains of desire dog them even in Arcadia, a 'graveyard of convictions' (291) and excoriation of pride, where a kiss can still make 'sheer futility' of 'finality' (285); even the venerated artist Poussin is subject to the undercutting presence of his mother, Mme Poussin, who is 'rinsed by time of every indignation' (281) and appallingly, cheerfully sexually unashamed and voracious. Thus, Barker's Arcadia is a place where each of the characters find their 'ego' challenged and strained to breaking point by these subjugations. Finally, Poussin expresses the determination 'If you hate the world ... You must invent another' (321) and he turns on Tocsin with a fierce resolve, until the agent of Death hangs from his own rope: a memorable instance of Barker's dramatic instinct for infinite reversibility of power. Without Tocsin's controlling terms of engagement, some of the characters seem released into irretrievability, while others persist, wilfully (Kalb's comment on Beckett – that his *oeuvre* is characterized by duality and his perceived 'negativity always stands tongue-in-cheek alongside a certain celebration of isolation' – is equally applicable to Barker

[Kalb 1989: 131]). *Ego in Arcadia* extends Barker's characteristic sense that history and the world comprise a series of unanticipated, but paradoxically and appallingly and even unenviably *vivifying*, catastrophes, where purpose and meaning are 'not to be found in the laws of nature, or in the plans of any external agent who made things that way'; 'it is our job to create them' (Carroll 2010: 374), here even beyond the apparent closures promised by death.

'We live in crushed time' remarks Sleev, the protagonist of Barker's *I Saw Myself* (2008) (Barker 2008: 53), remarking upon a catastrophic consciousness of emergency, common to the narratives of many Barker plays, evoking a ritualistic, dreamlike state of emergency and compression. If the enlightenment promises of 'progress' may be associated with 'accumulated slow change', Barker's theatrical 'catastrophism' offers an imaginative counterforce: an anti-empirical series of violent upheavals that challenge concepts of logical necessity and uniformity of law, space, time and process. This also involves characters experiencing a heightened sense of both a similarity (of location and situation) to those immediately around them, and also how their responses to this awareness throw into relief profound personal differences between them. This often involves an acute bristling, painful phenomenological immediacy to objects (as in Barker's 2003 compendium *13 Objects*), a sense of potential momentousness to (possibly terminal) interactions notwithstanding an intensifying, possibly infuriating sense of slow motion and a sense of feverish erotic suspension in which everything is tantalizingly just out of reach (in *I Saw Myself*, Sleev's paramour, whom she keeps naked in a wardrobe), or wilfully withheld until release, or else agonizingly deferred (Sleev's erotic encounters with her son-in-law, in opportunistic trysts that he consciously notes diminish from one minute to thirty seconds). Significantly, the performer of Smith in *Rome* is directed to undress '*with infinite slowness*' (Barker 1993: 209), suggesting her decision to ritualize her actions on her own (temporal) terms, abstracting them even as they unfurl a potentially erotic promise; *The Twelfth Battle of Isonzo* that depicts a duel between a (very old) man and a (very young) woman, who pursue and explore the deliberate prolongation of the pains and pleasures of eroticism through heightening anticipation and tension (rather than a more conventional rush towards the relief of climax). Barker's most feverishly and grotesquely comic exploration of catastrophic 'crushed time' is the opera libretto *Dead, Dead and Very Dead* (written 2005, staged with music by F. M. Einheit in Copenhagen, 2007), set in a plague-stricken city where a wealthy industrialist attempts to safeguard his art collection with a pistol, whilst his son marries the industrialist's former mistress, a fatally infected opera singer. In this situation, as I have noted elsewhere, time seems both to 'slow down (as energy flags and further decisive breakdowns are awaited) and accelerate (as [the characters] seek to do or say something particularly personally meaningful in the suddenly brief time available' (Rabey 2009: 226). The sense of mingled horror and disbelief is extended by the strangulation of a dog '*by slow degrees*' and the climactic grotesque and macabre appearance of the infectious bride, who removes a surgical mask in order to bestow a fatal kiss on the groom. The savage comedy of catastrophic time is foregrounded here, as all forms of conventional social meaning and responsibility are problematized by a ubiquitous *inability* to endure. The full ramifications of the crisis are explored by minute degrees, as suggested by the final song: 'When the roof caves in it waits a little bit', describing how imminent collapse may prompt some to try to flee, while others remain fatally oblivious to the slow significance of disintegration.

I Saw Myself and *Slowly* follow the processes of characters, characteristically Barkerian in being acutely and actively aware of the current moment, and the pressure of the past, but conscious that the future does not (yet) exist, and in their determinations to delineate their own narratives rather than have more conventional ones imposed upon them (also pertinent to the characters of *Dead, Dead and Very Dead*, except that they are denied this sense of future). The *cogito ergo sum* of Barker's characters seems to be expressed through their compulsions to develop intricately alternative possibilities, in order to respond dynamically to their situational juncture of change (in *I Saw Myself* and *Slowly*, a war that is drawing nearer). They seek to identify, and help create, a continuum of events that might best preserve their own sense of an individually discovered knowledge, style and (often posthumous) dignity: in short, a sense of becoming (or terms of disappearing). In *I Saw Myself*, the widow Sleev rallies her seamstresses to complete a transgressive tapestry, whilst conscious that if the enemy arrives 'the tapestry will be the first thing on the bonfire' (Barker 2008: 26). However, the possible ephemerality of this anti-conventional investment of their energies lends them urgency rather than paralysis; indeed, if Sleev's encroaching blindness (through eyestrain) incurs a 'loss of time' (44), she proposes intensifications in working patterns that may prove similarly damaging to her servants in 'the acceleration of a process' that, consciously, may prove 'a grotesque and comical redundancy' (53), yet is also proclaimed by even the most sceptical seamstress 'more important than we are' (66). Sleev's physical deterioration also accelerates with events (including a beating) so that, by the end of the play, she is manifestly and drastically more (prematurely) aged than at the outset, suggesting an intensely demanding *character time* whose rigours of concentration (self-consciously and willingly) surpass the conventional. It also permits her former lover Modicum to join the war, and return transformed by his experience, becoming her subjugator. However, Sleev is unrepentant and profoundly self-accepting, relying to her daughter's denuciations: 'the person you describe is no longer visible to me if I could walk the long yards of my own life I would say she lived like someone ill'; however, crucially, 'the illness [...] she experienced as ecstasy' (79), which lies beyond shame. Meanwhile, the 'small war' passed, 'the big war [is] now surely just fields away'(80); the stage direction, '*Time passes*' (81), yields to Sleev an unexpected revelation of her self in the suddenly heightened brevity of life and intensity of 'crushed time'.

In *Slowly*, four princesses (Sign, Calf, Bell and Paper) await the approach of ravaging barbarians, painfully aware that this is the juncture at which to end or extend their personal stories in time. The aptly named Sign argues for the triumphant significance of self-immolation through fire, placing the princesses beyond the desecrating reach of their enemies by rendering their bodies into ashes. Calf contrastingly argues for an artful, 'strong' disposal of their own dead but intact bodies, 'placed / not flung / clean / disdainful', striking shame into their attackers (Barker 2010: 86). However, the action of

Slowly follows the deceleration of consensus (like other Barker plays, but in particularly crystallized form), as the imminence of the threat steadily increases and perhaps accelerates. Calf focuses on a finality, 'We are disappearing', but Paper suggests a consciously appalling extension: they may be 'disappearing in one form/reappearing in another' (101), through artful ingratiation, on which her fearful sister Bell also fastens. A collective response to the crisis proves impossible, and the faltering of personal resolve is expressed when all except Calf '*stand and are still for some time*' (106) (which seems, in some ways, to be Barker's even more precisely existentially contextualized refraction of the final inaction presented by the end of Beckett's *Waiting for Godot*). Calf observes that their decisions may now be motivated more by (inter)personal contempt and resentment than by appeal to history or nation. Bell and Paper abscond; even Sign begs for the help of her remaining sister, Calf, in providing an image to assist in her terminal negotiation of 'intractable frustration'. Sign, '*fixed*', maintains 'I am going' but fails to do so, adds 'Slowly / [...] Slowly / but I'm going' (108) and realizes that Calf actively wants to be 'the subject of an atrocity', provocatively achieving a death, the shame of which will 'infect' the victory of her enemies and their descendants who will 'writhe and drown in the poisoned sink of their own history' (109). When Sign withdraws, Calf is alone, but realizes she also experiences a difficulty in dying on her own. In a play that emphasizes the crucial and mutual effects of the gaze (as, indeed, do Barker's *Gertrude – The Cry* and *I Saw Myself*), Calf's final appeal ambiguously positions the audience as confirmatory witness to her efforts, or repudiated barbarian, or both, with the action frozen in a harrowing incompletion (which is not the same as Beckett's arrested dynamism: the wistfully bathetic inertia of *Waiting for Godot*, the artistry in entropy represented by *Endgame*, the cyclical grating consignment of *Play*).

Found in the Ground (published 2001, staged 2009) is the dramatic work in which Barker, as both dramatist and director, extends his distinctive sense of rhythm as a primary dramaturgical factor, developing an extensively orchestrated choreography and scenography beyond the rhythmic and repetitive sequences, 'exordia', which he directs to preface his plays in performance (for example, the 'Wedding Machine' that introduced Barker's own production of *13 Objects*, described by Barker in Gritzner and Rabey 2006: 30–31) or the heightened ritualized sequences of action that suggest interpolations of the uncanny (such as Sopron's repeated cycle of actions in *Dead Hands* that characteristically 'Hang in the air / Like smoke' [Barker 2004b: 12]). *Found in the Ground* unfolds what I have termed a 'temporal landscape' (Rabey 2009: 155ff) – which then also seems to fold back in upon itself. Images and figures and '*industrial sound*' are released into rhythmic but unpredictable action (including a naked perambulating woman, a workman carrying books in a wheelbarrow that he empties into fire, flocking birds and three bandaged dogs that '*erupt*', barking, from kennels '*and travel downstage on wheels*' [Barker 2008: 123]). These motifs in action, and some characters' utterances, periodically recur like contrapuntal musical motifs, and are sometimes 'furthered, the torsion increased [...]' (Barker in Gritzner and Rabey 2006: 30–31). Toonelhuis, a dying Nuremberg judge attended by a chorus of nurses, ingests the remains of the war criminals he has condemned as if to evacuate them through this incorporation and so escape from the chaos of European history, in the knowledge that his biggest challenge, *'the ultimate dish'*, remains Hitler himself. However, Hitler and the war criminal Knox persist in rematerializing, in surprising and disarming ghostly forms (at one point Hitler appears as a baby, then in an ensuing scene appears simultaneously in adult form; indeed, this is the most protean example of Barker's recurrent interventions of posthumous but garrulous revenants from another age, also to be found in his plays *Fair Slaughter, Birth on a Hard Shoulder, Don't Exaggerate, Seven Lears, N/A* and *Two Skulls* – and, of course, all of the principal characters of *Ego in Arcadia*). Elisabeth Angel-Perez notes Barker's 'systematic blurring of the indicators of time', in which *Found in the Ground* may be his most extreme experiment, creating a temporal 'palimpsest' of indefinite shapes that 'locates the spectator simultaneously before, during and after Auschwitz' in its 'chiasmatic circularity' (Angel-Perez 2006: 143). Thus *Found in the Ground* represents, and re-presents, the feverish mayhem in both the compulsion to escape from history, and its apparent impossibility. When Toonelhuis dies, the contrapuntal spectres he has consciously or inadvertently released – Hitler and the headless woman representing war dead – persist, haunting the landscape; and Denmark, a frustrated librarian, ritualistically desecrates Toonelhuis's ashes, as if to consign and banish the judge, in turn, to history. However, the European history machine that *Found in the Ground* appears to be only reaches a point of release into endgame and entropy when Toonelhuis's valet slits the throats of the dogs, who *'do not protest, but sink at the knees'* (Barker 2008: 211), and he tears away their leashes. Even then, the landscape resounds to the nurses' echoes of Toonelhuis's words (and in Barker's 2009 production, a recorded voice inviting the audience to *'faites vos jeux'*, suggesting the game begins again, in other forms, and demands of choices). George Hunka observes how the play in performance challenges the audience to

> seek a perhaps impossible redemption in their own bodies, and in love and imaginative desire: to avoid the prostration and sexual self-degradation of idealists like Hitler and Denmark, to consider even the justice of a Toonelhuis as provisional, as the judge himself finds it at the end of his life. It is the melancholia of complicity in a bizarre human justice, a parody of the justice found, perhaps, only in the dead – in the 'ground' of the title of the play.
>
> (Hunka 2009)[10]

Barker's *Blok/Eko* (2011) again keenly testifies to the sense that it is 'not the length of life' but the 'intensity' that proves a factor of determination and discrimination (Barker 2011: 42); hence the ageing despot Eko consigns her most promising poet, Tot, to seven year's imprisonment rather than execution, conscious that his prolonged suffering will deepen his sensibility as an artist. Tot's seven-year imprisonment (during which he has lost an arm and generally sickened) is spanned by ten pages of script and a performance time of ten to fifteen minutes. However, this appears a continuous present of dreamlike (or nightmarish) condensation, in another remarkably extensive Barker work. *Blok/Eko*'s total stage playing time (of about two and a half hours) encompasses massacres, riots, falling regimes, public mourning rituals and counter-revolutionary reversals of edicts, frequently bringing the characters to conscious extremities of exhaustion, and struggles to poetic distillations of consciousness that go beyond rational terms. These distillations become strangely poignant in performance, as the characters strive to achieve, maintain and refine the self-conscious performance of a not always enviable enlargement of their capacities. Tot's dying speech, for example, resembles a bricolage of details possibly based on a dying flashback that suddenly recalled details from the perspective of his childhood, as if the fatal gunshot had opened his head and let out all his time[11]. Further examples are the ageing poet Blok's elaboration of self-conscious confinement in his terminal dedication to Eko; and the relatively superficial poet Pindar's final embrace of Nausicaa. Pindar's action serves to 'negate' the previous terms of 'his own existence', involving his reiteration of Nausicaa's word 'never', in ways which extend its reach and alter its value, but in different ways to the final irrevocable severance depicted in *King Lear*: in Blok/Eko, the repeated word 'never' suggests instead a selfless and hopeless commitment to the consciously abject (Barker 2011: 122).

Barker's compendium of 40 short plays, *The Forty* (2011), presents a series of brief crisis scenarios, all including junctures of suspension, where words break down and the (con)sequences of actions decay in the air and breaths between the characters, uncoupled, in their desperations, from the predominantly linear terms of social life and time (and, moreover, providing a succession of embodied images that may recall Wagner's intimation of how 'like the human body, the theatre exists in a paradoxical state of simultaneous vibrancy and decay' [Wagner 2012: 67]).

Barker's crystalline stage directions in *The Forty* frequently invoke a torsion within temporality, as demonstrated by these examples:

The gesture is maintained until it visibly agonizes her

She does nothing to assist him out of his dilemma, whilst knowing her own power over him

She resumes her relations with reality

When the scene has accumulated its whole quota of despair

An affectation of patience

She seems unable to move forward or back

Time hurts the unfulfilled lovers

(Barker 2014a: 294, 297, 302, 335, 337, 339)

The Forty studies, and invites the audience to study and scrutinize, interpersonal expressions of what might be termed 'the decay time of inhibitory postsynaptic potentials' (Buonomaro 2015: 332), and consequent wilful reformulations. These moments of suspension, abandoned and renewed/re-located initiative emerge from fictional situations that are often outlandish, indeterminate or surreal, yet present themselves to the audience for (surprising) recognition of what Wiles calls (in another context) 'comparable moments of pain' (Wiles 2014: 53), in which the audience may be reminded of feelings, in recall or in hypothetical anticipation, and how they might occur to others, in other times and places: again, surprisingly, with attention being focused on the temporal substance of what is *between* the usual identifications of words and actions. *The Forty* foregrounds the extent to which knowledge of time is predicated on 'effort and desire': on how, as Jean-Marie Guyau observes, we habitually estimate time 'on the basis of desires, our efforts, our own wills' (quoted by Droit-Volet 2014: 492). Furthermore, *The Forty* repeatedly dramatizes (and reformulates) how a hiatus may also constitute what Schneider calls an affective residue of other times, a resonance that crosses temporal boundaries 'as we touch things, persons, events that are no longer entirely "here"' (Schneider 2014: 44). This strange indeterminacy at the heart of theatre is perhaps best indicated by Barker in these terms:

> The play only appears to be about the living because the actors are living. The *characters* have never lived, nor by the same token, can they ever be said to be *dead*. Theatre is situated on the bank of the Styx (the side of the living). The actually dead cluster at the opposite side, begging to be recognized. What is it they have to tell? Their mouths gape [...]
>
> (Barker 2005: 20, original emphasis)

This connects with the way that Schneider proposes, not simply to remember the dead, but to involve the living in a crossing of 'a kind of threshold away from the strictly immediate present moment', a 'repeated gesture, an aged object, a clichéd phrase, an old letter, a footprint, a way of walking – all of these things, material and immaterial, might drag something of the no longer now, the no longer live, into the present, and drag the present into the no longer now' (Schneider 2014: 44–45).

In an essay from the 1980s, Barker sensed that plays are predominantly 'much too short'; 'One day a play will be written for which men and women will miss a day's work. It is likely this play will itself be experienced as work' (Barker 2016: 12).[12] This recalls Ernst Mach's 1865 suggestion that a specific sense of time involves the 'work of attention', the concentration of which Robert Hooke, in the same century, equated with the 'action of the soul' (Whitrow 1972: 17–18). Barker has also invoked 'the soul': 'not as an immortal form, not as a thing immune from damage, but as innate knowledge of other life' (Barker 2016: 62) – an imaginative capacity to envisage, speculate and develop possibilities *otherwise*. This leads him to project the precisely anti-commercial possibility of a play 'lasting seven days', which might itself create an impatience for 'The Play of an Entire Year' (Barker 2016: 215), a step further towards a refusal of laws, duties, obligations and compromise, but always suggesting another form of obligation, to the multifaceted, inconsistent and variable self.

Perhaps Barker's sense of 'the soul' here approaches that of Georg Lukács, who described tragedy as 'a science of death-moments, of conscious last moments when the soul has already given up the broad richness of existence and clings only to what it most deeply and intimately owns' (Lukács 1974: 161). As States observes in commentary on Lukács, tragedy is the most 'nonsocial' art form, 'at least from the standpoint of emotional logic', an event where 'what the audience shares' at specific moments and in the play at large is 'less important than what isolates each spectator vicariously in the experience'; and, though there may be contact points between what each spectator feels, the nature of the (usually silent) subjective reflections prompted by the experience remains 'a private thing, as metaphysical experience usually is' (States 1985: 175–171). This is very close to Barker's theatrical aesthetic.

> To walk unknowing where everything is known. To be immune to information. To recover ignorance from the superfluity of facts. To be ecstatically unpersuaded by the most compelling argument, even to the detriment of one's *interests*. Consequently, to desire tragedy, to experience tragedy as a need.
>
> (Barker 2014b: 2, original emphasis)

Barker's tragic spectator is both encouraged and isolated into reflection on the *absolute* privacy and subjectivity of their personal sense of time, a *terminal* perspective which the tragedy throws into relief. This develops Heidegger's sense of *Dasein*, the orientation of being towards death that generates a specific sense of temporality,[13] a process that offers 'both horizon and presencing', where a projective awareness of birth and death might 'enter creatively into every moment', horizontally and vertically, so that 'the time-frame is continuously reconstituted in the present' (Adam 1995: 76). Thus, tragedy offers (formally) limited and contained experiences, which are paradoxically delimiting and exhaustive in their resonances. These experiences include an element of isolating individuality for the spectator (they may evoke personally remembered action and inaction, personal notions of possibility and impossibility), possibly activating a consciousness of the extents to which we all live and die alone: a mindfulness of how the *subjectively temporal* dimensions of existence-as-process may be a key feature, to unlock possibilities of revised perspectives within (initially) the individual and (subsequently) her/his interactions. Thus, the tragic theatre offers 'the phenomenal moment where the private and the collective, the fictional and the real interpenetrate' (Schutz and Luckmann, as summarized in Adam 1995: 77).

Complicating shadows

'Time … what a tricky little fucker' remarks Larry, in Patrick Marber's *Closer*, complaining 'My head's in two places' (Marber 1997: 46). *Closer* selects and presents scenes from a four-and-a-half-year period, recurrent encounters between four specific characters, in a non-linear dramatic structure that foregrounds its own elliptical compressions. As Graham Saunders observes, in *Closer* as in Pinter's *Betrayal*, 'structure itself ultimately dominates over psychological characterization based on verisimilitude' (Saunders 2008: 54). Whilst the text and programme of *Closer* specify chronological relationships between scenes, these are not signalled explicitly or regularly by the characters' speech, actions or settings. The resulting sense of temporal dislocation denies the audience a superior or consistently ironic relationship in relation to the characters (who overtly seek to derive a stability of meaning from their desires, and fail). Rather, the effect is to bring characters and audience members *closer* in their experiences of unpredictably sudden and contradictory emotional shifts: most drastically in the scene featuring the line above, which plays out simultaneously in sections of the same space the consequential dissolutions of two relationships after a specific infidelity. In an earlier scene, Marber unfolds a distinctly spatial irony by collapsing the physical distance between two male cyberspace chatroom correspondents, invisible to each other but not to the audience, and generates comedy from the fast, physically decontextualized responses on which computerized interaction depends and thrives; a subsequent scene in a lap dancing club extends this sense of promised decontextualization that in fact involves and depends on simultaneous ironic surveillance. *Closer* activates an overt search for meaning over time on the parts of both characters and audiences, on the basis of the evidence provided (Rabey 2003: 201). The play also repeatedly demonstrates how rationalization founders on a sense of the restlessly enigmatic, which is associated with sexual desire and personified in the central character of Alice. She is a 'parallax' figure by which the others try to determine distances, but who nevertheless proves ultimately mysterious, even or especially when inscribed by the subjective gaze of the viewer. It emphasizes how Alice is a construction of various external subjectivities, but also her own, and her objective dimension, in which she nevertheless remains, is ultimately unfathomable.

One of the most ingenious modern plays in terms of discrepant temporality is the Irish dramatist Mark O'Rowe's *Howie the Rookie*. O'Rowe divides the unfolding of his narrative between two characters (unrelated but both surnamed Lee), The Howie and The Rookie. O'Rowe is here developing Conor McPherson's form of interwoven present-tense monologues by characters who are separated in time, space and awareness but whose lives connect unsuspectingly, mysteriously but significantly (exemplified by McPherson's *This Lime Tree Bower* [1995] and *Port Authority* [2001]).[14] However, O'Rowe ratchets up the tempo of the occurrence of significant events on a second-by-second basis, expressed by characters inhabiting an active present, so that the momentum of his plays acquires, at strategic moments, some of the headlong velocity and astounding, dizzying reversals associated with cinematic action movies, as well as an ominously momentous atmosphere of suspense, that 'Somethin's fuckin' comin'' (O'Rowe 1999: 27). The Howie is held responsible for negligence, which has contributed to the death of his younger brother. In a bid to restore a definite sense of consequence and justice, he attempts atonement by defence of his namesake (and former adversary) The Rookie from a more savage (and unreasonable) responsibility formulated by a gangland boss: as The Rookie remarks, The Howie 'helps' him in a way he doesn't 'understand', that is 'all a bit fuckin' mysterious' (41). However, the audience have *some* (but not *all*) of the pieces of the contextual time puzzle that informs and constitutes the breathlessness of the young men's lived experiences (like The Howie, they may find that details in the texture of the play 'spark' synaptically in their head, but do not immediately 'ignite' [43]). The discrepant perspectives of the two characters are most devastatingly poised at the end, when The Rookie visits the parents of The Howie to inform them of his (at least potentially redemptive and heroic) death, and is finally confronted by a video recording (signifier of the process by which The Howie's father distances himself from engagement with the immediacies of lived experience) of the (now dead) younger brother. The audience are left to imagine the process and repercussions of The Rookie reporting that a second son has died that night, a challenging act of imaginative 'completion', which the tautness of O'Rowe's theatrical writing nevertheless demands. Events and details accumulate and acquire a retrospective significance, though not in an essentially consistent way such as is provided by the reverse chronology of Pinter's *Betrayal* (the formal linearity of which, artfully, nevertheless brings us 'closer' to the characters than a forward motion, by making us wonder whether there is or can be such a thing, in human emotional relations as in anything else, as 'essential consistency' *over time*). In *Howie the Rookie*, the principally separated but occasionally overlapping perspectives of O'Rowe's two protagonists theatrically formalize and foreground an experience of temporal *discrepancy*, in its various manifestations, where (even individually) time is not single, but various and interpenetrative: comic, ironic, mysterious, astonishing and tragic.

O'Rowe pushes this premise further in his 2007 play *Terminus* that, like Caryl Churchill's *The Skriker* (1997), provocatively purports to extend a sense of time beyond the limitations of the human perspective, to incorporate a supernatural and demonic viewpoint. *Terminus* entwines the overlapping testimonies of three characters, including a serial killer who has struck a Faustian pact with the devil to enable him to sing masterfully (in mock-heroic parody not only of Marlowe's tragedy but of Thomas Murphy's 1983 play *The Gigli Concert*, which includes a similar premise). The killer is pursued by his own vengeful, severed soul, who has a brief supernatural tryst with a woman whom he caught plunging to her death above Dublin. She, in turn, is reborn (though the audience are privy to the bleak irony that the child's form that she adopts is terminally ill) and taken from the scene of her 'host' mother's death by her estranged 'former' mother, who herself possibly faces arrest for an isolated righteous killing. The wildly looping sense of ultimate consequence is aptly concluded by a duel between the killer and his soul: eviscerated and dangling from the aforementioned crane, the killer sings his last, momentarily commanding wonder from passers-by at his rendition of a kitsch power ballad (though perhaps more so by his circumstances), expressing a defiant sense of temporal epiphany that he insists (in defiant contrast to Marlowe's Faustus) will expansively redeem all to come: 'its bliss-inducing memory will do more for me to ease whatever suffering is in store for me when I enter Hell [...] I mean, I've heard tell that even the Devil remembered Heaven after he fell' (O'Rowe 2007: 48–49).

Dennis Kelly's *Love and Money* (2006) structures events in a reverse chronology, like Pinter's *Betrayal*, in tracing the dissolution of a relationship, but in more startling terms: the outwardly respectable and successful salesman David confides to a lover, via the decontextualizing disembodiment of an e-mail correspondence, that he 'assisted' the death of his former wife, Jess, out of a mixture of exasperation and material greed. The extremity of this premise is then traced back through different temporal contexts and developments, in each of which the shadows of financial pressures and addictive materialism are shown to have a consistently and remorselessly corrosive effect on the romantic idealism that Jess initially felt and professed – an idealism to which the play gives a final, poignant expression, but which is framed by its situation in this bleakly ironic structure, in demonstration of how ultimately antagonistic money is to love.

The aroused curiosity and element of 'detective work' involved in the (re)construction of a temporal context is an important element of much theatre: from the formulaically fictional Agatha Christie 'whodunnit', to the explicit body performance that challenges the spectator to situate an extreme and unsupported act in relation to both the artist and themselves. Simon Stephens's *Pornography* (2007) is a notable example of theatre that both elicits and ultimately thwarts this forensic approach, to fathom and rationalize extreme behaviour (in the case of *Pornography*, extreme behaviour that not only informed but also surrounded the 7/7 London tube bombings of 2005), 'from hindsight' as it were. One way Stephens resists closure is the way that he, like O'Rowe, mediates his events through an 'active present' of entwined monologues, as well as through unsettlingly non-located duologues. Stephens's theatrical processes involve a focus on phenomenological details that implies how 'everything acquires luminous significance in the light of what's to come' (Waters 2010: 83). Other variants on this theme – of seeking, if not understand rationally, then to approach and at least partly account for some traumatic event – are Analogue's *Beachy Head* (by Hannah Barker, Lewis Hetherington, Liam Jarvis, Emma Jowett and Dan Rebellato, 2010/2011) and David Greig's *The Events* (2013). *Beachy Head* begins with a pathologist, Rachel, alerting the audience to the rate at which 'people are dying all the time', including suicides (Analogue 2011: 21). From her professional viewpoint, 'Death is the problem which we're trying to solve', or, more precisely, she investigates 'what turns life into death, the forces that draw the living to their end', with the humanist objective, 'of course', of 'pulling people back from the edge' (22).[15] *Beachy Head* unfolds some of the residual 'stuff' – detritus, traces, 'ripples' (38) – of a life left behind by a suicide, Stephen, in ways that question Rachel's enlightenment perspective: as she describes the process of an autopsy, she acknowledges the equal importance of not seeing a body as 'stuff', quantifiable bodily tissue, as this is 'like seeing a painting just as paint' (64). A self-interested journalist, Joe, attempts to paint 'a picture' (69), constructing a 'backstory' on the basis of a video clip of Stephen, but in ways that intrude upon his partner's grief. The performer of Stephen is initially situated in the front row of the audience, and the play in production concludes by drawing specific attention to his vacated seat. *Beachy Head* suggests that any one of the varied assembled external perspectives on a lifetime (and its voluntary cessation) will be, however technologically impressive, well-intentioned or naturally motivated, an attempt to retrieve what is ultimately elusive, to reduce death to something manageable (from the pathologist's perspective, 'why one body shut down', not why a relative, friend or lover died [82]), whereas life, and death, remain *irreducible*, though immanent. Greig's *The Events* also attempts a reconstructive fathoming, in the wake of mass murder, even as the play testifies to the *irreversibility* of events, which cannot be mitigated. The play begins with the fantasy (from a performer who will later portray the murderer) of going back in time, to kill *en masse* in order to prevent later, worse global developments. However, the murderer remains a self-proclaimed 'void' into which the priest, Claire, who survives his atrocity, is 'drawn': 'a blankness out of which emerges only darkness and question' (Grieg 2013: 53). Indeed, Claire's humanist attempts to provide contextual accounts for his behaviour run aground, her impulses towards him alternating between the erotically redemptive, the punitively vindictive and the pragmatically lethal. Nevertheless, atrocity and murderer remain 'problems' she cannot 'solve': like *Beachy Head*, *The Events* aims to close some distance between characters and audience by dissolving conventional spatial divides (which also 'stand in' as metaphors of temporal divides): Grieg's play incorporates members of a local choir, specific to each community in which the play is performed. Both *Beachy Head* and *The Events* have an oddly neo-religious directive in their inclusive assembling of a self-conscious congregation to contemplate and admit something they must acknowledge as ultimately unfathomable. *The Events* may even seem to reinscribe, in its consciously limited circuit of actions, a position of liberal impotence, vocal harmonies and unison notwithstanding. My next chapter will engage further with the traumatic, in distinctly political terms.

Ed Thomas: Memory, desire and the parts you throw away

To paraphrase a Tom Waits song,[16] Ed Thomas's characters (seductively) tell you all their secrets, but they lie about their pasts (not always intentionally, or manipulatively). Thomas's mythic-political tragicomedies show how the necessarily selective faculty of memory (re)constructs the past, and how 'the past changes under the pressure of the present', and vice versa, to cite Hoffman's terms, which she resonantly develops: reconstruction not always as an inscriptive or controlling rewriting of facts, but 'placing experiential information in new – sometimes larger and richer – contexts', and so demonstrating how emotional memory 'entails acts of continuous autopoesis, or creative self-making' (Hoffman 2009: 108). Thomas's theatre of permanently fluctuating relationships shows how this subjective associative energy can generate both (self-)oppression and (re)invention. His characters speak in an engagingly energetic heightened realistic mode, but his dramatic events develop through less apparently natural time jumps and indeterminate locations that blend or alternate with a change of lighting, including overt references to 'dream sequences'. Indeed, it is appropriate in production to emphasize, through direction and scenographic design, the film noir and fantastic elements of Thomas's plays, which offer scenes that ask: 'is any given event a memory of a past or an imagination of a future?' His characters sift through their memories, in a bid to *shed* restrictions, like constrictive clothes or skins.

House of America (1988) is indicative of Thomas's subsequent drama in depicting how both predominant social relationships and microcosmic familial relationships are predicated on a submerged layer of history, stuck in a tragically arrested time of false cohesion and suppressed secrets. A mother deliberately withholds the fate of their father from her three children, who grow up on the edge of an open cast mine, naggingly conscious of how a concept of planetary speed and momentum is all that stands between them and extinction (Thomas 1994: 18). In a particularly haunting and expressionistic scene, one of the site labourers, surrounded by machines that resemble 'electric dinosaurs', complains of the loss of his head when he put it 'in the sand' at the age of 18, and its replacement with a different one, which it is now 'too late' to exchange (65–66). The siblings Sid and Gwenny are determined that the same will not befall them, and they abscond into a fictional timeline, based on expansive fantasies in which they are American Beat writer Jack Kerouac and his consort Joyce Johnson, in a bid to escape the limited options available under the immediately designated and circumscribed 'reality'. The labourer then unearths a head: of their father, killed and buried by their mother in order to instil and enforce a restrictive sense of belonging and identity for her children – her violent bid to arrest and control time, and deny loss and change (she goes mad, insisting on wearing Welsh national costume and clutching a plastic daffodil that promises to stay yellow forever). However, Sid and Gwenny's reflex into American mythology proves as deluded and evasive as their mother's retentiveness, another way to 'paper the walls' of their claustrophobic domesticity, until defensive intricacy hardens into enclosure. Their younger brother, Boyo, is shocked to discover that they have lost contact with the links between emotion and consequence: Gwenny is pregnant by Sid. In a particularly gruelling and memorable theatrical example of duration and counterpoint, Boyo strangles Sid to the sound of Lou Reed's song, 'Perfect Day': with its associations of slowed and idealized time, addictive self-forgetting and ultimate, undeferred retribution.

A sense of self-imposed enclosure and amnesia also pervades the layerings of identity in (what is nevertheless) Thomas's more ultimately optimistic play, *East from the Gantry* (1992), in which the central couple, Bella and Ronnie, have to remind each other of details such as their honeymoon location, and their brittle cheerfulness seems designed to keep fear and suspicion barely at bay (Ronnie has shot a cat, mistaking it for Bella's former boyfriend). The stranger Trampas initially seems to be a figure of Ronnie's fears and Bella's fantasies (they are both disposed to the intensities of erotic nostalgia or anticipation in preference to a distinct sense of the present); however, Trampas is suddenly (and paradoxically) individualized by his speech distinctly expressing lost opportunity in self-remaking, in which he reached for tomorrow but, transfixed, opened his eyes on the 'bitter silence of now' (Thomas 1994: 200). *Gas Station Angel* (1998) is Thomas's most ambitious and remarkable looping and overlapping of temporal perspectives in its tale of two feuding families, confused by a 'fucked up past' built on 'Secrets and lies' (Thomas 2002: 315). Thomas unfolds his narrative from several points of view, with the characters speaking directly to the audience in a disarming stand-up or cabaret style, inhabiting an active present (such as we also encounter in O'Rowe's entwined monologues and green's *random*). Characters often describe, explain and reassess events and details rather than simply enact, giving the play a conscious storytelling dimension of 'magical realism' as the story loops backwards and forwards in time[17]. The raconteur protagonist Ace explains how, when growing up, his own storytelling represented a dimension that he could control, a portal to an ultimately benign *nebenwelt* of '*tylwyth teg*'/fairies, magic and mystery, 'gaps' in literal definition and externally directed time (such as that micro-managed by even the local pub's new owner, Mr Entertainment), which may permit and invite each person to 'fill in the meaning' (369).[18] A shared pleasure in active imagination brings him into contact with Bron, daughter of a rival family (who can devastate an unwanted suitor by unfolding an accelerated projection of conventional romance, a consequentially emptied 'frozen time' to which his imagination would limit them, while 'time around' them moved on [374–375]). The charisma and rapport demonstrated by Ace and Bron exemplify how Thomas's theatre deploys language in order to reclaim its temporal importance, in all its variety and transformative energy (as does Ace's incantatory transfiguration of the sad boy Dyfrig, releasing him from his past into a sense of magical possibility, which counters the reductive, territorialized time marked out and sold by Mr Entertainment: Thomas artfully stipulates that both characters be played by the same actor). It transpires that Ace and Bron's antagonistic families are connected in unsuspected ways; thus, the secrets of the past constitute defining points of the present, *but* not completely. Ace's mother holds on to her idea of a parallel supernatural underworld (which is threatening, but not duplicitous as in Churchill's *The Skriker*), which Ace finally recharacterizes in a less fearful, regressive manner, permitting the release of the ghostly shadow of Bron's dead brother (whom his family associates with an inconsiderately idiosyncratic sense of time, potentially traumatizing in its effects on others: if extended globally, it would be catastrophic for the basic social orderings of multiple international time zones, 357–362). Together Thomas's latter-day Romeo and Juliet show it is possible to confront shameful secrets, release a divisive past, choose to see things differently, imagine change and survive, with the implication that their nation may do the same: the final image of their shared gaze is accompanied by '*the sound of the sea*', no longer in dispossessive tantrum, but (re)generatively rhythmic (406). All of Thomas's plays evoke a transforming or transformative landscape, location as time frame – either story event and/or encroaching and characterizing pressure – whilst eluding naturalistic specifics in scenography or staging. The sea in *Gas Station Angel* provides the most developed sense of this, as rhythmic perspective, beyond human resentments and restrictive shapes of time.

Thomas's *Stone City Blue* (2004) takes an acknowledged cue from the open theatrical forms of Sarah Kane's *Crave* (1998) and *4.48 Psychosis* (2000), in presenting a fragmented sense of self and time. A central consciousness ('Ray'), surrounded by Good and Bad Angel splintered shadow selves,[19] struggles to orient and perceive himself as a subject and find meaning in his life's remembered phases and events, which he selects for interpretation and revision from different perspectives, seeking new senses of connection and relief from 'temporal vertigo' (Segal 2014: 4). *Stone City Blue* aims to present a nightmarish experience of highly compressed time, in which an individual's temporal topography of continuity, succession and consequence has gone awry, resulting in a traumatic sense of disconnection and self-enclosure: 'the glue that's kept us [Ray's internal negotiators of meaning and structure] all together can't hold' so that the 'whole thing is turning in on itself', unsure of 'what is made up or memory' (Thomas 2004: 34–71). Ray acknowledges, 'I'm just the son of my father' (44), though this involves a history and memory of a husband and wife 'killing each other inside' because of their inability or unwillingness to communicate their fears and longings. We then follow the story of Ray's father, and his illness through cancer, which drives him to plead 'Forgive me' to the mirage of a betrayed wife who is no longer present. The voices of Ray seem to work their way out from a sense of guilt, of emotional murder of self and others, by reconnecting with a sense of a stone thrown into the 'river of time' (99), a continuum incorporating those who came before – forefathers, ancestors – in order to be able to forgive self and others, recover a sense of temporal fluidity so and ultimately make time, to express love.

Thomas consistently dramatizes psychic life as what the psychoanalyst Christopher Bollas describes as 'a kind of haunting', by ghosts who re-present the residues of intense encounters over a lifetime, meaningful but not always knowable or fully intelligible, contributing to 'life's mystery and the strangeness of being human' (quoted in Segal 2014: 24). Thomas's characteristic sense of the fluidity of life and possibility frequently involves him in critically mindful identifications of how men, even more than women, are culturally expected to remain and become more relentlessly, determinedly and notionally 'themselves' over time (I re-apply terms from Segal 2014: 118), and the ways in which this may constitute existential constraint.

Butterworth: Time past and time present

These two qualities identified with Thomas's theatre, in the paragraph above, are also salient to that of Jez Butterworth, who writes in as specifically an English context as Thomas does in a Welsh one. Nevertheless, both dramatists engage with their symbolical geologies with a distinctness of detail that intends to 'sound' a 'deep time' of wider (potentially universal) resonances.

Harpin observes that, whilst many recent site-specific theatrical and performance pieces have 'abandoned the epic time frames and panoramic settings of the traditional [state-of-the-nation play], they retain an unerring concern with the mechanics of state power and the root cultural identity that lies beneath', and, hence, 'what on earth national identity might mean any more' (Harpin 2011a: 65). Harpin proposes that Butterworth's play *Jerusalem*, though written for and first presented in a conventional theatre setting, demonstrates a similar 'preoccupation with geographical minutiae and the natural landscape', which itself challenges 'the non-spaces and boundary-less homogeneity of global capital and its devastating environmental consequences'; hence, its view of English country life is 'not in the spirit of nationalism or isolationism', but rather offers 'landscape as a prism through which to refract broader questions of culture, of identity, of place', a 'heightened geographical sensibility' that 'troubles the ancient ground upon which "here" and "now" might be built' (66).

This 'geographical sensibility' with regard to landscape and history is also powerfully present in Butterworth's earlier play, *The Winterling* (2006), in which a frozen forest landscape's temporal associations with authority, sacrifice and honour – represented formerly by a stone circle, burial mound and Iron Age fort – thaw and 'resurface' with new resonances (including, initially, fighter plane exercises and government directed mass exterminations of badgers) to contextualize the visit of contemporary bewildered middle-order gangsters, who, particularly because out of their 'comfort zones', strategically change frames of reference like poker players laying out successive cards. Wally nostalgically appeals to a sense of interpersonal order and continuity ('Nothing changes' [Butterworth 2011: 192]), which is significantly resisted by his former colleague, West (206). Wally's junior partner/apprentice, Patsy, strikes a (defensive?) pose of confident superiority over the former inhabitants of the landscape, who built and defended the fort, dismissing them pejoratively as 'history', 'yesterday's men' 'washed over' by the 'sands of time' (212). However, West knows the earlier violent sacrificial associations of the site and challenges Patsy to find the gumption to engage with this tradition: 'The skill. The knowledge [...] It's your turn' (218).

The second act of *The Winterling* has a structural function similar to that which Mark Taylor-Batty identifies in Pinter's *No Man's Land*: 'the subtle battle to gain advantage' in a given situation 'via manipulations of memory and imagined pasts', in which West here proves the strongest player, by finally and decisively 'insinuating himself into a dream' (Taylor-Batty 2014: 122–123). West wins the game, played with cards/terms of temporal identity, by actively rewriting the past to gain ground in the present, and so displacing the farmhouse's former occupant, his rights of tenancy and authority: 'taking all'. The dreamlike atmosphere of 'thaw' and (re)surfacing extends into the third act: Lue, the girl who lives upstairs in the farmhouse like an animal in her lair, recalls a vision of passing through the fort and seeing Patsy, immobile as a stone, then replaced by torn clothes, blood and bone. Wally reveals that the decisive test of loyalty for West will involve his killing and decapitation of Patsy, in exchange for his own survival (and West has earlier identified the grim imperatives of honour in this line of work, how he has tortured other men, as he was tortured by former colleagues). However, West spares Patsy and urges him to escape with Lue: West awaits Wally with an axe, and a stoic last-ditch resolution that recalls the former defenders of the fort, but also represents a resistance of hierarchy and its relentless gladiatorial demands. Thus, the events of Butterworth's play seem to strip away the temporal layers of the present-day fictional landscape, releasing older patterns of sacrifice, retribution and investment in new forms, strange even to themselves (a process that is also identifiable in Rudkin's 1960 play *Afore Night Come* [Rabey 2015: 88–89]).

Ed Thomas has spoken of his sense of time in his theatre as a disintegrating 'palimpsest', creating gaps that 'the reader has to fill in' to 'complete it morally' (Thomas, in Rabey 2006: 550). This also seems pertinent to Butterworth's *The River* (2012), in which the presences of women, who are brought to a specific cottage by a man, seem to overlap in the layered fluidity of the play's interactive associations. *The River* depicts an accumulated but shifting series of frames of temporal reference; it brings together, in a specified location, a compression of events that would normally be separated across an expanse of time. Its central image initially seems to evoke the sense of flow that is commonly associated with time, for example, as cited by Priestley: 'For Time as we know it, we need both change and not-change, some things moving and others apparently keeping still, the stream flowing and its banks motionless' (Priestley 1964: 64). However, a more specific image/principle of time may be at work informing this play. Butterworth's choice of epigraph, from T. S. Eliot's 'Burnt Norton', reflects how this specified section of the poem has been used as illustration of a quantum paradigm, in which principles of temporality, action and pattern are not clearly and consistently divisible, but exist in parallel, with aspects that interpenetrate and implicate each other. We will recall that the word 'quantum' stands for a unit of action that contains energy and time, and that 'quanta' are dynamic patterns of activities, energy patterns from which matter cannot be separated (Adam 1990: 58). Capra famously suggested how both action and the very notion of pattern are fundamentally temporal, also by reference to the same section of Eliot's poem: how, at subatomic level, 'the interrelations and interactions between the parts of the whole are more fundamental than the moving parts themselves' so that 'there is activity but there are no actors; there are no dancers, there is only the dance' (Capra 1982: 83). Accordingly, in *The River* narrative time is not linear but jumps unpredictably, skipping chronological frames as one woman replaces another, and The Man seems compulsively driven to try out all possibilities, situating himself temporarily but (generally) convincingly in various forms of relationships, which are never fully or finally actualized. The theatrical emphasis is, rather, on fundamental uncertainty and the relationship of mutual implication between the observer and the observed, where things can be described but 'reality' is never finally, exhaustively knowable or known. Butterworth's *The River* creates a theatrical prism where, to borrow and apply two phrases from Adam, time becomes '*a local, internal feature of the system of observation*', here specific to the play, '*dependent on observers and their measurements*' (1990: 56), both characters and spectators. By implication, the spectator is led to acknowledge her/his own reflexivity and relativity, including in her/his analysis and interpretations of *The River* a conscious awareness of their own 'symbol-constructing nature' and 'theoretical framework' (Adam 2004: 63). Indeed, Butterworth's play may imply that we might extend this conscious awareness to our wider extra-theatrical relations and interactions: our sense of time as *practice*.

Breaking the loop: McDowall's radical uncertainty

Alistair McDowall is one of the most striking emergent British dramatists in his depictions of how the normal rules need not apply; that is, how theatre can speculate about the suspension of the laws of physics and time, metaphorically suspending and questioning other forms and frameworks of behavioural determinism (such as the moral and political), in ways which suggest that determinism is itself a suspension of the imagination. McDowall's play *Brilliant Adventures* (2013) introduces two brothers, barely surviving in a dystopian (?) post-industrial edgeland, where the elder, Rob, profits from sale of drugs: a premise initially strikingly similar to Ridley's *Mercury Fur* (McDowall's boys' father has regressed to a feral pet, more canine than Beckett's Lucky). However, McDowall adds the science-fiction premise that the marginalized younger brother, Luke, has proved capable of building a time machine. This dramatic plot device might immediately be associated with simplistic utopian *ex machina* wish-fulfilment; however, McDowall shows how its existence begets significant ongoing complications for his characters, principally when it attracts the attention of a criminal profiteer, Ben. Luke is reluctant to use the machine (though Rob insists that not to use it is 'an insult to, to, *science*' [McDowall 2014: 35, original emphasis]), but his situation becomes more desperately pressurized, to discover some way of repudiating Ben's so-called materialistic 'realism' (voracious acquisition and control through fear, based on exerting destructive leverage involving money or sex or violence). Luke uses the time machine to create a second interventionist version of himself, returning from the future to change the situation through resistant (but limited) knowledge of the possibility of decisive action, which will itself project events into new sequential directions he cannot predict. Ingredients that might seem farcical turn more tragicomic under McDowall's applied theatrical pressure: the time travel premise cannot mitigate against other forms of threat, pain and loss experienced and expressed by the characters, in terms both poignant (when the father is briefly released from his broken form, to reminisce on better times, like Wilder's Emily) and harrowing (Luke and Rob suffer painful permanently disfiguring injuries at Ben's hands). Crucially, Luke has to convince Rob not to condemn himself (and those around) by/to making the same mistakes over and over again, to use his imagination rather than to pursue avoidance, notwithstanding the 'trouble' involved in choosing to make a situation *thoroughly and unpredictably* revolutionary: in this case, by decisively resisting Ben's moral and political presumptions, even in terms that may involve sacrifice and separation, in space and time.

McDowall's darker play *Pomona* (2014) ingeniously deploys what Rebellato describes as a 'disordered chronology' (Rebellato 2015) to engage the audience in a haunting and bewildering high-stakes hunt for meaning and value, set in a dystopian (?) gothic *noir* Manchester (artfully, the first speech concludes with a reference to a 'kind of a mysterious ending' [McDowall 2015: 8]). The play opens with Ollie being driven by Zeppo, a petty gangster and landowner who practises distanciation from the responsibility of knowledge (the contents of what he eats, the events that occur in his rented buildings), 'like a form of time travel' ([16], like Ben in *Brilliant Adventures*, Zeppo presumes everything can be bought [and few features of this world appear immediately to contradict him; like Rob, Zeppo survives and profits through imaginative self-disconnection]). Ollie, contrastingly, refuses to abandon her twin sister to whatever trouble she may be in. Behind them, a figure in the mask of Chthulu (H. P. Lovecraft's god of chaos) presides,[20] either (as in the script) momentarily distracted and placated by solving Rubik's cube puzzles, rapidly experimenting with alternating different alignments in order to find new permutations of consistent sequence; or else (as in Ned Bennett's production as it arrived at Manchester Royal Exchange theatre in October 2015) rolling polyhedral dice (associated with role-playing games) to cue the actions and initiatives of other characters.

In four scenes, a female performer plays Ollie; in three scenes, she plays her endangered twin. However, even the imparted information of a twin sister's existence will not entirely prepare an audience for the associated experiences of uncertainty, which will provoke attempted retrospective interpretations of particular scenes, yielding new points of possible significance. This reflects the dislocation expressed by the characters: Ollie says at one point, 'It's hard to recognise when your life is looping' (43), until at some point (perhaps the eighth loop of apparent repetition) a detail becomes noticeable and a figure 'pushes through the loop' (45) with a terrifying intimation, which is subsequently ignored by all others around: 'The loop fractures / But continues' (47). However, Ollie *or* her sister may be imaginary self-displacements from traumatic events, or else figures in a role-playing game. Similarly, the (female) character Keaton may be the vicious superior of Gale (who runs a brothel that extends into nightmarish depths of snuff movies and organ harvesting) charged with keeping the criminal empire intact, or Keaton may be The Girl, an urban legend harbinger of vengeful apocalyptic destruction, or both. The gothic noir of the setting permits a surrealistic disengagement of linear forms of time, which is both dreamlike / playfully enlivening (one character reappears as a seagull), and nightmarish / ominously enveloping (one character reports being imprisoned for no reason: the general climate of characters' vulnerability and susceptibility is one of several features by which the play erodes a secure distance from theatrical events that the audience may try to sustain). The play's final scenes raise further questions, as to whether some crucial intervention and salvation has been achieved (and by whom, on whose behalf), or not, and whether the first scene is about to be re/played with similar or possibly differently informed consequences,[21] reminding us that successful pretence and performance involve making the discontinuous and disparate appear to be continuous and consistent. Like the edgeland lacuna to which the play's title refers, *Pomona* presents the audience with haunting dialectical experiences of radical uncertainty, and with questions of moral consequence, of which they (like the characters, in their world of systematic disengagement, discomfortingly near to present intimations) must finalize a decisive interpretation, alone. However, *Pomona* also indicates (like *Brilliant Adventures* that also demonstrates an embattled but surprising, and so potentially transformative, sibling loyalty) that only an action that is *unpredictable* in its (potentially self-sacrificial) courage and mutuality might break the loop of deterministic damage and degeneration. In this respect, *Pomona* provides an apt hinge into the more overtly political sphere of reference constituted by our last chapter.

Notes

1   One lens through which to view the theatrical work of the nature(s) considered in this chapter might be appropriately provided by terms that Hunka associates with the 'metaphysical': where 'the subject spectator' perceives an object/moment 'from a number of metaphysical

perspectives as time progresses: but the object changes as well, relocating itself from place to different place in the metaphysical landscape', so that as 'more and more about that object becomes known, that knowledge undermines the subject's certainty that he knows just what the object is'. This creates a 'dynamic of conflict' predicated on 'the understandable urge to hang onto what is known in fear or trembling of approaching the unknowable, that which can't be defined and probably can't be presented on a stage anyway' (Hunka 2014).

2 Favorini suggests Beckett theorizes habit and memory as 'self-preservational' 'responses by the human organism to escape victimizing at the hands of time', although his characters are 'struck erratically by the lightning bolt of involuntary memory, when the consolations of habit or reminiscence are withdrawn' (Favorini 2008: 185–186).

3 http://www.phillipzarrilli.com/trainapp/index1.html accessed 4/8/2014, and Zarrilli, Phillip B. (2000), *When the Body Becomes All Eyes* Oxford: Oxford University Press India. Zarrilli's delineation of 'slow theatre' (with reference to Ōta Shōgo's *The Water Station*) is also pertinent to our considerations: Zarrilli, http://exeuntmagazine.com/features/the-water-station-living-human-silence/ accessed 30/10/2015.

4 Some readers may be surprised that Michael Frayn's acclaimed play *Copenhagen* (1998) does not loom larger in this study. I feel that, while Frayn's play is laudable in its insistence that physics has an irreducibly political dimension in both paradigms and application, its dramatic form and contextualization of its characters, in a reflective yet reiterative 'afterlife', tend to obscure problems of consequentiality and determinism, even as it strives to present an insistently humanistic and reconciliatory image of contradictory complementarity.

5 Her question, as to what he is doing 'at this time of night?' (Pinter 1991a: 362), becomes a repeated enquiry in Pinter's drama, as characters undertake nocturnal activities at what others sense are disturbing *times* (in *The Caretaker, Silence, The Homecoming* and *Moonlight*).

6 All these factors also appear in Jez Butterworth's short play, *Leavings* (2006), on which, see Rabey (2015: 89–91). The dreaming, reappearing dog in Pinter's *A Kind of Alaska* also suggests something that is trying to be faithful, but proves imperfectly biddable – like memory.

7 Adam observes how listening to popular songs of earlier periods 'allows us to relive experiences of many years ago. We need to recognise, however, that the contemporary reliving is always inclusive of the intervening years, that these years are fundamentally implicated and resonate through the experience' so that the 'relived experience is different because of it'. She adds, the same principle applies 'when we watch a Shakespeare play, or look at a photograph album': 'the past is reconstituted in the present, making the past as revocable and hypothetical as the future' (Adam 1990: 143). Favorini suggests that, if Beckett's characters look at memory microscopically, so that small things appear bigger, Pinter's characters look at memory telescopically, so that something large appears smaller (Favorini 2008: 194).

8 On Pete Atkin's album *Winter Spring* (Hillside Music, Bristol, 2003). Pinter's political (re)contextualization of a Beckettian trope (here, compulsive dissociation) has a possible parallel in David Edgar's play *The Jail Diary of Albie Sachs* (1978). I have noted previously how Edgar's play deploys Beckettian elements, 'sensory deprivation and heightened perception, and the mutual interrogation of rational motivation and physical contingency', and makes

the audience focus on an unusual *duration* of apparent inactivity, but in a political rather than metaphysical context, out of which the protagonist fashions purpose and meaning (Rabey 2003: 118).

9 In these respects, Pinter's play and protagonist anticipate, and may have influenced, Neilson's *The Wonderful World of Dissocia*, considered in the next chapter.

10 Hunka observes elsewhere, 'Time is the creator of memory and the limit of our consciousness. The more time passes, the less is left to us. We are aware of that. The theatre is not a place for the young' (2013).

11 Tot's expressionistic speech at his Stygian moment of death recalls for me Shroeder's observation on Harriet's farewell speech in Wilder's *Pullman Car Hiawatha*: 'Seen from this unique, retrospective viewpoint, time passes imperceptibly in an accumulation of details with significance only for the person involved' (Schroeder 1989: 62). However, it does so whilst suggesting that this may possibly be true for us all, in ways that might constitute a final particularity and defiance of generalization.

12 'The true "cost of a thing," wrote Henry David Thoreau, "is the amount of what I will call life which is required to be exchanged for it." And the true value of a thing is the amount of life we are willing to exchange for it' (Kalb 2011: 22).

13 Adam notes how writers such as Irigaray and O'Brien have criticized Heidegger's 'being unto death' as an inappropriately masculine approach to time, which excludes birth and time generation. It may be that Barker's perspective in *Death, The One and the Art of Theatre* eludes at least some of these criticisms of Heidegger, in that Barker criticizes the contemporary cultural fear and denial of mortality, which writers such as King associate with patriarchal civilization, and repositions centrally – in his own idiosyncratic ways – the figure of the desired woman ('The One') who is patriarchally marginalized or demonized as an incessant reminder of mortality and the limitations of exclusively male definition (Adam 1995: 146).

14 O'Rowe's *Our Few and Evil Days* (2014) suggests a further extrapolation of McPherson, specifically his plays *Shining City* (2004) and *The Seafarer* (2006), in suggesting how the past impinges inextinguishably on the present, in the spectral form(s) of a supernatural revenant.

15 Robin Soans's play *Crouch, Touch, Pause, Engage* (2015) also brings its dual protagonists to the edge of suicide – in one case, a clifftop – at the point of interval, to consider their terms of persistence in the second half. Soans's wider dramatic strategy involves assembling a montage of perspectives, over time, on the rugby player Gareth Thomas: a strategy of temporal fragmentation in order to see a subject more whole in their less widely acknowledged chaos, which is also at work in Rudkin's *Cries from Casement* (1972). I submit that the 'modern-classic' paradigm of this is Orson Welles's film *Citizen Kane* (1941).

16 'Tango 'till They're Sore'.

17 I am grateful for Ben Howarth's observation on how Thomas creates an illusion of fluctuating time in his plays: when characters, who represent different (temporal) perspectives on events, meet; and then a character's conversation with one partner flows into an engagement with a different one, but the rhythm of flow continues, rather than having to start afresh.

18 *Gas Station Angel* (1998) anticipates Butterworth's *Jerusalem* (2009), in that it dramatizes a wide range of a specifically located community: characters poised precariously between

the directives of an invasive council (and the degenerate machinations of a publican's conscious exploitation) and the warily respectful invocations of an older authority, a supernatural world.

19   The published text, based on the first production, documents four performers, two of each gender. My own 2008 production of *Stone City Blue* involved, and distributed lines between, 15 performers of differing genders. Themes in the play that emerged in rehearsal included: people want to mould or shape others, or else shrink away from them; mechanical married couples try to fit together, then find that they push apart; people withdraw from the promise and challenge of each other; they can't give because they can't accept; they adopt and/or impose a deafening, blinding, deceiving, taunting grin.

20   This figure may be interpreted retrospectively as another gangster, Charlie, who is later shown to have a similar mask; or as Keaton wearing Charlie's mask (as in Bennett's production as it arrived at Manchester Royal Exchange theatre in October 2015); or else it may be the dramatic manifestation of the malign supernatural.

21   In this respect, *Pomona*'s ending evokes for me the ending of Patrick McGoohan's final episode ('Fall Out') of his innovative television series *The Prisoner* (1967-8), which permitted the final interpretation of the protagonist's escape, but also permitted the final interpretation of the protagonist's recapture, and the whole 'loop' of events beginning again (the 'cyclic' form of McGoohan's text depicting the process of 'struggle of every one of us to maintain our individuality within society' [Gregory 1997: 176–177]).

Interlude 2

The Clock in the Forest: *Jerusalem* Unenclosed: A Case History

I have written elsewhere (Rabey 2015: 111ff) on senses of time in Butterworth's *Jerusalem* (2009), but it seems appropriate to return to Butterworth's most acclaimed play, and Harpin's context of argument, by way of a case history based on seeing the play situated anew: at Shobrooke Park, Crediton, on 28 June 2014, the last performance in the final venue of an English West Country tour (May–June 2014) of open-air site-specific performances[1] undertaken by The Common Players in co-production with Exeter Northcott Theatre, directed by Anthony Richards. This 're-imagining' of Butterworth's play (as described by the programme cover[2]) took place in specifically rural outdoor settings, not so as to inforce a limiting sense of geographical literalism, but to make the play available to those who lived closer to its fictional setting (than the play's original places of staging, The Royal Court and Apollo Theatres in London) and localized concerns, and to attempt a resonantly – even mythically – expansive situation of the play at the epicentre of a midsummer festival.

As spectators approached the country park site of Shobrooke Park, they were greeted by signage directing them to the 'fair' (at the edge of which Butterworth's play takes place); then, from the other side of the central amphitheatrical field, the sounds of live performances by musicians (local to the specific town of performance); and then the welcoming vista of a range of lakeside stalls selling locally produced food and drink. This provided the extended setting for a full performance of Butterworth's three-act play, in which each act was punctuated by musical interval and preceded by a mumming play. In Richards's production, the principal theatrical action took on a stunt bike ramp (painted with an extravagant fabulous 'Johnny Rooster Byron' emblem imposed upon a St. George's Cross) and the back of a lorry, which were used to elevate performers, situated next to the 'foreground' area in front of Rooster's caravan (and 'disclosure space').

Kalb notes how it is 'no coincidence that long productions tend to occur in summer, as their slowed-down experience of time replicates benefits that many people seek in vacations, such as travelling with other people to share common experiences with them', and 'relishing elongated days to commune with nature' (Kalb 2011: 16), and the promised likelihood of drier weather is of course another factor. The Common Players' production of *Jerusalem* indeed benefited from these contextual associations at the performance I attended, but the contexts of landscape and time moreover conducted and amplified the resonances of the play itself, which includes the implication that a sense of time (and history) as process is only possible 'after we have transcended dualistic thinking in which we oppose change and persistence, synchrony and diachrony' (Ingold, quoted in Adam 1995: 27). *Jerusalem* involves conflicts of past and present associations, and asks how these might be reinvigorated, discarded and/or synthesized to create and hand on a meaningful future. Richards's production drew out, in its fortuitous specifics of place and time, the sense of Butterworth's play as offering what Adam terms a 'timescape': an extension of landscape perspective to 'develop an analogous receptiveness to temporal interdependencies and absences' (Adam 1998: 54).

Applying Adrian May's terms, I suggest *Jerusalem* begins with a tragicomic view of 'anxiety about what the world is coming to' when the (social and political) world 'ignores the strength of what it suppresses' (May 2011: 63); a tragicomic premise comparable to Adam's point of departure, identifying how 'the combination of existential threat, scientific uncertainty and government bungling causes paralysis in the afflicted, preventing them from engaging in constructive thought and purposive action' (Adam 1998: 3). *Jerusalem* ends in apocalyptic style, in terms that May associates with the mythic confrontation with the dragon, an event that involves identifying the monstrous in the 'good' and the good in the 'monstrous': the play *Jerusalem* might also be seen as a dramatic poem of 'the present being haunted by the Shadow of the greatness of the past, and somehow betraying it' (May 2011: 62ff–63). The protagonist Byron plays the role of mythological Trickster to the hilt, as 'boundary crosser and boundary creator' who lies and steals shamelessly, not so much to 'get away with something or get rich' as – like myth itself – 'to disturb the established categories of truth and property' (Hyde, quoted in May 2011: 96–97).

Whereas Ian Rickson's original stage production of *Jerusalem* picked out and foregrounded Rooster's Wood and the caravan as a capacious, verdant clearing in a somewhat 'Jacobean' indeterminate darkness, Richards's open-air production demonstrated how the play was also amenable to a more 'Elizabethan' approach, involving occasional boisterous spectacle, interludes and mutually visible spectators. Richards's production also set the characters within and against a landscape of animal life and natural light, stretching as far as the eye could see, and beyond. The first act opened and played in bright evening light, with a chorus of more than a dozen 'Green Men', playing percussion, converging from the outskirts onto the playing space; they then froze, rapt, to listen to Phaedra sing the opening invocation, Blake and Parry's anthem 'Jerusalem', on the back of the lorry, which then cut to the playing of amplified rave music, and the further action.

The 'Green Men' (and women – in fact performed by all members of the company not otherwise on stage) returned for the production's ending: after Byron's climactic curse, a startling conflagration engulfed his caravan (more spectacularly than in the Apollo production, prompting audience gasps), with not only smoke billowing but also high flames leaping from it (its structure, I was informed, had been specially constructed by a sculptor to permit this in successive performances). Then, Byron (or his irrepressible spirit?) reappeared, to take his place amongst the 'Green Men' for final drumbeats and applause. Whereas Rickson's London production of *Jerusalem* finally emphasized gruellingly bloody sacrificial tragedy, Richards's production thus finally chose to strike a festive midsummer note, enfolding Byron into folklore associations of resurgent figures who are celebrated even as they are apparently destroyed, from John Barleycorn to Guy Fawkes, or who cheat death, like Mr Punch outwitting and killing The Devil.[3]

However, it was in intervening moments of the narrative where Richards's production, and its setting, interacted most memorably in distinct confluences and counterpoints of human time and natural rhythms. Not all of these could be completely premeditated and guaranteed. On the occasion I attended, there was an ominous rumble of thunder as the Professor announced his intention to set off to the fair. There were massed cries from a flock of birds, rising from the lake, as Byron claimed to 'have eyes everywhere'. Similarly, birdsong was particularly audible in the pauses after Byron's declaration, 'I ain't goin' up the fair today', after which the sounds of his klaxon siren died away into a silence illustrated by a blood red sunset, and owl cries followed his action of burning the summons. Alongside these capacities for theatrical serendipity were some resonantly definite decisions: the electric lighting was switched onto the performance area to begin Act Two (Phaedra's rendition of the song 'Werewolf', for which she was surrounded by the bordering dim shapes of 'Green Men'); at Byron's invocation of the 'black eyed boys' of his dead and buried forefathers, all characters looked out at the surrounding darkening hillsides; in Act Three, Davey's instruction, 'Smell that', encouraged spectators to be similarly aware of night air (and they actually saw the performer of Wesley leave the central playing area and jump into the bordering lake after announcing his intention to swim); and the delivery of Byron's climactic curse allowed time for all to hear a dimension of respondent echo, suspended in the landscape. The Common Players' production of *Jerusalem* thus overcame my major reservations about open-air site-specific performances: they may sometimes (though not always) involve a loss of sonic and scenographic focus, and rhythms slackening through mutual distraction. This final performance at Crediton constituted a triumphant example of theatrical narrative in specifically contrapuntal interaction with its setting, in both space *and* time: a 'host' space (a conscious synthesis of nature and human theatrical sculpture into amphitheatre shape), literally echoing with 'ghosts'[4] at its furthest reaches, and beyond. It thus presented a theatrical timescape, in that it reversed the dominant cultural emphasis 'on visible materiality at the expense of what is latent, immanent and hidden from view': an emphasis promulgated when 'countryside and meadows, mountains and forests, wild animals and birds' are referred to exclusively as 'the *products* of nature', 'externalised outcomes of processes' and 'de-contextualised physical phenomena without activity or process' (Adam 1998: 12, original emphasis). This was an event that emphasized the essential importance and vitality of temporality and context, in re-presentations and re-imaginings of living phenomena and processes.

Notes

1　Other open-air locations on the tour were: Knackershole Theatre, Dulverton; Torre Abbey, Torquay; Kentisbeare; Hatherleigh; Moretonhampstead; Lewdown; Hannah's at Seale-Hayne, Newton Abbot.

2　'Re-locating' or 're-situating' might have been more precise, if we are prepared to consider each production of a play a 're-imagining'.

3 The tragic sacrificial aspects of Butterworth's play alludes to ancient folklore motifs: Robert Bly notes the complicating feelings likely to be evoked by the European Middle Ages pageant story of the Wild Man who enters the town, disregards threats and rejects offers of inclusion, refuses to give up his forest life and 'leaves town to the cheers of the young men and the exuberant dancing of the lovers'; only for the pageant to end on a more ominous note, 'a mile out of town', where the townspeople meet the Wild Man, put his costume on a straw man and throw it into a lake, in ritual execution (perhaps the vestiges of a previous actual execution in the community [Bly 2001: 249–250]).

4 The terms 'host' and 'ghost' were developed in the contexts of site-specific performance by Cliff McLucas and Mike Pearson, and are succinctly introduced in McLucas (2000: 128).

Chapter 5

Time Out of Joint

My final major chapter considers time and temporality as resource in an age of centralization, as instrument of group interaction and as political currency, and how this might be re-presented theatrically. I will consider some examples of theatre that deal with/in the problematization of time as a notional limitation of our lifespans and possibilities, and how these entwined concepts are defined in terms of social prioritization and allocation. For some, as Borst comments, time 'holds out the prospect of enjoying the most arbitrary things, while for other it offers the prospect of lacking the things they most need' (Borst 1993: 132). However, as Griffiths points out, there are 'thousands of times, not one'; to 'say any one time is *the* time is both untrue and highly political' (Griffiths 1999: 2, original emphasis). Gipson-King observes with admirable succinctness: if 'perceptions of time reflect worldview, then depicting time *differently* can challenge that worldview and potentially challenge the institutions that perpetuate and profit from the dominant temporal paradigm' (Gipson-King 2013: 154).

One of the principal political 'confidence tricks' under which we labour is how industrial society, and its combination of clock-time, scientific laws and a money economy, has 'de-temporalised the temporal, fixed the ephemeral, transformed transience into permanence, and thus created a simulacrum of immortality and omnipotence' (Adam 1998: 70). For example, James Gleick points out how it is 'no accident' that the Directorate of Time, an agency of the United States military based in Washington, belongs to the Department of Defence, because knowing 'the exact time is an essential feature of delivering airborne explosives to exact locations – individual buildings, or parts of buildings – thus minimizing one of the department's standard euphemisms, collateral damage' (Gleick [1999] 2000: 7). The modern nation state justifies its accumulations of information, and predication on what it characterizes as *protective* control, on the basis of its promises to ensure that the future can be rendered predictable (and thereby controllable, pre-emptively if necessary). Assurance in survival is thus purveyed as a matter of making things conform to our expectations, but assisted by externally imposed frameworks of regulation.

So, in an application of 'reverse engineering' (to use a term from Tim Price's play, *The Radicalization of Bradley Manning*), tasks for theatre might encompass a demonstratively embodied retooling process, aiming to re-temporalize the temporal, demonstrate as provisional what is purportedly 'fixed', emphasize the transience of the supposedly permanent, expose the intrinsic flaws of the systemic ideologies underpinning current power structures and manifest the surprising possibilities that are alternative to what is widely supposed to be, and promoted as, natural, just and inevitable (not least, to preserve an ostensible 'security'). As Hoffman observes, when we consciously (re)consider time in practice, what is 'at stake is not only the public sphere, but the politics of experience' (Hoffman 2009: 13).

The lyrics to Paddy McAloon's song 'Elegance' (1984) shrewdly identify one facet of time authoritarianism:

There are those whose time
Is due for swift decline
If you can't find the spot
Where their time stops
Just ask who built the clocks.[1]

Timebends and countermyths

Bigsby describes Arthur Miller's objective as a theatrical 'timebend' (adapting the title from Miller's autobiography): 'the folding of time together [to] bring past and present into immediate contact', with 'the assumption [...] that meaning is a product of such interactions, that the parallel universes of "now" and "then", once brought into contact, generate significance, speak to each other in the language of memory' (Bigsby 2005: 126).

Thornton Wilder's allusion to the sense of tenuous relief with which people might emerge from a depression 'by the skin of their teeth' is further investigated, with foregrounded references to time, in Miller's *The American Clock* (1980). Miller's briskly far-reaching play recalls Wilder's *Our Town* in its fluidly anti-naturalistic evocations of various locations and mobilization of many characters (over 40 in *The American Clock*).[2] Miller's explorations of spatial relations under the heightened pressure of time is furthered in *Playing for Time* (1985) that similarly opts for demonstrative and anti-illusionistic changes of scene and costume, in order to present a selective dramatic representation of imprisonment in a concentration camp, where perceptions of time may alternate between extreme repetition and – particularly for characters under death sentence – extreme acceleration.

The American Clock foregrounds two senses of time: the image of a national 'doomsday clock', a measure of risk and precarity that may provide a warning 'countdown' to extensive social disaster; and the national sense of capitalist social economics as a mechanism offering inevitable continuity and impervious buoyancy (as for some, believing 'For them the clock could never strike midnight' [Miller 1983: 2]). Miller's wide but specific theatrical tapestry challenges several characters' presumptions of faith in the prevalent system: Lee's sense that life was a matter of 'individuals' working hard to make 'the right goods' and so becoming 'well-off' (16); the question of whether the strike action of Iowa farmers, aiming to 'create scarcity and raise prices' is 'conservative' or 'revolutionary' (25); even the businessman Robertson is mindful of the precariousness of any success, when he closes the first half of the play by recalling observations, from his more comfortably located window, of the shanty towns and encampments of the unemployed, along the banks of the Hudson river. Whilst deducing 'people still blamed themselves rather than the government', Robertson is conscious that 'there's never been a society that hasn't had a clock running on it and you couldn't help wondering – how long? How long would they stand for this?', and he vocalizes the ticking of a clock that he claims was almost audible, 'in the air', on such nights (41), extending into the interval distinctly social senses of mounting pressure, impatience and fragility.

One of Miller's achievements in *The American Clock* is to dramatize events representing a definitely specific time and place, which nevertheless are likely to float free from exclusive application, and provide connections with fears and hopes experienced in other countries, at other times. His characters' senses of temporal possibility might nevertheless be described as characteristically American in their presiding senses of resilience, buoyancy and energetic optimism, but any sense of possibility is also shown to be crucially subject to external determining social and political forces:

LEE: How could there be another war?
JOE: Long as there's capitalism, baby.

(43)

Again, Robertson, though individually successful, is depicted as mindful of the erosive duration of the economic depression: 'a whole generation was withering in the best years of its life' (55), which informs an urgency of concern among the activist characters that disaster might not be averted, as when one admits, 'I'm afraid there isn't going to be time to save this country' (65). However, one African-American character observes that even the extents and effects of crisis may be shaped and channelled politically to effect delay; he reflects wryly, 'the main thing about the Depression is that it finally hit the white people', when 'us folks never had nothin' else' (50). Another, Irene, addresses a crowd and tries to instil a sense of responsive urgency: even if they are instinctively resistant, and think they are 'so educated' they would 'sooner die than say brother', Irene insists that the 'Time has come to say brother'; that their best recourse for survival with dignity is unified, orchestrated, collective action.

Robertson finally reflects on the odds of the recurrence of an economic depression, with a finely poised awareness of human capacity to learn; he finds it hard to imagine a comparable future economic disintegration, 'but of course there is no limit to human stupidity' (81). He reflects that during the leadership of President Roosevelt ('a conservative, traditional man who was driven to the Left by one emergency after another' [81]), the country, somehow, achieved a sense of agency rather than impotence. This harks back to an earlier scene in which characters are encouraged by listening to the words of Roosevelt, in a radio broadcast, professing his intention to steer government away from the paradigm of a 'mechanical implement', something absolute and external to human subjectivity (like the functionalist and saturnine figuring of clock-time), towards 'the vibrant personal character that is the embodiment of human charity' and reciprocity: crucially, forms of *generosity* with time, rather than its sale or saving, necessary in this instance to relieve the unemployed of the 'dark fear' that 'they are not needed in the world' (53). One of the questions raised by Miller's play is the importance of the terms of how one might count and value human time, including that spent in work. Zoe Williams observes how 'hardworking' has become a denomination and award of 'morality, citizenship, respect and status', though this may equate honour with measures of economic profitability, social opportunity and consumption (Williams 2015) that are, in turn, defined by social opportunity. 'Minimum wage' work, and being a domestic carer, are onerous and demand many hours, but do not entitle workers to the circumstances and facilities of those with more highly *valued* skills; activities such as engaging in exercise, reading poetry and attending theatre may be demanding, even strenuous, but do not accrue financial reward. The system of value is just that: a system, geared towards self-perpetuation. The very title of Miller's play, *The American Clock*, indicates how it might be appropriate to analyse the valuing of time in a nation's cultural politics, and to consider how it may differ from another's.

Favorini observes how Edward Bond frequently opposes the mythologizing of the past by 'constructing countermyths', as do David Hare and Howard Brenton (Favorini 2008: 72). These dramatists 'bend time', not just to effect an informative historical dialectic, but to enable one predominantly authoritative 'version' of political meaning to be brought into critical collision with a consciously disruptive alternative. For example, Bond's play *Early Morning* (1968) constitutes his sustained confrontation with the associations and (subsequent) Conservative reanimations of 'Victorian values', imperial ideology reconfigured as the 'false memories' of national tradition that Bond deconstructs, lest it fix into a restricted political sense of present and future possibilities like a badly set broken limb. Bond's play is one of the most scarifying examples of theatrical deconstructions of British national identity and iconography of its period (see Poore 2012, particularly his section 'Staging the Empire', 46–66); this seam of Bond's work is also visible in his plays *Narrow Road to the Deep North* (1968), *Lear* (1971), *Bingo* (1973) and *Restoration* (1981).

Hare's *Plenty* (1978) employs a non-linear, looping chronology to present a political framework for analysis of what 'being English' might constitute for its fictional protagonist, Susan, in the period following World War II. Hare's play selectively assembles a timescape, based on personal junctures of despair and decision, which also contextualizes Susan's individual sense of impatience, frustration and dislocation within a wider context of post-war social experiences of women and men. Hare artfully deploys a sense of enigmatic nonconformist sexuality to provoke curiosity in the first three scenes (who is the naked man in the first scene, in 1962? How might Susan's relationship with Lazar develop from their tense intimacy in the second scene, in 1943? Why is Susan travelling with a different, unseen man and pretending to be his wife in the third scene, in 1947?). Susan's impatience with the decorum and compromise of post-war England propels her into increasingly violent confrontations with representatives of these forces: confrontations that form a temporal contour of tragic disillusionment in mid/late twentieth-century England. This effect is heightened by a scene depicting Susan's disconnective meeting with Lazar (now a compromised conformist) in 1962. The scenographic closures of this scene open up into a flashback to her wartime idealism under pressure, with the French Resistance, in 1944, and a coda of her poignant assurance that the world (and England) will change, becoming more mature and emotionally articulate: 'There will be days and days and days like this' (Hare 1978: 86). One might transfer John Peter's comments on Pinter's *Betrayal* (which premiered the same year) to Hare's *Plenty*: the 'final effect is nightmarish: as if you realised with a shudder that what you have just been through were only about to begin' (quoted Megson 2014: 230). However, there is a crucial difference, in that Hare's play maps a sense of personal despair and erosion of ill-founded relationships onto a decline in national political integrity, suggesting that Susan's tragic thwarting is a microcosmic consequence of a general increasing expediency in the social values that surround her; but that this is only fully visible, and discernible, over (a life) time.

Howard Brenton is determinedly less tragic in his neo-/romantic theatrical initiatives. His most notorious play, *The Romans in Britain* (1980), assembles three contrapuntal episodes of invasion and its aftermath, implying potential parallels: in 54 BC, skirmishes on the edge of the Roman Empire's military arrival in Britain; in 1980 AD, an English officer's disastrous covert mission in Republican Ireland; in 515 AD, collapse and opportunity in the wake of the Saxon invasion of England. If Hare characteristically tends to depict tragic enclosure, Brenton is drawn towards impulses of surprising excavation, transformation (the monstrous metallic Romans inspire fantasies of inhuman neo-animalistic strategic mutations in response [Brenton 1996: 6, 54[3]]) and startling temporal leaps (impulses manifested in Brenton's early 1972 play *Hitler Dances*). The audience may be startled by how initially self-consciously engaging characters, such as Conlag, Daui and Chichester, are demystified and brusquely terminated.[4] This is particularly disconcerting as it is possible for the audience to interpret the narrative thread set in 515 AD as Chichester's drunken, unhinged rapture/epiphany of personal and national shame; however, its events continue after his unceremonious shooting, and the dismissal of his English presence as a manifest crime to Irish soil. This leaves the audience 'unhinged' in time and possibility, and the play concludes with the fugitives' speculative myth-making, hastily constructing the ideal figure of Arthur.

In several subsequent plays, Brenton takes wilfully erratic imaginary flight from contemporary 'Block-age' ('A blocked age. Rage, blocked' [Brenton 1996: 157]). *Thirteenth Night* (1981) is an underrated 'dream play' about the possible achievements and compromises of a future Labour government, depicting achievements and expediency provocatively entwined; more light-heartedly, *Greenland* (1988) imagines a semi-utopian future in which contemporary representatives are shown to be imaginatively limited 'fools of time' (or the fearfulness that they associate with time). Brenton has acknowledged, 'I am fascinated by heroes and heroines who were ahead of their time', who 'could not know the future, of course', but who extend, from the intrinsic limitations of their temporal perspective, a tradition of personal political revolt contributing to larger upheavals (Brenton 2010: 8).

Brenton's *In Extremis* (2006) enfolds the legendary lovers Abelard and Heloise into this radical historical perspective, and the play ends, not with tragic death and separation, but enduring transmission to the future. Heloise finally admonishes an Abbot, Bernard, for trying to reclaim Peter Abelard as part of his own life story ('You are all story, Abbott. You are not really living at all' [Brenton 2006: 89]), but she tells him that Peter produced an autobiography, in which he features, and letters:

Full of our love and pain, and our hopes to live a better life. There are copies translated into every language in the world. *(Taking the Penguin paperback edition out of her habit.)* Look, here's one in English, eight hundred and fifty years from now.

She holds the Penguin book out to BERNARD, who stares at it, then out to the audience.

(90)

Brenton's mischievous breaking of the historical barrier and redrawing of the time frame that would conventionally distance characters from audience continue in his play for the Globe Theatre, *Anne Boleyn* (2010), which features several instances of neo-Elizabethan frame-breaking (*'They are sliding into an embrace. They break away and, holding hands, announce the interval'* [Brenton 2010: 69]) and direct address, as when Anne finally tells the audience, 'Dear demons of the future', that 'We must all die, so die greatly, for a better world, for love', before concluding 'Oh, I can't see you any more. And now you can't see me. Goodbye, demons. God bless you all' (Brenton 2010: 115).

Bond: Time as blood money

The dramatist-director Edward Bond suggests that 'Self-consciousness creates a future and so a sense of morality: imagination is the knowledge given by time that we live and die' (Bond 2000: 15). Thus Bond suggests that it is precisely a self-conscious engagement with the boundaries (social and mortal) imposed on our possibilities that might, at best, generate the conscious friction of imagination. He also suggests that paradigms of time are principal examples of how social limits can be internalized. *Red Black and Ignorant*, the first of his trilogy *The War Plays* (1985), begins by identifying crucial aspects of the human temporal consciousness: 'Alone of creatures we know that we pass between birth and death' (Bond 1998: 3). We anticipate and nurture the existence of children with a concern for what to transmit for and into a future; yet humans also have the capacity to kill children, and adults, systematically. Bond notes how 'the subjective human image is also a limit', something that 'joins us to society' but also 'stands between us and our needs'; however, we 'not only interiorize the human image, we exteriorize it and perform it', in order to 'apprehend the external world and behave in it', either acceptingly or questioningly (266). Bond's *Red, Black and Ignorant* projects immanent possibilities into a charred cultural future after a nuclear conflagration, showing speculative scenes from a fractured social life that the protagonist 'did not live' (5); in the last scene, the characters address the audience ('You who live in barbarous times') to state that 'If we'd lived we wouldn't be content with your savage stupidities', presumptions that kill future generations in the name of a notional but illusory 'freedom' ('you went on building your house with bricks that were already on fire' [39]). This (purportedly *rational*) framework of temporal distance – the depiction of a possible future in order to create a critically impatient perspective on, and detachment from, conformity in contemporary limitations – is a dramatic strategy that links Bond to Shaw. Bond's urgency in identifying the importantly pivotal nature of the audience's 'here and now', and of the future importance of their actions in relation to this temporal and spatial juncture, is a principal feature of what, furthermore, links him to Brecht (specifically, Brecht's injunction to immediate response, 'What is the rule, recognise it to be an abuse / And where you have recognised abuse / Do something about it!' [Brecht 1977: 35]).

In a letter, Bond writes of a sense of sudden estranging recontextualization, provoked by action, which he terms 'accident time': a juncture when 'the questions change'; 'It's not a matter of solution but of understanding: the geography changes and you are in a different place because the same place is now different' (Bond 2001: 167). This 'accident time' has possible contact points with the 'catastrophic time' described by Lingis, a suspension of the habitual terms and pace of seeing and responsive action, which I have identified in Barker's theatre (Rabey 2009: 15–17). Bond's other recent theoretical statements provide further indicative contexts for his development of a sense of time within human self-consciousness. In his 'Notes on Imagination' Bond writes of how a child has a 'map of the world', a topographic self-contextualization; however, authority then 'inscribes the adult world onto the child's map', incorporating ideology by transposing the child's 'map' to 'the world of ownership and authority' (Bond 1995: xvi). In his essay 'The State of Drama', Bond claims:

The human mind seeks to inscribe the intellectual on the lyrical. I think this is the source – and actually the nature – of self-consciousness [...] In isolation both intellect and lyric are inhuman [but] there is a logic in the relation which only drama can enact. Truth is not instantiated by facts because values are astonishingly mutable, and so the meaning not just of ideology but even of use constantly changes. That's why we have to talk of human truth – but human truth is in fact reality, it's what enables the self to be conscious of itself. This is how the objective and the subjective are bound together in history.

(Bond 2010: 1)

One way of thinking about Bond's distinction between the intellectual and the lyrical might be in terms of objective (socially designated) space/time and subjective (personal) space/time. Bond increasingly opposes the affirmative term 'drama' to the essentially commercial sphere of 'theatre', similarly to how Barker refers to 'theatre' as opposed to his own radically dislocatory and tragic 'art of theatre'. Drama might re-present to the audience, in physical forms, how the friction between different temporal and spatial perspectives and claims constitutes the given terms of a society. This friction might be analogous to what Schneider calls the 'scrim' between the here and 'now' of the character's time and the performer's time, and the audience's sense of the here and 'now', when theatre encloses 'one time within another' (Schneider 2014: 40).

Bond claims that (lyrical) emotion and intellect meet in a 'gap' of sensed resistance (Bond 2010: 1), which might be the dramatized discrepancy between personal and social space/ time – or else, in exclusivity 'each will justify itself in its own terms'. Indeed, Bond states it is this dramatic meeting in 'the gap' that 'creates imagination in the self's raw reality', in instantaneous realization of knowledge, whereas the received facts, interpretations and narrative rationales of history and ideology are re-presented in 'the lag of time' (Bond 2010: 2). Thus, state, religion and ideology 'lead by the glove on the hand'; however, Bond suggests drama is 'the glove inside the hand – it gives each of us our particularity but also our shared ontology and so guides us to democracy' by indicating 'the logic of humanness' (3). Bond's strange but resonant image, of an indicative 'glove inside the hand', might suggest an alternative consciousness of time (perhaps relatable to Barker's concept of 'the soul', though Bond rejects this term as authoritarian [Bond 1995: xxvii]) that renders provisional the immediate social permutations of morality, creating a *delimited* consciousness[5] that Schneider also approaches:

> In the theatre at least, if not in also in everyday life, emotions or feelings or even thoughts are displaced off of a *real* event to take place in a time that is not strictly delimited to 'now' or to 'then'.
>
> (Schneider 2014: 47, original emphasis)

Bond also claims that 'Auschwitz' – which, for him, constitutes both a time and a place – cannot be culturally countenanced by twenty-first-century consumer capitalism, which dismisses it as 'unimaginable'; however, what is repressed will return in symptoms and postures of dis-ease, *unless* fully countenanced in the present, by means of a properly investigative drama (Bond 2012: 3) (and I am here also reminded of Barker's excavatory drama, *Found in the Ground*). Bond suggests that drama offers a way out of this social and cultural trauma of infantilization, through exploration of past in relation to present and future:

> In it we retrace the steps of our cultural psychosis. The process of understanding the insane obliges us to understand ourselves. It is as if we met ourselves face to face in the first second of the future, in the time and place of drama. Drama fashions our consciousness. All great civilizations create the drama that sustains them. And a civilization is created when it comes to terms with its past.
>
> (Bond 2012: 4)

Elsewhere, Bond describes drama as 'the fictive replication of the duality of self' which enacts 'the human imperative' (Bond 2014b: 2) in a way that is crucially 'trans-historical':

Conscious humans have to dramatise themselves and it follows from our self-consciousness that there must be a 'principle' to structure this self-dramatisation. Tragedy provides this 'principle' by creating human meaning. This meaning does not relate to any particular historical culture or society. It is trans-historical [...].

(Bond 2014b: 2)

In several ways, Bond's theoretical statements remind me of Antonio Negri's political essays, as collected in the volume *Time for Revolution*. Negri describes 'reality as a constrained unity, *that is, dominable space*', based on the 'fundamental *reduction of time to space*' (Negri 2013: 30, original emphasis). Bond's earliest plays *The Pope's Wedding* (1962) and *Saved* (1965) dramatize social power and contention primarily in terms of space: confinements, restrictions, jealousies, incursions and occasional acceptances. However, several of Bond's later plays present physical depictions of one socio-temporal perspective impinging upon another: the aforementioned *Early Morning* (1968) shows historical figures from Victorian England inflated to bloated monsters of consumption, still dominating the country's landscape and misshaping grotesquely its present definitions of possibility. *Lear* (1971) presents an image of a state 'order' that is fundamentally inscriptively violent and cyclically self-perpetuating, in a play that scrambles temporal indicators (its Shakespearian root, World War I trench warfare, more modern technology such as aerosols, the *Oedipus at Colonus* echoes of the final section) to create a trans-historical reach and reverberation. Whereas *The War Plays* (1985) present spectral figures who are harbingers of the (a?) future, *At the Inland Sea* (1995) initially seems to present the imaginary incursion of a revenant from the Holocaust into the secure historical studies of a modern day boy; however, the Old Woman disorientatingly tells the boy 'I'm not yet born. One day I will be' (Bond 1997: 30), suggesting that the preconditions for systematic genocide are not historically finite and distantly unrepeatable: *au contraire*, the boy's mother expresses a well-meaning but authoritarian refusal to imagine, for the sake of preserving a notional 'security' in terms of the immediate social context. Bond is here dissolving the separations of domestic walls and historical periods, in terms that seem akin to what Negri identifies as revolutionary in Marx's philosophies, where the '*traditional relationship of time to space is definitively overturned*', so that space is 'temporalized' and 'becomes dynamic' (Negri 2013: 35, original emphasis).

Negri's writings might conceivably be construed as a critique of Adam's model of the multiplex timescape. I am thinking here of when Negri criticizes attempts at 'paradigms of the totality of temporal involvement', which arrive at 'an immanent *relative definition* of time, as a *relationship of times*' (37, original emphasis): a series of contradictory claims that are '*not resolved but given as resolved*' by their unified depiction as a definable spectrum, and so presented as '*solution*' (38, original emphasis). However, one might counter that the principles of selection for inclusion in a timescape are crucial here: the events that Bond (or Hare, or Churchill, or Price) chooses from various possibilities for inclusion in a timescape play may (indeed, will) themselves reflect politically significant reaction, decision, choice and action.[6] This would then not necessarily be incompatible with Negri's political objectives and 'temporal territory', which characterize time as 'not relation, nor residue, nor subtraction', but a bid to perceive 'the ontology of the proletariat and its possibility of self-valorization', a process of 'liberation' (77) based on 'the relation between body and bodies' (105). Indeed, Negri's ideas of 'the *kairòs* of bodies that create truths through *praxis*' (178) may be related to the anti-oppressive theatre initiatives of Augusto Boal and Jennifer Hartley, in exploring a 'dynamic pluralism in so far as it is submitted to the rule of antagonism', 'a cross-section of this determination of being, a constitutive moment whose internal joyousness we must grasp' (105) – a formulation that seems particularly relatable to Boal's Rainbow of Desire programme. At times, I feel Negri resembles Bond in his highly idiosyncratic mobilizations of theoretical terms (Negri's uses of 'common' and 'teleology', Bond's uses of 'postmodern' and 'reality'), and in how impacted assertions sometimes prevail over clearly and engagingly (con)sequential argument in the theorizings of both (the ways that both refer to 'truth', Negri's generalization that the history of the poor is 'always revolutionary' [199]). However, there is identifiable common ground, in relation to a sense of time, where Negri writes of glimpsing 'another history', the sense of which may be 'grasped only from the instants of *kairòs*' that leads to 'the refusal of work, of understanding and of the limit' (199).

This might indicate an appropriate portal into Bond's play *Coffee* (published 1995, staged 1997), a particularly searching excursion through the nightmare of post-Auschwitz history extending into present and possible future warfare: its protagonist Nold has a definitely settled sense of space (his upstairs flat) and time ('good job. Tech one day a week' [Bond 1995: 2]) that is profoundly unsettled by the incursion of Gregory, a bandaged man who leads Nold through his door and into an unfamiliar forest (the most startling and haunting example of Bond's recurrent use of a motif most widely associated with Lewis Carroll's Alice stories, in which a figure from another space/time activates a curiosity and initiates an odyssey: see also *Tuesday, Have I None* and *The Under Room*). Nold's inquisitiveness is piqued; though disorientated, resentful and puzzled, he tells Gregory, 'If I go back now I'll spend the rest a' me life wonderin where I'd a got to if we'd gone on' (4). However, Gregory purports not to recognize Nold, to Nold's further consternation ('Yer must remember me! I followed yer!' [6]). This sense of territorial dislocation and temporal uncertainty is not concerned not only with questioning Nold's sense of ownership and identity (as it might principally be, in a Pinter play) but with opening up a traumatic landscape of reflexes into ownership, hierarchy and authority, as played out by a Woman, her daughter and the doll onto which the daughter displaces saturnalian cruelty; and by Gregory (who now appears unbandaged and younger), commanding a squad of soldiers into which Nold is enfolded. The effect is of one predatory world enclosing another in its relentless consumption (the Girl says, 'Under the pebbles there's another world', from which a hand tugs down the hapless [15]), even as Nold tries to fix his experiences in time, recollecting that 'Two days ago I was sittin at my table by the window – everythin in its place' and maintaining 'I'll find it, it's still there' (19). Later, however, he is driven to ask 'Tell me why I'm 'ere! 'oo I am!' (33).

The action of *Coffee* shifts to Nold's embroilment in the systematic machine-gunning of civilians under Gregory's command, which Bond (wisely) specifies the audience to delineate imaginatively, as offstage details.[7] The play's nightmarish condensation of time and effect develops into a scene in The Big Ditch, an underworld of the dead where The Woman and The Girl reappear, abject flotsam among the corpses. But this is where ties of lethal command and atrocious consequence are broken: Nold shoots Gregory, the Woman releases her hold on The Girl. Back in 'Daylight', Nold finds another room, in another house, belonging to the family of a man he killed: making the grim, tenuous assertion, 'I survived' (87), crucially, by rejecting complicity in tyranny. Nold's stepping out of conventional space/time means that his (and our) perspective on socially endorsed atrocity is not something that can be reduced to a single remote historical occurrence,[8] nor to the bleak determinism of a possible future scenario (as in *Red, Black and Ignorant*). The space/time he encounters is disturbingly *adjacent* to our own. As Bond says, 'value comes from the imagination *because* it cannot be stabilised by closure', but remains dualistic and dialectical (Bond 1995: xxvii, original emphasis). *Coffee* finds a memorable dramatic form for destabilized trans-historical time, an imaginary place and juncture from which moral and political self-determination may occur, against the otherwise prevalent odds and forces of capitalist authoritarianism and its consequences in human nihilism.

The adjacency and relation of the world of *Coffee* to our own brings us to consider questions of the respective positioning of art (theatrical and otherwise) in relation to the world itself and the world it creates. Jean-François Lyotard indicates in his reference to Paul Klee's suggestion that art does or need not merely imitate nature in mimesis, but can create the idea of a world *somewhat* pivotally apart, a '*Zwischenwelt*' (the German preposition *zwischen* denoting between- or inter-). This leads Lyotard to the positing of a '*Nebenwelt*' (the German preposition *neben* denoting 'beside/next to/apart', but also suggesting a space/time possibly less central, more marginal and therefore 'under the radar' of official definition, so to speak): a world in which 'the monstrous and the formless have their rights', to claim a space and time, 'because they can be sublime' (Lyotard in Benjamin 1989: 202).[9] This tragic *béance* or 'disclosure space' in time is the pivotal juncture I have elsewhere identified in terms (Rabey 2004: 55) that provide the title for our consideration of Anthony Neilson's 'entry point' into a surreal and initially playful, but darkening, *nebenwelt*…

Neilson's *The Wonderful World of Dissocia*: 'Inside-between the carvings of the clock'

By way of contrast to Bond, the Scottish dramatist-director Anthony Neilson claims the use of comedy as a possible 'delivery system' for more serious themes, in developing his own 'increasingly absurdist' agenda (Neilson 2008: ix). Neilson's play *The Wonderful World of Dissocia* (2004/2007) is a vivid experiment with a manifestly subjective perspective: it invites the audience to share the viewpoint of Lisa, who feels a sense of dislocation and listlessness on return from a trip to New York, involving the (widespread and objectively explicable, but still subjectively mysterious) experience of the 'loss' of an hour in transit. Neilson makes explicit his playful parallels with Carroll's *Alice in Wonderland* as well as *The Wizard of Oz* and C. S. Lewis's *Narnia* stories, echoing other fairy tale and fantasy narratives that involve an aperture in conventional time, by which one might step or swing through into a parallel world. Lisa acknowledges a sense that her life is 'out of balance', reflecting how she has 'difficulty in managing commitments' (Neilson 2008: 203). Victor (a spirit guide in the business of 'temporal mechanics', who recalls both Sigmund Freud and Carroll's White Rabbit) tells her that it is she, not her watch, that is an hour slow (204), and charges her to restore balance by embarking on a quest to retrieve the spare hour, a 'source of tremendous energy' (205) that she should 'never doubt or deny' (206) as hers. The hour has been relocated to Dissocia, a realm of space/time that lends the narrative of fantastic quest further aspects of a child's eye view (Neilson specifies that the scenographic design should incorporate a large raked expanse of domestic carpeting to mimic a widespread memory and perspective, in infancy, upon the world, 196). The unfolding *nebenwelt* also adds unsettling details to technological time-savers (such as lifts and underground trains) that are familiar, but whose overall interrelations of working are just beyond the conscious details of most human comprehension. Neilson furthermore incorporates tropes and echoes of traditional pantomime and vaudeville popular theatre forms (slightly dated, and thus recalling childhood for many) that are developed in ways characteristic of Neilson's theatre, in that surprising developments push slightly but steadily against their comic forms, towards the breaking point of such forms. For example, the comic double act of the 'insecurity guards' provides a surreally humorous image for the airport security checkpoint, which fuses ludicrous paranoia with an effective totalitarianism: drugs are not a matter for the guards' concern (indeed, like the professional arbiters of normality in Joe Orton's 1969 farce *What the Butler Saw*, the guards claim they 'couldn't function without them' [Neilson 2008: 213]), but they are wary of feathers or pants that might be used to tickle or strangle pilots. They acknowledge that the general situation is 'nerve-wracking' because the country and government create circumstances beyond individual control: 'It's the war, you see' ('There's a war on?', 'There's always a war on' [211]), even as they demand obedience in return for a notional security (the swearing of an oath of allegiance to Queen Sarah, who protects her subjects from the Black Dog King). However, Lisa realizes the fallacy at work in this social confidence trick: 'That's the problem with insecure people: they just tell you what you want to hear' (227).

Further on her odyssey, Lisa sings 'What's an Hour', a song lamenting her separation from her boyfriend Vince, which acknowledges the notionality of time measurement (*chronos*), 'I know an hour is just a construct / Concocted by an order-hungry race / I'm familiar with the work of Stephen Hawking / (Though I'm not sure I would recognise his face)', but also missed erotic opportunity (*kairos*): 'An hour is simply three thousand / Six hundred seconds / That I / Could have spent / With you' (Neilson 2008: 229). She is then clustered by 'timeflies' (which tend to bother anyone who is having fun in Dissocia) and 'the Scapegoat', a Carroll-like mythical creature who is usually and purposefully blamed for things he has little, or nothing, to do with, but who now finds himself obsolete and neglected in a war where everybody 'blames the enemy for everything', so that there is 'nothing for a scapegoat to do' (234). The Scapegoat appears both pathetic and comic, until he tethers Lisa and tries to rape her, becoming 'the Judas Goat'. This disturbing turn of events is momentarily interrupted when Jane appears. She is a bandaged and impossibly cheerful representative of the Council's Community Crime Initiative, volunteering herself to be beaten, anally raped and urinated upon (compressed into the euphemism, 'BAUed') on Lisa's behalf in order to make the statistical number of crime victims fall: a darkly satirical parody of how government offices are not concerned with truth, damage and culpability so much as with meeting statistical targets. The thoroughly instrumentalized Jane fails to see that crime need not happen ('Right, well, I'm not actually in the position of deciding Council Policy? I'm just the victim' [240]). Jane's offstage ordeal (the *'awful'* sounds and duration of which deliberately challenge the surreal satirical humour of this displaced violence) overshadows the fairy-tale sentimentality of a bear's serenade to Lisa. Jane then offers to drive Lisa to the Lost Property office, in search of her hour, and proves she is also blithely capable of unquestioningly inflicting, as well as receiving, violence; in response to an attack, Jane drops a novelty bomb, an explosive that incinerates everything in a five-mile radius, such as people, children and houses, but leaves 'a scorch mark in the shape of a cat', or rhino, or 'little koala bear' (248). At the Lost Property office, she encounters Argument and Inhibitions (two men reminiscent of Carroll's Tweedledum and Tweedledee) who dispute how to sabotage a wild goose chase: Inhibitions observes that a wild goose chase means 'you're hunting for nothing, how can you sabotage that?'; Argument shares the knowledge of his work as a saboteur: 'You let loose – some geese!' (259). This (like most, if not all, of Lisa's experiences in Dissocia) transpires to be part of a conspiracy to distract Lisa from apprehending her lost hour, as one Dissocian confesses: 'Dissocia is the life your hour generated … And if you reabsorb your hour … Dissocia will die' (263). Lisa tries to insist 'you can't hold me responsible' (264); however, her unique ability to withstand sonic attacks unprotected suggests she may be Queen Sarah, the legendary saviour of this world (parodying the many myths and fantasies in which an apparently ordinary child in one world and time proves an unlikely hero in another). Notwithstanding Lisa's presence, the cacophonous Dissocians are slain by the encroaching menace of the rival Black Dog army – of whom her boyfriend Vince appears to be King.

This concludes the first half of *The Wonderful World of Dissocia*, in which the noisy and deliberately childish surface energy is increasingly challenged by intimations of horror associated with war. Neilson thus suggests the ultimate fragility of various forms of *kitsch* escapism, ludicrous but ineffectually panicky assurances of security, displacement of blame and denial of responsibility, which may be required to support (and distract from) a country's war effort in a distant, and distanced, land (such as Britain and America's military interventions in Afghanistan and Iraq at the time of the play's premiere, and in other places subsequently). The comic and parodically sentimental songs also add surreal vitality to this paranoid world, as in the novels of Thomas Pynchon (whose novels such as *V*, *The Crying of Lot 49* and *Gravity's Rainbow* similarly ask: what is more terrifying: the presence, or the absence, of consequence in the form of a conspiracy?).

The starkly contrasting second half of Neilson's play is monochromatic, quiet and slow, evoking the enveloping inertia, resignation and time of 'drift' associated with periods spent in hospital or institutional care. Lisa's sister, Dot, blames Lisa for her absorption in 'selfishness' (279). Vince deterministically insists that 'This is what happens when you come off the medication', 'Sooner or later you end up here' (283), then claims she resents him for nagging her. Lisa explains that her release into another world and space/time is 'like the siren song': 'so lovely' it's worth getting 'smashed up' for (284). Finally Lisa holds a toy bear in bed, '*at peace*', but the music and coloured lights of Dissocia again become gradually discernibly at play, suggesting '*There is little doubt that she will return to her kingdom*' (285).[10] Here (and in his other plays), Neilson challenges the notion that 'the imaginary turns "objective" time or "natural" time into subjective time'; rather it 'works *between* the two terms, but the gap it creates is not necessarily the gap between "subjective" and "objective"' (Kristeva 1996: 308, original emphasis) (nor is any theatrical event). *The Wonderful World of Dissocia* playfully (but seriously) deconstructs this objective/subjective binary and choice, and presents a theatre *somewhere/when* in between: a personal fissure in the definitions of a presumed and pre-emptive lack of political agency, a crack in which carnivalesque forms of time are uproariously and hideously stretched out, embodied and spatialized.[11]

Once upon a time: Churchill's traumatic dystopias

Caryl Churchill's plays are often concerned to depict disjunctions of subjectivity, based on divergent senses of time: Alec in her play *Owners* (1972) resists incorporation into others' agendas by insisting 'You talk about the past and future but it doesn't apply. Here I am now' (Churchill 1985: 31). Carney describes this as a manifestation of 'utopian selfhood' that suggests Churchill's 'desire to explore the theatrical (im)possibilities' of liberation from dominant chronology'[12] (Carney 2013: 188, 189). This is more thoroughly formalized in her play *Traps* (1977), which seems an experiment in dissolving irreversible linear time to present what would normally be considered incompatible possibilities, in the manner of the play's central image of the Möbius strip, which offers a transformative frame of reference and reconciles what would appear to be impossibilities in space and time (Carney 2014: 315). Carney observes how *Traps* is, more specifically, 'at once dystopian and utopian' in its depiction of the tragic 'malaise and despair of English life' (190) that makes time and space subjects of fear (Churchill 1985: 94), as well as a more Dionysian bid to suspend its distinctive presumptions of consequence. The non-orientable combination of temporal features is discernible in several subsequent plays by Churchill: *Cloud Nine* (1979) hinges in its depiction of events from Victorian times to 1979, with the stipulation that 'for the characters' it is only 25 years later (Churchill 1985: 248), as it delineates instances of (utopian) personal release and how these are shaded by (dystopian) new forms of repression. *The Skriker* (1994) sets the human frame of reference within a larger, ancient and supernatural temporal context (represented in the original production's direction by Les Waters and scenographic design by Annie Smart as locating the human world within a bleached cube, bordered by the wider realm of the occasionally incursive fairies' contrapuntal processes). The Skriker's offers to Josie and Lily rework Faust's pact with Mephistophilis: the vengeful damaged spirit thrives on further damage, accelerated by a sense of human impotence that increases in relation to war and ecological catastrophe. Lily's mistaken sense of her personal power makes her try to appease the Skriker, who projects Lily into a future of desolation and deformity (suggesting a nuclear winter), where she is reviled by her own granddaughter for being the representative of a stupefied generation sleepwalking into wreaking irrevocable environmental destruction. Churchill's *Far Away* (2000) develops this dystopian sense of a world at accelerative war, reflecting and intensifying the polarizations of human moral binaries. The human tendency to disclaim and evasively situate an offensive Other as 'far away' in time and space (contrary to all apparent evidence) leads to a collapsing of boundaries and moral compression, in which weather, gravity, light, rivers and silence are reanimated as inscrutably malign resurgent forces recruited by one side or the other. *A Number* (2002) plays upon the extent that a clone, like a human being, constitutes both 'a repetition' and 'a difference' (Carney 2013: 226): so, we might note, does a subsequently recollected memory, and a theatrical performance. Salter assures his cloned son that he is not just his source-predecessor 'all over again', although Salter wanted 'one just the same because that seemed to me the most perfect' (Churchill 2002: 14). However, the original son also senses himself as a discard: after taking a sample cell, 'you threw the rest of me away' and 'had another one made' (17). The existence of these estranged siblings calls into question the degree to which Salter might have 'managed better' and 'tried harder' with them (32, 34). The rejected (possibly traumatized) first son kills his successor, and then himself, disrupting Salter's capacity to revise evasively his terms of connection to others by consigning him to a sense of irrevocable loss. Another clone, Michael is, however, fundamentally untroubled by Salter's revelations of his nature, and his unknown father's grieving attachment to the dead: distinctively, Michael accepts a sense of points of both contact and inevitable loss that constitute varying junctures of a lifetime, without embittered senses of envy or exclusion.

Churchill's *Love and Information* (2012) takes the form of a series of ironic playlets, satirical projections of how various contemporary figures attempt to arrange and make sense of their experiences over time, but their dealings are marked by senses of personal and/or interpersonal disconnection: ranging from the most basic personal disjunction ('You don't know where I put the car keys, do you?' [Churchill 2012: 76]) to traumatic adherence unmitigated by time (46). The playlets also suggest how a reduction of experience to 'information' (such as sex [49]) – a potentially consistent category of what is recordable and therefore predictable – systematically diminishes human will and agency (65): as in the instance of an implicitly dysfunctional reliance on technology and video recordings in order to preserve memories (34–35). It is informative to compare *Love and Information* with Barker's slightly earlier compendium, *The Forty*, which eludes constriction to any specific or consistent historical junctures and presents a series of extreme experiences (principally unforeseen confrontations with death, resistance, pain, resilience and beauty, recalling Freud's quotation of the aphorism 'Experience consists of experiencing that which one does not wish to experience' [quoted by Segal 2014: 179]). Paradoxically, Barker's figures, in stepping outside their normal temporal patterns and selves, present images of the human extraordinary *in extremis* that spectators may find strangely emotionally resonant, notwithstanding Barker's deliberate defamiliarization of contexts. Churchill's figures in *Love and Information* are identified as contemporary by their verbal references and assertions, which define them (rather than their actions; in contrast to the actions that define Barker's characters, sometime in defiance of their words) as attempting to 'manage' and regulate experience through the limitations of a vocabulary of familiarity and predictability, which forestalls transformative interaction. Hence the dominant ironic effect and salutary tone of *Love and Information*, which increasingly resembles a satirical catalogue of contemporary cultural evasiveness, foolish mistakes and disconnective narcissisms that are restricting, rather than expanding, human capacities: suggesting (in a manner notably more aloof than Barker's) what self-limiting fools these contemporary mortals can be.

The time that does not heal

Luckhurst interprets Churchill's *Heart's Desire* as depicting a family 'trapped in a continued enactment of a repressed trauma' (Luckhurst 2015: 139) (which might seem to link it thematically with O'Neill's *A Long Day's Journey into Night*, Albee's *Who's Afraid of Virgina Woolf*, Williams's *The Two-Character Play*, Thomas's *House of America* and green's *born bad*). This might be extended to the symptomatic reflexes of characters in Churchill's *Traps*, *Cloud Nine*, *Fen*, *The Skriker*, *Far Away* and *A Number*, in which traumatized subjective temporality is contextualized in relation to wider political events, which demand but defy personal 'closure', in terms of Caruth's definition of trauma, which seems particularly pertinent to Churchill's theatre: 'an overwhelming experience of sudden or catastrophic events in which the response to the event occurs in the often delayed, uncontrolled repetitive appearance of hallucinations and other intrusive phenomena' (Caruth 1996: 11).

The shifting and transformative frameworks of theatre make it a particularly apt medium through which to explore both the depiction of subjective temporality undergoing traumatic reflexes and ways in which these reflexes might be politically contextualized. Recent British dramatic examples include Jonathan Lichtenstein's *The Pull of Negative Gravity* (first staged 2004) and *Memory* (2006), Simon Stephens's *Pornography* (first staged 2007), and several plays by Sarah Kane,[13] Philip Ridley and debbie tucker green. Lichtenstein's *Negative Gravity* returns to the pivotal moment in which two brothers toss coins to decide who will join the army in Iraq, and plays out variant versions – imagined/ idealized and real/shattering – of the return of the soldier, Dai, after being wounded in action. Dai is physically disabled and traumatized ('The things I have seen! It doesn't go away!' [Lichtenstein 2006: 44]); furthermore, he is also a traumatic figure to his family and home community (like the protagonist in Sean O'Casey's play, *The Silver Tassie*, staged 1929), who compulsively and dependently re-presents his own abject body, until his mother and fiancée reflexively adhere to the grief he has instilled even after his release into death. The (re)performative quality of traumatic suffering finds an analogous framework in Lichtenstein's *Memory*, in which we see professional actors rehearsing a play (also titled *Memory*, perhaps recalling the vertiginous nomenclature of Williams's *The Two-Character Play*). The play depicts parallel political upheavals in pre-war Germany and contemporary Bethlehem: a refinement, through repetition and amendment, of the presentation of 'past' sufferings, which challenge assimilation and the resumption of a distinct narrative of the 'present' ('trauma theory suggests a performative bent in traumatic suffering itself – the trauma symptom is a rehearsal, re-presentation, re-performance of the experience of the trauma-event, which irrupts unbidden into the sufferer's daily life', Wallis and Duggan 2011: 2). Thus, conventional links and distinctions between past, present and future are questioned, to be re-presented: as Lichtenstein's director-figure remarks, 'The recovery of memory is a present-day activity. It's not the past. Memory occurs in the present [and] must live in the present and it must be truthful' (Lichtenstein 2006: 8). This, in turn, raises the question: 'truthful' to *whose* terms of identity and narrative?

Duggan suggests the term 'trauma-tragedy' for theatre, which does not only re-view 'a historical moment of trauma', but attempts 'to bridge or reduce the gap between historical moment, its witness' and traumatic experience (Duggan 2012: 57). This presumably involves problematizing habitual and normative distanciations in time and space, and, for example, resisting evasions of political and social responsibility such as those which are critically identified by Churchill in *Far Away* and by McDowall in *Pomona* (Miller's approaches to dramatizing the traumatic events and aftermath of the Holocaust, including the *Kristallnacht* to which Lichtenstein's *Memory* also refers, are considered thoughtfully by Forsyth 2008). I suggest that Katrin, the protagonist of Barker's *The Europeans* (1987), provides a striking example of a theatrical character who consciously and compulsively re-performs the terms and consequences of her pain and violation, in public contexts that defy her assimilation into the closure of state pageantry of 'history'. Katrin discomfortingly reduces the 'gap' between herself and her witnesses, challenging them to formulate the reconciliation which she repudiates.

Simon Stephens's play *Pornography* (2007) provides a notable instance of what Duggan describes as 'a mode of performance which not only represents trauma in ways which echo the structures of trauma-symptoms, but also addresses it without moral commentary' (186). *Pornography* re-presents time(s) (and, indeed, specific London locations) with which a contemporary spectator is likely to have personal associations: the juncture between the announcement that London was to host the 2012 Olympic Games and the bombing of a bus and tube station on 7 July 2007 (which killed 56 people, including the four bombers involved). However, Stephens approaches and develops this sense of moment (and momentousness) in consciously surprising ways: six (transposable) scenes in which characters, who remain ultimately unknowable, present their various perspectives on dislocation and disconnection. Engagingly unpredictable in their emotional precision, these characters are not fully 'contained' by conventional theatrical exposition or closure, which provokes the audience to remember, speculate and consciously attempt to generate (personal, political and social) contextual meaning.

This effect may have some affinities with what Luckhurst describes, the ways in which trauma challenges the capacity for narrative knowledge in relation to past, present and future: 'in its shocking impact trauma is anti-narrative, but it generates the manic production of retrospective narratives that seek to explicate the trauma' (Luckhurst 2008: 79).

I agree with Booth that theatre offers a (literally synthetic, yoking disparities) structure for the temporary containment, limitation and confrontation of that which defies comprehension (Booth 1983). I have one reservation about Duggan's terms in suggesting that theatre and performance 'can make an attempt to bear witness to trauma that enables an audience to bear witness to their own traumas by accessing them precisely through *inadequate* theatrical representations' (Duggan 2012: 114, original emphasis). I would suggest a distinctive (re)inflection: the theatre of Shakespeare, Barker, Churchill, Stephens, green and others considered here offer *precisely incomplete* and *artfully elliptical* re-presentations, which are 'inadequate' only in terms of the prevalent norms of closure that constitute conventions – conventions both artistic and political.

Anna Harpin writes insightfully on how Philip Ridley's plays distort time and space, even as they follow a series of apparently irreversible fictional events enacted in 'real-time':

The collapse of organized memory and eschatological framing at once eschew and focus time. The preoccupation with nightmarish re-enactment and repetition dictates the rhythm [of events] and creates a rip tide within the performance that drags the characters repeatedly to violent crises.

(Harpin 2011b: 107)

This dynamic is discernible from Ridley's first play, *The Pitchfork Disney* (first staged 1991), in which an ageing but regressive brother and sister fluctuate between approaching and withdrawing from confrontations with the consequential. In this they resemble the brother and sister in Tennessee Williams's *The Two-Character Play* (staged in amended versions 1967–75), who similarly find that what they fear nevertheless gnawingly calls into question the theatrical walls of their compulsively performed self-enclosure, become concerned that the world outdoors might unbalance their delicate terms of arrested equilibrium, and conclude in what might be termed a tender admission of defeat (dynamics that prove re-emergent in Ridley's later plays, *The Fastest Clock in the Universe*, *Mercury Fur* and *Dark Vanilla Jungle*). Andrew Wyllie has traced how all of Ridley's plays for adult audiences are to some extent concerned with 'the role of memory in achieving or losing an adult identity' (Wyllie 2013: 65ff, an issue that will recur in our later consideration of

Price's *The Radicalization of Bradley Manning*). Schroeder's terms of analysis of Williams's play are also applicable to Ridley's plays: their present situation is explicable only in terms of a 'continually influential, partially unfixed and unfixable past' that the characters only feel able to investigate through insistently framed retrospective play (Schroeder 1989: 120). *Mercury Fur* (2005) presents a dystopian world that is nightmarish in both external social circumstances and internal causal logic based on memories, so that both have collapsed into a 'fragmented, hallucinatory whole', where the only escape from susceptibility to a 'terrifying present' is by characters locking themselves into a form of temporarily comforting resistant play, which offers 'the illusion of controlling time' but may ultimately make them time's victims (Schroeder 1989: 121).

In the future shattered London of *Mercury Fur* – a landscape where museums are looted, zoos are broken open for the monkeys to be shot and flaming zebras run down Brick Lane – psychotropic butterflies have become both favoured drug and currency; their palliative erasure of memories includes a political past that might constitute the present and near-future of the theatre audience before the 'riots' started (135). Through the cumulative effects of a significantly nebulous political history and consuming the butterflies sold by his brother Elliot, Darren thinks Kennedy was married to Marilyn Monroe and won the war by dropping bombs that 'turned all the Germans into Chinkies', 'or something' (Ridley 2009: 114). Elliot maintains that life is 'easier for the young' because they remember less of 'how it was'; it is precisely the memory of better possibilities and alternative circumstances, 'good stuff', that 'fucks you up' (139) by creating a sense of injustice. Elliot and Darren maintain a resilience based on a love that they express in ritualistic terms of violence and self-destruction (91) and wry humour ('the ancient Egyptians believed that, after you die, you travel to another place', 'Like Southend?' [102]). This equilibrium seems positive when compared to Naz's memory of his mother, who sentimentally cries over a melted snowman, but is pragmatically unfazed when their neighbours 'got chopped up' (106), and the blind Duchess's desperate assembly of her own narrative identity from the plot of *The Sound of Music*, trying (but failing) to keep at bay her traumatic recall of her husband trying to kill her children (probably Elliot and Darren) 'to save them from this terrible place' (162)[14]. The most appalling manifestation of fantasy is The Party Guest's elaborate scenario of sadistic power, in which he employs Spinx and the brothers to be complicit; however, Spinx lets slip that they do not have the leeway of 'next few weeks' to organize future events, because The Party Guest's company are pulling out all integral personnel to another country before the napalm bombing of London begins, to be followed by army occupation. When their friend becomes the substitute prey of The Party Guest, Elliot and Darren can be complicit no longer: they resist, and Darren shoots The Party Guest. As the threatened bombing starts, Darren revives his childhood game of optimistic exploration, Space Invaders, and his ritual expression of endearment with Elliot, who does not respond, but aims a gun at Darren's head as the '*fire and bombs get louder*' (202). This image of symbiosis, turned antagonistic (which may recall for some the ending of Pinter's *The Dumb Waiter*), suggests that Elliot's lethal stance may be his final act of a protective love for Darren, refusing palliative escapism and sparing Darren a future on the vested terms of 'order' (187) supported by The Party Guest and his kind: a defiantly consequential act, eluding the systematic victimization and dominance associated with their location in place and time.

I would propose debbie tucker green as the foremost post-Kane trauma-tragedian, in her interrogations of the given forms and terms of 'facts', 'truth' and 'reconciliation', and insistent manifestations of personal wound, socially located. If Kane deliberately subverts the consistency of the social contexts of her plays (most strikingly in *Blasted*), green is contrastingly concerned to locate and express (in non-literal, non-linear terms) trauma as powerfully subjective personal response to an appallingly, reductively consistent social context (a point of contact between green, Bond and Kane's *Cleansed*). Favorini's observation is relevant here, how the 'narratives that shape traumatic memory are frequently contested and provocative, and they sometimes deliberately construe to hold a trauma culturally unintegrated and unassimilated' (2008: 228). green's plays frequently depict characters struggling to be appropriately reactive to some unseen traumatic event, and now actively exploring, in the moment, the catastrophic time of their own shock: moreover, green's plays re-present, in terms of personal subjective temporality,[15] the effects of cultural dis-integration.

My second chapter has foregrounded green's *random* (2008) as a case study in this respect, but her other works also artfully play off interpersonal temporal disjuncture against spatial proximity (not least to the audience in appropriately intimate stagings). *dirty butterfly* (2003) compresses time and space in depicting its characters as adjacently uneasy (overlapping verbally, sonically and otherwise 'Bleedin' thru' [green 2003: 7]), but resolutely and complicitly disconnective from suffering ('not infringin' [4]), until consciously 'turned' (26) by the admission of cyclical physical damage, at a suddenly pivotal juncture. Jo's traumatic (literally, leaking) body impinges on the prevalent 'clean' categorizations of space and time, and so may open up a possibility of difference between 'morning' and 'afternoon' (51).

green's *generations* (2005) is a startlingly condensed (30-minute) depiction of three generations of a black South African family, almost all of which die, in ways that shatter natural expectations of sequence, as a non-specified AIDS pandemic creates specific unbridgeable gaps of personal absence. green's theatrical specifications set up different patterns of inclusion: '*live vocals*', ideally provided by a '*black South African choir*', preface and underscore the central performance of consumption of the family nucleus (who playfully and poignantly refer to the transformative processes of 'cooking'), and call out specific members to join the dead, manifesting what Osborne describes as 'a distorted rites of passage, a frozen liminality of the undead and the soon-to-be', who nevertheless remain visible at the periphery of the performance space (Osborne 2015: 172). This may be a surprising juncture to indicate a continuum that also includes Thornton Wilder's *The Long Christmas Dinner* and *Our Town*, and to J. B. Priestley's *Music at Night*; however, like Priestley's play, green's *generations* uses a musical framework to unify a consciousness of transition between the living and the dead, and, like Wilder's plays, dramatizes a sense of individualized temporal specifics within a larger context of universal liminality. The significant difference is that green challenges the audience member to 'jump' the imaginative 'gap' of non-specification, and re-perceive these repeated familial disjunctures of *generations* as potentially socially *avoidable*, in their traumatic relative *untimeliness* if not in their ultimate occurrence. Osborne observes, with particular resonance for our framework of considerations, how the characters of *generations* function as 'Everyman/woman' in ways that underline 'the catastrophe's entrance at every level of society' in ways that are ultimately 'tragically equalising', but these are significantly unlike the 'socio-economic conditions' (Osborne 2015: 172) that have catalysed the catastrophe. green's plays defy the prevalent social promise of so-called 'closure' by insisting on individual right to a political-poetical elaboration that holds open and extends a wound in time: sometimes through verbal delineation of disquiet, sometimes through what her stage directions specify as an '*active silence*' of physical impulse revoked, braced or physicalized.

green's *truth and reconciliation* (2011) places the personal experience of suspension, waiting (for permission and/or acknowledgement and/or confirmation), in a variety of political contexts, where the 'need' to know/ask/hear/speak actually becomes antithetical to the liberal humanist goal of what will 'help' people 'live with' something, attain an 'appropriate' sense of its consignment to the past and thereby a healing unification. In green's theatre, time does *not* heal: nor should it, or its evocation, when social circumstances are fundamentally different, and personal lives are irrevocably changed by the traumatic eruption of social faultlines (which nevertheless may be claimed or identified as someone's personal 'fault' [green 2011: 56]). The last two scenes of *truth and reconciliation* permit temporary dissolution of the boundary between the living and the dead, as two dead characters, haunting those responsible for their deaths, insist on the compulsive discovery of a truth that will defy reconciliation.

green's *hang* (2015) depicts the protagonist's character's purposeful cause (which was specifically and personally 'caused' [green 2015: 63]) to resist the bureaucratic procedures of abstraction and generalization (and proffered sympathy based on role-play scenarios) with which she is besieged following a crime. Instead, she retains her problematizing status as 'unsettled, unsettle-able, *unsettling*' (green 2015: 24, original emphasis) in her choices in reaction to the unseen obscene. In green's own production of *hang* at the Royal Court Theatre, Marianne Jean-Baptiste played the protagonist, appropriately and electrifyingly, as having a relentlessly faster personal timing than those surrounding her, evidenced by compulsive tremulous movement (for example, of hand-cleaning) even (or particularly) in moments of silence, and as she wryly mocked the proffered terms and processes of 'development' (32). The protagonist decisively nominates hanging as the method of execution of the offender, preferably implemented by someone 'shit at maths' (60), and so likely to undermine the technical objectives of brisk efficiency and extend the time of the offender's suffering. Her final decision to read the offender's letter begs the question: can she, will she, revoke her issue of sentence in the time remaining before execution, as is her right? *Should* she let her insistently personal vehemence be modified by time, or reject liberal humanist arguments of (and impulses to) forgiveness as disgracefully, unjustly paralytic?

Rudkin: The once and future

David Rudkin is the modern dramatist who creates for audiences the most far-reaching and estranging temporal dislocations, extravagantly bending the conventional grammar of time, in ways that are at once excavatory (of another time) and reverberative. Rudkin frames his selected dramatic junctures within unusually precise, imaginatively specific elemental and physical contexts, where the usual points of reflection, witness and reference – including the sun, moon, tide and stars – are refracted, distorted, dimmed, surprisingly projected or kaleidoscopically fragmented, in order that audiences might re-approach and re-cognize anew their own cultural and political perspective in history, and their wider possibilities, which frequently involve the dissolution of the binary distinction between the sacred and the profane, and their unification in (social and theatrical) practice (indeed, Rudkin's work might be cited as a remarkable theatrical harrowing of Kristeva's call for 'the analysis of the potentialities of *victim/executioner* that characterize each identity, each subject, each sex' [Kristeva 1981: 34, original emphasis]). An important aspect of Rudkin's theatrical project is the political analysis of how a cultural ethic can be rendered self-destructive by 'individual psychopathologies which have come to inform our entire cultural ethic and cosmic suicide' (Rudkin 1995–6: 97), through a purported (and deceptive) elimination of the shadow; theatrically this involves exposures of how

> the clearances of another age continue, but sometimes in a less obviously visible form: the alienation of people from their nature and their ecosphere, an effect integral to the capitalistic process, continues unabated, no less corrosively for the fact of its being invisible, a subtle eating away at the very fabric upon which we depend, until a race of dispossessed people effectively becomes part of the landscape.
>
> (Rudkin 1995–6: 96)

This narrative task – which we might readily associate with Adam's 'timescape perspective' – is profoundly characteristic of Rudkin's wider *oeuvre* in various media (notably, his 1974 television film *Penda's Fen*), in its archaeological impulse to delve and divine through perceptual obstacles and its dramatic impulse to manifest an interrogatory coexistence between various layers of time: what Rudkin describes as 'looking at the surface' of a landscape 'as though it were a filter through which you could just glimpse a previous layer' (Rudkin in Sandhu et al. 2014: 16). His dramatic process activates presences that call into question the habitual distinctions between the objective and the subjective, not least in terms of temporal distinctions, interpretations and narrative identities.

Furthermore, Rudkin's most innovative stage plays – *Afore Night Come* (1962), *The Sons of Light* (1976), *The Triumph of Death* (1981), *The Saxon Shore* (1986), *Red Sun* (2003) and *Merlin Unchained* (2009) – all extend these processes into explorations characteristically conducted in the pressurized time of a nocturnally darkening or darkened auditorium, in which the (conventional, but here refigured as initiatory) dimming of (artificial) light involves self-relocation by unusual means and senses, before the theatre 'house lights' rise in release from this purposefully selective time (and the endings of *The Sons of Light* and *The Saxon Shore* presage the break of lights of day into the renewed cycle of a next day). The promises and forces of a fundamentally illusory and dispossessive enlightenment are countered by a faith in other ways of seeing, and acting, expressed by the exhortation of Rudkin's Merlin: 'Let there be Night!' (Rudkin 2011: 196).

In Rudkin's *The Sons of Light*, John rouses the subterranean slaves from their Platonic-Manichean underworld by telling a story of a white bird, which embodies *kairos*: an apparition presaging opportunity of inclusive transformation, to be grasped or lost irrevocably. The epigraph of (and subsequent character utterance in) Rudkin's play *The Triumph of Death* cites, and contradicts, the opening of L. P. Hartley's 1953 novel *The Go-Between*, 'The past is another country: they do things differently there'. Rudkin transforms this into a perfectly reverberative theatrical paradox: 'The past is another country. The past is not another country' (Rudkin 1981). *The Triumph of Death* dramatizes the cultural enshrinement of time as a restrictive system of work ethic and social economics based on ordeal, penance and reinvestment, rather than festive liberation or reward. It does so by taking the form of a 'triumph', a medieval pageant of tableaux interpreting the present by reference to the past, depicting the chameleonic resurgence of the necrophilous force of control ('death' as embodied in the literally *vicious* female figure of Mother Manus and her acolytes), whilst drawing a parallel with Percy B. Shelley's final and unfinished poem *The Triumph of Life* (1822) that ironically depicts systematic human corruption and obsessive limitation of self and nature. Wilcher succinctly observes the play's refutation of political claims to enlightenment: it identifies the confidence tricks by which successive regimes deceive self and others 'into thinking that process is progress, and that its own ideological perspective is an improvement on the less civilized culture of its predecessors' (Wilcher 1992: 576). The first fatal social estrangement identified by the play is the ongoing war against 'the Saracen', demonized infidel whom the religious despot Papatrix directs his children to oppose in war, and thereby prove themselves of 'good' purpose, giving earthly shape to the 'Will Above' (Rudkin 1981: 2). This starting point is based on the thirteenth-century Children's Crusade, the disastrous expedition to expel Muslims from the so-called 'Holy Land', an initiative that has many subsequent parallels in forcible bids to claim cultural authenticity (which show no signs of abating since the play's premiere). Two scholarly characters debate how the Saracen may also claim to be made in the image of his god, but deduce that contradictory revelations cannot both be true: 'As well the Sun revolve around two earths' (3); for their existence to be vindicated, they must engage in war, 'mortal test of our validity': 'It is the challenge of our time' (4).

However, '*the Crucified Risen JESUS*' then appears to the audience, introducing himself as 'Me. Whom you each make, in your own moral image' (4). He also appears to Stephen of Cloyes (based on a French peasant boy inspired to lead the second movement of the crusade), and continues to raise (rather than answer) questions as to how one may put 'Death and Devil in his place' and gain 'life eternal' (5). Stephen's vision is 'interpreted' by Mother Manus, who channels and directs his ardour to a fatal end in Jerusalem; she reassures Papatrix that, accordingly, no crusaders have survived to return home: 'Their estrangement dies with them. That's the beauty of war' (8). However, as she proclaims a 'rational' age (the 'moral problem' of the Saracen subdued), the audience encounter the forest-dwelling descendants of some returned (maimed and crazed) survivors; a rural people who scent a 'death' from the direction of (the future world, represented by) the audience (8). This pagan commune is based on a benign inter-relationship with the Sun and soil, but the crippled girl Jehan becomes one of Rudkin's recurrent 'go-betweens' – a figure who painfully bridges two worlds – by glimpsing a world beyond the forest (located in the audience's space/time) where people fetishize Christ's suffering and live by money, 'the shit of toil' (16). A contrasting view of 'toil' and time follows: Enester, a young Renascence duke, assumes the mantle of Pan in order to preside over a gathering of the forest dwellers. He castigates one for his self-removal from co-operation in communal work: a parasitic disavowal that leeches the time of his fellows, from their possible fruitful work, to the distraction and burden of 'fruitless work', time spent in guarding against him: a 'deathly' schism ('for it spells the beginning of the end of the world' [Rudkin 1981: 31]). Later, Enester appears in contrasting guise as The Lord (in visual terms that evoke William Holman Hunt's painting 'The Light of the World', though this Lord deliberately promises nothing[16]), relating to the scattered survivors of Pan's coven further ways in which man becomes 'our own enemy': by fashioning 'loftier drudgeries to mesh himself', as 'though for fear, in idleness, some well in him might open, and his dark water rise' (42). The forest people 'found a time to play' and 'toiled, to live' as opposed to the man who builds upwards and around himself the 'unacknowledged tower of his own unalienable bondage', the investment and wages of fear: who 'finds work for his time' and 'lives to toil', until the 'skies above his world are red with burning' (43). Finally, a feminized Martin Luther appears, deduces the terms of man's flight from consciousness of his own mortality and accepts there is 'no garden above'. The dismissal of present time involves pursuit of a mirage: to 'quench this life, that we are given and have, for a yonder life that we shall never: what else is that but Satan's victory?' (51). However, even this rational Luther proves institutionalized, ultimately turned catatonically inwards, in an asylum over which Mother Manus presides.

The Triumph of Death suggests how and why no single vantage point of place or time can – or should – presume to constitute exclusively 'the centre of the world' (16), even as it suggests there is 'no escape from history' (51), but history in this play (and Rudkin's other work) is associated with existential questions, and choices, rather than with deterministic consequences in territory, space and time. Rudkin's deliberately stipulated doublings in *The Triumph of Death* work in a diametrically opposed way to the dramaturgy of Caryl Churchill's *Light Shining in Buckinghamshire* (1976), which dissociates performers from consistent association with specific roles, in order to emphasize collective interpretation (though this may also hinder identification of narrative consequence) in performance. *The Triumph of Death* orchestrates the reappearances of performers through a stipulated series of roles, so that physical presences and vestigial associations recur, and are modulated in both associative and surprising terms, like musical motifs, over the duration of the performance, suggesting expansions and contractions in the ostensible 'progress' of the human sickness, to seek to inherit, 'fix' and control the world (however, Churchill's *A Number* works to conscious effect the accruing associations of a given performer, over theatrical time, in a variety of fictional roles). *The Triumph of Death* remains one of the most prophetic and discomfiting achievements of the modern theatre.

I propose an approach to Rudkin's *Merlin Unchained* (2009), and its protagonist, via the most temporally shattering line in English-language theatre. In Shakespeare's *King Lear*, the Fool remains onstage, fictionally alone on the heath, in order to utter words 'which are to theatrical nature as the storm is to the natural world' (Booth 1983: 40): a prophecy of how the 'realm of Albion' will come 'to great confusion', a speech that nevertheless eludes any predictable conclusion and ends with the words, 'This prophecy Merlin shall make, for I live before his time' (Shakespeare 2007: 2043). These eleven words explode 'the chronological limits of the fiction and, indeed, all divisions between character and actor, character and audience, past and present, past and future, future and present', implying that 'any sense we have' of our temporal location 'is false' (Booth 1983: 43). Rudkin's *Merlin Unchained* gathers and furthers these resonances, and indicates how temporal location is also political location.

Merlin (who according to some accounts lived his life backwards in time) is the figure of British myth primarily associated with the ability to glimpse, open and even become confounded within portals between different time zones (and these aspects of his combined imaginative appeal and consequent troubling otherness reverberate discernibly in the successively regenerating fictional television character, Dr Who[17]). But the Arthurian legends, as an epic whole, are notable for their pivotal self-location in 'once and future', a spellbinding effect of immanence noted by Priestley: the Arthurian web of narratives seems 'to wander in and out of Time', suggesting that the 'magic place' may be 'around any corner' (Priestley 1964: 165). Elsewhere in his book *Man and Time*, Priestley delineates an opposing polarity of vested interests in mired fixation, which he terms 'The Fortress': 'citadel of science, technology, positivism', from which the so-called 'climate of opinion' is controlled:

If we feel we are tied to chronological time, that is where the tying was done. If we appeal against this servitude, that is where our appeal will be rejected. It is the home of science as a dogmatic system and a colossal vested interest [...] This is very much the Fortress style. Conquest is all. Having conquered land and sea, we are now conquering space, more and more of it. As soon as we have conquered the moon, we must make plans to conquer the planets [...] Hag-ridden by our idea of Time, the narrowest and worst man has ever had, secretly feeling humiliated, we have to be conquerors, bulldozing our way towards a receding glorious future.

(Priestley 1964: 181, 186)

This also corresponds to Rifkin's sense of 'fortress futures in which artificially controlled time frames are imposed on the rhythms of nature' (Rifkin 1987: 208), how political tyranny 'in every culture begins by devaluing the time of others', imposing a pyramidal hierarchical structure in which 'some people's time is more valuable' (196) and other's more expendable. Priestley and Rifkin's analyses anticipate precisely that which Rudkin's protagonist opposes in *Merlin Unchained*: the city of Garganel, with its Global Online Distribution (G.O.D.) Tower, and, of course, much more that has manifestly occurred in our world since Priestley's and Rifkin's times of writing. *Merlin Unchained* is a play both 'anti-Newtonian' in its fracturing of time and space and two-hundred-year-old protagonist, and also 'firmly rooted in historical realities and historically real landscapes' (Rudkin 2011: 71). Its first half contrapuntally presents (a) Merlin (now himself traumatically severed from his past and frozen in time, repressing intimations of magical and tragic episodes from Arthur's court) in the Celtic borderland forestry of late seventh-century Britain; and (b) a sisterhood of fundamentalist assassins in their desert stronghold (based in historical details from thirteenth-century Northern Persia), seeking, under guidance of abbess Albatusa, their transfigurative glory in a murderous 'hour of light'. Merlin and Albatusa are both consciously *separative* from the world and time of the audience, and opposingly so: Merlin believes night to be 'Time of seeing' (110), Albatusa holds noon to be the 'Zenith of our Lady's unwavering light supreme' (99). Significantly, Albatusa's order has imprisoned Almazen, a scientist who (heretically, to the assassins) pursues deductive knowledge based on nocturnal observations of the stars. Merlin also scrutinizes the stars for encouragement, intimations and warnings (part of the archaeoastronomical seam in Rudkin's play, which is consistently and dramatically mindful of convergences and alignments between architecture, landscape, stars and planets, as well as individuals). If the thawing of the year and the visits of his wolfboy companion Sirius seem to presage a gradual unlocking in Merlin, the pressure of time is more ominous for Almazen and her disguised son Perseus, whose visible maturation threatens their fatal exposure. Merlin reclaims the harp that signifies his calling, and leaves his time, drawn through a 'gateway' portal by the Green and Golden Lady (one of the presiding genii of place that Rudkin's psychogeographical drama is often concerned to glimpse, as in *Penda's Fen*), in order to cross centuries and confront the vision of Garganel, 'City of Dreadful Light'. Albatusa invokes and summons a different 'genie': Abeminoth, a demonic figure of destructive 'terminal light' who, once released, cannot be contained by his discoverer.

In the second half of *Merlin Unchained*, the two timelines, each projected into its own future, converge. Merlin and the audience find themselves in the dystopian world of Garganel, which becomes gradually apparent as an imaginative projection of the audience's 'Here and now' (Rudkin 2011: 72): a place vibrating to industrialized hammerstroke, amplified commentary on share prices, machine gun fire and ambulance sirens, where the topological dimension and space/time of subjectivity and inwardness (seemingly intrinsic to the sense of self) is itself colonized (in a deathly triumph of capitalist consumerism). The inhabitants, 'abjects', are physically subordinated to an illusion of 'absolute time' outside and beyond the human realm, predicated on the power and rationale of market economics (thriving on the creation, even as it promises the satiation, of needs), over which Abeminoth is enthroned (in his human guise of media mogul, McAbendroth). In this world, there is no such thing as 'unoccupied time' as all denizens are wired into a central bank of de-composed consumerist imagery, through fetishistic attachments to sub-systemic technical 'supports' that subjugate their owners to the circular priorities of intrusive diffusion: a potent dramatic image of how the 'leisure industries (an oxymoron maybe, but no contradiction) fill time, as groundwater fills a sinkhole', leaving its citizens awash in 'the old rubble and shiny new toys' (Gleick 2000: 10) of their notional civilization and constant artificial momentary present (with no visible sky or nature to discern time of day or year). Merlin, though bewildered by his new environment, reconnects with memories of contrasting times and places (though he denies personal contact with Shakespeare, adding 'Alas, I live before his time...' [Rudkin 2011: 161]). The surrounding 'abjects', such as a girl he encounters, believe themselves dependent on the G.O.D. Tower to put and hold anything in their heads (in their imposed imaginative restrictions, they recall the Pit workers in Rudkin's *The Sons of Light*). Abeminoth/McAbendroth meanwhile plans to render obsolescent the moon, deemed 'irrational' and redundant in its waxing and waning, to 'decommission' and replace it with his own totalitarian technological construction, 'eye into all human souls and source of all earth's dreams' (174).[18] Only one in McAbendroth's inner sanctum dares to express dissent from this project: a Japanese neuro-physiologist who cites the (obscure but factual) example of a crab that is behaviourally dependent on rhythms associated with high and low tide (her/his analysis has striking parallels with that of Whitrow in his seminal study *What is Time?* ([1972] 2003: 39–42), which also illustrates an inner capacity for the measurement of time by living organisms, 'biological clocks', by tracing how lunar and semilunar cycles 'may be explicable in terms of the interaction of circadian rhythms with tidal rhythms', 42). The generative processes of the crab thus provide 'one modest microcosmic image' of the naturally developed and developmental processes that 'a macro-managerial decision can destroy' (Rudkin 2011: 184): as such decisions must, to attempt their contrary (but rootless) self-validation.

A crucial confrontation occurs at Stonehenge, the English megalith primarily associated with a sacred embodiment of time and space that transcended the human individual: here proposed dramatically as an edifice formerly assembled by Merlin to measure time through angles of light and welcome its festive occasions. This is the territory for Merlin's defiance of the purported ushering in of a 'new age' through the launch of McAbendroth's man-made moon (a reflective membrane of tin). However, Merlin's Shakespearean blank-verse curse meets only ridicule; he discovers that a sharper weapon is scorn, instigating an irreverence among the onlookers, which proves decisive in breaking the glamour and function of this satellite that promises unity and concordance on specifically and exclusively materialistic terms: the false moon falls. In the ensuing darkness, Merlin challenges the alarmed and resentful 'souls of Garganel', as well as the theatre audience, to discern shapes (Merlin tells them, 'You have nothing. / And what did that light you grieve for do, / But blind you to the nothing that you have' [201]). As he seemingly transforms to birdlike form to attack and destroy the G.O.D. Tower, the girl whom he formerly encountered realizes her own capacity to 'put' and keep his image in her head, through time.

Now freed from her captivity in the desert fortress, Almazen presents a scientific lecture on early paradigms of the universe, reminding her audience of their own perspectives of change: while we may 'smile at these primitive cosmologies', 'at that very moment of landmark insight when we think we know, / we too are arrived only at a threshold / of the further unknown' (206). The incessantly questioning terms of her process and her respect for natural forces avoid idealization, and so importantly challenge her son Perseus's resentful allegation that she is irresponsible. Tragically, Perseus now opposes her search for knowledge with a Luddite fundamentalism, developed from those of Albatusa's order, which demonizes his mother, and he seeks the simplicities of 'eternal love' through the toxic ideology of the suicide bomber, which dismisses the sanctity of life. However, the experience of the afterlife that Perseus fanatically brings upon himself proves less exclusive and hierarchical than he anticipated: this eternity contains his ideological opposites too, and is based on an infinite duration of re-evaluative learning.

The last scene of *Merlin Unchained* shows its protagonist awaking to a sense of mortal restriction that the portals in time have (been?) closed behind him. His wife insists he '[s]trive no more', let the world 'be': a rhetoric of accommodation, in all directions, which involves Merlin's incorporation into Christian mythology, and thereby assimilation into a narrative of management and control that his doctor-therapist admits is intended to placate and restrict 'the peasants and schoolchildren of tomorrow' (218). Merlin repudiates the 'bargain' as a fundamentally Faustian confidence trick, which involves the reduction of the full 'restless' terms of humanity and animality, to a contrastingly compliant 'solemn, saintly dust'. Without his former temporal agility, Merlin appears caught between worlds: even as Sirius signals his dimly-heard sympathy, Merlin is demonized to 'beast' by a more fearful age where political duplicity has severed words from their moral moorings: responsibility, honour and *consequence*. He is killed by those who would, in fear and ignorance, reject their own gateways to other worlds. Merlin's tragedy is counterpointed by Sirius's intimation that he is Merlin's younger self to come: as Merlin exits from this world, Sirius picks up his harp and sets off on whatever will prove to be his own way, 'down the roads of time' (226).

Sirius's assumption of the bardic role (however stigmatized it may be) sounds a final keynote that is crucial to Rudkin's theatre and drama and temporal politics: the importance of transmission: transmission of deeply informative identifications, stories that deal with the unseen, things crucially done and undone, and carry notions of how people can define themselves in consequences (all of which contravene the standard historical, and so intrinsically dispossessive, forms of 'received wisdom'). It is logical that some of Rudkin's recent work has taken his drama outside of the theatre, to where voices might be imaginatively located in a landscape, though not in the audience member's immediate (and perhaps apparently *inconsequential*) perception of that landscape. Rudkin's development of a series of ten sonic 'place-prints' involves individuated audience members listening to short audio plays on headphones whilst they traverse specific physical locations and landscapes: audio plays that aim to dissolve the sensed habitual temporal barriers between the listener and an imaginative reanimation of the named and buried dead, and prompt a revisioning of actions and consequences, formerly undertaken in that place. This is Rudkin's own archaeological excavation of what might be – to borrow the terms of a Barker play title –

'found in the ground': an exhumed psychogeography that sonically manifests alternative terms and forms of history, reframing the subject matter through provocations of 'pictures in the head'.

For the purposes of this study, I will confine myself to consideration of 'Here We Stay', set in the Derbyshire village of Eyam[19]: the sole Rudkin 'place-print' to have reached the public domain at my time of writing (in a live presentation at Eyam parish church, 18th July 2015[20]). 'Here We Stay' is, in Rudkin's own words, a place-print which 'overlays the Eyam of now with the Eyam of the plague time', 'as preparation for a visit, or simply as an evocation of the village and its ordeal' but primarily organized as an 'audio-guide for visitor on foot' extending to particular sites of narrative significance. The audio track approaches the dwellings from the intimate perspective of Pestis, a feminized and satanically invasive figure of contagious Death (her assurances reminiscent of a vampiric regeneration of Mother Manus from *The Triumph of Death*). Rudkin's narrative 'peoples' the modern landscape with detailed views of its former inhabitants, and their steady infection and sickening by plague, in 1665, but Pestis also emphasizes the extensiveness of her powers and finitude of her prospects, and how they cancel the distance between that conjured time and our own:

> Oh you think: what a terrible time to live,
> where I can be so rampant.
> 'Time'?
> What is a 'time'?
> I am at once in your Then
> and in your Now and in your To Come.

A roll-call of the names of the village dead suggests an unremitting avalanche of personal grief and loss, the staggering accumulative force of which the listener is left to imagine (in reminder that 'each name / even the tiny day-old child, / is *someone…*'), while Pestis calmly observes 'let rich and privileged, with their better means, outrun me. / I am more at home among the poor', particularly the 'god-fearing and sociable' who are so potentially contagious in their gatherings. Determined to 'fight this', the Reverend Mompesson preaches at outdoor gatherings, the congregation standing 12-foot apart: the listener hears an address in his voice as they are invited to consider the setting of 'Pulpit Knoll' in present-day Eyam. Mompesson explains how the villagers should adopt and enforce a collective quarantine to prevent plague spreading more widely, not in a spirit of passive acceptance or resignation, but of decisive agency by which to 'save the world': an active manifestation of '*SOCIETY*', distinct from the 'herdlike obedience', and the circulation of filthy money, by which Pestis thrives. Mompesson further instigates the cleaning of all coins in a boundary well, sensing that their catastrophe is a task, from which to draw some as yet unsuspected and otherwise unformulated deduction. The villagers' active respect of boundaries confounds and infuriates Pestis ('The insufferable self-discipline of these people! Have they no selfishness?'). Still, however, the litany of dead within Eyam rolls on, and when at last the plague's progress abates, Mompesson soberly repudiates Pestis's frustrated shriek '*afar*' that 'There is no such thing as society'[21]; Mompesson wonders 'In time to come: shall others / have the "society" in them to do as we did?'. Pestis, routed on this occasion, waits, and considers her next move:

I tell you:
in your Now, and in your To Come,
I see so many a visitation afflict your earth:
and each a consequence
of heedless choices your more 'scientific' kind have made.

Though Pestis has the literal 'last word', she does not win the battle (as did Mother Manus in *The Triumph of Death*). To paraphrase words from Rudkin's play *John Piper in the House of Death* (1987, 1991), 'Here We Stay' informs the listener of ways to 'know' and recognize Death, to 'hate' and 'disbelieve each word she speaks', and how 'their living duty is to disobey' her expectations and foreclosures: particularly when apparent in the modern contexts of drives towards globalization, 'whose worldwide damage amplifies rather than compensates for the erosion of local identities and interests' (Chesneaux 1992: 70). 'Here We Stay' furthermore deploys the form of the audio play in what might be considered as a radically Protestant way (reflecting Rudkin's tradition of upbringing), in that it involves the listener in individuated (and at least somewhat isolated) consideration of a congregation who defy division: locating the listener across imaginative space/times where they are alone with their potential unmaker. The listener is invited to consider possible (formerly, actual) terminal and lonely circumstances, and to consider how similar circumstances might challenge her/his own individual will – in what is a hard but nevertheless identifiable tradition of those who have lived and resisted before – to awaken the unsuspected disobedient within her/himself.

Rifkin: Searching for the new 'time rebels'

In Wesker's *The Old Ones*, one character observes in 'the age of computers, the problems are different' (Wesker 1980: 151). Like this comment, Jeremy Rifkin's 1987 book, *Time Wars: The Primary Conflict in Human History*, seems more prescient with the intervening years. Rifkin examines contemporary issues of power in terms of a battle over 'the politics of time' (Rifkin 1987: 2) and aims to identify tendencies (which are overlooked by discourses that conceive of politics in primarily spatial terms) through his focus on relatively 'unexplored temporal dimensions' of political processes (to provide a firmer foundation for an 'eventual synthesis of space/time politics' [5]).

Consider, for example, Rifkin's observations in 1987 on the potential effects of a 'nanosecond culture': what he identifies as a fourth era of time consciousness, which orders life in terms (supplanting those of the seasons, the stars and the clocks) of the computer. The computer deals primarily in temporal measurements that can be conceived of, but not experienced distinctly or directly, by human consciousness: the acceptance of 'expedience as a substitute for participation'; the transformation of discretionary time (associated with the pleasure principle, savouring an experience, and with historical reflection) from amenity to luxury; a world of novelty, fast projection and abstraction that involves the professional devaluation of others' time in order to increase production quotas, increasing superficial conveniences but requiring that we become 'more detached, self-absorbed and manipulative in relation to others' (11–12) as a 'reality principle' of necessary compromise. With less need for 'face-to-face interaction to order the sequence, duration, rhythm and tempo' of modern life, Rifkin suggests, people will rely on the computer as both 'form of communication and time frame through which to relate to their fellow human beings' and find increasing difficulties to 'slip back into face-to-face interchange' (19), except to 'relate to each other entirely in terms of information exchange' (20). Do any of these predictions seem to you more, rather than less, recognizable in social life since 1987?[22]

In a scenario in which accumulation of information has become associated with evolution of consciousness (and security), Rifkin also indicates potential consequences for traditional (non-centralized) senses of history, commemoration (which honours past experiences), reflection and memory: all things that may seem too slow, and therefore uneconomical and unnecessary, 'to a child who has come to think of the past as a code', as data suspended in a medium 'that can instantaneously be called up whenever past information is necessary to fulfil a momentary need' (26); this child will accordingly regard time as mere utility, 'instrument to secure output' (80). Rifkin suggests that as long as human beings 'remain the agents of change, future events can never be totally controlled by pre-established schedules' (98). However, some computer programmes now require no human participation, after their initial design, in implementing further processes of manufacture or delivery (99). This ultimately eliminates the importance of active human involvement and participation in the unfolding of a predetermined future, and undermines subjective memory of past experiences (as 'users rely less and less on their personal memories of past experiences and events as a guide to future actions and become more reliant on the data stored in the programme's memory bank' [100]). By 'automating the unfolding of future events', the computer programme introduces 'a new level of determinism into the social process', beyond the clock or the calendar, which may reduce the individual to 'the narrow confines of preprogrammed scenarios' and models of reality laid out for her/him (101). This context of social maintenance through predetermination abstracts the individual from natural time/s, detaches them from subjective temporality, and even from contextual memories of a government or political party's former political promises and commitments, in a schedule that valorizes expediency and urgency (160). Rifkin suggests that this temporal deprivation and decontextualizing of experience from history creates the conditions for 'a new form of social control', because it makes its victims 'totally manipulable, ready to accept blindly their inquisitors' definition of past and future' (166), and thus ultimately pave the ways for 'fortress futures', artificially controlled time frames based on imposed autonomy (208).

However, Rifkin is crucially not deterministic, and this is notably apparent in his critique of Marx's argument that it is material conditions that inevitably dictate changes in economic, social and political relationships. Rifkin observes that 'the age we live in is so steeped in a materialist consciousness that we cannot possibly imagine the idea that time considerations might play as important a role in the political process as economic considerations':

> The mind, however, is more than a passive captive of its physical and material surroundings. The mind is continually initiating change by fashioning new temporal orientations, and these new dimensions interact with the changing material conditions to help shape the context for the kind of economic, social, and political realities that emerge. Temporal transformations accompany and, on occasion, even precede material transformations.
>
> (132)

Rifkin may occasionally seem rhetorically overly romantic, even superheroic, in his messianic invocation of 'new time rebels' (5) who might emerge to refashion a 'vision of the future' (208), but his subtler model of expansive freedom involves a theatrical image for an empowering re-presentation of possibility, self and others: a process that will 'move society onto the centre stage of a new world drama where we might become writer and director as well as actor' (150).

Hoffman makes a similar point, about the inherent abstractions involved in increasingly predominant technological emphases on multiplicity and simultaneity: how the 'impersonal, indeed virtual, gaze of scattered interlocutors hypothetically noting fragmented bits of one's activities' is 'not the same as the embodied attention of another person, taking in what you are saying and following the thread of your story'; the gaze of the witness offers a contrasting intersubjectivity, which 'like subjectivity, requires precisely a deepening and development of knowledge rather than its mere accumulation' (Hoffman 2009: 175–176). I suggest theatre specifically foregrounds this element of intersubjectivity in the artistic encounter, and this has particular implications for an age that tends to submerge individual agency under a bombardment of more highly valued mediated information. It is not pre-selective 'information' that we lack: it is the temporal frameworks to derive deductive knowledge from intersubjective experiences, and the courage to draw conclusions in consequential action.[23]

Reverse engineering: *The Radicalization of Bradley Manning*

Tim Price's play *The Radicalization of Bradley Manning* (first staged 2012) focuses on struggles towards freedom in both self and society, particularly the struggle to become adult: informed and developed to a point capable of autonomy. Price explores these themes through events that depict both the promise and the loss of control, as thrown into relief by the 'electronic present' of computer-driven networking instantaneity and simultaneity (Adam 2004: 120), through appropriate theatrical form, which is fluid and looping in time, location and casting (Price specifies the central role of Bradley be played by each member of the mixed-gender ensemble of performers). The play's central dynamic is transition: sometimes precisely connective, sometimes nightmarish (when the human imagination loses control over its manifested consequences), sometimes depicting the remembered and imagined traumas, experiences and strains of a very particular person's adolescent and young adult life: a dynamic enhanced by National Theatre Wales's first site-specific performances of the play, situated in the school premises, principally the gymnasium, of Tasker Milward School, Haverfordwest, which was attended by (the now Chelsea) Manning as a boy. This setting provided a highly resonant crucible for the events of Price's play, 'a fictional account based on a true story',[24] which offers a speculative timescape based on the imagined memories of Chelsea Manning, who in May 2010 leaked information to the worldwide web in order to provoke a reassessment of military actions in Iraq. Appropriately the very first scene mobilizes contending and contradictory verbalized 'blizzard' impressions of (the then) Bradley Manning, in order to provoke the audience into an intrigued, puzzled and investigative attitude. Thereafter the scenes are presented in a selective and compressed chronology of significant experiences, choices and decisions, principally alternating between Bradley's formative schooldays and his brief military career. This contextualizing framework formally suggests the condensations that might be associated with the subjectivities of a central individual's temporality, in opposition to the commodification, compression, colonization and control (Adam's 'four Cs', 2004: 124) of industrial time, which finds its ultimate expression in military hierarchical temporal relations: neither of which, Price's play suggests, are without their contradictions and paradoxes, despite their assurances. Scene One of the play offers a glimpse of the systematic displacement of a military prison, to which Bradley is consigned: the nausea of undifferentiated time, which might constitute one aspect of the prison's punitive function, is intensified by regulative demands that purposefully disrupt his body clock by depriving him of sleep or exercise. Another form of undifferentiated time is represented by Bradley's work at a 'McJob', a minimum-wage service industry post (a sympathetic detail when this is increasingly, for many, a social rite of passage or means of funding study, at the least). However, Price's play in performance, like theatre at its best, aspires to offer sharply *differentiated time*, in nuances both of narrative, and of group and individual performances. *The Radicalization of Bradley Manning* constitutes a theatrically formalized relayed testimony that encompasses 'real' microcosmic historical details (including recorded fatalities) and adds the ethical dimension of the complicating personal perspective (Manning's, as activated and articulated selectively by Price) that provides unusual contexts for what have been normatively designated 'extreme and criminally irresponsible' actions, and the constructive and complicating processes and consequences of enquiry.

When Bradley lends his computing skills to the US military, he finds out how their efforts in transport, transmission and transplantation, all aimed to increase mastery of situations, in fact issue in a decrease in control (Adam 2004: 146): their purported forms of space-eliminating interconnectivity have an impact on the fragility of local social networks, so that their means of attempted control undermine their own ends – as in Scene Twenty-three when Bradley realizes that a military operation designed to identify and detain 'more insurgents not less' is, in fact, targeting the wrong people – protesters accusing the Iraqi government of corruption (Price and Wasserberg 2015: 120–121). This scene, and the ensuing one in which Bradley discovers a circulating video clip of an Apache helicopter shooting civilians, confront him (and the audience) with questions of meaning, which beg choices in reaction. Bradley expresses the impulse for the finititude of the recorded war crime to be somehow reversible: 'We're supposed to make sense of it. / *(Silence)* / All I can think … every time I watch it, I think …/ *(Beat)* / Maybe *this* time they'll get away' (124, original emphasis). The video clip provides an ultimate example, and consequence, of the military's spatio-temporal dissociation, a process that involves 'abolishing perceptions of what is local and unique' (Chesneaux 1992: 22). The next scene shows Bradley at school, refusing complicity in an action with which he disagrees, which – ironically *and* significantly – borders a lesson on how people 'found themselves at pivotal moments in history and had no choice but to act – such was the power of their convictions' (127). Bradley's mutinously principled response to this delineation of a Welsh tradition of radical revolt leads into Scene Twenty-Six, his adult arrival at conviction that military mistakes that are proving fatal to civilians should not be concealed in the name of 'professionalism': 'The world can't be like this, or I can't be in it' (131). After Bradley takes action by leaking the clip, all surrounding performers fall and '*form the dead bodies who have haunted BRADLEY*', then one by one rise to personify the 'layers' of his former selves in time, giving shape to former classifications whilst also showing their provisional natures (137–138): this individual timescape is marshalled alongside and against the play's immediately subsequent depiction of the systematic processes of punitive reduction and disintegration that are occurring in Manning's cell, through repetitive questioning,[25] in the remarkable Scene Thirty (138–142). This scene involves 48 iterations of an ostensibly concerned question to which Manning is required to respond, and requires the performers (and audience) to explore a gruelling ordeal of distinctive nuance of resolve. Superficially, this section takes the form of (near) repetition: but only superficially. In performance, it becomes a process (much as Manning's earlier repetition of his → her own name seems to have re-endowed it with the plasticity of a verb, of questionable process, or even performative excoriation) of differentiated tones and times: of the patrolling Marine's disingenuous insistence, of Manning's defiance, fragility, despair, resolve, in permutations and sequences to be decided upon and expressed, by the performers, interactively, *in the moment*. The scene is a demonstration of rhythm as a means to the experience of a dialectical duration.

Price's play concludes by looping back to Bradley's last day at school, providing a retrospectively poignant ironic context for his professed idealism: 'If I want to help people, make the world a better place I can't think of anywhere better than the U. S. army' (144).

However, the whole play's arc provides a larger, further recontextualization of these last words, and of Bradley's youthful expression of fatalistic determinism – 'I don't have a choice Miss' (144) – which resonates with his (significantly contradictory and beleaguered, if acclaimed) experience of role-playing a member of a tradition of Welsh radicals, who 'had no choice but to act – such was the power of their convictions'. This calls fatalistic determinism into question, as do the wider events of Manning's life. Like Rudkin's *Cries from Casement* (1972), Price's *Radicalization* strategically and purposefully avoids (indeed, fractures) imposed linear chronology and categorization, in order to see their subject(s) more holistically (if polemically and dramatically, in their principles of selection). In *Radicalization*, transition is not limited to a matter of linear consequence: the last line of many scenes acts as a springboard to the next, whereby an utterance or proposition, or an aspect of a situation, is then contextualized differently in/by time. Thus, expansive theatrical frames of reference remind us that there is 'no objective realm from which to conduct acontextual investigations'; rather, it is deeply significant how we 'theorize the social relations of time past and present, their geneses and projected futures', particularly in analyses of contemporary situations and projected consequences, where 'theory' – and theatre – 'intersects an open process' and so 'reflexively alters condition and outcome' (Adam 2004: 152), here relativizing and recontextualizing 'the present' and its political edicts. This is highly pertinent to theatre that is both speculative and consequential in its address to the past, the contemporary and the ongoing (and which links them questioningly in the continuum of a non-deterministic timescape). *The Radicalization of Bradley Manning* is an outstanding example of this, which focuses on a living figure, in transition and in process of challenging boundaries, on so many levels.

Price's subsequent play, *Teh Internet is Serious Business* (2014), considers further the hinge opportunities for 'control/loss of control associated with the network society', where strategic instantaneity and trans-national connectivity offer 'entirely new temporal limits', within which it is possible to expose 'fault lines of logic' and provoke reflections unlikely to be provoked or sustained by the vested interests of science or politics in their socially prevalent forms (Adam 2004: 148). Part of the play's paradox, and artful challenge, is to physicalize the playful freedom which is possible in intersubjective relations that are nevertheless separated by distance (though only momentarily by time).

Price's theatrical work thus continues to investigate multiplicity and the active inter/personal construction of knowledge. His plays, like the others considered here, constitute examples of how, in bringing together what other forms of analysis and imagination might set apart, and in rendering visible what other definitional boundaries might exclude, theatre may be uniquely well placed/timed, in its precise distinctions of time, to (re)present negotiation and contextual process; to resist dualistic categorization and objectification; to move, through its own precise forms of distinctions, beyond the boundaries of separatist distance and absolutes; and to manifest forms of difference and divergent resonance, independencies and interdependencies – the challenges of dis/continuity, embodied.

Notes

1 From the Prefab Sprout album, *Swoon*. I have made consistent efforts in approaching possible copyright holders for this quotation.

2 Miller seems here particularly influenced by Wilder's sense of what Schroeder identifies as 'the equal validity of multiple temporal contexts', dramatized by combining and synthesizing 'Brechtian theatricality, Elizabethan flexibility of space, and expressionistic distortions of time and perspective', in order to portray the interaction of 'concurrent yet rival perspectives on the passage of time' (Schroeder 1989: 59). However, Miller is perhaps more concerned to be forensically and deductively selective in his presentations of time and perspective, seeking to eliminate the extraneous in order to identify underlying but discernible political forces and social consequences. Wilder is the dramatist more interested in expressionistic distortions, to dilate and expand the value of the ephemeral and seemingly trivial moment, and thereby, as Schroeder observes, its value and potential significance in 'creating history' (74).

3 Brenton's images of fantastic human-animal transformation reach their apogee in *Sore Throats* (1979).

4 This effect prefigures the disconcertingly unconventional 'mortality rate' of leading and supporting characters in the BBC television drama series, *Spooks* (2002-11), on which Brenton was one of the first principal writers.

5 In another essay, Bond presents another image for the distinctive and fertile 'gap' in the human consciousness (which he opposes to animal consciousness, which has a less developed sense of past, present and future):

> Think of two boxes, separate but side by side. One box is imagination in the mind and the other is the natural world (in parts of which we live) and its laws of cause and effect. The laws are installed in the self as the sense of reality – and, in the same way, in the imagination. Imagination could be fantasy if the consequentiality of the laws of the natural world were not integrated in the mind of the self as the consequentiality of morality. They are repeated in this way not because we are part of the natural world, which we are, but because we also are not. These two boxes are contiguous but absolutely separate – except in drama. Drama occurs in the gap between the two. Since we are vulnerable and mortal, objective reality (the natural world and its laws) is naturally dominant – except in drama. In drama imagination is dominant and it uses the laws of nature, and their counterpart in the moral imperative to be human, to create humanness. When the self confronts the gap, and in this way enters it, imagination has the reality of the objective world. The self finds the gap totally alien – and it is there that it finds its self.
>
> (Bond 2014a: 3)

6 In contrast, for example, the American dramatist Bernard Slade's comedy of sexual manners *Same Time Next Year* (1975) foregrounds personal transitions in its sporadically reconnecting protagonists: social change provides a significant informing context for these transitions, but the focus of Slade's play is personal rather than political.

7 Bond based this scene on a massacre conducted by Nazis at Babi Yar, near the Ukrainian capital of Kiev, and a soldier's personal expression of disgust at his task, by spilling coffee, a currency of privilege (Bond 2012: 5).

8 This would suggest, such a massacre did, and could, only occur at Babi Yar, where there is no historical record of any comparable moral mutiny (Mangan 1998: 91).

9 I am indebted to Lara Kipp for drawing to my attention Lyotard's responses to Klee, and for her translation of the German prepositions.

10 In some respects, *Dissocia's* provocations were echoed by the BBC Wales television speculative drama series *Life on Mars* (2006–7) and *Ashes to Ashes* (2008–10), created by Matthew Graham, Tony Jordan and Ashley Pharoah, in which the odysseys of the protagonists also suggested that a subjective world, and a private mythology, might ultimately be preferable (at least for the first protagonist, Sam Tyler) to the monotony and hollowness of present-day promises of order, security and control (*Ashes to Ashes* revealed that the questers' apparent time slippage to an alternative 1970s/80s *nebenwelt* constituted a spacetime of limbo or purgatory before ultimate release into deliverance). In 2011, Neilson pursued further some of the preoccupations and impulses identifiable in *Dissocia* when he directed a fiercely, vividly provocative production of Peter Weiss's 1963 play *Marat/Sade* for the Royal Shakespeare Company. The production assumed a contemporary setting for its turbulent and literally uncontainable subversion of anodyne patriotism, which featured many details (such as cameras, video screens and tasers) updated to a present-day 'surveillance society' promising a 'war on terror': begging the question, what is madness, in a totalitarian age when a hypocritical regime depends and thrives on promising its citizens a merely vicarious existence.

11 One might compare Thomas's *Gas Station Angel*: Ace's personal sense and development of a story-shaped supernatural world in between the forces of the council and the fairies.

12 Carney's suggestion that Churchill is exploring the possibility of 'liberation from the temporal' (189) strikes me as not quite accurate. Her plays, from *Traps* to *A Mouthful of Birds*, *The Skriker* and *Far Away*, seem to me, rather, to be explorations of how subjective experience becomes an ultimate reality for both characters and audiences.

13 The extensive amount of existing secondary material on Kane (and what appears to me increasingly as her *theatre of melancholia* in terms similar to those outlined in Segal 2014: 195–196) dissuades me from adding to it on this occasion, in an already large and crowded study. However, with reference to the themes of this chapter, I refer the reader to Alex Mangold's Ph.D. thesis: *The Empty I: Sarah Kane and the Aesthetics of the New Tragic* (2010), Aberystwyth University: http://cadair.aber.ac.uk/dspace/bitstream/handle/2160/5865/The%20empty%20I_Mangold_abstract.pdf?sequence=1 accessed 20/08/2015.

14 I am grateful for Georgia Hayward's observations: on how Ridley does many things at the same time in *Mercury Fur*, creating polyrhythmic layers which only add to the ambiguity and confusion of time and space. Caught between the traumatic time before the dramatic events (distorted by nostalgia) and the impending and emergent apocalyptic sense of time to come, the play's dramatic present is dominated by a sense that is running out for all the characters: Elliot has not had time to find a venue for the 'party', nor Darren to attain the appropriate personal mood, nor Lola to finish making a costume, nor the Party Piece to regain full consciousness. The disturbing transformations of *Mercury Fur* (caterpillar to lethal

butterfly, ice cream van to vendor of lethal drugs) extend to the destruction of an ancient bowl showing a human sacrifice, like that which the characters are planning. The political point is clear: cultural memory is what prevents humans repeating mistakes of the past.

15 Osborne notes how green's 'language repetition' and 'subtle reformations' and active silences suspend audiences in an 'unremitting dramatic temporality' (Osborne 2015: 170).

16 Rudkin's Lord seems to express a starkly Protestant ethos: 'Bereft of the Catholic belief in redemption and the expectation that sins can be undone through confession, Protestants had to come to terms with the harsh reality of a unidirectional, cumulative, irreversible time where every action counted, where every digression meant an irrevocable step on the path to damnation, every good deed was one step closer to grace' (Adam 2004: 45).

17 One of Britain's most popular, enduring and regenerating television drama characters, Dr Who is an ultimately benign alien 'timelord', whose abilities promise some 'escape from relentless chronology, from the ticking away of youth and health and high spirits toward senility and extinction' (Priestley 1964: 110). However, writers, directors and performers involved in the series have discerned and dramatized how the Doctor's power and control must be erratic to be engaging, and how his sense of time gains an unusual poignancy when set against the human travelling companions, and their 'youth and health and high spirits' that carry them irrevocably towards the 'senility and extinction' that he (just about) defies. Much of the character-based resonance of the series *Dr Who* concerns possibilities of regeneration: how a torch might be passed from one age, or alien, or actor, to another.

18 Storylines involving stealing or destroying the powers of the Moon have subsequently appeared in the films *Despicable Me* (directed by Pierre Coffin and Chris Renaud, 2010) and *Oblivion* (directed by Joseph Kosinski, 2013), and, on television, in an episode of *Dr Who* ('Kill the Moon', 2014).

19 Eyam is also the location of a theatre play by Don Taylor, *Roses of Ayam*, staged 1970 and adapted for television by the author in 1973. The unattributed Wikipedia entry on the play intriguingly observes that 'In some productions each corpse reappears in ghostly white make-up until the audience is surrounded by keening': an effect that, if pursued, suggests some anticipation of debbie tucker green's durational effects specified in her play *generations* (2005). See http://en.wikipedia.org/wiki/The_Roses_of_Eyam (author unknown), accessed 25/11/2014.

20 Rudkin describes how the formal reading presented by the New Perspectives Theatre Company of Nottingham, on 18th July 2015 was 'not a play-reading in the simple sense', nor 'a staging', as 'This is an audio piece, and not to be physicalised nor choreographed', yet 'the director, Jack McNamara, was called on to endow it with physical presence'. Rudkin continues,

> The readers were seated separately amid the congregation in different parts of the church, each with a discreetly lit lectern and script, and miked so that each could speak quietly as though into the listener's ear. Occasionally, as appropriate, one or other character would stand to speak. Pestis presided from a dais at the west end of the aisle. Mompesson was opposite, at the transept, in his pulpit. Far opposite Pestis, in the choir, a violinist improvised a soundscape of spare, eerie sounds, to set the scene at the beginning, and at

the end to shape it away, and very sparingly to punctuate the performance at appropriate points throughout. Between these performers, the aisle became a cavernous emptiness, given hope by one flame that burned throughout.

Rudkin, e-mail to the author: 30/07/2015

21 Pestis's words here echo a notoriously reductive assertion by the former Conservative Prime Minister of Britain, Margaret Thatcher, which continues to inform the political presumptions of her sympathizers.

22 See also Chesneaux for prophetic observations on specifically modern combinations of 'narcissism and gregariousness' (1992: 40, 124–125). I can date as 2011 the juncture when I would convene a first day of rehearsal with students and observe that, instead of risking or attempting initial and necessarily uneasy and stumbling conversation with each other, they would rather take atomized refuge in consulting their iPhones in order to feel and appear secure and purposeful, and hence mature and poised, until such time as they would next receive centralized information.

23 Here I am consciously and significantly adapting Lindqvist, as quoted by Jay Griffiths (1999: 188). Compare the point made by another Griffiths, Charlotte (2015):

> Perhaps the most politically radical thing theatre is doing, this spring of 2015, is not airing the issues of the day, but insisting its audience sit in a place, with our fellow humans, watching other humans doing and speaking, being moved to pity and fear. And insisting its audience do so, furthermore, without recourse to email, Twitter or Facebook, without, for a span of time, contributing to the algorithmic churn of Google. That, maybe, is the small, true act of resistance that all theatregoers undertake.

24 Price, 'Disclaimer', on an unnumbered page prefacing the 2012 Methuen edition of the single-play text, *The Radicalization of Bradley Manning*. My subsequent references will be based on the revised edition of the text in Price and Wasserberg's anthology as cited.

25 I refer back here to my comments on Beckett's Godot, and its depiction of 'marking time in deference to an inconsistent (despotically vague and/or wilful?) authority' (p. 147). Like David Edgar's *The Jail Diary of Albie Sachs* (1978), Price's *Radicalization* (re)locates the theatrical experience of enforced waiting, for characters and audience alike, in contexts that are not *metaphysically*, but rather *politically*, existential.

Inconclusion: Repent, Harlequin ...

Stolen moments

One Sunday night in 1995, I stood in the wings of a theatre, in the company of my fellow actors, waiting to go onstage to start the final performance of a production, and I suddenly thought: one day all of these people will be dead. Now at least one of them is. Perhaps a specific theatre performance is a consciously brief encounter between strangers, audience and production team, with a sense that time is the witness, at an event that specifies ephemerality and resurgence, endurance and fragility: 'The play is dead, long live the play' (Rabey 2004: 72).

This connects with the sense of 'temporal dualism' identified by Wagner, who notes how 'while defined on one hand by its material immediacy' any performative art is 'equally defined on the other hand by its transience', just as life is 'impossible to fully define in the absence of its opposite, death'; the theatre, in its foregrounded senses of transience and subjective time, might be 'be defined by a movement toward a death', but 'only insofar as we understand a link between death and time' (Wagner 2012: 134). Marlowe's Faustus provides a heightened sense of this: 'the more prescient the experience of death, the more palpable the manifestation of time', which is 'at its most material, it is most present, just as it expires'; and 'in the theatre, it is expiring all the time (135). However, this is a perception which *The Winter's Tale* presents (exposes?) as (inevitably) partial and subjective (as is any perspective), in the experiences of the shepherds, and Leontes, contradicting (if only briefly and locally) the figure of time as movement towards death. But I agree with Wagner's deduction that Shakespeare's theatre consciously presents different forms of time as 'bodied forth, in all their complexities', 'encounterable', 'something we can meet and feel ourselves in the presence of' (11), and I have sought to extend this observation to other forms of theatre.[1]

This is important because, as Barbara Adam observes, 'concern with the multiple time dimensions of our lives is no mere theoretical, academic exercise; rather it is a strategy for living':

Recognizing time running out as our creation, temporal time as present-creating becoming, and both as fundamental to our lives enables us to re-view the mutual implication of time and health and gives us choice for action [...] clock time's invariable repetitions confront us with that which is irrevocably gone, with the relentless entropy of physical processes and with absolute finitude.

(Adam 1995: 54)

Theatre may, at best, render visible the processes of temporality, what Adam terms 'present-creating becoming' and its ongoing importance, and it can potentially do so less expensively and more resourcefully and quickly than other more literalist electronic media, though it must necessarily do so on a more locally physical scale: a limitation that might also, sometimes, be a source of specificity and strength. Its basis in relatively small but transformative resonances of energy suggests some possible affinity with emergent 'string theory', which characterizes all constituents in the universe in terms of vibrating strings of energy, and so suggests that even the 'theatre of reality in which gravity acts would take place on a quantum stage' (Powell 2015; for further discussion of temporality and string theory in contemporary performance, see Woycicki 2011).

Arstila and Lloyd note how the temporal processes of 'subjective time' are 'subject to a broad and unruly relativity', in which the cognitive connections afforded by the social fabric of perception are subject to explicit time and timing – which is 'multifaceted, inconsistent and variable', full of dissociations and 'divergent judgments', so that the image of the 'metaphorical flowing river' of time might more aptly be 'replaced by a sputtering fireworks display' (Arstila and Lloyd 2014: 658). Theatre is the domain of explicit time and timing; and of all the self-conscious qualities above: a synchronized interaction of jointly focused subjectivities which might best be summarized as a collective exploration of 'unruly relativity'.[2] Theatre might be likened to an hourglass, in that its 'evolving internal state is in itself the indicator of passing time' (Arstila and Lloyd 2014: 326), and that time will proceed beyond us, as Prigogine indicates:

> [The big bang] was an event associated with an instability that produced our universe. It marked the start of our universe but not the start of time. Although our universe has an age, the medium that produced our universe has none. Time has no beginning, and probably no end.
>
> (Prigogine 1997: 6)

In the meantime, Priestley sought to remind his audiences and readers that properly informed decisions and choices cannot be separated from an integral awareness of human relations with time, and that renewal of consciousness, expansion of possibilities and enjoyment of life are not possible unless 'our minds and personalities' develop outside the constraints of 'totalitarian states and systems, narrow and authoritarian churches, and equally narrow and dogmatic scientific-positivist position'; indeed, that 'all three are bearing down on us now', so that while humanity has 'always lived in jeopardy, our present position is unusually precarious' (Priestley 1964: 308). These words seem to me to be no less prescient than when written.

However, it is also salutary to recall Howard Barker's observation that counters the fetishization of urgency: 'The effects of the work of art are characterized by *delay*...' (Barker 2005: 103, original emphasis). This is particularly provocative if extended to challenge modern presumptions surrounding sustained focus of attention, response time and formulation in professional, social and personal contexts of electronically mediated information overload. Barker's Prologue to his (first of several) marathon theatrical works, *The Bite of the Night* (Barker 2014a: 9–10 and 2016: 28–9), centralizes the response of a woman theatre spectator member who is, crucially, less rapidly dismissive than her colleagues in what, and for how long, she is prepared to entertain and contemplate, prior to finalizing and stating a categorical position in relation to that with which she has engaged. In selecting and considering my examples of theatre, I have found myself in agreement with Jonathan Kalb, who contends that, all too often, theatre artists incorporate and internalize the levelling, ironizing and trivializing effects fundamentally characteristic of screen-based media:

> fitting their once defiant imaginations to pseudosubversive institutions of consumerism, adopting the contours and limitations of media even in their nonmediated work, and settling into the habit of 'thinking small' to keep on the good side of information purveyors. The most malignant syndrome I see around me now is not self-importance but rather puniness of ambition, clipped talons, and shrunken horizons. Hence my urgency to find and chronicle meaningful exceptions. The productions discussed [...] dare to evoke the monumental in a postmonumental era [...] To me, however, they all found astonishingly intelligent and ingenious ways to accommodate monumentality without sacrificing scepticism. Indeed theatre generally has a built-in protection against excessive self-importance in its ephemerality – its bombast is written on the wind – and most of these productions turned that to deliberate advantage too [...] by establishing a fascinating tension between some awe-inspiring central vision and underlying awareness of its provisional, hypothetical, or interrogative nature.
>
> (Kalb 2011: 190)

Fortunately, we should all be able to think of instances of contemporary performance that have used technological supports to astonishing, unpredictable and highly original effects. Unfortunately, I, for one, can also think of instances of contemporary performance that have foregrounded their own dependency on fetishized 'sub-systems' of self-conscious modernity, which are, as such, 'primarily concerned with the fixing of their own value' (Chesneaux 1992: 78), crucially in extra-(or even anti-)theatrical terms. I agree with Klaic's proposition that the more theatre 'churns out its stuff in unison' with the other 'cultural industries', 'factories of collective consciousness, such as film or television', then 'the more irrelevant it becomes' (Klaic 2002: 145).

One (but not the only) strategic point may be not to try to make art in a vacuum or in an ideologically hostile or indifferent system, or even to explain it on other people's terms, but to create a specific (even unique) context for it, temporal or otherwise. If theatre practitioners neglect (and implicitly accept) an externally formulated and imposed sense of context, then they end up working on other people's terms: usually, trying to make theatre acceptable or attractive by making it relate to/as much like screen-based media as possible. I am wary of scientific (enlightenment) identifications of paradigm shifts, proclaiming that 'the world/

terrain/discourse has changed utterly', if they tend to support current cultural, political and economic priorities as if they are the end result of a deterministic Darwinism. Whilst the world may have changed utterly from one perspective, or alternatively stayed the same from another, theatre is well placed to locate, and corporeally based to express, the pertinence of the perspective that is not dominant. I can imagine an argument that could dismiss any artefact or event as anomalous in this time now, belonging to an antiquated paradigm: in other words, so not immediately or obviously relevant to immediately recognizable (that is, commercial) priorities. We might counter: the point is how much time you give it, to consider it, engage with it. People older, younger, richer and poorer than us will tell us there is no longer the time to do 'that' nowadays. So we have to be able to say why it should be made and engaged with.

Tadeusz Kantor's words remain prescient:

the highest freedom
which is demanded
by art
will not be understood,
or even deemed necessary. [...]
Freedom in art
is a gift neither from
the politicians
nor the authorities.
Freedom is not bestowed
upon art by the authorities.
Freedom exists inside of us.
We have to fight for freedom
within ourselves,
in our most intimate interior,
in our solitude,
in our suffering.
It is the most delicate domain,
the domain of the soul and spirit.

(Kantor 1993: 204)

Therefore, not wishing to be under-ambitious, I would propose a (hermeneutic, ethical) approach to theatre as time practice, which adapts Kearney's three tasks for the imagination: 'to discriminate between a liberating and incarcerating use of images, between those that disclose and those that close off our relation to the other' (Kearney 1988: 390) – a historical approach, to transfigure the present by 'refiguring lost narratives and prefiguring future ones' to 'offer ways of breaking the stranglehold of the dominant modern ideology of progress – an ideology which has tended to reduce the multiplicity of historical experiences [times] to a single totalizing doctrine [mechanical clock and computer time]' (393–394); a narrative task that not only recalls forgotten 'others' from history but equally demands the continual reinterpretation of the self through narrative identity, which 'in contrast to egological identity (permanent *same*ness) includes change and alteration within selfhood' and which casts 'each one of us as a narrator who never ceases to revise, reinterpret and clarify his own story' (395–396, original emphasis). These objectives have points of contact with Lepecki's objectives for dance studies: to 'track the coexistence of multiple temporalities' and 'multiple presents' within the temporality of theatre performance; to 'expand the notion of the present' beyond 'entrapment in the microscopy of the now' or the predeterminisms of an exclusive melancholy; 'to the extension of the present along lines of whatever still-acts, to reveal the intimacy of duration': tasks which he identifies as both theoretical and political (Lepecki 2006: 131).

Thus we may never lose sight of the interrogatory figure/force that Kennelly terms 'The Wild Streak' (Kennelly 2013: 112–114), which might also provide an apt personification of theatre.

Envoi: Give me just a little more time

On the other hand, Arnold Wesker's poem 'All things tire of themselves' finds at least some consolation that all proves unsustainable in/by time: not only 'the singer's joy', but also tyranny, recrimination and weeping.

> Only this knowledge remains:
> That all tires of itself
> All recreates
> Nothing sustains
> But knowing this is so.
>
> (Wesker 2008: 74)

Barbara Adam suggests that the 'conceptual re-presentation and construction' of 'temporal complexity, historically contextualized' might be the task of social theory (Adam 2004: 150), a task inevitably 'political in its processes of re-presentation and its social consequences' (152). I submit that this is also the principal task of theatre, more innately than any form of theory, because theatre involves and demonstrates – precisely, physically and distinctively – how the 'abstract and the lived become inseparable' as soon as imagined conceptions are 'activated in practice and the materialized ideas are inserted in processes' (143). I write this in conscious resistance of how, as Chesneaux observed and foresaw, 'the political role of the critical observer has given way to the view of the view of the intellectual as social guidance and social maintenance consultant' (Chesneaux 1992: 121), working within directives based on a purely economic approach to time: the bigger the quantity and the shorter the production time, the better for business. If 'theatre troubles linearity with repetition' (Schneider 2014: 45), theatre also involves challenging stasis with activity, powerlessness with agency (and, if something designates or implies you powerless, the most responsible human course is to challenge it). Theatre artfully reminds how tomorrow need not be like today, or yesterday, unless in ways that are actively chosen; it resists fatalism (and is therefore revolutionary, in individual terms) by offering an embodied range of both continuity and discontinuity, inviting us to participate in both, further, as we step out.

As we now should, from this horologist's labyrinth…

Don't reduce time
By dividing it into lives
Time must be sculpted
More slyly
Just as you carve a lover's
Pleasure
With your tongue

(Rabey 2008: 38)

Notes

1 Lepecki considers Siegel's identification of a (dance) performance, as an event existing at 'a perpetual vanishing point', in that it 'disappears in the very act of materializing' (Siegel 1972: 1), as a significant forerunner to Phelan's proposition that live performance lives only in the present, 'plunges into visibility' and 'disappears into memory, into the realm of invisibility and the unconscious where it eludes regulation and control' (Phelan 1993: 148). However, Lepecki insists that *the present is to be found in whatever still-acts*, citing Bergson's sense of duration, an affect of temporality, as 'defined less by succession than by coexistence' (Lepecki 2006: 130, original emphasis). I refer again to Mangan's observation that to 'remember the past is, whether we like it or not, to perform a creative act in the present' (Mangan 2013: 124).

2 The image of the sputtering fireworks evokes, for me, the final tableau of Barker's *The Europeans*, in which trickling bursts in the darkness frame two protagonists who are explicitly dissociative and specific in their timing.

References

Adam, Barbara (1990), *Time and Social Theory*, Cambridge: Polity Press.
—— (1995), *Timewatch: The Social Analysis of Time*, Cambridge: Polity Press.
—— (1998), *Timescapes of Modernity*, London: Routledge.
—— (2004), *Time*, Cambridge: Polity Press.
Analogue (Hannah Barker, Lewis Hetherington, Liam Jarvis, Emma Jowett and Dan Rebellato) (2011), *Beachy Head*, London: Oberon.
Angel-Perez, Elisabeth (2006), 'Facing Defacement: Barker and Levinas', in K. Gritzner and D. I. Rabey (eds), *Theatre of Catastrophe: New Essays on Howard Barker*, London: Oberon, 136–149.
Arstila, Vallteri, and Lloyd, Dan (eds) (2014), *Subjective Time*, Cambridge, MA and London: MIT Press.
Artaud, Antonin (1958), *The Theatre and its Double* (tr. M. C. Richards), New York: Grove Press.
Aston, Elaine (2011), 'debbie tucker green', in M. Middeke, P. P. Schnierer, and A. Sierz (eds), *The Methuen Drama Guide to Contemporary British Playwrights*, London: Methuen, 183–202.
Augustine, Saint (1998), *Confessions* Book XI (tr. H. Chadwick), Oxford: Oxford University Press.
Ayckbourn, Alan (2002), *The Crafty Art of Playmaking*, London: Faber and Faber.
Bachelard, Gaston (1994), *The Poetics of Space* (tr. M. Jolas), Boston, MA: Beacon Press.
—— (2000), *The Dialectic of Duration* (tr. M. M. James), Manchester: Clinamen Press.
Barker, Clive (2000), 'The Ghosts of War: Stage Ghosts and Time Slips as a Response to War', in C. Barker and M. B. Gale (eds), *British Theatre Between the Wars 1918-1939*, Cambridge: Cambridge University Press.
Barker, Howard (1987), *Gary the Thief/Gary Upright*, London: John Calder Publishers.
—— (1993), *Collected Plays: Volume Two*, London: Calder Publications.
—— (1996), *Collected Plays: Volume Three*, London: Calder Publications.
—— (2004a), *The Ecstatic Bible*, London: Oberon.
—— (2004b), *Dead Hands*, London: Oberon.
—— (2005), *Death, The One and The Art of Theatre*, Abingdon: Routledge
—— (2008), *Plays Four*, London: Oberon.
—— (2010), *Slowly/Hurts Given and Received*, London: Oberon.
—— (2011), *Blok/Eko*, London: Oberon.
—— (2014a), *Plays Eight*, London: Oberon
—— (2014b), *These Sad Places, Why Must You Enter Them?*, London: Impress.
—— (2016), *Arguments for a Theatre* (4th ed.), London: Oberon.
Barrie, James Matthew (1931), *Dear Brutus*, London: Hodder and Stoughton.

Beckett, Samuel (1986), *The Complete Dramatic Works,* London: Faber and Faber.

Benjamin, Andrew (ed.) (1989), *The Lyotard Reader,* Oxford: Blackwell

Bennett, Susan (2013), *Theatre and Museums,* Basingstoke: Palgrave.

Billington, Michael (2004), 'Magic for a Cynical Age', http://www.theguardian.com/stage/2004/mar/04/theatre3/ accessed 18/11/2014.

Bigsby, Christopher (2005), *Arthur Miller: A Critical Study,* Cambridge: Cambridge UP.

Bly, Robert (2001), *Iron John,* London: Rider.

Boal, Augusto (2002), *Games for Actors and Non-Actors* (tr. A. Jackson, 2nd ed.), London: Routledge.

—— (2005) *The Rainbow of Desire* (tr. A. Jackson), London: Routledge.

Bogart, Anne (2014), *What's the Story,* Abingdon: Routledge.

Bond, Edward (1995), *Coffee,* London: Methuen.

—— (1997), *At the Inland Sea,* London: Methuen

—— (1998), *Plays: 6,* London: Methuen.

—— (2000), *The Hidden Plot,* London: Methuen.

—— (2001), *Edward Bond: Letters 5* (ed. Ian Stuart), London: Routledge.

—— (2010), 'The State of Drama', http://www.edwardbond.org/Theory/theory.html/ accessed 21/10/2014.

—— (2011), 'Four Little Essays on Drama', http://www.edwardbond.org/Theory/theory.html/ accessed 21/10/2014.

—— (2012), 'The Third Crisis', http://www.georgehunka.com/essays/edward-bond-the-third-crisis/ accessed 23/10/2014.

—— (2014a), 'The Institute of Drama', http://www.edwardbond.org/Theory/theory.html/ accessed 21/10/2014.

—— (2014b), 'The Mind Field', http://www.edwardbond.org/Theory/theory.html/ accessed 21/10/2014.

Booth, Stephen (1983), *King Lear, 'Macbeth', Indefinition and Tragedy,* New Haven and London: Yale University Press.

Borst, Arno (1993), *The Ordering of Time* (tr. Andrew Winnard), Cambridge: Polity Press.

Bradley, Karen K. (2009), *Rudolf Laban,* Abingdon: Routledge.

Brater, Enoch (2011), *Ten Ways of Thinking about Samuel Beckett,* London: Methuen.

Brecht, Bertolt (1977), *The Measures Taken and other Lehrstücke* (tr. R. Manheim), London: Methuen.

Brenton, Howard (1996), *Plays: Two,* London: Methuen.

—— (2006), *In Extremis,* London: NHB.

—— (2010), *Anne Boleyn,* London: NHB.

Buonomaro, Dean V. (2015), 'The Neural Mechanisms of Timing on Short Timescales', in V. Arstila and D. Lloyd (eds), *Subjective Time* Cambridge, MA and London: MIT Press.

Burroughs, William S. (1968), *The Ticket that Exploded,* New York: Grove Press.

Burton, Harry (2014), 'The Curse of Pinter', in M. Taylor-Batty, *The Theatre of Harold Pinter,* London: Bloomsbury, 192–214.

Butterworth, Jez (1998), *Mojo & A Film-maker's Diary,* London: Faber.

—— (2011), *Plays: One,* London: NHB.

Callender, Craig, and Edney, Ralph (2010), *Introducing Time,* London: Icon.

Capra, Fritjof (1982), *The Turning Point,* London: Wildwood House.

Carlson, Marvin (2003), *The Haunted Stage,* Ann Arbor: University of Michigan Press.

Carney, Sean (2013), *The Politics and Poetics of Contemporary English Tragedy,* Toronto and London: University of Toronto Press.

Carroll, Sean (2010), *From Eternity to Here,* Oxford: Oneworld.

Carson, Anne (1998), *Eros the Bittersweet,* Champaign: Dalkey Archive.

Caruth, C. (1996), *Unclaimed Experience: Trauma, Narrative and History,* Baltimore: John Hopkins UP.

Cawley, A. C. (ed.) (1977), *Everyman and Medieval Miracle Plays,* London: Dent.

Chesneaux, Jean (1992), *Brave Modern World,* London: Thames and Hudson.

Churchill, Caryl (1985), *Plays: One,* London: Methuen.

——— (2002), *A Number,* London: NHB.

——— (2012), *Love and Information,* London: NHB.

D'Arcy, Margaretta (2005), *Loose Theatre: In and Out of My Memory,* Crewe and Victoria: Trafford.

Davis, Jessica Milner (2003), *Farce,* New Brunswick: Transaction.

Derrida, Jacques (1992), *Given Time. 1: Counterfeit Money* (tr. P. Kamuf), Chicago: University of Chicago Press.

Dreyfus, Hubert Lederer (1975), 'Human Temporality', in J. T. Fraser and N. Lawrence (eds), *The Study of Time II,* New York: Springer Verlag.

Droit-Volet, Sylvie (2014), 'What Emotions Tell Us About Time', in V. Arstila and D. Lloyd (eds), *Subjective Time,* Cambridge, MA and London: MIT Press.

Dufourmantelle, Anne (2007), *Blind Date: Sex and Philosophy* (tr. C. Porter), Urbana and Chicago: University of Illinois.

Duggan, Patrick (2012), *Trauma-tragedy,* Manchester: Manchester UP.

Edgar, David (2009), *How Plays Work,* London: NHB.

Elam, Keir (1980), *The Semiotics of Theatre and Drama,* London: Methuen.

Eliot, Thomas Sterns (1975), *Collected Poems 1909–1962,* London: Faber and Faber.

Ermarth, Elizabeth Deeds (1992), *Sequel to History: Postmodernism and the Crisis of Representational Time,* Princeton: Princeton UP.

Escolme, Bridget (2006), *The Shakespeare Handbooks: Antony and Cleopatra,* Basingstoke: Palgrave Macmillan.

Evans, Gareth Lloyd (1964), *J. B. Priestley: The Dramatist,* London: Heinemann.

Favorini, Attilio (2008), *Memory in Play,* Basingstoke: Palgrave Macmillan.

Forsyth, Alison (2008), 'The Trauma of Articulation: Holocaust Representation in *After the Fall* and *Broken Glass*', in *The Arthur Miller Journal,* vol. 3, no. 2, 41–60.

Fraction, Matt, and Zdarsky, Chip (2014), *Sex Criminals: One Weird Trick,* Berkeley: Image Comics.

——— (2015), *Sex Criminals: Two Worlds, One Cop,* Berkeley: Image Comics.

Fraps, Thomas (2014), 'Time and Magic: Manipulating Temporal Subjectivity', in V. Arstila and D. Lloyd (eds), *Subjective Time,* Cambridge, MA and London: MIT Press, 263–85.

Frayn, Michael (1998), *Copenhagen,* London: Methuen.

Gale, Maggie B. (2008), *J. B. Priestley,* Abingdon: Routledge.

Gipson-King, Jay (2013), 'History in an Age of Fracture: Catastrophic Time in Barker's *The Bite of the Night*', in D. I. Rabey and S. Goldingay (eds), *Howard Barker's Art of Theatre*, Manchester: Manchester University Press.

Gleick, James (2000), *Faster: The Acceleration of Just About Everything*, London: Abacus.

Goddard, Lynette (2015), 'debbie tucker green', in J. F. Deeney and M. Gale (eds), *Fifty Modern and Contemporary Dramatists*, Abingdon: Routledge, 220–4.

Gould, Stephen Jay (1987), *Time's Arrow, Time's Cycle*, London: Penguin.

green, debbie tucker (2003), *dirty butterfly*, London: NHB.

—— (2008), *random*, London: NHB.

—— (2011), *truth and responsibility*, London: NHB.

—— (2015), *hang*, London: NHB.

Gregory, Chris (1997), *Be Seeing You*, Luton: University of Luton Press.

Grieg, David (2013), *The Events*, London: Faber.

Griffiths, Charlotte (2015) 'Theatre: the Nation's Debating Chamber', *The Guardian*, 06/03/2015. http://www.theguardian.com/stage/2015/mar/06/political-theatre-nations-debating-chamber/ accessed 17/08/2015.

Griffiths, Jay (1999), *Pip Pip: A Sideways Look at Time*, London: Flamingo.

—— (2015), 'What's the Time?', in *Radio Times*, no. 4738 (vol. 364) (28/3–3/4/2015), 9.

Gritzner, Karoline, and Rabey, David Ian (eds) (2006), *Theatre of Catastrophe: New Essays on Howard Barker*, London: Oberon.

Hammer, Anita (2008), 'Imagination and Memory in the Theatrical Space', in *Consciousness, Literature and the Arts*, vol. 9, no. 3, https://blackboard.lincoln.ac.uk/bbcswebdav/users/dmeyerdinkgrafe/archive/hammer.html/ accessed 16/12/2014.

Hammond, Claudia (2012), *Time Warped*, Edinburgh: Canongate.

Hare, David (1978), *Plenty*, London: Faber.

Harpin, Anna (2011a), 'Land of Hope and Glory: Jez Butterworth's Tragic Landscapes', in *Studies in Theatre and Performance*, vol. 31, no. 1, 61–73.

—— (2011b), 'Intolerable Acts', in *Performance, Research*, vol. 16, no. 1, 1–3.

Hawking, Stephen (1988), *A Brief History of Time*, London: Bantam.

Hoffman, Eva (2009), *Time*, London: Profile.

Hoffman, Piotr (1993), 'Death, Time and History: Division II of *Being and Time*', in C. Guignon (ed.), *The Cambridge Companion to Heidegger*, Cambridge: Cambridge University Press, 195–214.

Höpfl, Heather (1982), *The Subjective Experience of Time with Particular Reference to Time-Bound Institutions*, Ph.D. thesis: University of Lancaster.

Hume, David (1739), *A Treatise on Human Nature*, https://ebooks.adelaide.edu.au/h/hume/david/h92t/B1.4.6.html/ accessed 01/05/2015.

Hunka, George (2009), 'Found in the Ground', http://www.georgehunka.com/barker/howard-barkers-found-in-the-ground/ accessed 06/11/2015.

—— (2013), 'Theater, Time and Memory', http://www.georgehunka.com/drama/theater-time-and-memory/ accessed 07/11/2015.

—— (2014) 'Time and the Metaphysical Perspective', http://www.georgehunka.com/drama/time-and-the-metaphysical-perspective/ accessed 06/11/2015.

Jackson, Joe (1999), *A Cure for Gravity*, London: Anchor.

Jacques, Elliot (1982), *The Form of Time*, London: Heinemann.

Jha, Alok (2013), 'What is Heisenberg's Uncertainty Principle?', *The Observer*, 10/11/2013, http://www.theguardian.com/science/2013/nov/10/what-is-heisenbergs-uncertainty-principle/ accessed 29/09/2014.

Jones, Emrys (1977), 'Introduction' to William Shakespeare, *Antony and Cleopatra*, Harmondsworth: Penguin.

Kalb, Jonathan (1989), *Beckett in Performance*, Cambridge: Cambridge University Press.

—— (2011), *Great Lengths*, Ann Arbor: Michigan University Press.

Kantor, Tadeusz (1990), *Further on, Nothing: Tadeusz Kantor's Theatre* (ed. M. Kobialka), Minnesota: Minnesota University Press.

Kearney, Richard (1988), *The Wake of the Imagination*, London: Hutchinson.

Kennelly, Brendan (2013), *Guff*, Tarset: Bloodaxe.

Kiper, Dasha (2015), 'The Deviousness of Dementia', *The Guardian*, 20/10/2015, http://www.theguardian.com/society/2015/oct/20/the-deviousness-of-dementia/ accessed 09/11/2015.

Klaic, Dragan (2002), 'The Crisis of Theatre? The Theatre of Crisis!', in M. M. Delgado and C. Svich (eds), *Theatre in Crisis?*, Manchester: Manchester UP.

Klein, Stefan (2008), *Time: A User's Guide*, London: Penguin.

Kristeva, Julia (1981), 'Women's Time' (tr. A. Jardine and H. Blake), in *Signs*, vol. 7, no. 1, 13–35, http://www.jstor.org/stable/3173503/ accessed 07/02/2010.

—— (1996), *Time and Sense: Proust and the Experience of Literature* (tr. R. Guberman), New York: Columbia UP.

Lakoff, George, and Johnson, Mark (1980), *Metaphors We Live By*, Chicago: University of Chicago Press.

Landes, David S. (1983), *Revolution in Time: Clocks and the Making of the Modern World*, Harvard: Belknap.

Lash, S., Quick, A., and Roberts, R. (eds) (1998), *Time and Value*, Oxford: Blackwell.

Lefebvre, Henri (2004), *Rhythmanalysis: Space, Time and Everyday Life*, London: Continuum.

Lehmann, Hans-Thies (2006), *Postdramatic Theatre* (tr. K. Jürs-Munby), Abingdon: Routledge.

Lepecki, André (2006), *Exhausting Dance*, Abingdon: Routledge.

Lewis, Gwyneth (2010), *A Hospital Odyssey*, Tarset: Bloodaxe.

—— (2015), *Quantum Poetics*, Hexham: Bloodaxe.

Lichtenstein, Jonathan (2006), *The Pull of Negative Gravity*, New York: Dramatists Play Services.

—— (2006), *Memory*, London: Nick Hern Books.

Limon, Jerzy (2010), *The Chemistry of the Theatre: Performativity of Time*, Basingstoke: Palgrave.

Lingis, Alphonso (1994a), *The Community of Those who have Nothing in Common*, Bloomington: Indiana University Press.

—— (1994b), *Abuses*, Berkeley and London: University of California Press.

—— (2000), *Dangerous Emotions*, Berkeley and London: University of California Press.

Lippincott, Kristen, et al. (1999), *The Story of Time*, London: Merrell Holberton.

Luckhurst, Mary (2015), *Caryl Churchill*, Abingdon: Routledge.

Luckhurst, Roger (2008), *The Trauma Question*, Abingdon: Routledge.

Lukács, Georg (1974), *Soul and Form* (tr. Anna Bostock), Cambridge: MIT Press.

MacNaghten, Phil, and Urry, John (1998), *Contested Natures*, London: Sage.

McAuley, Gay (2000), *Space in Performance: Making Meaning in the Theatre*, Ann Arbor: Michigan UP.

McDowall, Alistair (2014), *Brilliant Adventures*, London: Bloomsbury.

—— (2015), *Pomona*, London: Bloomsbury.

McLucas, Cliff (2000), 'Ten Feet and Three Quarters of an Inch of Theatre', in N. Kaye (ed.), *Site-Specific Art*, London: Routledge.

Malkin, J. R. (1999), *Memory-Theatre and Postmodern Drama*, Ann Arbor: Michigan UP.

Mangan, Michael ([1987] 1989), *Christopher Marlowe: Dr Faustus*, Harmondsworth: Penguin.

—— (1998), *Edward Bond*, Plymouth: Northcote.

—— (2013), *Staging Ageing*, Bristol: Intellect.

Marber, Patrick (1997), *Closer*, London: Methuen.

Marlowe, Christopher (1969), *The Complete Plays* (ed. J. B. Steane), Harmondsworth: Penguin.

Mason, Paul (2014), 'The Unending Economic Crisis Makes Us Feel Powerless – and Paranoid', *The Guardian*, 19/10/2014, http://www.theguardian.com/commentisfree/2014/oct/19/unending-economic-crisis-powerless-paranoia/ accessed 20/10/2014.

May, Adrian (2011), *Myth and Creative Writing*, Harlow: Longman/Pearson.

Marx, Karl, and Engels, Friedrich (1976), *Collected Works Vol. 6*, London: Lawrence and Wishart.

Mead, George Herbert (1959), *The Philosophy of the Present* (ed. A. E. Murphy), Illinois: Open Court.

Megson, Chris (2014), '"Who the Hell's That?" Pinter's Memory Plays of the 1970s', in M. Taylor-Batty, *The Theatre of Harold Pinter*, London: Bloomsbury, 215–31.

Michon, John A. (1985), 'The Compleat Time Experiencer', in J. A. Michon and J. L. Jackson (eds), *Time, Mind and Behaviour*, Berlin and New York: Springer-Verlag, 20–52.

Miller, Arthur (1981), *Collected Plays*, New York: Viking Press.

—— (1983), *The American Clock*, London: Methuen.

Milton, John (1972), *The Poems of John Milton* (eds J. Carey and A. Fowler), London: Longman and Norton.

Mitchell, David (2014), *The Bone Clocks*, London: Sceptre.

Mölder, Bruno (2014), 'Constructing Time', in V. Arstila and D. Lloyd (eds), *Subjective Time*, Cambridge, MA and London: MIT Press, 217–38.

Moran, Caitlin (2014), *How to Build a Girl*, London: Ebury.

Mortimer, Ian (2014), 'The 10 Greatest Changes of the Past 1,000 Years', *The Guardian*, 30/10/2014, http://www.theguardian.com/books/2014/oct/30/10-greatest-changes-of-the-past-1000-years/ accessed 31/10/2014.

Mumford, Lewis (1971), *The Myth of the Machine: The Pentagon of Power*, London: Secker & Warburg.

Negri, Antonio (2013), *Time for Revolution*, London: Bloomsbury.

Neilson, Anthony (2008), *Plays: Two*, London: Methuen.

O'Reilly, Kaite (2014), *Woman of Flowers*, Twickenham: Aurora Metro.

—— (2016), *Atypical Plays for Atypical Actors: Selected Plays*, London: Oberon.

O'Rowe, Mark (1999), *Howie the Rookie*, London: NHB.

—— (2007), *Terminus*, London: NHB.

Osborne, Dierdre (2015), 'Resisting the Standard and Displaying her Colours: debbie tucker green at British Drama's Vanguard', in M. F. Brewer, L. Goddard, and D. Osborne (eds), *Modern and Contemporary Black British Drama*, Basingstoke: Palgrave, 161–177.

Parry, Gwenlan (1979) *Y Twr*, Llandysul: Gomer.

Pearson, Mike (2010), *Site-Specific Performance*, Basingstoke: Palgrave.

Phelan, Peggy (1993), *Unmarked: The Politics of Performance*, London: Routledge.

Phillips, Ian (2014), 'The Temporal Structure of Experience', in V. Arstila and D. Lloyd (eds), *Subjective Time*, Cambridge, MA and London: MIT Press, 139–58.

Pinter, Harold (1991a), *Plays: One*, London: Faber and Faber.

—— (1991b), *Plays: Two*, London: Faber and Faber.

—— (1997), *Plays: Three*, London: Faber and Faber.

—— (1998), *Plays: Four*, London: Faber and Faber.

Poliakoff, Laura (2012), *Clockwise*, London: Methuen.

Poore, Benjamin (2012), *Heritage, Nostalgia and Modern British Theatre*, Basingstoke: Palgrave.

Powell, Corey S. (2015), 'Relativity versus Quantum Mechanics', *The Guardian*, 4/11/2015, http://www.theguardian.com/news/2015/nov/04/relativity-quantum-mechanics-universe-physicists/ accessed 04/11/2015.

Price, Tim, (2015) *The Radicalization of Bradley Manning*, in T. Price and K. Wasserberg (eds), *Contemporary Welsh Plays*, London: Bloomsbury.

Priestley, John Boynton (1964), *Man and Time*, London: Bloomsbury.

—— (1969), *Time and the Conways and Other Plays*, Harmondsworth: Penguin.

Prigogine, Ilya, and Stengers, Isabelle (1997), *The End of Certainty*, New York and London: Free Press.

Pynchon, Thomas (1963), *V*, London: Jonathan Cape.

—— (1966), *The Crying of Lot 49*, New York: Bantam.

—— (1973), *Gravity's Rainbow*, London: Jonathan Cape.

—— (2006), *Against the Day*, London: Jonathan Cape.

Quinones, Ricardo (1965), 'Views of Time in Shakespeare', in *Journal of the History of Ideas*, vol. 26, no. 3, pp. 327–352.

—— (1972), *The Renaissance Discovery of Time*, Harvard University Press: Cambridge.

Rabey, David Ian (1997), *David Rudkin: Sacred Disobedience*, Abingdon: Routledge/Taylor and Francis.

—— (2003), *English Drama Since 1940*, Harlow: Longman/Pearson.

—— (2002–3), 'The Theatrical in the Sexual, the Sexual in the Theatrical: Some Parallels and Provocations', in *Essays in Theatre/Études Théâtrales*, vol. 21, no. 1&2, 63–78.

—— (2004), *The Wye Plays*, Bristol: Intellect.

—— (2006), 'Ed Thomas: Jazz Pictures in the Gaps of Language', in M. Luckhurst (ed.), *A Companion to Modern British and Irish Drama 1880–2005*, Oxford: Blackwell, 541–550.

—— (2008), *Lovefuries*, Bristol: Intellect.

—— (2009), *Howard Barker: Ecstasy and Death*, Basingstoke: Palgrave Macmillan.

Rackin, Phyllis (1991), *Stages of History*, Routledge: London.

Read, Alan (2003), *Theatre and Everyday Life*, Abingdon: Routledge.

Rebellato, Dan (2015), 'Pomona', http://www.danrebellato.co.uk/spilledink/2014/11/22/pomona?rq=pomona/ accessed 01/09/2015.

Richardson, Brian (1987), '"Time is Out of Joint": Narrative Models and the Temporality of the Drama', in *Poetics Today*, vol. 8, no. 2, 299–309.

Ridley, Philip (1997), *Plays: One*, London: Methuen.

—— (2009), *Plays: Two*, London: Methuen.

—— (2014), *Dark Vanilla Jungle*, London: Methuen.

Rifkin, Jeremy (1987), *Time Wars*, New York: Henry Holt and Company.

Righter, Anne (1967), *Shakespeare and the Idea of the Play*, Harmondsworth: Penguin.

Rudkin, David (2001) *Afore Night Come*, London: Oberon.

—— (1981), *The Sons of Light*, London: Eyre Methuen.

—— (1981), *The Triumph of Death*, London: Eyre Methuen.

—— (1986), *The Saxon Shore*, London: Methuen.

—— (1995–6), 'Burning Alone in the Dark: An Interview with David Rudkin', in *Planet*, vol. 114, 91–99.

—— (2011), *Red Sun and Merlin Unchained*, Bristol and Chicago: Intellect.

Ryan, Katy (2015), 'Prison, Time, *Kairos* in Langston Hughes's *Scottsboro, Limited*', in *Modern Drama*, vol. 58, no. 2, 171–193.

Sandhu, Sukhdev (2014), '*Penda's Fen*: A Lasting Vision of Heresy and Horror', *The Guardian*, 14/11/2014, http://www.theguardian.com/tv-and-radio/2014/nov/14/pendas-fen-heresy-horror-pastoral-horror/ accessed 22/11/2014.

Sandhu, Sukhdev S., Evans, Gareth, and Fowler, William (eds) (2014), *The Edge is Where the Centre is: David Rudkin and* Penda's Fen*: A Conversation*, Brooklyn: Texte und Töne.

Saunders, Graham (2008), *Patrick Marber's 'Closer'*, London: Continuum.

Schechner, Richard (1969), *Public Domain*, New York: Discus/Avon.

—— (2006), *Performance Studies* (2nd ed.), New York and Abingdon: Routledge.

Schneider, Rebecca (2014), *Theatre & History*, Basingstoke: Palgrave Macmillan.

Schroeder, Patricia R. (1989), *The Presence of the Past in Modern American Drama*, London: Associated University Presses.

Schutz, Alfred, and Luckmann, Thomas (1973), *The Structures of the Life-World* (tr. R. M. Zaner and H. T. Engelhardt Jr), London: Heinemann.

Scott-Heron, Gil (2000), *Now and Then*, Edinburgh: Payback/Canongate.

Seremetakis, Nadia (ed.) (1994), *The Senses Still*, Chicago: University of Chicago Press.

Segal, Lynne (2104), *Out of Time*, London: Verso.

Shakespeare, William (2007), *The RSC Shakespeare Complete Works* (eds J. Bate and E. Rasmussen), Basingstoke: Macmillan.

Sheldrake, Rupert (1990), *The Rebirth of Nature*, London: Century.

Siegel, M. B. (1972), *At the Vanishing Point*, New York: Saturday Review Press.

Sierz, Aleks and Ghilardi, Lia (2015), *The Time Traveller's Guide to British Theatre*, London: Oberon.

Smith, Irwin (1969), 'Dramatic Time versus Clock Time in Shakespeare', *Shakespeare Quarterly*, vol. 21, no. 1, 65–69.

States, Bert O. (1985), *Great Reckonings in Little Rooms*, London: University of California.

Stephens, Simon (2009) *Plays: Two*, London: Methuen.

Stevenson, Juliet (2014), 'How I Learned to Love Beckett', *The Guardian*, 02/10/2014, http://www.theguardian.com/stage/2014/oct/02/juliet-stevenson-samuel-beckett-happy-days-young-vic/ accessed 02/10/2014.

Stoppard, Tom (1986), *Jumpers*, London: Faber and Faber.

—— (1993), *Arcadia*, London: Faber.

Stuart-Hamilton, Ian (2011), *An Introduction to Gerontology*, Cambridge: Cambridge UP.

Taylor-Batty, Mark (2014), *The Theatre of Harold Pinter*, London: Bloomsbury.

Taylor, Steve (2007), *Making Time*, Cambridge: Icon.

Thomas, Edward (1994), *Three Plays*, Bridgend: Seren.

Thomas, Ed (2002), *[Selected] Work '95-'98*, Cardigan: Parthian.

—— (2004), *Stone City Blue*, London: Methuen.

Thompson, E. P. (1967), 'Time, Work-Discipline and Industrial Capitalism', in *Past & Present*, vol. 38, no. 1, 56–97.

Trigg, D (2012), *The Memory of Place: The Phenomenology of the Uncanny*, Ohio: Ohio University Press.

Vanden Heuvel, Michael (1991), *Performing Drama/Dramatizing Performance*, Ann Arbor: University of Michigan Press.

Wagner, Matthew D. (2012), *Shakespeare, Theatre and Time*, New York and Abingdon: Routledge.

Waits, Tom (2014), *Tom Waits: The Ultimate Music Guide*, J. Mulvey (ed.), London: IPC Media/Uncut.

Wakefield, N. (2014), 'Time-specificity of Performance', *Choreographic Practices*, vol. 5, no. 2, 183–197.

—— (2016), 'Time-specificity of the Future of Performance', *Maska*, vol. 30, no. 175–176, 6–13.

Waller, Gary F. (1976), *The Strong Necessity of Time: The Philosophy of Time in Shakespeare and Elizabethan Literature*, Mouton: The Hague.

Wallis, M., and Duggan, P. (2011), 'Editorial: on Trauma', *Performance Research*, vol. 16, no. 1, 1–3.

Waters, Steve (2010), *The Secret Life of Plays*, London: NHB.

Weitz, Eric (2016), *Theatre & Laughter*, Basingstoke: Palgrave Macmillan.

Wesker, Arnold (1976), *Three Plays*, Harmondsworth: Penguin.

—— (1980), *Plays Volume Three*, Harmondsworth: Penguin.

—— (2004), *Letter to Myself*, unpublished premiere production script.

—— (2008), *All Things Tire of Themselves*, Hexham: Flambard.

Whitrow, G. J. ([1972] 2003), *What is Time?*, Oxford: Oxford University Press.

Wickham, Glynne (ed.) (1976), *English Moral Interludes*, London: Dent.

Wilcher, Robert (1991), *Understanding Arnold Wesker*, Columbia: University of South Carolina Press.

—— (1992), 'The Communal Dream of Myth: David Rudkin's *The Triumph of Death*', in *Modern Drama* 35, 571–584.

—— (2010), 'Dying for Love: the Tragicomedy of Shakespeare's Cleopatra', in K. Gritzner (ed.), *Eroticism and Death in Theatre and Performance*, Hatfield: University of Hertfordshire, 28–43.

Wilder, Thornton (2007), *Collected Plays and Writings on Theater,* New York: The Library of America.

Wiles, David (2014), *Theatre & Time,* Basingstoke: Palgrave Macmillan.

Williams, Richard (2009), *The Blue Moment,* Norton: New York and London.

Williams, Tennessee (1976), *The Theatre of Tennessee Williams, Volume Five,* New York: New Directions.

Williams, Zoe (2015), 'We Don't Work to Live, We Live to Work. Why Don't We Say So?', *The Guardian,* 09/10/2015, http://www.theguardian.com/commentisfree/2015/jun/09/we-dont-live-to-work-we-work-to-live-why-dont-we-say-so/ accessed 09/06/2015.

Wilshire, Bruce (1982), *Role Playing and Identity: The Limits of Theatre as Metaphor,* Bloomington: Indiana University Press.

Wittman, Marc (2014), 'Embodied Time', in V. Arstila and D. Lloyd (eds), *Subjective Time,* Cambridge MA and London: MIT Press.

Worth, Katharine J. (1972), *Revolutions in Modern English Drama,* London: Bell.

Woycicki, Piotr (2011), 'Temporality and String Theory in Imitating the Dog's *Kellerman*', in *International Journal of Performance Arts and Digital Media,* vol. 7, no. 1, 23–42.

Wyllie, Andrew (2013), 'Philip Ridley and Memory', in *Studies in Theatre and Performance,* vol. 33, no. 1, 65–75.

Zarrilli, Phillip B. (2009), *Psychophysical Acting,* Abingdon: Routledge.

—— (2015), '*The Water Station*: Living Human Silence', http://exeuntmagazine.com/features/the-water-station-living-human-silence/ accessed 30/10/2015.

Zarrilli, Phillip B., Daboo, Jerri, and Loukes, Rebecca (2013), *Acting,* Basingstoke: Palgrave.

Index

A

Adam, Barbara 4, 11, 13–6, 20–5, 32–5, 38, 44–5, 47–9, 53, 61–2, 66–75, 88–9, 92, 97, 114, 116, 141, 150, 153, 165, 176, 185, 189, 193–5, 199, 207, 220, 231–3, 236, 241–2, 245

Albee, Edward, 214

Analogue, 179–80
  Beachy Head, 179–80

Angel-Perez, Elisabeth, 173

Aristotle, 11, 23, 87

Arstila, Vallteri, 11, 17, 50–2, 242

Artaud, Antonin, 34, 67

Aston, Elaine, 59

Atkin, Pete, 165

Augustine, Saint, 94, 147

Ayckbourn, Alan, 12, 109, 128–31, 138

B

Bachelard, Gaston, 12, 17, 20, 27, 53–6, 76, 79–80, 169

Bacon, Francis, 30

Barba, Eugenio, 53

Barker, Howard, 23, 46, 54, 56, 79, 81, 134–5, 142, 147–8, 155, 158, 165–76, 189, 205–6, 214–6, 226, 242–3, 246
  Birth on a Hard Shoulder, 173
  Bite of the Night, The, 166–7, 243
  Blok/Eko, 173–4
  Brilliance of the Servant, The, 168
  Castle, The, 81, 168

Dead, Dead and Very Dead, 170–1
Dead Hands, 168, 172
Defilo, 167
Dog Death in Macedonia, 142
Don't Exaggerate, 173
Ecstatic Bible, The, 166–8
Ego in Arcadia, 134, 169–70, 173
Eloquence, An, 167
Europeans, The, 215, 246
Fair Slaughter, 173
Forty, The, 46, 174–5, 214
Found in the Ground, 172–3, 206, 227
Gary Upright, 54
Gertrude – The Cry, 135, 172
Hated Nightfall, 168
He Stumbled, 168
House of Correction, A, 168
I Saw Myself, 170–2
N/A, 173
Rome, 166–7, 170
Seven Lears, 167, 173
Slowly, 168–9, 171–2
Stalingrad, 167
Swing at Night, The, 167
Twelfth Battle of Isonzo, The, 142, 168, 170
Two Skulls, 173
(Uncle) Vanya, 167
Und, 168
Ursula, 76, 167
13 Objects, 170, 172

Barrie, J. M., 106–7, 110, 115
  Dear Brutus, 106–7, 110, 115
Barrow, Isaac, 89, 97
Bate, Jonathan, 99, 103
Beckett, Samuel, 43, 46, 62–5, 71, 89, 128,
    137, 142, 147–56, 159, 162, 164, 169,
    172, 186, 188–9, 237
  Acts Without Words, 46
  Breath, 46
  Endgame, 144, 150–2, 154–5, 172
  Footfalls, 152–3, 162
  Krapp's Last Tape, 62–5, 128, 137, 142,
    151–2, 159
  Molloy, 149
  Not I, 154–5, 164
  Ohio Impromptu, 155
  Play, 154–5, 169, 172
  Rockaby, 153–5
  Silence, 159–60, 162
  That Time, 128, 151–2
  Waiting for Godot, 89, 142, 147–50, 152,
    172, 237
  What Where, 155–6
Benjamin, Andrew, 209
Bennett, Ned, 186–7, 190
Bennett, Susan, 12
Bergson, Henri, 38, 53, 63, 88, 129, 246
Berlioz, Hector, 98
Bigsby, Christopher, 200
Billington, Michael, 137
Blake, William, 117, 122, 194
  'Jerusalem', 117, 122, 194
Blum, H. F., 88
Bly, Robert, 196
Boal, Augusto, 22–3, 208
Bogart, Anne, 49–50, 53
Bollas, Christopher, 183
Bond, Edward, 22–3, 75, 142, 202, 204–9,
    218, 234–5
  At the Inland Sea, 207
  Bingo, 202
  Coffee, 208–9
  Early Morning, 202, 207

  Have I None, 208
  Lear, 142, 202, 207
  Narrow Road to the Deep North, The,
    202
  Pope's Wedding, The, 207
  Red, Black and Ignorant, 204–5, 209
  Restoration, 202
  Saved, 207
  Tuesday, 208
  Under Room, The, 208
  War Plays, The, 204–5, 207
Booth, Stephen, 54, 101, 134, 136, 216, 233
Borst, Arno, 199
Bradley, K. K., 38
Brater, Enoch, 76
Brecht, Bertolt, 37, 57, 159, 205, 234
Brenton, Howard, 82, 202–4, 234
  Anne Boleyn, 204
  Greenland, 203
  Hitler Dances, 203
  In Extremis, 204
  Magnificence, 82
  Sore Throats, 234
  Romans in Britain, The, 203
  Thirteenth Night, 203
Brookes, Mike, 37
Buonomaro, D. V., 174
Burroughs, William S., 82
Burton, Harry, 12, 158
Butterworth, Jez, 21, 73, 81, 129, 136, 183–5,
    188–9, 193–6
  Jerusalem, 21, 81, 183, 189,
    193–6
  Leavings, 188
  Mojo, 129
  River, The, 136, 184–5
  Winterling, The, 184

C
Capra, Fritjof, 56, 69, 185
Carlson, Marvin, 12, 76, 137
Carney, Sean, 212–3, 235
Carroll, Lewis, 162, 208, 210–1

Carroll, Sean, 16, 19, 21–22, 34–5, 88–9, 98, 132, 162, 165, 170
Carson, Anne, 17, 103
Caruth, C., 214
Cawley, A. C., 92–4
Chekhov, Anton, 117–8, 128, 157
    Cherry Orchard, The, 117–8
Chesneaux, Jean, 228, 232, 237, 243, 245
Christie, Agatha, 46, 179
Churchill, Caryl, 45, 51, 130, 135, 137, 178, 182, 207, 212–6, 222–3, 235
    Blue Heart, 45, 137
    Cloud Nine, 212–4
    Far Away, 130, 213–5, 235
    Fen, 214
    Light Shining in Buckinghamshire, 222
    Love and Information, 213–4
    Number, A, 213–4, 223
    Owners, 212
    Skriker, The, 135, 178, 182, 213–4, 235
    Traps, 51, 212, 214, 235
Common Players, The, 193–6
Crimp, Martin, 90–1
Csikszentmihalyi, Mihaly, 38

D
Daboo, Jerri, 155
Dahl, Mary Karen, 50
Davis, Jessica Milner, 141–2
Dawkins, Richard, 162
Dear, Nick, 136
Derrida, Jacques, 93
Descartes, René, 26
Doran, Gregory, 81–2
Downing, Richard, 42
Dreyfus, H. L., 50
Droit-Volet, S., 175
Dr Who, 223, 236
Duffy, Carol-Ann, 93, 135
Dufourmantelle, Anne, 49, 102–3, 136
Duggan, Patrick, 215–6
Dunne, J. W., 105–6, 109, 115, 118, 136
Dylan, Bob, 57, 76

E
Eco, Umberto, 87
Edgar, David, 36, 51–3, 75, 91, 188, 237
    Jail Diary of Albie Sachs, The, 188, 237
Einstein, Albert, 66, 88, 134, 138
Elam, Keir, 35, 76
Elias, N., 69
Eliot, T. S., 106, 108, 136, 185
Engels, F., 32
Ermarth, E. D., 12
Escher, M. C., 51
Escolme, Bridget, 104
Euripedes, 142
Evans, Gareth Lloyd, 118
Everyman, 90, 93–4, 101

F
Favorini, Attilio, 102, 137, 188, 202, 218
Fielding, David, 130
Flannery, Peter, 144
Forsyth, Alison, 215
Fraction, Matt, 75
Franklin, Benjamin, 32
Fraps, Thomas, 51
Fraser, J. T., 15, 24
Frayn, Michael, 156, 188
    Copenhagen, 188
Freud, Sigmund, 57, 105, 107, 210

G
Gale, Maggie B., 116
Ghilardi, L., 36
Gipson-King, Jay, 50, 88, 91–2, 166, 199
Gleick, James, 33, 87, 199, 225
Golding, William, 138
Gould, Stephen Jay, 4
green, debbie tucker 21, 58–60, 69, 148, 181, 214, 216, 218–9, 236
    born bad, 214
    dirty butterfly, 218
    generations, 218–9
    hang, 219

random, 21, 58–60, 69, 90, 181, 218
truth and reconciliation, 218–9
Gregory, Chris, 190
Grieg, David, 179–80
 Events, The, 179–80
Griffiths, Charlotte, 237
Griffiths, Jay, 4, 30, 32, 56, 199, 237
Griffiths, Trevor, 21
Gurdjieff, George, 105
Guyau, Jean-Marie, 175

H
Hare, David, 124, 202–3, 207
 Plenty, 124, 202–3
Harpin, Anna, 183, 193, 216
Hartley, Jennifer S., 208
Hawking, Stephen, 13, 25, 133, 210
Haynes, Todd, 57
Hayward, Georgia, 235–6
Heidegger, Martin, 26, 88, 176, 189
Heisenberg, Werner, 147
Hoffman, Eva, 11, 14, 21, 26–7, 29, 34, 38, 44,
 49, 63, 68, 74, 101–2, 162, 180, 200,
 230
Hooke, Robert, 175
Hopkins, H., 22
Howarth, Ben, 189
Hume, David, 51
Hunka, George, 173, 187–9
Husserl, Edmund, 19–20, 88
Hyde, Lewis, 194

I
Ibsen, Henrik, 108, 167

J
Jackson, Joe, 43
Jacques, E., 49
James, Clive, 165
James, William, 51
Janet, Pierre, 54
Jean-Baptiste, Marianne, 219
Jha, Alok, 147

Johnson, Mark, 32–3, 68
Jones, Emrys, 102
Jonson, Ben, 141
Joyce, James, 114
Jung, C. G., 107

K
Kaiser, Georg, 108
Kalb, Jonathan, 13–4, 18–19, 36, 93, 124, 155,
 166–7, 169–70, 189, 193, 243
Kane, Sarah, 90–1, 161, 182, 214, 218,
 235
 Cleansed, 161, 218
 Crave, 161, 182
 4.48 Psychosis, 182
Kant, Immanuel 11, 54
Kantor, Tadeusz, 76, 137, 244
Kearney, Richard, 67, 244–5
Kelly, Dennis, 178–9
 Love and Money, 178–9
Kennelly, Brendan, 245
Kesey, Ken, 144
Kiper, Dasha, 142
Kipp, Lara, 235
Klaic, Dragan, 243
Klee, Paul, 209
Klein, Stefan 11, 16–7, 26, 29, 32, 37–8, 63,
 65, 89, 98, 154
Kristeva, Julia, 30, 156–7, 161, 212, 220

L
Laban, Rudolf, 38
Lakoff, George, 32–3, 68
Landes, David S., 30–1, 38
Layzer, David, 120
Lefebvre, Henri, 26
Lehmann, Hans-Thies, 90, 135
Leibniz, G. W., 30, 88
Lepecki, André, 26, 38, 245–6
Lévi-Strauss, Claude, 67
Lewis, C. S., 210
Lewis, Gwyneth, vii, 69–70
Lichtenstein, Jonathan, 214–5

Memory, 214–5
Pull of Negative Gravity, The, 214–5
Limon, Jerzy, 21, 37, 52, 55, 68, 75, 91–2, 132
Lingis, Alphonso, 156, 168, 205
Lippincott, Kristen, 50, 87
Lloyd, Dan 11, 17, 50–2, 242
Locke, John, 30
Loukes, Rebecca, 155
Luckhurst, Mary, 214, 216
Lukács, Georg, 175–6
Lyotard, Jean-François, 205

M
MacNaghten, Phil, 16, 25, 32
McAloon, Paddy, 200
McAuley, Gay, 73
McCarthy, Cormac, 138
McDowall, Alistair, 185–7, 215
   Brilliant Adventures, 185–7
   Pomona, 186–7, 190, 215
McGoohan, Patrick, 190
   Prisoner, The, 190
McLucas, Cliff, 196
McNamara, Jack, 236–7
McPherson, Conor, 177, 189
   Port Authority, 177
   Seafarer, The, 189
   Shining City, 189
   This Lime Tree Bower, 177
McTaggart, J. M. E., 138
Mach, Ernst, 175
Mangan, Michael, 4, 34, 95–7, 136, 141–2, 144, 235, 246
Mangold, Alex, 235
Mankind, 94, 101
Manning, Chelsea, 230–3
Maratain, Jacques, 55
Marber, Patrick, 176–7
   Closer, 176–7
Marlowe, Christopher, 94–8, 124, 136, 142, 178, 241
   Dr Faustus, 94–8, 124, 126, 130, 136, 142, 178, 241

Marx, Karl, 32, 89, 107, 207, 230
May, Adrian, 194
Mead, G. H., 45
Megson, Chris, 148, 156–7, 159, 162, 203
Merleau-Ponty, Maurice, 88
Michon, J. A., 15
Miller, Arthur, 107, 108, 137, 200–2, 215, 234
   American Clock, The, 137, 200–2
   Death of a Salesman, 137
   Playing for Time, 200
   Timebends, 108, 200
Milton, John, 29
Mitchell, David, 89
Mölder, Bruno, 51
Molière, 91
Moran, Caitlin, 128
Mumford, Lewis, 31–4
Murphy, Thomas, 178
   Gigli Concert, The, 178

N
Nash, Ogden, 87
Negri, Antonio, 49, 72, 75–6, 138, 207–8
Neilson, Anthony, 137, 189, 209–12, 235
   Realism, 137
   Wonderful World of Dissocia, The, 189, 209–12, 235
Norris, Rufus, 93

O
O'Casey, Sean, 215
O'Neill, Eugene, 107–8, 214
O'Reilly, Kaite, 15, 143–4
   Cosy, 143–4
   Woman of Flowers, 15
O'Rowe, Mark, 177–9, 181, 189
   Howie the Rookie, 177–8
   Our Few and Evil Days, 189
   Terminus, 178
Orton, Joe, 210
Osborne, Dierdre, 218–9, 236
Osborne, John, 81
Ouspensky, P. D., 105

P

Parks, Suzan-Lori, 91
Parry, Gwenlyn, 121
Pavis, Patrice, 37
Pearson, Mike, 19, 23, 26, 36–7, 89–90, 94,
    196
Peter, John, 203
Phelan, Peggy, 246
Phillips, Adam, 62
Phillips, Ian, 52
Pinter, Harold, 44, 91, 129, 142, 147–8,
    156 65, 176, 178, 184, 188–9, 203,
    208, 217
  Ashes to Ashes, 129, 164–5, 235
  Betrayal, 44, 91, 162–4, 176, 178, 203
  Birthday Party, The, 157
  Caretaker, The, 157, 188
  Dumb Waiter, The, 157, 217
  Homecoming The, 129, 157–8, 161, 188
  Kind of Alaska, A, 162, 164, 188
  Landscape, 159
  'Last to Go', 157
  Lover, The, 157
  Moonlight, 162, 188
  Night, 160
  Night Out, A, 157
  No Man's Land, 129, 162, 184
  Old Times, 160–2
  Silence, 158–60, 162, 188
  Slight Ache, A, 157
Plato, 20, 141
Poliakoff, Laura, 143–4
  Clockwork, 143–4
Poore, Benjamin, 202
Potter, Dennis, 160
  Blue Remembered Hills, 160
Powell, Corey S., 242
Price, Tim, 199, 207, 217, 230–3, 237
  The Radicalization of Bradley Manning,
    199, 217, 230–3, 237
  Teh Internet is Serious Business, 233
Priestley, J. B., 3, 5, 18, 22, 48, 74–5, 94,
    105–6, 109, 111, 115–123, 129, 131,
133, 137, 142, 153, 162, 164, 185, 218,
    223–4, 236, 242
  Dangerous Corner, 119
  Ever Since Paradise, 118
  I Have Been Here Before, 119–20
  Inspector Calls, An, 119
  Johnson over Jordan, 118
  Linden Tree, The, 118–9, 120, 142
  Music at Night, 118, 140, 218
  Time and the Conways, 111, 116–23, 129,
    153, 162, 164
Prigogine, Ilya, 11, 35, 53, 56–62, 66, 69, 72,
    76, 92, 242
Proust, Marcel, 156
Pynchon, Thomas, 87, 212

Q

Quinones, Ricardo, 24, 89–90, 118, 135

R

Rabey, David Ian, 22, 29, 37, 67, 87, 121, 144,
    168–70, 172, 177, 184, 188–9, 193,
    205, 209, 241, 246
Rabey, Isabel, 76
Rackin, Phyllis, 132
Ramis, Harold, 48
  Groundhog Day, 48–9
Ravenhill, Mark, 74
Rebellato, Dan, 179–80, 186
Richards, Anthony, 193–6
Rickson, Ian, 194
Ridley, Philip, 130, 142, 186, 214, 216–8,
    235–6
  Dark Vanilla Jungle, 216
  Fastest Clock in the Universe, The, 216
  Mercury Fur, 130, 186, 216–8, 235–6
  Pitchfork Disney, The, 216
Rifkin, Jeremy, 16, 18, 23, 223–4,
    228–30
Righter, Anne, 99
Rudkin, David, 74, 142, 167, 184, 189, 220–8,
    233, 236–7
  Afore Night Come, 184, 220

Cries from Casement as his Bones are Brought to Dublin, 189, 233
'Here We Stay', 227–8
John Piper in the House of Death, 228
Macedonia, 142
Merlin Unchained, 142, 220, 223–7
Penda's Fen, 220, 224
Red Sun, 220
Saxon Shore, The, 220–1
Sons of Light, The, 220–1, 225
Triumph of Death, The, 220–3, 227–8
Ryan, Katy, 76

S

Sandhu, Sukhdev, 220
Sartre, Jean-Paul, 169
Saunders, Graham, 176
Schechner, Richard, 90, 94, 97
Schneider, Rebecca 3, 13, 18, 20–1, 23, 35–6, 50, 131–2, 154–5, 175, 206, 245
Schroeder, Patricia R., 13, 35, 93, 107–8, 189, 217, 234
Scott-Heron, Gil 4–5, 59
Seremetakis, N., 26
Segal, Lynne, 43–6, 62, 141, 143, 148, 182–3, 214, 235
Shakespeare, William 12, 19, 22, 28, 33–4, 45–6, 64, 76, 80–2, 89, 91, 98–106, 112, 125, 130–2, 134–6, 216, 223, 225, 235, 241
   All's Well that Ends Well, 100
   Antony and Cleopatra, 80, 102–5, 142
   As You Like It, 21
   Comedy of Errors, The, 98
   Coriolanus, 80
   Cymbeline, 28, 101
   King Lear, 12, 33–4, 76, 101, 174, 223
   Hamlet, 19, 68, 81–2, 102, 135
   Henry IV, 132
   Henry V, 45, 90, 102, 112–3, 131–2
   Love's Labour's Lost, 80, 90, 98–100, 105, 136
   Macbeth, 101, 135
   Measure for Measure, 100–1
   Merchant of Venice, The, 100
   Midsummer Night's Dream, A, 129
   Pericles, 101–2
   Rape of Lucrece, The, 134–5
   Taming of the Shrew, The, 100
   Tempest, The, 33–4, 98, 101–2, 105
   Titus Andronicus, 22, 80
   Twelfth Night, 100, 129
   Two Gentlemen of Verona, The, 100
   Winter's Tale, The, 80, 102, 106, 143, 241
Shaw, Bernard, 80–1, 114–5, 119–20, 130–1, 137, 205
   Back to Methuselah, 114, 130–1
   Caesar and Cleopatra, 115, 130
   Heartbreak House, 80–1, 115, 130
   Saint Joan, 130
Shelley, Mary, 136
Shelley, Percy B., 167, 221
Siegel, M. B., 246
Sierz, Aleks, 36
Simpson, N. F., 114
Slade, Bernard, 234
Soans, Robin, 189
   Crouch, Touch, Pause, Engage, 189
Sophocles, 142
Specian, Eric, 110
Spufford, Francis, 105–6, 136
Stanislavski, Konstantin, 165
States, Bert O., 23, 25–6, 37, 63, 90, 118, 128, 134, 176
Stein, Gertrude, 35
Stengers, Isabelle, 56–7
Stephens, Simon, 179, 214–6
   Pornography, 179, 214–6
Stevenson, Juliet, 148
Stoppard, Tom, 130, 132–4, 138, 165, 169
   Arcadia, 132–4, 165
   Jumpers, 138
Storey, David, 144
Strindberg, August, 108
Stuart-Hamilton, Ian, 141

T

Taylor, Don, 236
Taylor, Steve, 17, 162
Taylor-Batty, Mark, 159, 161–4, 184
Thomas, Ed, 70–2, 76, 142, 148, 180–4, 189,
    214, 235
  East from the Gantry, 181
  Flowers of the Dead Red Sea, 70–2, 76
  Gas Station Angel, 181–2, 189, 235
  House of America, 180–1, 214
  Stone City Blue, 182–3, 190
Thompson, E. P., 32
Toller, Ernst, 108
Trigg, D., 17, 36

U

Urry, John, 16, 25, 32

W

Wagner, Matthew D., 17–21, 23–4, 26–7, 64,
    79, 81–2, 89–90, 92, 95, 97, 102, 105,
    124, 132, 174, 241
Waits, Tom, 13, 36, 180
Waller, Gary F., 24
Wallis, Mick, 215
Walton, K. L., 52
Wasserman, Dale, 144
Waters, Steve, 35, 47, 90–1, 179
Weill, Kurt, 87
Weiss, Peter, 144, 235
Weitz, Eric, 43, 141–2
Weller, Paul, 5
Welles, Orson, 189
Wesker, Arnold, 60–2, 70, 109, 121–8, 137–8,
    142, 147, 228, 245
  'All things tire of themselves', 245
  Caritas, 124
  Chips with Everything, 121
  Four Seasons, The, 121–2, 124
  Friends, The, 124, 126, 147
  Kitchen, The, 60–2, 70, 109, 121

Letter to a Daughter, 126
Letter to Myself, 126–8
Old Ones, The, 124–7, 228
Roots, 126
Shylock, 142
Their Very Own and Golden City, 122–4,
    137–8
Whitelaw, Billie, 155
Whiting, John, 80–1
  Saint's Day, 80–1
Whitrow, G. J, 14–5, 24–5, 27–9, 34, 88–9,
    92, 95, 97, 119–20, 135, 175, 225
Wicks, Victoria, 155
Wilcher, Robert, 104, 138, 221
Wilde, Oscar, 48
Wilder, Thornton 4, 105–15, 137, 186, 189,
    200, 218, 234
  Long Christmas Dinner, The, 109–12,
    115–6, 218
  Our Town, 108, 112–5, 200, 218
  Pullman Car Hiawatha, 112–3, 115, 189
  Skin of Our Teeth, The, 90, 114–5, 137, 200
Wiles, David, 3, 25, 27, 53, 129, 136, 165,
    167, 175
Williams, Tennessee, 107–8, 214–7
  Two-Character Play, The, 214–7
Williams, Zoe, 202
Wilkins, George, 101–2
Wilshire, Bruce, 18, 21
Wilson, Nicola, 143
Winnicott, D. W., 45
Wittman, Marc, 43, 45
Worth, Katharine J., 118
Woycicki, Piotr, 242
Wyllie, Andrew, 216

Z

Zarrilli, Phillip B., 43, 53, 154–5, 188
Zdarsky, Chip, 75
Zeller, Florian, 143
Žižek, Slavoj, 43